THE PRINCE AND HIS LADY

The Prince and His Lady

The love story of the Duke of Kent
and Madame de St Laurent

by

Mollie Gillen

SIDGWICK & JACKSON
LONDON

SBN 283 48428 4

Printed in Great Britain
at the St Ann's Press, Park Road, Altrincham
for Sidgwick and Jackson Limited
1 Tavistock Chambers, Bloomsbury Way
London, W.C.1

Historians are unnecessary. That was the brusque opinion of Wellington after Waterloo, on finding that 'history' usually meant travellers' tales—legends, hearsay, even the wildest fiction picked up from tourists, peasants, publicans, old soldiers, anybody ready to spin a yarn over a glass of grog. Today we would not automatically despise such sources provided they were rigorously checked.

Who was Madame de St Laurent? Her biographers, with a gift for story-telling and an eye for colourful legend, have hitherto been unable to resist certain family traditions, arising in all innocence many years ago, and never checked against places or dates—those austere guardians of historical truth. Until the publication of this new biography we have only been able to suspect who Madame was *not*. Her lover, Prince Edward Duke of Kent, and later the father of Queen Victoria, has incidentally suffered from caricature out of all proportion to the genuine eccentricities of his character. The fact that he was at times an unpopular public figure has rubbed off on to his private life, building a legend in which his greys have become black, and her greys white. His beautiful 'Madame de St Laurent', thrown over after years of faithfulness, has found plenty of champions to leap to her defence and at his throat. If she had been just another Mrs Jordan (King William IV's ex-actress-mistress), it is implied, there would have been more excuse for chucking her for the chance to produce an heir to the throne. But 'Madame de St Laurent'! How dared he treat so badly an aristocratic lady, only a little less blue-blooded and certainly much better brought up than himself?

The mills of history grind slowly but they grind exceeding small. Nemesis has been hanging over Madame's legend-writers for some years. Now Mrs Gillen has proved to be the instrument through which it has decided to strike.

In writing an introduction to this remarkable book I may perhaps be allowed to declare a lively personal interest. When I was writing my biography of Queen Victoria between 1960 and 1964, I was aware that there was more to 'Madame de St Laurent' than met the eye. Her charm was unassailable; but her pedigree? Professor Aspinall was deftly releasing the first cat from the bag (as he has released so many others in his brilliant editions of the letters of King George III and his sons) and it was in this context that I described the story of Prince Edward's lovely lady as a 'bare wall' up which the ivy-leaves of legend had found it tempting to climb. I myself mentioned a few of the legends, particularly one which had been used against Queen Victoria, giving her character a falsely malicious twist.

When I heard, therefore, that Mollie Gillen was determined to get behind the ivy, however much travel and research it demanded (and it was to demand a great deal) I welcomed her enterprise as something really worth while—history instead of romancing. Not that *The Prince and His Lady* has turned out to be destructive of romance. Quite the contrary. Madame's true story is in many ways stranger than the fiction it replaces and her romance more touching and less meretricious.

I must not give away Mrs Gillen's discoveries prematurely. Nevertheless, two instances of the way she works and of her results may be be mentioned safely.

Why, I asked her, was the Prince's lady called 'Madame de St Laurent'?

'I have never found the answer to that', she wrote back; 'I checked her birth date to see if Laurent was her patron saint, but no: there was nothing in Besançon [her home town] which could account for it —no church, no street, or such like. I postulated that she may have had a first lover of that name, and I checked the various biographical dictionaries in France, coming up with two possible men called St Laurent. They were both contemporary with Madame, and both engaged in occupations that could have brought them into contact with her; but as all this was very "iffy", I have not at present been able to pursue it far. I don't think Prince Edward chose "St Laurent" because he knew he was going to serve in Quebec: he had got Madame to Gibraltar before he heard that his suggestion of Quebec was being granted.'

And so in all honesty Mrs Gillen leaves this bit of the wall still bare. But I back her to find the answer.

The second example of her method concerns legends: quite another matter. She sees them as often comically vulnerable, like the one which made Madame live to 106. The answer to this was simple but laborious. She just had to find the legendary lady's actual grave.

At long last we have the truth about Queen Victoria's father and his mysterious French lady; I revelled in Mrs Gillen's detective skill.

ELIZABETH LONGFORD

CONTENTS

Foreword		v
List of Illustrations		ix
Acknowledgements		xi
Author's Note		xiv
Preface		xv
Genealogical table		xvi
INTRODUCTION: The Legends		1
Part One—THE TWENTY-SEVEN YEARS: 1790–1818		9
Chapter	1 'I look for a companion'	11
	2 Beginnings	26
	3 Quebec	35
	4 'The stupendous wonder of this country'	51
	5 Mutiny	59
	6 Goodbye to Quebec	69
	7 Action	80
	8 Sojourn at Halifax	93
	9 'The bells rang for an hour'	108
	10 The Duke of Kent	119
	11 Farewell to dreariness	132
	12 Disaster at Gibraltar	144
	13 Into the wilderness	156
	14 The quiet years	163
	15 Domestic happiness	175
	16 Last years in London	189
	17 Brussels	204
	18 Parting	213

Part Two—AFTERWARDS   227

Chapter 19   Separate paths   229

            20   Tragedy   242

            21   Madame alone   251

                EPILOGUE   259

Appendix : The Facts   266

The Mongenet family tree   283

Bibliography   284

References   290

Index   303

LIST OF ILLUSTRATIONS

Madame de St Laurent	*facing page* 8
Prince Edward	*facing page* 9
Marquis de Permangle	*facing page* 80
Casernes, Besançon	*facing page* 80
General Wetherall	*facing page* 81
General Wetherall in old age	*facing page* 81
Captain Shuttleworth	*facing page* 81
Gibraltar	*facing page* 96
Quebec	*facing page* 96
Ignace-Louis de Salaberry	*facing page* 97
Charles de Salaberry	*facing page* 97
De Salaberry miniatures	*facing page* 97
De Salaberry miniatures	*facing page* 97
Halifax, Nova Scotia	*facing page* 160
Ruins of the Lodge, Halifax	*facing page* 160
Madame's commonplace book	*facing page* 161
The church at Besançon	*facing page* 161
Castle Hill Lodge	*facing page* 176
Kensington Palace	*facing page* 176
Place Louis Quinze	*facing page* 177
116 rue de Grenelle	*facing page* 177
Mongenet family	*facing page* 208
Sir John Wentworth	*facing page* 209
Lady Wentworth	*facing page* 209
Place Royale, Brussels	*facing page* 224
Cemetery of Père Lachaise, Paris	*facing page* 224
Duke of Kent	*facing page* 225

ACKNOWLEDGEMENTS

To Her Majesty the Queen must go my first grateful thanks for the gracious permission given me to see in the Royal Archives those papers that concerned the Duke of Kent's association with Madame de St Laurent and with his life in Canada. To the Canada Council I owe the means of carrying to completion the preliminary research that had shown me the possibility of finding the truth behind the legends. I am grateful to *Chatelaine* magazine and its editor, Mrs Doris Anderson, for permission to make use of discoveries from the early research undertaken for my original article, and also for leave of absence in which to continue the search. To no one do I owe more than to Mr Robert Mackworth-Young, C.V.O., librarian at Windsor Castle, for his enthusiastic interest and co-operation; and to his staff in the Royal Archives headed by Miss Jane Langton.

From those with private papers I received only the utmost courtesy. Madame la marquise de Permangle entertained me in her home and gave me every possible assistance. The comte de Wurstemberger undertook a special trip to London to make the de Vincy papers available, and later welcomed me as a guest at his villa at Menton. Lord Harcourt brought to his London house the massive, leather-bound volumes containing the royal correspondence. Lord Fitzwilliam arranged for me to see relevant family papers at the Sheffield Central Library, where Mr John Bebbington and his staff offered me every facility. The Robert Owen Papers were opened to me at request by Mr D. Flanagan at the library of the Co-operative Union in Manchester. The Directors of Messrs Coutts and Company, through their archivist Miss Veronica Stokes, gave me access to their files of relevant royal correspondence.

Mr Anthony Neale went to endless trouble to produce the papers of his great-grandfather the Reverend Erskine Neale, one of the duke's earliest biographers. To Mrs Cecil Woodham-Smith I owe a special debt for drawing to my attention the vitally important documents among the Melbourne Papers in the Royal Archives. Lady Audley procured copies of letters from the duke to her ancestor Admiral Sir Ross Donnelly, and Madame Marie-Térèse Pierregrosse, the present owner of the Château de St Philippe in Savoie, sent information and photographs, as did also members of the de Salaberry family. To Lord Mountbatten and Lady Longford I owe special thanks for unfailing encouragement and interest from the beginning, and to Mr Arnold McNaughton of Montreal, whose interest in royal genealogy sparked the whole project.

I have also to thank the staff of many libraries and archives: the British Museum, Public Record Office, Ealing Public Library, India Office Records, Garrison Library (Gibraltar), Bibliothèque Nationale (Paris), Bibliothèque Publique et Universitaire (Geneva), Bibliothèque Royale (Brussels), Newberry Library (Chicago), Archives de la Martinique, Public Archives of Canada, Public Archives of Ontario, Archives du Québec, Public Archives of Nova Scotia, University of Toronto Library, Metropolitan Toronto Public Library.

I am infinitely grateful to all the county archivists of Britain who were unstinting of time and effort in answer to my inquiries. I could not have made progress at all without the tireless researches made by archivists on the Continent. Madame Nicole Felkay, Archives de la Seine; Mademoiselle F. Joigneault, Bibliothèque Municipale de Besançon; Monsieur Paul Hamon, Bibliothèque Municipale de Grenoble; Monsieur Perret, Archives du département de la Savoie; Mr John Searle, editor of the *Gibraltar Chronicle*; Monsieur Jean Ferrandier, secrétaire général adjoint de la Mairie du 7e arrondissement de Paris; Madame Françoise Barré, Archives du département des Landes; Monsieur Louis Espinasse of Toulouse, a gracious correspondent and host. Miss Winifred Binning in Edinburgh and Mrs Beatrice Pugh in London ferreted out necessary records with skill and devotion. Mrs Eve Jennings of the Greater London Record Office was a tower of strength, as were also Mr Gerard Young of Bognor Regis, Miss Norma Lee of Quebec, and Monsieur Jean-Daniel Candaux of Geneva.

The undaunted efforts of the librarian of the Royal United Service Institution, Mr J. R. Dineen, aided by a legion of regimental secretaries and the good will of private families, unearthed invaluable portraits of officers associated with the Duke of Kent. My grateful thanks go to Lieutenant-Commander J. A. Shuttleworth, D.L., for the portrait of Captain John Shuttleworth; to Lieutenant-General Sir Edward Wetherall for the portrait of his great-great-grandfather Sir Frederick; to His Excellency the Governor and Commander-in-Chief of Gibraltar, to whom I owe the courtesies that opened to me the original Garrison Orders books of the Command.

Of the kindness of the members of Madame's own family, descendants of her brothers Claude-Charles and Jean-Claude, I cannot say enough. Professor André Brun of the Faculté de Droit et des Sciences Economiques, Université de Lyon, gave me permission to make use of the documents in his possession—a letter to Madame and her Commonplace Book—and Monsieur Michel Diday, *conseiller à la Cour d'Appel de Lyon,* and his brother Charles of Annonay, gave me heartwarming welcome. To Madame Valentine Botok-Berlioz I am deeply indebted for permission to publish the portrait of her ancestor Jean-Claude Mongenet and his family.

I am grateful to the following authors, editors and publishers, and others who have allowed quotation from their books and papers: Earl Fitzwilliam and Earl Fitzwilliam's Wentworth Estates Company and the City Librarian, Sheffield City Libraries, for the Wentworth Woodhouse Muniments; Simon Fraser, Esq., for the Spencer Stanhope Collection in the Sheffield City Libraries.

I would also like to thank the following publishers who have allowed quotation from their books: Cambridge University Press for extracts from *Letters of George IV* and *The Later Correspondence of George III* edited by A. Aspinall; Cassell and Co. Ltd. for extracts from *Correspondence of George Prince of Wales* edited by A. Aspinall; Hollis and Carter for extracts from *The Letters of Mrs. Fitzherbert* edited by Shane Leslie; McClelland and Stewart for extracts from *A Mountain and a City: the Story of Hamilton* by Marjorie Freeman Campbell; John Murray (Publishers) Ltd. for extracts from *Lord Granville Leveson Gower Private Correspondence* edited by Countess Granville and *The Creevey Papers* edited by Sir H. Maxwell.

There are many more, too numerous to mention, and some of them unknown by name, who have aided and encouraged me with interest and information. I would like to think that all of these will feel they are included in my most sincere and heartfelt gratitude.

Toronto   MOLLIE GILLEN
April 1970

Where printed material has been quoted, I have retained the original spelling and punctuation. In quoting from manuscript sources, I have updated punctuation, but not spelling, and retained only enough capital letters and underlining to preserve the flavour of the style. All translations from the French are my own, except that published in the Report of the Public Archives of Canada for the year 1946, and, of course, those letters printed in Dr Anderson's *Life of the Duke of Kent* of which the original manuscripts are not now available.

It is almost impossible to describe the sense of drama and suspense that has accompanied every stage of the research for this book. Few excitements, I have found, can equal that of the arrival through the mail-slot of an envelope that might contain a copy of some ancient manuscript documenting absolutely what had been half-suspected, or a letter from some stranger with the next clue to the solution of a mystery—the origin and ultimate destiny of that royal mistress known as Madame de St Laurent, a lady whose life had become encrusted with so much legend. There was nothing more fascinating than the discovery, by clue leading to clue with the suspense of a detective story, of the people of her family; some whose life-span overlapped at one end my own, at the other end that of people who had known and talked with the duke and his lady.

And what could offer more magic than to walk the streets where she so often had walked in the city of her birth, to pass through the doors of those buildings in Paris where she had lived and died, and to handle the letters and turn the pages her hands once had touched?

It will be obvious that I disagree with the usual verdict on the character of the duke. A largely unjustified unpopularity in his own time has hardened around him like cement: the man who emerges from his letters and the opinions of his friends has faults and pomposities, but for all that he is a man who earned the loyalty of those who knew him well, and was as honest a person as most of us can claim to be.

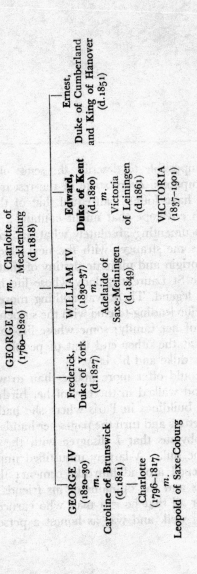

Genealogy chart of George III and his family

GEORGE III *m.* Charlotte of
(1760–1820)   Mecklenburg
                 (d.1818)

GEORGE IV   Frederick,   WILLIAM IV   Edward,   Ernest,
(1820–30)   Duke of York   (1830–37)   Duke of Kent   Duke of Cumberland
m.   (d.1827)   *m.*   (d.1820)   and King of Hanover
Caroline of Brunswick   Adelaide of   *m.*   (d.1851)
(d.1821)   Saxe-Meiningen   Victoria
                                       (d.1849)   of Leiningen
Charlotte   (d.1861)
(1796–1817)
m.   VICTORIA
Leopold of Saxe-Coburg   (1837–1901)

The legends

On 19 May 1818, someone—man or woman—whose handwriting has not yet been identified, sat down in London and wrote, in French, a charming warm-hearted letter of sympathy and understanding to a lady who had been known for the past twenty-seven years by the name of Madame de St Laurent. It was then exactly two months since circumstances had parted her from the man to whom for all of those years she had been a joy and a comfort, and whom she was never to see again. Edward Augustus, Duke of Kent, had chosen a path of duty (and perhaps also a way out of his financial problems) which meant much heartbreak to her and to himself, but more to her, for he would have a new and (as it fortunately turned out) congenial companion to console him after his marriage to Marie Louise Victoire, widowed Princess of Leiningen.

The royal bridegroom had just left London for Coburg where the first of two marriage ceremonies would take place on 29 May. He had, in fact, landed in Calais the day before the unknown writer—friend to the Duke and Madame both—took up his pen to write to the duke's beloved companion.

On 19 May 1968, therefore, exactly 150 years afterwards, it has seemed appropriate to begin the true story of a love affair that has been shrouded in mystery until now, and about which much has been written, mostly in error. It is a story of genuine affection, of a love that could be called ill-fated except that twenty-seven years of happiness together do not fall to the lot of many humans. Perhaps, when the letter reached her in her Paris apartment in 1818, Madame was able to take comfort from what it said to her, and be grateful for what

B

the gods had given her, though they had taken it away at the last.

Everyone said she was beautiful. She was talented, gentle and well-bred. In May 1794, Governor John Wentworth wrote from Halifax, Nova Scotia, in a private letter to his friend John King, Under-Secretary of State in London, 'She is an elegant, well bred, pleasing, sensible woman, far beyond most . . . I never yet saw a woman of such intrepid fortitude yet possessing the finest temper and refined manners.' (1) In 1806 a young protégé wrote from London to his sister in Quebec, 'She is certainly the most kind, the best natured and the most amiable of all women; the beauties of her mind can only be equalled by those of her lovely person.' (2)

She was known as Alphonsine Thérèse Bernardine Julie de St Laurent de Montgenêt, Baronne de Fortisson—'Madame St Laurent', wrote Governor Wentworth, 'with an hundred names and titles' (3)—the companion for twenty-seven years of Edward Augustus, fourth son of King George III of England.

But who was she?

Madame's personal history is offered in greatest detail by McKenzie Porter in a book entitled *Overture to Victoria*. (4) In this account she was born in France in the late 1760s at St-Laurent-sur-Mer, in the Norman department of Calvados, but was raised in Martinique on sugar plantations owned by the de Montgenêt family. Here she received her education in a convent school, La Maison d'Education pour les Jeunes Personnes, fellow-pupil (though younger) of the girl who would become the Empress Josephine of France. Back in France, she married her cousin Jean Charles André de Mestre, baron de Fortisson, and in 1789, to escape the Revolution, fled with him and their baby daughter Melanie to the safety of Geneva.

Here the glamorous and flirtatious Julie captured the heart of the young English prince who was pursuing his education in the Swiss city. After the prince's debts had forced him into an unauthorized return to England in January 1790, and subsequently to a kind of banishment in the garrison of Gibraltar, he called on his naval brother the Duke of Clarence for assistance to smuggle Julie, her husband and child, to Gibraltar from Switzerland via Toulon and a British warship. There, while the disapproving but helpless baron acted as his aide-de-camp, the prince's indiscretions with Julie finally aroused the indignation of the garrison commander, Major-General Charles O'Hara, whose irate reports to the King caused the prince to be posted to the distant garrison of Quebec. The baron de Fortisson, at last reaching the limit of his tolerance, refused to accompany his erring wife and her lover across the Atlantic, and the prince, with Julie and her baby daughter, embarked in May 1791 for Canada. In her association with the prince,

she was known as Madame de St Laurent, a name taken, it was
suggested, from her birthplace.

Thus Mr Porter. Over the years since the Duke of Kent parted from
Madame the legends have been growing, first whispered among the
members of certain families, and finally bursting into print in the pages
of journals and books, that from this union were born children whose
descendants—deliberately unrecognized by a vindictive Queen Victoria
—today still carry the royal blood of the Hanovers. Two of these—two
sons, Robert Wood and Jean de Mestre, said to have been given into
the care of foster-parents whose names they took—have gained the
acceptance of authorities, and appear as children of the duke and
Madame in the trusted pages of such reference books as the *Oxford
Companion to Canadian History and Literature*. Evidence for the
claims of five others, presented by one writer or another as sufficiently
strong to be accepted as true, has been offered for consideration:
Isabella Hyde, William Goodall Green and his sister Louisa, and John
and Mary Rees.

Isabella Hyde, because she was seventy-four when she died in 1865,
thus indicating the year of her birth as 1791, would have been the first-
born of the seven children attributed to the duke and Madame. (5)
Two theories have been offered for her background, though no evidence
other than family tradition exists to prove either of them. The first
of these suggests that she was born on board a warship, possibly
Ulysses or *Resolution*, the ships that brought the prince and his
regiment from Gibraltar to Quebec in 1791. (6) In Quebec she was
placed in the care of the Ursuline nuns, and later sent to Martinique
where she was brought up by Madame's mother on the de Montgenêt
estates. In the second account, Isabella was sent, not to Martinique,
but to Jamaica, to Hyde Hall, 'the estate of the East or D'Este, family
—related by marriage to Lord Clarendon Hyde' [*sic*]. Both accounts
agree that around 1800 she was taken to London to live in Kent
House, a Knightsbridge residence where it is known that the prince
set up an establishment for Madame.

Isabella eventually married a man named John Whyte—'that
Colonel John Lionel Whyte/who/came from service in Jamaica with
the Royal Dragoons/to England/, to be there stationed with the 46
Foot Regiment, South Devon, under Lord Morley.' (7) Despite this
precise identification, descendants have believed that 'Whyte' was a
cover name, assumed to protect the anonymity of the duke's 'daughter',
and that money arriving regularly from some unknown source in
England might have been a pension paid by Queen Victoria to her
father's illegitimate offspring. In 1843 John Whyte inherited from his
brother James Matthew an estate in Hamilton, Ontario: it was sug-

gested that James Whyte had left his honourable post and plantations in Jamaica to build the beautiful home, Barton Lodge, on The Mountain in Hamilton, for the residence of this royal child. Isabella's daughter Emily (among other evidence believed conclusive) also bore 'a remarkable resemblance' to Queen Victoria.

About the birth-date of Robert Wood, one of the two sons whose royal parentage has been widely accepted, there is some confusion. Porter, in *Overture to Victoria,* says it took place in 1793 'early in the year' : but a memorial window in the Church of the Holy Trinity in Quebec City erected by his son William Frost Wood gives it as 10 August 1792. The royal child, it was said, was baptized at 'Christ Church Anglican Cathedral in Quebec City,' and the failure to discover, to this day, any record of birth or baptism has been attributed to the mysterious disappearance of the relevant page from the church register after the Duke of Kent's legitimate daughter Victoria came to the throne.

The senior Robert Wood, to whom, it has been believed, the eldest son of the prince and Madame was entrusted as foster-child, was identified as having been a chief petty officer of the Royal Navy who had served with Prince Edward's elder brother Prince William. Having accompanied the latter on his visit to Quebec in 1789, said Porter, the young Wood took a French-Canadian bride and settled in Canada, where he would later be employed by Prince Edward, and still later, through the prince's influence, become 'door-keeper at the Legislative Assembly'. (8)

The second son attributed by Porter to the prince and his lady was given the name of Jean de Mestre (a family title of Julie's husband who, by an astonishing coincidence, turned up at the prince's feet, decapitated, on the Martinique battlefield in 1794). The news of her husband's death was dispatched to her at once by the prince's courier Robert Wood, who had accompanied his master to the West Indies. It was suggested that the young couple (Prince Edward was twenty-seven, Julie was thought to be about the same age) visited Martinique together later in 1794, taking the new baby to be brought up by Madame's mother, and that as Julie was now free, they were married there by a Roman Catholic priest, the prince using the name of Armstrong.

The young Jean de Mestre was sent to school to the Jesuit College in Philadelphia at the age of seven, and associated during his growing years with aristocratic French emigrés in Martinique, the United States and England, escorted on his journeys to the latter place by none other than the foster-father of his 'brother' Robert Wood. Though he inherited the de Fortisson property in France, he eventually became a British subject and settled on Crown lands given to him by Queen

Victoria in Australia, whither he had gone as a member of the French consular corps.

Of the two children named Green, the boy, William Goodall Green had been mentioned in *The Shy Princess* by David Duff (who also referred to the son known as Robert Wood). (9) The child who took the name of Green, said Duff (agreeing that the information was not authenticated) was born in 1792 in Quebec. Documents that might have supported his claim and which (including the certificate of marriage between the duke and Julie) had been given to him with ill-grace by the Duchess of Kent after the duke's death, were said to have been removed from him at gunpoint in Canada by masked men who threatened him and forced him to sign an agreement never to press any investigation into his parentage.

A genealogical chart drawn up by the late Mr George Laidler of Hamilton, Ontario, and lodged in the Public Archives of Canada, added two children born in Halifax and known as John and Mary Rees. It included Robert Wood, William Goodall Green, *Laura* Green and Isabella Hyde. Laidler did not mention the boy Jean de Mestre. His information augmented Mr Duff's (and endorsed Mr Porter's account of her birthplace) by stating that Julie had been 'Princesse de Normandie'.

The evidence was persuasive : it seemed not incredible that such children had indeed been born of so long and apparently so happy a relationship, though it remained puzzling that they would have been unacknowledged and so widely scattered.

In the Green claim were some of the same elements as in that for Isabella Hyde—documents missing or deliberately destroyed (a destruction attributed similarly to the malice and embarrassment of Queen Victoria and her mother the Duchess of Kent), remarkable likenesses to the Royal Family, pensions arriving from unexplained sources. The traditions of the Green descendants were almost more confused than those of Isabella Hyde. One story said that the prince and Julie (this time a well-born French-Canadian) had eloped and been married at Dunkirk, a small community on the outskirts of Buffalo, New York. When the time came to separate, the prince was said to have told Julie to cover her identity by taking the name 'Green'. With the two children (known as William Goodall and *Louisa* Green), Julie thereupon went to England. There, under the name of Elizabeth Green, widow, she married Thomas Esdaile, member of the London banking family, in July 1809. After Thomas died in 1811, she lived on at his London home, 72 Baker Street, and at Sudley Cottage, his residence in Bognor, Sussex, until her death in 1835, when she was buried in Chichester Cathedral.

Other details varied. One of the duke's letters had mentioned that Madame had a sister : the name was given variously as the Comtesse de Jensac and the Countess de Jeansan. (10) The Green tradition said she had a sister *Madeline* who was married to Lieutenant-General George Glasgow of the Royal Artillery. This couple was said to have attended the prince's marriage to Julie—this time at St Paul's Episcopal Church in Halifax, Nova Scotia. Another story gave Julie's *maiden* name as Green, daughter of William Green who had owned considerable property around Albany, New York, who had sent his three daughters to Quebec at the time of the Revolutionary War, and who was later drowned crossing a river or lake, the title deeds to his lands carefully stowed in his baggage.

An article in the *Berwick Advertiser* on 19 November 1918 recorded the death of William Goodall Green's grandson William George with an account of his royal descent. In this account, the prince and Julie were morganatically married in *Montreal* in 1792 after Julie had escaped from the convent on the shores of Lake Erie where she had been secluded by her father. Of the two children, the boy was said to have been the elder. He often recalled (it was reported) sitting on the knee of his grandfather King George III, from whom he received gifts, including a gold watch. Other family tradition set Louisa's birth a year *earlier* than her brother's, and recalled her memory of being in Spain when her brother was a baby (this was significant because of Prince Edward's association with Gibraltar).

The next generation of William Goodall Green's descendants struggled diligently and tirelessly to prove their descent and claim to the Kent title, gathering every bit of information possible about their background. William Goodall Green had been appointed Deputy-Assistant-Commissary-General in Quebec in 1813, claimed by his descendants as preferment due to his royal ancestry. When the Duke of Kent died in 1820, it was said, William's mother (now Mrs Julie Esdaile) wrote to her son that 'he had better come to England to look after his interests'. Sent by his mother to the Duchess of Kent to get some papers the duke had left for her, he was believed to have been so rudely treated by his 'father's' widow that he vowed he would never again approach the Royal Family.

Of the children named Rees in Halifax little was known that could be considered as evidence for royal birth except the tradition. It seemed likely that a similar confusion existed : trinkets and furniture treasured because they were thought to have belonged to royal Edward and his love, handed down to blood descendants : uncertainty about birth-dates, whispers about true parentage : the ever-recurring 'likenesses' to the Royal Family : vanished documents ruthlessly destroyed by a queen ashamed of her father's liaison—more of these same elements would probably be presented to support the Rees claim. Was there a grain of truth in all these kernels?

The only available information (up to the publication of Porter's book) about Madame's fate after she had parted from her royal lover had appeared in a biography of the duke published in 1870 by Dr W. J. Anderson, a Quebec historian, which preserved an invaluable correspondence between the Duke of Kent and Madame and their Quebec friends, the de Salaberry family. Seeking some account of what had become of 'the amiable lady who for upwards of a quarter of a century presided over the domestic arrangements of the Duke' to be added as a postcript to his book, Dr Anderson had asked Colonel de Salaberry, grandson of Ignace-Louis (the duke's friend) for his latest information. The Colonel agreeably searched through his papers and found a letter written to his father by General Baron de Rottenburg on 3 March 1819, in which he had stated 'Madame de St Laurent has retired to a convent'.

Porter's book offered a new version of her later life. After a few years of grief in her Paris convent, he said, Julie had emerged to enjoy a quiet social life as the Comtesse de Montgenêt, with her family estates at St-Laurent-sur-Mer and her own title restored to her by Charles X. (11) From among numerous suitors, though she was now in her mid-fifties, she chose a second husband (or third, if she had indeed been married to Prince Edward) in Prince Prospero Colonna, Russian member of a famous Italian family. Colonna's two sons lived in New Orleans: Julie's daughter Melanie had married a New Orleans engineer named Levison or Lewison. The happy couple visited their children in the southern states, and Julie's son Robert Wood in Quebec. Friendships in Quebec kept them there for three years before the prince, on a trip to Russia, was drowned at sea. Quebec held Julie's happiest memories and her heart. She settled in the summer home at Montmorency Falls where she had lived with Prince Edward early in the 1790s, visited from time to time by both her sons, and lived there peacefully until her death in 1872 at the age of 106.

So the legends have grown. But where a Mrs Hyde is buried, where a Mrs Armstrong, where lies interred a Princess Colonna who lived to be 106, where even a Mrs Esdaile (a search of Chichester tombstones and the cathedral records did not bring her resting place to light) no one seemed to know. And where the body of Alphonsine Thérèse Bernardine Julie de St Laurent de Montgenêt, Baronne de Fortisson?—who she was, how old, where and when she met her prince, what her life was after their parting, and what the day of her death—these were mysteries still to be solved.

* * *

None of the stories is true. She did not retire to a convent in France, in Belgium, or in Smyrna (as one story suggested). She did not die in Bognor in 1835 nor in Quebec at the age of 106. She was never married. She had no children at all, though she had at least three lovers. And by the last of these, though he left her to marry another, she was beloved until the day of his death.

Alphonsine Julie Thérèse Bernardine de Montgenêt, Baronne de
Fortisson (Madame de St Laurent).
Credit: Archives du Québec.

Prince Edward (later Duke of Kent), Halifax 1796, painted by S. Weaver.
Credit: Nova Scotia Legislature Library.

Part One

The twenty-seven years

CHAPTER ONE

I look for a companion

Early in January 1790, London society was astonished and intrigued
by the sudden arrival in the city of the young Prince Edward, his
Majesty's fourth son, who had been pursuing his studies in Europe.
Tongues wagged, the public prints speculated, and on 28 January a
young officer stationed at Woolwich passed the latest gossip to his
brother, a captain with the Royal Fusiliers stationed in the Isle of Man.

'By this day's paper,' wrote Ashton to John Shuttleworth, 'I find
you have chang'd your Colonel (*Prince Edward*), who leaves London
tomorrow for Portsmouth accompanied by the *Prince of Wales* in order
to join the Southampton frigate, now waiting to carry him to
Giberalter [*sic*] to join his regiment viz. *2nd or Queen's* (lately Colonel
Jones's, who is now to be your Colonel) I dare say you will be happy
in the exchange—as he is reported to be very extravagant, have run
himself in Debt in various places abroad, to the amount of Twelve
000 Pounds as reports go, He has incurred His Majesty's displeasure
which is the reason given for his quitting England in so great a
Hurry . . .' (12)

Though Ashton Shuttleworth was wrong about the exchange of
colonels (Prince Edward was temporarily Colonel of the Queen's
Regiment but remained Colonel of the Royal Fusiliers, an appointment he had received in April 1789) his other information was more
nearly accurate. But the twenty-two-year-old prince had more on his
mind than the debts he had run up.

He had whipped his horses across Europe early in January in a
wild and unauthorized trip by coach, accompanied only by Mr Sturt,
'son of the Member for Dorsetshire', and delayed by a broken axle and

boisterous weather in the Channel which he had crossed by ordinary
packet-ship. (13) Arriving at Nerot's, a small hotel in London, in the
cold hours of early morning, he had sent to his eldest brother an urgent
plea for help. He would have been here forty-eight hours sooner, he
said, except for accidents on the road. Mr Sturt, by whom this message
would be delivered, would explain 'the singular reasons that obliged me
to depart so quickly from Geneva'. He was counting on his brother's
kindness, and would do whatever he suggested. (14)

He was to be kept waiting for two nervous weeks before being at
last received into the royal presence, unable, because he had not been
officially presented after a four-year absence from home, to attend the
grand ball and supper given by the Prince of Wales at Carlton House
on the evening of his arrival, nor the brilliant Drawing Room to celebrate the Birthday of his mother the Queen (which Mr Sturt attended,
arriving in 'a very elegant Post Chariot, painted and striped of a fine
yellow, with full Arms and Supporters, in silver circles, and rich silver-
plated work all over the body'). He was probably still suffering from a
sense of shock when he finally faced his justly angry father in the
uncomfortable fifteen-minute interview he was allowed on the evening
of 28 January : for he now had to acknowledge that he had left in
Geneva an illegitimate baby daughter, whose young mother had died
in childbirth not more than six weeks earlier.

The papers had made much of the unexpected arrival, wondering,
surmising, hinting, sneering at each other's misinformation, and at last
ponderously admonishing. Rumours had been circulating just before
his dramatic appearance in London, that the prince was about to
embark on various continental visits from the starting point of Geneva,
where he had been pursuing his studies for the past two years. Now
his unexplained presence, the stony silence preserved by Windsor, the
warmth of his reception by what the papers termed 'the band of
brothers', the Prince of Wales, the Dukes of York and Clarence, all
were sucked dry of any possible meaning. The prince had contracted
huge debts—£14,000, £20,000—which his Majesty had undertaken
to pay. He would take his seat in the House of Lords next session as
Duke of Lancaster. He had (had not) been at the Prince of Wales's
gala. He had (had not) paid his respects to their Majesties in an interview 'truly interesting on both sides'. He was lodged at Carlton House,
at St James's, at the Duke of York's. It was agreed that he had grown
very tall, in stature full six feet two inches, and in his figure, air and
manner—'singularly engaging and affable'—he resembled the King
more than any of his royal brothers.

On Saturday, 16 January, only two days after his arrival, the
General Evening Post had sprung a sensational story.

'The return of an Illustrious Gentleman to this country has, it is said, excited some displeasure in very Great Persons. Permission was not given for this visit, and the departure of the young gentleman, it is thought, will be the necessary step to appease the resentment!

'An incident of a pathetic nature operated in a degree to induce him to leave Geneva: a young lady, of French birth, is said to have engaged a share of his attachment, and after an intimacy of some duration, she appeared in a state of pregnancy.

'Her death happened a short time since; she died in childbed, and left a charming little girl behind her. During her indisposition, the unremitted [sic] care and solicitude shewn by her admirer, demonstrated a heart rich in the finest feelings of nature!'

Five days too late, on the 21st, the *World* attempted a contradiction. 'It was not any affair with any Lady, as has been falsely asserted, that induced Prince Edward "to take the Royal Family by surprise"— because we do not believe that any one of that family . . . knew of the Royal Adventure.' The King had in fact been informed, though not in time for preventive action. Prince Edward's governor Lieutenant-Colonel George von Wangenheim wrote urgently on 5 January to say he had discovered the intentions of his young charge, had remonstrated in vain, and now suggested to the King that the prince, feeling neglected by his father's failure to write for nearly two years, and seeking parental kindness rather than strict justice, hoped to explain his severe embarrassments in person. (15)

The King was not notably regular with his letters to any of his absent sons, and for much of the past two years had been fighting his own agonizing battle with physical and mental illness. But apart from the prince's affair of the heart—and with perhaps some excuse because of Wangenheim's tight control of his available pocket money—the young man had sadly abused his first freedom from restraint by making extravagant financial commitments that would haunt him for the rest of his life.

On the heels of this message came word from the Prime Minister, Mr Pitt, in a letter dated the 14th, 'that the report which had been conveyed to your Majesty respecting Prince Edward proves to be well founded, and that his Royal Highness landed yesterday morning' at Dover. The same day Lord Chancellor Thurlow reported to the badly distressed King an interview he had had with the two eldest princes and their delinquent brother, when 'the language of all the Princes was as satisfactory as so untoward an occasion would admit of'. (16)

While Prince Edward—surely somewhat subdued—took what comfort he could from the reunion with his brothers and nostalgic visits to Windsor, Hampton Court and Kew, urgent letters flew between the Queen's House and Downing Street, and anxious audiences were given to decide on suitable discipline for so sad a fall from grace. A destination (Gibraltar), a ship to take him there (*Southampton*) and as immediate a date of departure as could be arranged. 'With regard to the frigate for conveying Edward to Gibraltar', wrote the King to Mr Pitt on the 19th, 'I cannot think it so material whether he embarks preferably at Portsmouth to /or?/ Plymouth as that he should as soon as possible quit London'. (17)

He did not get his interview with the King until the evening of Thursday the 28th, and then only because of the efforts of his brothers and Mr Pitt. 'The sensations which this interview occasioned in the breasts of both father and son', said the *Public Advertiser* with truth, 'are more easily conceived than expressed'.

The prince had spent some time earlier that day in one of those kindly acts which were to be characteristic throughout his life, visiting in his Newgate prison cell the instigator of the notorious 1780 riots, Lord George Gordon, with whose nephew the Marquis of Huntley he had been friendly in Geneva. Next evening he set off for Portsmouth, travelling in a carriage lent him by his brother Prince William with whom he had dined earlier: William also lent him the cook from *Pegasus*.

If he was chastened by his recent experience, his welcome at Portsmouth where *Southampton* had been hastily fitting out was well calculated to restore his self-esteem. Admiral Roddam had had orders to receive him as a Prince of the Blood, and the immensity of the throng that impeded his progress from carriage to lodgings suggested the wisdom of spiriting him out through a different door when he had to leave, to the disappointment of thousands. After two days of harbour tours and a variety of civic entertainment, he was seen off by 'a beautiful assemblage of Ladies' at the Hulk Stairs, including, probably, Sally Martin, an early love of his brother Prince William's and daughter of the Commissioner of the Dockyard, at whose home he had dined the night before. *Southampton* sailed at noon on 1 February amid bands playing, banners flying and a continual cloud of gunsmoke.

With the prince on *Southampton* went Captain Charles Gregan Craufurd, one of his brother the Duke of York's equerries. 'In the company of a gentleman of such merit, and so nice a sense of honour, his Royal Highness cannot fail of finding a most agreeable companion, and a very useful friend', said the *General Evening Post* on 4 February. He was to be a temporary adviser, companion and guardian, to keep some kind of check on a young man now known to be headstrong and high-spirited, but (it was hoped) biddable. 'I think he may be led',

Captain Craufurd reported after he had been with the prince for a month, 'but I am certain he never will be drove.' (18) His recent escapade had resulted partly from the heady effect of freedom from family restraints in a new and exciting milieu where his rank and good looks attracted flattering adulation, partly from the galling new controls exercised by the gentlemen placed in charge of him. The programme for the young prince that had sent him to Luneburg, Hanover and Geneva for military and other studies had been planned with a good deal of thought and concern by the King, but his 'bear-keepers' (his own phrase) headed by Lieutenant-Colonel von Wangenheim, who had been recommended by the Duke of York, had succeeded only in irritating their princely charge.

Despite the rapidity with which Prince Edward was hustled out of the kingdom, his father's concern was manifest in the arrangements made for his term at Gibraltar. Captain Craufurd proved so congenial a companion that the prince tried hard but unsuccessfully to persuade him to remain a member of his family. Colonel Richard Symes, who had accepted the King's command with some trepidation, and departed reluctantly from his estate at Ballyarthur, County Wicklow, to replace Craufurd as mentor to the young man, had to refuse the same invitation when, a year later, the prince wanted him to go with him to Canada.

It was evident that he was abashed and mortified by his disgrace. His letters to his father were genuinely repentant. Always after reprimand, the young prince honestly meant to do better and was quick to acknowledge the error of his ways. But, like his far more extravagant and always more worldly-wise elder brothers, he had been brought up aware of the pomp and ceremony of the princely estate without the slightest attempt to equip him with any financial competence, and it was his over-spending rather than his flirtations that had brought down the wrath upon his head. 'The youthful vanity of wishing to have everything about him better, more showy, and in greater abundance than other people is his chief error', wrote Captain Craufurd with considerable foresight. 'He appears good humoured; he receives and seems to attend to advice on subjects that relate to his conduct here as a Prince & a Colonel of the Garrison; he neither drinks nor games in the least; but in certain points of expence, such as horses, furniture &c. he is impatient of control; this is his passion, but in the indulging of any other he seems by no means inclined to excess.' (19) This judgement would remain true all his life.

He had been welcomed with royal honours on 24 February at Gibraltar, where the garrison, 'His Royal Highness Prince Edward His Majesty's 4th son being arrived in the Bay', had been getting spit-and-polish orders for the event. Then, posted to the command of the

Queen's Royal Regiment, he relinquished his royal rank and assumed the regular duties of his military one, on garrison duty every other day as Colonel of the day. He was now receiving a first-class military training, which was planned to fill up a considerable portion of his time. (20) What was left of it was filled with the carefully supervised dinners, suppers, balls, with which the Commander-in-Chief, General Charles O'Hara, fêted the prince and the whole of the garrison.

Prince Edward had lodged with the General for the first week, breakfasting, dining and supping with him, but by 2 March he had begun to live in his own house, which he set about furnishing with an enthusiasm somewhat dismaying to Captain Craufurd. The King's care in selecting suitable companions for his fourth son had not been extended to include realistic financial arrangements. The £500 advanced to Captain Craufurd to get the prince established in Gibraltar, though meant to be a temporary measure, was pitifully inadequate, and raised fears in the Captain's mind that a false economy would defeat the good intentions surrounding the prince's rehabilitation. Craufurd did his best to control reckless spending, but was remarkably sympathetic to the young man's position.

'If, in spite of all my endeavours, the furniture should exceed what his Majesty wishes, I can only say that in one scale you must place the saving a moderate sum of money, in the other, the danger of defeating the purposes of H.R.H.'s journey hither. The limits of this place are very confined; the amusements of it few . . . were he not then to be *égayé* here as much, and made as comfortable as the place will admit of; allowed to indulge in a certain degree his little whims, which, whether childish or not, equally constitute his amusement, I own I apprehend the worst consequences, such as his becoming quite disgusted with the place, and his acting in opposition to the King's commands.' (21)

Earlier in the same letter, Craufurd had summed up the situation well. 'He is between two and three & twenty, of course no longer a boy. He feels this, and seems very anxious to be on the footing of a man in every respect: immediate control therefore will not do; art and good management must supply its place; and the great thing in my mind is to endeavour the accomplishment of our principal ends, keeping him at the same time in good humour. Should he once become disgusted with us, the thing is over; from that moment he will never listen to a word we say, and purposely act in opposition to what we wish.'

Prince Edward appeared to be more than willing to co-operate, anxious to regain his father's esteem and respect. He had agreeably followed advice against accepting an invitation (to which he had been looking forward) to head the Masonic Lodge in Gibraltar early in his stay there, and agreed to some supervision of the guests who would be 'fit persons among the Officers . . . to invite to his little parties'. He attended punctiliously to his military duties, gaining everyone's commendation.

Colonel Symes took over from Craufurd in mid-May, and his letters, beginning with apprehension that the prince was prejudiced against him, were able to contain increasingly favourable reports over the next six months to his friend Major-General Richard Grenville, through whom the news of his son's progress was reported to the King.

The continued failure to settle the amount of Prince Edward's income was to be the Colonel's major grievance, and perhaps Pitt's faulty advice at the time of the young man's dispatch to Gibraltar must bear part at least of the blame—not only for the prince's difficulties at that time, but for his later distress with debts. 'Perhaps your Majesty may think it adviseable [sic] to defer settling anything finally on this head till Col. Symes, or any other officer whom Your Majesty may select, is sent out to Gibraltar, and . . . by these means there will be an opportunity of receiving more particular information from Genl O'Hara,' Pitt had written when the urgent matter of the disposal of the young delinquent confronted them. 'In the meantime Genl Grenville seemed to suppose that his Royal Highness could not have occasion for any large sum, probably not more than five hundred pounds, as, on his first arrival at Gibraltar and till his establishment could be fixed, a table would be kept for him by Genl O'Hara. A farther sum of five hundred pounds might also, as Genl Grenville conceived, be proper to be advanced to Capt Crawford [sic].' (22)

Symes proceeded to deal with the prince with the most admirable tact and delicacy and soon won the young man's confidence and respect. Like Craufurd, he appreciated that the prince's youth, his inexperience and his rank, rather than any real defect of character, were the chief causes of his present situation: and though he deplored the expenses already incurred by the time of his arrival, he agreed that they were not altogether Prince Edward's fault. On 21 May he wrote to Grenville: 'In the expense which the Prince has incurred here, too much money has no doubt been spent, but less thrown away than I had imagined. To look for a well regulated and judicious œconomy from one of his age and disposition would be vain: it is therefore only to be wished for, but not yet to be expected.' (23)

By November he was able to point out that Prince Edward had reduced the number of his servants, had bought no more horses, had got rid of the greater number of musicians he had imported, and that

C

'the debt contracted before my arrival . . . has in no instance increased'.
But he also added that the prince had expected (not unreasonably) that
his establishment would be at least as much as his Geneva allowance,
and had spent accordingly : that he had promised the King to moderate
his extravagance if the debts were paid and a regular sum transmitted
to him : and that some of the expenses to which he was committed were
unavoidable. His regiment alone (the 7th or Royal Fusiliers had been
sent to Gibraltar at his request) was a constant drain on his purse. 'If
its being here fortunately contributes to his instruction and employment
it also engages and always must a part of his income.' A large
Portuguese squadron in the Bay for several months meant additional
entertaining. 'In his mode of living, when alone, nothing can be more
plain, or simple, when he entertains either the Garrison or strangers
he will be magnificent.'

In short (or rather, at length, in eighteen pages of exposition)
Symes reported improvement and pleaded extenuating circumstances.
The prince had been rushed out of England too fast for proper provision to be made for the way he was to live, said Symes, and having
landed without any furniture he had even had to hunt around for
what was needed to prepare meals for himself and any guests he might
wish to entertain. 'The Principles and practice of just Economy . . .
are only to be acquired in the school of the world, with which Princes,
and men of high rank, are not always sufficiently acquainted to derive
the advantages of which they often stand in need in the management
of their affairs.' He had been sent to Gibraltar, after all, to get him
away from bad influences : until now he had been just like a boy let
out of school, who had decided to make up for his former restraints
by running a bit wild. 'What follies do we not see, every day, committed by youth under similar circumstances, and for which allowances
must be made,' concluded wise Colonel Symes. (24)

The colonel found no lessening of the ardour and attention, reported
by Craufurd in March, with which the prince was going about his
regimental and garrison duties. He paraded the guard-duty members
of his regiment every morning at seven (earlier in summer), and on
alternate mornings took charge of the whole garrison guard of about
600 men : busied himself with reports and detail work : sat on General
Courts-Martial : made the rounds of the various districts with the
Field Officer of the day : and studied the regulations and fortifications,
all under the careful eye of O'Hara and Craufurd or Symes.

But however industrious in his duties, the tall, handsome, blond,
blue-eyed prince had a need of other diversions. He had written to
the Prince of Wales on 29 February [sic] about the bareness of his
quarters, pleading for furniture. 'Barring the two beds and the chairs

which my brother William was so good as to give me, my whole quarters consist of bare walls . . . if you would favor me with a little furniture of any kind, particularly two or three dozen of red leather chairs, and a few mahogany tables with some common carpets & floor cloths, as well as half a dozen common looking-glasses with gilt frames, it will be of all presents the most acceptable that you can make me.' (25) But furniture was not his greatest lack.

In June he told his brother that though he was 'upon the whole' satisfied with his situation, he was lonely. 'There is one very essential requisite towards rendering the life of a young soldier happy, in a solitary place like this, I mean, a partner for his leisure hours, which, selon mon gout, I am incapable to provide myself with here. You know, that is a point I am not easily satisfied about; for I despise every sensual enjoyment, which one might procure when the object of it is a prostitute, in short I look for a companion, not for a whore. I know, you will laugh at my strange out of the way ideas, but consult your own heart, and then reflect, with this sentiment, if it is possible for me to live solus very contented in a fortress like this, where, even those who love the bawdy house are obliged to practise much self-denial.' (26)

Although Prince Edward would always have an eye for a pretty face and, like many a happily married man, would not be averse to a temporary arrangement from time to time, he was essentially a one-woman man all his life. To the end of achieving some kind of permanence—the only kind possible for a young man of his rank and station—he now dispatched his valet on a mission of the utmost importance and consequence, designed to relieve the loneliness that bothered him.

On 9 July, the watchful Colonel Symes reported to Grenville.

'Moré, the Prince's valet . . . is returned here this morning with Made Dubus, sister to a young woman who lived with the Prince at Geneva, and by whom he had a daughter. The ostensible cause of this journey was to convey the child to its Father—the real one, to procure a Mistress in the Aunt, to whose care on the death of the mother, the child was left at Geneva, but has died on the voyage from Marseilles hither. I hear this Lady possesses some talents for Musick to which her sister was bred, and by which she supported the family. A musical intercourse produced the former intimacy, and has occasioned the Prince to wish that she might replace her sister. Moré, the valet, who is his Master's confidential agent in this Business, gives the Prince to understand that Mademoiselle Dubus means to play the Lucretia in this piece and return to Marseilles, to engage in Musick as a profession, and that her inducement for undertaking so long a journey and voyage was purely from motives of affection to her niece and to mark her respect for the Father, which she could not have carried into execution had not her own Father attended as her protection.

'This history you will conclude, as I do, calculated to enhance in the eyes of the Prince the merit of her coming, and the sacrifice she makes, in becoming his Mistress, when her talents enable her to live in Independance, and with reputation. This visit you perceive will occasion a change in the Prince's situation, and an addition to his expense, of which we were ignorant when I left England; It is an Evil none of us could prevent and all that can be done is to guard as much as possible the Prince's pockets, already drained, from being wholly exhausted.'

The realistic colonel was not entirely opposed to the prince's solution of his problem. In fact, he could see some virtue in it.

'In other respects, the introduction of this female may prevent greater ills, it is not to be expected that a young man of his age will lead a life of celibacy, and we have our ladies here, as well as with you, equally ready to sacrifice their reputation and the peace of their families to the vanity of such a conquest. Craufurd can instruct you how strongly the Prince's smiles have been contested by our rival Queens, his attentions at that time gave rise to scandal, which has since increas'd to a degree as to induce me very sincerely to wish for the arrival of this female as the only means by which he might be directed from pursuits the consequences of which must have involved him in difficulties without end, and proved dangerous as well as disgraceful.

'In a choice of difficulties, we are happy to have recourse to the least. In my own opinion, the Prince is likely to suffer less, in every point of view, at present, than before, and more so as I hear the newly arrived is not endowed with such attractions as are likely to make a very strong impression.'

No wonder the harassed and conscientious colonel added that his present situation was 'the most arduous and irksome I was ever placed in . . . under the pressure of constant anxiety from the desire I have to act in conformity to the King's wishes'. (27)

The mother of the dead child had been a young French actress named Adelaide Dubus, who on her death left the baby in the care of her sister Victoire. A legal agreement which provided for pensions for both the girl's father and sister had also stated that the child was not to become an actress and was to be brought up a Protestant. It also retained for the prince the right to have his daughter, born on 15 December 1789 and christened Adelaide Victoire Auguste, brought to him whenever he so requested. (28)

The arrangement, however, to have Mademoiselle Victoire replace her dead sister did not turn out as well as the prince had hoped. Whether she refused to sacrifice her virtue on terms he was prepared to meet, or whether her charms were not sufficiently appealing, nothing came of the plan. The lonely prince began to look around for another companion, and this time with greater success than he could have dared to hope.

By October he had grown restless and unhappy and tired of the Rock. His health in Gibraltar's hot weather constantly distressed him with the bilious attacks from which he was never to be entirely free, and the confinement was becoming tiresome for one whom Captain Craufurd had found 'so lively a Prince'. To his friend Lieutenant-General Sir William Fawcett, the Adjutant-General, Prince Edward wrote on 18 October with various suggestions for relief. He would be ready, he said, to go to any part of Germany, France or Switzer-land if the King did not approve his return to England, 'or to pass that time in rambling over those three countries . . . without fixing my residence in any part.' Or, if his regiment could be sent to Quebec, he would be content to stay there until recalled. (29)

By January next year, though still on the Rock, he was writing to his brother the Duke of Clarence in quite a different tone. Something had happened that had settled his restlessness, filled the gap in his life.

'I feel this want of resources perhaps less than any man, for I manage with the assistance of a little music, a few books, & a little small talk with four or five officers, who constantly live in my family, to fill up as chearfully as I can those moments when professional business does not occupy me. Besides I have at present a young woman living with me who I wrote over to, to come from France to me, who has every qualification which an excellent share of good temper, no small degree of cleverness, & above all, a pretty face & a handsome person can give to make my hours pass away pleasantly in her company.' (30)

The young woman was the lady known in all the prince's future letters as Madame de St Laurent. He had apparently entrusted to a gentleman in his confidence and identified in his letters only as M. Fontiny (or Fantiny) the delicate commission of finding someone to be his companion in exile. Fontiny appears to have discovered her in

Marseilles, and his letter to the prince enclosing one from the lady herself seems to have described her in such glowing terms that Prince Edward, enchanted, could hardly wait for her arrival in Gibraltar. Fontiny, with what he must have thought was immense tact, had engaged her as a singer, and planned to have her accommodated in Gibraltar, with her maid, in an apartment in the town. The prince, on 23 November, imperiously disillusioned him.

'As the commission with which I charged you to find for me a young lady to be my companion and mistress of my house was very detailed, and the talent for music which I wanted her to have was not at all the chief object which I had asked you to watch for, you must have understood quite well that I was much put out to see that you had contracted an engagement with a young person who should, according to the instructions that I had given you myself in writing, and of which I have carefully kept a copy, have in my home a much higher status than would be afforded to her by any professional contract; but I was even more upset when I read on the small note that you enclosed in your letter that you wanted Mlle de St Laurent, with her maid, to be lodged in an apartment in the town and not with me. I confess to you quite plainly that I do not know to what to attribute this way of acting on your part, when you have heard from my own lips more than twenty times before you left for Marseilles that under no consideration would I ever consent to lodge under another roof than mine the person who would become my companion and my friend. But I wish to consider that you have acted in these two matters without thinking, and on condition that you correct your error by exactly carrying out the orders that will be given to you by Beck, I am disposed to forget what should with good reason have displeased me on your part; consequently as you wish not to appear in this affair, stay with the musicians at Malaga until Captain Nicolas has ended his business and puts to sea for here. Come with them, and no one will notice that you had anything to do with Mlle de St Laurent.' (31)

To Mademoiselle herself, Prince Edward wrote on the same day.

'The moment I received your kind letter enclosed with M. Fontiny's, I knew I must immediately send my confidential servant, Beck, to meet you at Malaga and make sure that nothing should delay you and postpone the pleasure I will have in welcoming you here.

'I dare flatter myself that in signing your contract you felt it was only a simple form you had to observe purely out of delicacy for

Fontiny's sake; I hope also that from the moment you receive this you will be convinced that your arrival will be welcomed with all the respect of which a young man is capable who is consumed with happiness at making your charming acquaintance, and of the respect of all my friends and my family whose eagerness will prove that they have no deeper wish than to win your friendship and offer you theirs. Please then accept my recognition of the courage you have shown in undertaking such a long and tiring journey. At the same time, honour me by not refusing the first favour I ask of you—to come as quickly as you can, with just your maid and my confidential servant, who will have the honour of being your guide; it will bring me the happiness of seeing you very soon, and in taking immediately the place I have planned for you, you will give me the best proof of your affection. I wait with open arms to place in your hands the running of my little establishment, only do not forget that a bed and a few chairs in a cottage are all that make up the small estate of a soldier. Having made your contract with a soldier, you must make up your mind to carry the knapsack and not dream of the broidered coverlets of kings and the great of this world. Awaiting the pleasure of welcoming you, I will keep the cottage warm and expect that from the moment of your arrival our life will begin to be happy and content.' (32)

The news of the latest arrival put the long-suffering Colonel Symes into a flutter. On 27 December he wrote in consternation to General Grenville.

'Since I wrote to you last Monday on the subject of Canada, I am happy to find by letters from England that the Prince's wish and request to go there in the spring is likely to be comply'd with. For his sake I most sincerely wish it may take place, and have promoted the idea to the utmost of my power. . . .

'With the promise I have obtained from the Prince of his ceasing any further importation from England, I now wish France had been included, from whence, a Lady is just arrived whose company here at present would have been very well dispensed with. Had she arrived five months since, her coming might have had a good effect, and have prevented what has nearly produced a great deal of mischief, which to avert in part has cost me both infinite pains and extreme anxiety. Craufurd will have explained to you the origin of this business, and on that account the departure of Mademoiselle Dubus was unlucky and therefore to be regretted. This female companion will have less claim to his future attention or pecuniary supplys, having made this visit perfectly to suit her convenience, as her late keeper—a countryman of her own who calls himself the Marquiss de Permangle—she quitted at Malaga from his being unable to defray her expenses. She seems near thirty, well-looking, has been in England, with whom I have not learned, but resembles a woman I have seen with Lord Cholmondeley.

'The Prince at present talks of her going with him from hence, but before that can take place I hope he will grow tired of her, and move without the Embarras of such an Incumbrance.

'I don't think he is disposed to be much the Dupe of women, and had he remained here this might have answered a good purpose. When that is not to happen, I regret what now has taken place as much as I should have formerly been pleased with such an arrival.' (33)

The Colonel continued to fuss and worry, but all to no effect. He suggested to Grenville in January that perhaps Mademoiselle could be bought off. 'As the lady came here merely to suit her convenience —and to pick up what money she can—what think you of making it her interest to leave him? We can touch no other string, and I own I think two or three hundred pounds for this purpose would be well disposed of.' (34)

But Mademoiselle could not be bought off. Less than a week later the Colonel had almost given up hope of prying her loose from the prince. 'I shall leave no means untried to dissuade his R. Highness from taking along with him the female who has lately joined him here—and which he seems at present resolved on. We must therefore look on it as an evil which at present possibly cannot be removed, and act accordingly.' He was not happy about the prospect of 'the ills arising from a mixture of wives and mistresses' on the ships that were to take the prince and his regiment to Canada. (35)

On 14 February Gibraltar Garrison Orders announced the removal of the 7th Regiment of Foot or Royal Fusiliers to Canada in the coming spring, and ordered that it hold itself in readiness for embarkation. After a month of tossing in Gibraltar Bay, held ('for our sins', wrote the prince) from mid-May to mid-June by contrary winds, his Majesty's fourth son left the garrison with (except for his debts) a reputation redeemed by hard work and good behaviour. 'This whole garrison agree in giving Prince Edward the most perfect character, and declare that his conduct as a Prince and Coll. of Regt is worthy of example,' the Hon. George Keith Elphinstone had reported to the Prince of Wales in January (36) and private letters from Colonel Symes confirmed the judgement.

The prince had been fêted with some magnificence by a ball and supper on 11 May, organised at a total cost of about £360 (two guineas from each officer, an account which the meticulous Captain Shuttleworth was still settling in Quebec in 1792). With dancing till midnight, singing and band music, 'the gay uniforms of the different regiments, and the attire of the belles' decorating the ballroom, and a special canopy for Prince Edward of pink silk ornamented with silver, the affair was a brilliant climax to his term on the Rock. (37) Omission of any reference in the report to 'this female companion' followed the usual discreet pattern, but the Lady, at the height of her undoubted beauty, was probably one of the loveliest of the belles at the ball.

Prince Edward sailed at last on 24 June, with a retinue (reported *The Times* of 29 July) 'rather domestic than Princely; a French Lady, his own man, and a Swiss valet, composing his whole suite'. He sailed on board the forty-four-gun frigate *Resistance,* which with *Ulysses* had been ordered to carry the regiment to its station in North America. With him on board *Resistance,* carefully listed in the ship's muster book, sailed his servants Philip Beck, John Woolmer and Robert Wood. And *Madame* de St Laurent. (38)

CHAPTER TWO

Beginnings

She was not a 'Princesse de Normandie'. She was not from Normandy at all, but from the Franche-Comté, child of respectable family born in Besançon where her parents before her had been born, and where they would die knowing nothing of the exotic islands of the West Indies where 'de Montgenêt' plantations would come to exist in the fabric of unimagined splendour to be woven around their name.

When the guns had fired on Tower Hill in London soon after noon on 2 November 1767 to announce that the Queen was happily delivered of a Prince—the largest child, Lady Mary Coke recorded in her journal a few days later, that the Queen had ever had—Thérèse-Bernardine Mongenet was a small girl growing up in a small provincial city deep in France, where English news hardly penetrated.

Just before the new prince was born, a mournful procession had started from Charing Cross for Greenwich down the river. A hearse drawn by six dun horses with white feathers on their heads preceded the empty state coach of Edward Augustus, Duke of York, whose body, landed that morning from one of his brother the King's yachts, was to be brought to town with an escort of Horse Guards and noblemen for interment in Henry VII's chapel at Westminster.

The death of the twenty-eight-year-old Duke—'aussi triste qu'inopinée'—at Monaco on 17 September was important enough for the 7 October issue of *Affiches et Annonces de la Franche-Comté* to have brought the news to the citizens of Besançon, snugly tucked into a loop of the Doubs river in the mountain district just below the Swiss border. (39) News of the birth of the young prince of England who would bear his royal uncle's name did not reach so far afield, but it was to be of infinite importance to the little girl who, now just past her seventh birthday, had been baptized with the names Thérèse-Bernardine in the parish of St Paul on 30 September 1760. (40)

Thérèse-Bernardine was the middle child of five offspring of Jean Mongenet, an engineer in the department of highways (*ponts et chaussées*) and his wife Claudine Pussot. Her only sister, Jeanne-Beatrix, was thirteen when the English prince was born, her elder brother Claude-Charles twelve. The two younger ones were Jean-Joseph-Suzanne, aged five, and Jean-Claude, two.

What kind of child she was, and what her appearance, has to be deduced from her subsequent history. That she was pretty—even beautiful—is attested by a host of those who knew her during her years with Prince Edward, and by the history of her young womanhood before she met the prince. Being French, she was probably dark-haired, and perhaps dark-eyed, though there is a hint at a later date that her eyes may have been blue. She must have been a lively, precocious little girl, quite soon aware of her power to charm the young artillery officers stationed in the four solid barracks buildings that formed a rectangle around the parade ground beside the old church of St Paul.

The family name appears on all legal documents—birth, death and marriage certificates and wills—simply as *Mongenet,* though from time to time many members added a *de* or inserted a letter and a circumflex to write it as *Montgenêt.* The name was an ancient and honourable one in the Franche-Comté, and supplied several emigrés from the Revolution, including a *conseiller au Parlement*, an artillery officer a canon and a curé. (41) It also surfaces in civil and religious records—a Madame de Mongenet who magnificently endowed the church of Sainte-Madeleine in 1746, the Charles-François-Benoit de Montgenêt who was *conseiller honoraire au parlement de Besançon* in the 1780s. But Thérèse-Bernardine's family seem to have been solidly bourgeois, good middle-class stock with enough education to enter the professions and to equip the children with the arts and graces of the day.

Besançon was ancient already when Thérèse-Bernardine grew up there in the 1760s. It had been Vesontio, city of the Sequani, when Caesar came to Gaul. It had been the free imperial city of Frederick Barbarossa, an imperial capital of Charles-Quint and Philip II of Spain. Not far up the old Roman road, known to her as Grand'Rue as it is today, Thérèse-Bernardine could clamber among the ruins of a Roman theatre only a short distance from the sharp climb to the Roman arch called Porte Noir. Many of the worn grey mansions she would pass on Grand'Rue had been standing for more than two centuries when she was born. Not far around the curve of the river (nothing is

very far in Besançon) the embankment of the Quai Vauban would take
her to the Pont Battant, past the unbroken lines of tiered windows in
the houses looking out over the Doubs and across to l'Eglise Sainte-
Madeleine. A church had stood on the site of her own church of St
Paul since the year 630, several times rebuilt or repaired. Today a
museum, it had a tower when Thérèse-Bernardine knew it in the open
space at the end of the rue St Paul.

Besançon was a lively little city for a small girl to grow up in.
Notable visitors arrived and were taken with ceremony to the Casernes
de St Paul, and the officers from the garrison paraded and made
exciting cavalry charges. The notable visitors were then taken up
to the Citadel built by Vauban at the end of the seventeenth century
and crowning the rocky mass nearly 400 feet above the city, and guns
were fired and targets shot at, and sometimes mortar shells were
cleverly lobbed into a barrel set on top of a pole. When Thérèse-
Bernardine was only six, one of the visitors had been the Hereditary
Prince of Brunswick, who was married to a sister of the King of
England.

There was the library on Grand'Rue at the Place Saint-Pierre,
owned by Sieur Charmet and later by his widow, which not only
offered books (did she first become acquainted here with the *Oeuvres
complettes de M. de Voltaire*?—and the *Elemens de la langue Angloise*
which she spoke with perfect ease in later years?) but also acted as a
clearing house for advertisers in the Besançon journal. She could easily
picture—and perhaps with determination to own one herself some
day—the magnificent two-wheeled carriage offered for sale in July
1771, lined with sky-blue velour, with blinds and window-panes on
each side and harness for two horses. She might wonder who was the
young man looking for work as secretary to a Seigneur, the lady seeking
a hydraulics engineer to install fountains and cascades in her garden,
the officer of dragoons who sought a seat in someone's carriage going
to Paris (and vow she would go there herself some day).

Le sieur Suard (on Grand'Rue, of course) advertised, as well as
his perfumes, his baths near the promenade of Champmars the other
side of the city, where one would find aromatic and agreeable odours.
Le sieur Pelletier, surgeon dentist (Grand'Rue), undertook treatment
of teeth and gums, and all kinds of dentures of the greatest perfection.
On the rue Neuve, le sieur Pierre-Georges Bertrand, organist at the
church of St Maurice, offered lessons on the harpsichord, violin,
german guitar, flute and flageolet. Thérèse-Bernardine would receive
many compliments in later years on her fine singing : if she was also
accomplished as an instrumental performer—as she probably was—
some Besançon musician like le sieur Bertrand could take the credit.

She was fourteen when the Regiment d'Infanterie de Monsieur in garrison at Besançon and commanded by the Marquis de Saint-Simon celebrated its centenary with one of the most brilliant festivals the city had ever seen, beginning on the day after Christmas with a solemn mass at the church of Sainte-Madeleine. It is hard to believe that the vivacious girl who would sacrifice reputation for elegance and ceremony and the aristocratic company of the society she chose to mix with would not have been standing on tip-toe among the vast crowd gathered to see the regiment marching in formal parade to the church. She might, even at those tender years, have been among the guests who joined the officers afterwards at the supper prepared in their quarters, illuminated for dancing all through the night.

She was just past eighteen when the city went wild over the birth of Marie Antoinette's first child (though it was sincerely regretted that the child was not a prince), and in the decorated streets the crowds quenched their thirst at city fountains running with wine. In 1781, when she was twenty-one, she heard the bells ring out for the birth of a prince at last—that young prince who would be Dauphin until his death eight years later left the title to his younger brother, the tragic little Louis Capet.

In 1780 the big event had been the visit to Besançon of Monseigneur le duc de Chartres, who would be the notorious Philippe Egalité of the Revolution looming ahead. The twenty-year-old Thérèse-Bernardine was to be an intimate friend of his son Louis-Philippe, duc d'Orléans, for almost forty years: but now, even if the influence of the baron de Fortisson, whose mistress she became prior to 1786, won her a privileged position, she could have been little more than a spectator at the festivities.

In England the young prince whose destiny was to be linked so closely to hers was growing up under the privileges and restraints of a royal childhood. His life was neither as unhappy nor as formal as some of his biographers have suggested, and many of the theories explaining his father's attitude towards him are erroneous.

The anecdote most often quoted as pathetic illustration of Prince Edward's rejection by his father is one from the journal of Lady Mary Coke. The little boy was being told about the devotion of the Duke of Ormond to his dead son Ossory. Weeping when he heard that Ormond would not change his dead son 'for the best living son in Europe', the prince wondered if his own parents would say the same of him in case he were to die, and then, before he could be answered, said: 'As I am a child I suppose not, but if I live to grow up, perhaps they wou'd say the same.'

This story about Prince Edward's unhappy childhood, handed down

from biographer to biographer, has a poignant ring, but it suffers from
a basic flaw. The prince who wept was not Edward. It was Prince
Frederick, his father's favourite son. (42)

King George III and Queen Charlotte appear to have given their
children a carefully supervised upbringing, with a simple and sensible
diet, lots of fresh air, and a progressive introduction to the society and
etiquette with which they would be surrounded in later life. From an
early age they were taken to the formal Drawing Rooms at St James's
Palace and Buckingham-house. It was in 1772, when he was only
five, that the little boy's comical remark on being told he was not to
go to Court that day so amused Lady Mary Coke: 'Then I suppose
I am not well: I must button up & Take care of myself.' His precocity
in talking at a year old had amazed the same lady in 1768, and again
in 1769, when she recorded that 'His Majesty's youngest Son talks
everything, tho' I believe he is but a year & half old'. (43)

Excessive formality of behaviour was not practised except in public
or as a part of their training to act the proper role of princes and
princesses. The weekly promenade around Richmond Gardens 'in
pairs', often interpreted as an example of deadly conformity, was
balanced by the free play in the children's own gardens. Mrs
Papendiek, whose father had accompanied the young Queen Charlotte
to England for her marriage in 1761, and who was born just a
month before Prince William, has recalled how she used to enjoy
playing with that little prince during her childhood ('I was always
rather impatient with anything that kept me from the royal nursery').
(44) The King and Queen liked to sit in the room while the children
had dinner, and often at other times. Mrs Delany drew an equally
pleasant picture of informal domesticity in 1785. 'I have been several
evenings at the Queen's Lodge, with no other company but their own
most lovely family. They sit around a large table, on which are books,
work, pencils, and paper . . . the younger part of the family are
drawing and working, &c & the beautiful babe, Princess Amelia . . .
sometimes in one of her sisters' laps; sometimes playing with the King
on the carpet.' (45)

If we can believe contemporary gossip published at the time of the
old King's death in 1820, the young Prince of Wales was not afraid,
when he was about ten years old, to yell 'Wilkes and No. 45 for
ever!' at his father's door before making a speedy retreat. It was
hardly necessary to add, said the writer, that His Majesty laughed
heartily at the incident 'with his accustomed good-humour'. (46)

Only when his sons left boyhood behind did the King, like many
another father, discover that they were hard to handle. Then, lusty
with approaching manhood, aware of their rank and easily led to

forbidden delights by courtiers only too willing to vie for royal favours, they began to present problems to their father.

Prince Edward's future had been planned with great care and as much wisdom as human limitations could apply. Intending to send his son to Luneburg in Hanover for continued studies and the beginning of his military education, the King had begun in mid-1784 to consult with his second son Prince Frederick to select 'an Officer of rank to place about Edward'. Prince Frederick himself was in Europe at the time, with headquarters at Hanover, where he had been sent in 1781 to receive his own military training. Among other alternatives, he suggested Lieutenant-Colonel George von Wangenheim of the Horse Guards, 'as fit a man as can be found, as he is not only a very good officer but besides is exceedingly entertaining in conversation and has very much the manners of a gentleman'. (47)

During the months before his departure from Greenwich in the royal yacht *Augusta* on 20 May next year (48) the young prince, now turned seventeen, was beginning to appear in public more often. He had probably been among those members of the Royal Family attending the performance on Saturday 2 January of the annual New Year's Ode by the Poet Laureate, and the Court and Drawing Room which followed, when the fashion was reported to be 'poppy-coloured satin waists and trains', heads ornamented with ribbons and flowers to match. He was certainly present at the Queen's Birthday, officially celebrated in January, where the gentlemen mostly wore velvets, the ladies 'rich fancy satins and new manufacture of Irish tabbinets and poplins elegantly trimmed', and the King appeared in a gold-embroidered scarlet coat glittering with diamond star and 'George'. (49)

Public opinion was not sure whether to approve this migration to the Continent of British princes, but made the best of it. On 18 May the *Morning Chronicle* commented: 'There was a time when the English would not be pleased to see their Princes go in such numbers to reside out of the country; and much less so since the accession of the reigning family to see them live in Germany; but now that they have a native Prince on the throne the English are not afraid of foreign attachments, which during the reigns of the last two monarchs, influenced the Councils of the nation much more than a regard to its real interests. On the arrival of Prince Edward in Hanover there will be three sons of our King residing in his Electoral dominions.'

The week of his departure he was given a fine family send-off. The Queen turned her actual birth date into a special State ceremonial on Thursday 19 May, so that her fourth son could say farewell to the nobility. On Tuesday he had gone *en famille* (his royal parents and five of his sisters) to the King's Theatre to a performance of *Orfeo,* probably the one by Gluck. An uncommonly crowded house at Drury Lane next evening (the younger ladies with 'an immensity of white feathers on their heads') attended his last public appearance with their Majesties and three of the princesses to see Mrs Siddons in *As You Like It.* The King was attired in a pea-coloured silk laced with silver. Prince Edward wore pale pink.

Prince Frederick, now the Duke of York, had been busily occupied in preparing for Prince Edward's reception, advising against his father's first plan to send his young brother to Göttingen, since the young men all lived separately there, 'and the Professors have very little more than a nominal authority over them, so that there does not pass a day without some very great excess or other being committed'. He wondered 'if it would not be very risking to send a young man who has never been in the world before to such a place, where he shall hear every day of these excesses and where he will in a manner be obliged to keep company with the very people who commit them'. (50)

The King's nervousness had been aggravated by the behaviour in Europe of his third son Prince William, whom the Duke of York was shepherding back to England by the yacht that delivered Prince Edward. The King had been writing some very stern letters indeed about Prince William's levity, his debts and his irresponsible behaviour. 'I had hoped', he wrote on 6 May, 'reflection must by this time have convinced you of the impropriety of your conduct'. (51)

The twenty-two-year-old Duke of York may have sounded rather too avuncular to his two juniors. To his father he wrote about Prince William on 1 April: 'There never can be any real alteration for the better in him till he has been kept for some time under severe discipline.' (52) And about Prince Edward, on 3 June: 'I think him very much grown and improved in every respect. To be sure he is as yet very little accustomed to the ways of the world, but that is so much the better, as it will be much easier to put him in the right way and to keep him in it.' (53) The young duke had even gone so far as to do some virtuous tut-tutting to the King about the behaviour of his elder brother the Prince of Wales, with whom he was later to ally himself in opposition to his father. Though he himself had been only eighteen when first sent abroad, and his habits had been little more exemplary in moral terms than those of his brothers, he seems to have indulged them with far greater circumspection, at least at this period of his life.

Prince William, it appears, having seen (temporarily) the error of his ways, gave his younger brother 'some very good advice' at the reunion of the three brothers in Harburg, for which Prince Edward was not particularly grateful: he told his father that the Duke of York's reception of him 'I cannot help saying, was much more friendly than William's'. He settled down in Luneburg, however, with the best intentions of meriting his father's commendation, writing home about his social activities—shooting, dancing, dining, music—and his studies. 'Every morning in the week, I study 4 hours, 1 in German, 1 in law, 1 in artillery, and one in history; and also 1 hour every evening, 3 times a week upon religious subjects, and 3 times a week the Classicks.' (54)

In accordance with the King's plan he was moved (rather unwillingly) to Hanover in the spring of 1786, where he was established early in June in the Fürsten Haus. Immediately after his arrival he was invested as a Knight of the Garter in a ceremony before the King's Hanoverian throne improvised by his brother the Duke of York, who had been reporting qualified approval of his junior's progress. 'I understand that Edward is grown quite a giant', wrote his sister Princess Augusta to Prince Augustus a few months later. 'If so I hope he will never be *a Grenadier* or else he will be quite a frightful sight.' (55) Apart from trouble with stomach complaints, he seemed to be doing well. But by mid-July 1786 it was apparent that his private and personal behaviour left a good deal to be desired. His Luneburg debts had come to light and begun to catch up with him.

For Thérèse-Bernardine Mongenet in Besançon the year 1786 was, apparently, a fateful one also. An attachment far more attractive than that to the baron de Fortisson had offered itself in the person of that 'countryman of her own who calls himself the Marquiss de Permangle'.

Philippe Claude Auguste de Chouly, Marquis de Permangle, twenty-seven at the time of his posting to Besançon as a Lieutenant in the Royal Regiment of Artillery, would have seemed a very glamorous young man indeed, even to a girl who by now had accustomed herself to association with officers and gentlemen. Born of an ancient and wealthy Limousin family, lordly owner of more than one château (the family de Chouly de Permangle were 'seigneurs de Monchasty, Béchadie, Frédières, Brie les Champs, Boubon, Grand et Petit Permangle, Champagnac et autres lieus' at least since the fifteeenth century), he had been admitted to the Ecole Militaire in 1766 after presenting his family credentials to the Juge d'Armes de France. An ancestor had been governor of Limoges in 1670. He was related to Mirabeau, to whom an uncle had been godfather. On graduation, he had become a Mousquetaire du Roi and Chevalier de l'ordre Royal et Militaire de Notre Dame de Mt Carmel et de St Lazare.

Tall, handsome and arrogant, Philippe Claude seems to have easily cut out the earlier contender for the charms of Thérèse-Bernardine,

D

to the bitter and public resentment of the baron de Fortisson, who took civil action against his rival. The document of record, so far regrettably untraced but obviously in existence today in the hands of a collector, surfaced in 1964 as Item No. 3210 in Catalogue No. 167 of Saint-Hélion of Paris: 'Action of the baron de Fortisson against the marquis de Permangle who lured away his mistress, 1786, piquant details given by the plaintiff, contemporary manuscript.' Though the errant mistress is not named, the known facts exactly fit Thérèse-Bernardine. It would be stretching coincidence too far to imagine that two different women at the same date had been successfully charmed away from a baron de Fortisson by a marquis de Permangle. (56)

With Philippe Claude, Thérèse-Bernardine travelled in France and to England, where the marquis, whose estates and fortune had been swallowed up in the early days of the Revolution, was reduced by economic necessity to becoming a maker of salads (was Thérèse-Bernardine indeed the lady Colonel Symes had seen with Lord Cholmondeley?). Other evidence than the Colonel's supports his presence in Malaga in 1790, where he evidently accompanied his mistress from Marseilles on her way to join Prince Edward. In 1815, when he was petitioning the French Secretary of State for War for the Cross of St Louis, he stated that he had emigrated first to Spain before deciding to join his brother in Germany. (57)

For whatever reason and by whatever means he managed to get to Malaga, the penniless marquis could no longer afford a mistress in 1790. Whether or not Thérèse-Bernardine left him with regret, she also had to look around for another means of support. The offer from Prince Edward by M. Fontiny came just at the right moment.

Henceforward Thérèse-Bernardine would be known to the world as Madame de St Laurent, referred to always by the prince by that name, by others often simply as 'Madame'. What he called her in private has not survived, and none but the scantiest clues point to the name Julie. She signed her letters 'J' de St Laurent: another hand than hers and possibly at a later date scribbled 'Julie' in the margin of the baptismal record of young Edward de Salaberry, her Quebec godson, in 1792. She is called 'Julia' in a poem written to 'Madame De St L——t' in 1811. Whatever the name she adopted, whatever the circumstances that brought her into Prince Edward's life, the relationship was to prove almost as permanent as marriage.

CHAPTER THREE

Quebec

The Quebec to which Prince Edward and Madame came in August 1791 had almost not become a possession of Britain. Still French in appearance and culture beneath a busy overlay of British merchants and government officials, the province had just missed being returned to France by the Treaty of Paris of 1763. 'Some are for keeping Canada, some Guadaloupe,' Pitt is reported to have said during the time of decision, when the West Indian merchants were lobbying against the competition that would be offered by additional sources of sugar. 'Who will tell me which I shall be hanged for not keeping?'

Though the city was becoming something of a haven for American loyalists thrown out of office by the War of Independence, the French seigneurs were active and influential in the energetic social life of Canada: indeed, did much to give it its tone, its air of elegance. Since early in the seventeenth century the land along the St Lawrence river had been industriously developed and farmed by the *habitants*, in the narrow strips that some visitors thought were romantic. The trading empire of France had extended by canoe and bateau and the personal courage of the *voyageurs* into the fur lands of the unexplored northern interior.

English newcomers were fast being integrated into the population of Canada. The cities of Montreal, Trois Rivières, Quebec became almost cosmopolitan centres: crossroads for merchants, traders, adventurers, seamen, soldiers, farmers: a stage for the performances of political figures, religious leaders, schoolmasters, importers, publishers, ladies and gentlemen of fashion. They had their own rivalries, their own social conventions that governed the pattern of official functions and the intercourse of the various levels of rank and order in the community.

Already the names that would thread the fabric of Canadian life for generations to come were appearing in the local journals. In the *Quebec Gazette* in English and French from 1764, the *Montreal Gazette* from 1785, the *Quebec Herald* in English from 1788 they appeared beneath official notices, as signatories to petitions, as agents for sales and purchases, names that would sound like a roll-call of the community leaders of the day : de Salaberry, de Lanaudière, Mabane, Sewell, Monk, the Lymburners, the Panets, Dambourges, Finlay, Toosey, Goodall, Duchesnay, Allsopp, a host of new names mingling with the old. Towards the end of 1786, when Sir Guy Carleton returned to Quebec as Governor and Commander-in-Chief of British North America under his new title of Lord Dorchester, much of the energy of the inhabitants was being devoted to unravelling a tangle of interests, pulled this way and that between the merchants, the Canadians, the Protestants and the Catholics, the lawyers and the military.

On the *Thisbe* frigate with Dorchester was William Smith, newly appointed Chief Justice of Quebec. Smith, who had just spent a year and a half in London waiting for government action to compensate his losses as a New York loyalist (he had been appointed Chief Justice there in 1779) was delighted with the Quebec he saw on arrival.

'This Colony is all Town upon the Banks of the River, 90 miles below this, & 180 above it to Montreal', he had written a week after landing. 'They use a Calash in summer, which is a coarse sort of Double Chair, and a Cariole in Winter or Chairot-Box upon a Slay. The Roads are so good, that the Calashes run 8 Miles an Hour, and also every where practicable for a Chariot in the Environs of this City, very beautifully disposed by Nature, & not meanly improved.'

Together with instructions to his wife Janet about the sort of furniture and supplies that should be ordered to supplement what was available locally, the number and kind of servants to bring with her, Smith sent reports of the housing conditions in Quebec. 'Our Winter is commenced', he wrote early in December, '& yet I was never less sensible of the Frost—the Stoves of Canada in the Passages, temper the air through all the House—I sit ordinarily by a common Hearth, which gives me the Thermometer at 71 or 72, nearly Summer Heat. The close cariole & a Furr Cap & Cloak, is a Luxury only used on Journies—the Cariole alone suffices in Town. The Route of last Thursday demonstrates this—50 Ladies in high Head Dresses, and not a lappet or Frisse discomposed.' (58)

Almost every traveller passing through Quebec had nice things to say about the city and about the inhabitants of the province, perhaps because what they found was so different from the primitive conditions they may have expected. Many later visitors would attest to the accuracy of the description by Frances Brooke, author of that lively novel *The History of Emily Montague* in 1769: 'Nothing can be more striking than the view of Qubec as you approach; it stands on the summit of a boldly-rising hill, at the confluence of two very beautiful rivers, the St Lawrence and St Charles, and, as the convents and other public buildings first meet the eye, appears to great advantage from the port. The island of Orleans, the distant view of the cascade of Montmorenci, and the opposite village of Beauport, scattered with a pleasing irregularity along the banks of the river St Charles, add greatly to the charms of the prospect.' (59)

Superbly located on its great jut of rock pointing downriver, the basin below the Château St Louis a scribble of spars and masts in summer, in winter a waste of tumbled ice floes safe for crossing only in January and February, Quebec was a city of spires and turrets, fortress walls and buttressed buildings above the clustered dwellings and shops of Lower Town. The narrow streets, the open market place, the guarded city gates, were not unlike many of the provincial towns of France. And when Chief Justice Smith wrote in November 1786 about 'these French folks, the gayest animals upon Earth', he was echoing the baroness Riedesel's comments of not many years earlier: 'The Canadians are hospitable and cheerful; they sing and smoke the whole day.' (60)

This was the Quebec to which *Ulysses* and *Resistance* brought Prince Edward and Madame, their servants and the Royal Fusiliers, on 11 August 1791, seven weeks out from Gibraltar. An observer noted in his diary that his Royal Highness 'received the compliments of the citizens, clergy, magistrates and military in the New Salon of the Castle without speeches, swords, guns or ceremony'. (61) The deficiency in ceremonial was probably noticeable to anyone who had witnessed the festivities that had excited the city during Prince William's visit when, as captain, he had brought *Pegasus* upriver in 1787. 'The Prince is here', Thomas Aston Coffin had written then to his friend Colonel Winslow in Fredericton, 'has been recd in great Pomp—Balls, Dinners, Suppers, Fireworks &c take up our whole attention'. (62) The Lieutenant-Governor, Brigadier-General Hope, had been on the beach to meet Prince William with all the city's dignitaries, and the prince, preceded by the five officers appointed as aides-de-camp by Lord Dorchester, passed between troop-lined streets to Fort St Louis and yet another royal salute. 'Great Preparations for Elumination going

on', wrote James Thompson, Overseer of Public Works, as the prince's
ship lay in the bay the day before. He noted next day, 'it was astonishing what numbers of well dressed Ladies were crowded in every
Window along the Streets through which the Prince passed'. (63)

Four years later, in 1791, after his morning meeting with the
leading male citizens, it was Prince Edward's turn to be introduced
in the afternoon to the ladies of Quebec, no doubt all of a dither in
a furious rivalry of frills and flounces. It was unlikely that Madame
would have been present at such a formal first presentation, especially
in a community under the social domination of Lady Dorchester, a
daughter of Lord Effingham and 'the proudest woman of her days'.
The pretty girl from Besançon would live all her days with her prince
in a strange sort of twilight, flitting like an almost invisible woman in
and out of personal letters but never appearing in official reports or
the public press (except infrequently as a choice item of gossip, or,
with an anonymity that deceived no one, as Madame de St L———t).
Any recognition given to her would offend the conventions, mock
accepted morality, reduce the value of respectability. Few except the
most rigid would fail to acknowledge her privately, seek her favour
(though she seems to have behaved with admirable discretion in using
any power she might have exerted), accept her invitations. But she
never appeared upon any official stage in Quebec.

On this day of her arrival, however, there would have been many
curious eyes from many windows cast upon this fashionable beauty
whom they would have seen treated with obvious deference by minor
but important officials and members of his Royal Highness's family.
A buzz of questions would have flown that night from parlour to
parlour. Who? . . . Why? . . . What treatment should she be afforded?
Much the same kind of soul-searching had exercised the ladies of
England in making agonized social decisions about their public attitude
to Mrs Fitzherbert after the rumours of her marriage to the Prince of
Wales. 'Will you go about with his mistress, or do you mean to
countenance and support such a marriage?' anxious Lady Spencer
had written to her daughter Georgiana, Duchess of Devonshire, in
February 1786. 'Better to remain out of town till people are grown
more accustom'd to the thing, and . . . have set you an example.' (64)

Among the curious crowd in 1791, no doubt, watching the prince
and his suite come up from the landing place, were a jovial, gregarious
merchant named Henry Juncken and a pretty *Quebecoise*, Eliza Green,
who would play a minor part in the royal visitor's life at a later date.
Henry Juncken had had something to say about this young lady a
couple of years earlier, jotting down in his journal for 21 January 1789
an anecdote that had amused him.

'Mr Terrill called upon us this morning & was with us for some time, I mention this on purpose because of the Pleasantry of his comming to town at this time, he as usual had his son with him . . . as he passed by Greens he was called upon by them and desired to take Greens Daughter with him to town, now it is to be observed that their Daughter had her Bastard Child with her, she being kept by some officer as a Lady of Pleasure, good manners & Politeness which is his character, would not permit him to Deny her that Favour, and therefore he took her in, but as he did not like to be seen in company with her, riding in his own Sleigh for fear of a Reflection by the Vulgar, he under some Pretence alighted a good Ways ere he came to town, and caused his Son to Drive along and bring the Lady to her lodging, whilst he followed on foot, we saw the son drive by with a Lady not knowing & wondering who she is, some little while after, Mr Terrill came in relating the affair as above said, which raised a laugh, wherein he joined.' (65)

The army officers and men serving brief terms of service in the garrison, the merchants who came from England on temporary visits or on longer but still impermanent posting to guard the interests of their London-based companies, these men offered to Quebec girls the glamour of a great unknown outside world in exchange for a fleeting relief from loneliness. Quebec church registers are full of the evidence of human frailty. Many a name known today for devoted public service appears in baptismal records, preserving for posterity the illegitimate but understandable lapse of one of its forebears. Eliza Green had borne one bastard child at this date. She would bear another, that child believed to have been Prince Edward's.

If Madame could not share the prince's honours, there was much to occupy her time. French-speaking, she would have understood any comments overheard on her route from shore to the house assigned to the prince at 6 St Louis Street (if he would not have had her accommodated separately in Gibraltar, it was unthinkable that he would do so here). She would hardly have missed being a proud and happy member, if perforce anonymous, of the 'great concourse of spectators' at the Parade before the Castle where her prince, having formed his regiment on the beach after disembarkation, and marched them up from the Lower Town with drums beating and music playing, commanded them in person for a review by His Excellency Lord Dorchester and His Honour General Clarke.

The Dorchesters, in the throes of imminent departure for a visit to England, must have found the week a crowded one. As well as the prince a delegation of about forty Indian chiefs with Sir John Johnson and Colonel Brant had arrived with complaints from the Confederated Western Nations about border encroachments by the United States, and Dorchester met them at the Castle on Sunday evening to receive their address. He promised them, in his answer next day, faithfully to represent their situation to his Majesty, presenting the prince to them in a ringing introduction. 'Brothers! Here is Prince Edward, son of our King, who has just arrived with a chosen band of his Warriors, to protect this Country. I leave him second in command of all the King's Warriors in Canada and he will also take care of you.' (66) The young warrior's princely stature and his undeniable position as son of the great British King their Father would be impressive to the Indian visitors.

On the evening of Thursday the 17th, the Dorchesters departed on HMS *Alligator*, the citizens of Quebec having been treated to a fine marine carnival in the morning, when the prince, in a barge with the Royal Standard flying and attended by two other boats with pendants, boarded *Alligator*, circling it and the other two King's ships and receiving salutes from all of them both coming and going. There followed a series of smart military reviews and presentation of addresses; General Clarke tactfully waited a few days before taking the oaths of office and entering on the duties of Commander-in-Chief, to allow Lord Dorchester time to get clear of the boundaries of the colony.

Meantime there was a settling-in process to busy the prince and his lady. There were a few pieces of Judge Adam Mabane's furniture in the house on St Louis Street rented by the prince for £90 a year: several mahogany tables of various sizes, a large cherry-tree sideboard table with drawers, a pair of looking glasses, some fire-irons, stoves, pipes, a pair of sconces, 'two old Red Damask Window curtains' and eight old mahogany chairs which, at the time of the judge's death five months later, were 'at Mr Wyles the Carpenters to see if they could be mended'. (67)

Madame would be kept busy installing any furnishings they had brought with them, ordering what else they needed, receiving the troops of tradesmen with their samples, comparing for value and attractiveness the fabrics for curtains, carpets for floors, fine furniture for reception rooms; exclaiming over the exquisite craftsmanship of made-in-Quebec silverware. There would be time, perhaps, for excited letters home—all of Madame's letters were animated. To the parents in Besançon (68) (her father may have died before this date, but her mother still lived); the sister she would not see again for twenty-six years; the older brother by now established in Grenoble as highways engineer in the Département de l'Isère and about to be married (in

October) to the Demoiselle Euphrosine Elisabeth Jeanne Cavillon, daughter of another highways engineer. Madame continued in touch with her family by whatever means were possible in those difficult days. A younger brother would have much cause for gratitude in later years.

In between ceremony (for the prince) and domestic affairs (for Madame) there were the new sights and sounds and customs to marvel at and the new names to learn. Though she would neither have curtsied to Lord Dorchester in the receiving line at Castle balls, nor accepted the kisses on both cheeks that Chief Justice Smith had noticed His Lordship jealously reserving for himself, the prince's companion was to become known as an elegant and admirable hostess at suppers and parties in the St Louis Street house. The many who could not bring themselves to accept Mademoiselle, the prince's light-o'-love, could, if they wished, persuade themselves there was no need to ostracize that charming lady Madame de St Laurent, the baronne de Fortisson, graciously and respectably filling a necessary position as hostess in his Royal Highness's official establishment. Besides, they grew to like and admire her for her own sake.

Her friendships with women in Quebec were probably always private. She presided at the prince's table among guests who were almost always male. The prince never attempted to insist on her public reception anywhere, and those ladies who refused to countenance a situation not open to social recognition were spared the embarrassment consequent upon her presence. René Boileau, member for Kent County of the first parliament of Lower Canada, left in his *Cahier de notes* a table plan of one such dinner on 21 November 1793, when Madame sat at the head of the table on the prince's right, and Boileau (one of thirteen male guests) on his left. (69)

All Quebec society enjoyed driving out into the surrounding country-side, down the narrow streets between the solid sensible grey houses, out through St John's Gate, St Lewis Gate, Palace Gate, into an extensive prospect 'diversified by a variety of hills, woods, rivers, cascades, intermingled with smiling farms and cottages, and bounded by distant mountains which seem to scale the very Heavens'. The favourite place for picnics was Montmorenci-falls, just over an hour's ride from the city, in summer its thunder gemmed with sunlight, in winter a scene whose capture was attempted by the quill or pencil of many a passing traveller. 'The torrent, which before rushed with such impetuosity down the deep descent in one vast sheet of water, now descends in some parts with a slow and majestic pace; in others seems almost suspended in mid air; and in others, bursting through the obstacles which interrupt its course, pours down with redoubled fury into the foaming bason below, from whence a spray arises, which, freezing in its ascent, becomes on each side a wide and irregular frozen breast-work; and in front, the spray being there much greater, a lofty and magnificent pyramid of solid ice.' (70)

Here a former governor, General Sir Frederick Haldimand, had had a house built, 'his favourite residence', and at the suggestion of his friend the baroness Riedesel he had added in 1782 a little summer house opposite the falls themselves, 'a small house, which was, as it were, suspended upon the cataract . . . The foundations of the house consisted of eight strong beams, laid athwart, beneath which the cataract hurried down with tremendous velocity. The situation of this house afforded an awful, but majestic sight. The noise was so tremendous, that it was impossible to remain long within it.' When there appeared to be no takers for the sale of 'the elegant Villa of the late Sir Frederic Haldimand K.B. delightfully situated near the Falls of Montmorenci in the Parish of Beauport with the Farm-house, and other buildings, and all the lands thereunto belonging', (71) the prince rented it as a summer residence. His guests would follow the path of the baroness to view the splendour, climbing the steep ascent over rocks connected by little bridges like a scene from a Chinese wallpaper.

Quebec citizens devoured the daily journals avidly, reading, along with local items, the news from the civilized world whose habits and customs they were trying to perpetuate on the fringe of a wilderness. The sad King of France and his pale Queen had lost their dash for freedom at Varennes, reported a special communication in the *Quebec Gazette* of 29 August. The Duke of York was being married to the Princess Frederica, eldest daughter of the King of Prussia: Sir Gilbert Elliot wrote to his wife that 'there never was heard, seen, or read of such a passion as the mutual one of the Duke and Duchess'. (72)

Mr Jouve, professor of music and lately arrived in Quebec with His Highness's band, was offering lessons vocal and instrumental, especially the French guitar, 'very easy to learn and very pleasant, as in a very short time one may learn enough to accompany the voice with it'. His Excellency General Clarke set off on a three-week tour to the upper parts of the province, and when he returned, watched Prince Edward hand out good-conduct medals to soldiers in his regiment. In England a messenger from the Secretary of State came posting into Weymouth with a letter for Colonel John Graves Simcoe (awaiting a fair wind to board *Triton* and brooding over his inability to obtain the rank of Brigadier-General because of the prince's presence in Canada) which told him he was to be Lieutenant-Governor of Upper Canada following the newly planned division of the Province of Quebec.

In Quebec city the social whirl was speeding up. The prince and

Madame watched the blue skies deepen, saw the first delicate skin of ice form over puddles, the mist of breath hang upon the air, watched the drizzle of rain and sleet, the first snow turn to slush in the streets. The soldiers stamped frostily on the parade ground, marvelled at the intensity of the Canadian cold, which almost stopped their breathing, and grumbled at the long parades and the prince's orders that forbade the wearing of their caps down except when on duty.

The city was clothed in gala dress on 2 November for the first of the three princely birthdays it would celebrate, with illuminations and a ball at the Castle. A week later Mrs Simcoe on board *Triton* now at anchor in the great basin of Quebec, 'looked out of the Cabbin window & saw the Town covered with Snow & it rained the whole day . . . I was not disposed to leave the Ship to enter so dismal looking a Town as Quebec appeared through the mist sleet & rain. . . . Quebec is divided into Upper & Lower town. The latter is inhabited by Merchants for the Convenience of the Harbour & Quays. They have spacious Houses 3 stories high built of dark stone, but the streets are narrow & gloomy. . . . The Upper Town is more airy & pleasant though the Houses in general are less.' (73)

That night the prince wrote to his father in his neat careful writing to thank him for the letter delivered by Colonel Simcoe after *Triton* had finished her blustering voyage, in which the King had offered to pay off the Gibraltar debts. 'I have at present reduced my expences so as to be able by April next to acquit in full the whole of the debt I left behind me at Gibraltar on my embarkation for this garrison: so that should your Majesty graciously chuse to afford me any assistance, I should presume to hope you would approve of my employing it towards clearing a part of my most unfortunate Geneva incumbrance.' (74)

He had been very good about his debts, earning the commendation of Colonel Symes, who in September had written to the King about 'the cheerful and manly manner with which his Royal Highness gave up more than half the income your Majesty allows him to pay his debts and to enable him to do so, having made a proportional reduction in his expences'. (75) But if half one's income goes to pay off past expenditure, and one is still expected to live up to the whole of one's income to maintain the standards of one's rank and estate, one ends up running just to stay in the same spot. The prince's regimental band (always his pride and joy) cost him a sum varying from £500 to £800 a year. (76) With some justification he considered it necessary to keep up royal appearances, an expensive occupation in a society that would have despised as niggardly and parsimonious anything less from a King's son.

His regiment also provided entertainment for the community by concerts, dances in the barracks, music for church services and even amateur theatricals (of which Colonel Simcoe disapproved as being unsuitable employment for officers). There was no doubt that the regiment was an asset to Quebec. 'The Fusileers are the best dancers, well dressed & the best looking figures in a Ball Room I ever saw. They are all musical & like dancing & bestow as much money, as other Regts. usually spend in wine, in giving Balls & Concerts which makes them very popular in this place where dancing is so favourite an amusement, that no age seems to exclude people from partaking of it.' (77)

People visited each other or made country excursions (often across the chunky river ice to the Island of Orleans) in the covered carioles that had so delighted Chief Justice Smith in 1786 ('I shall buy one tomorrow, in which I can lay abed my whole Length') (78), bundled from top to toe in bear skins or buffalo skins, the men in beaver coats, the ladies in long cloaks lined with fur or padded with down. Winter picnics were the rage. 'It is the custom here', recorded Mrs Simcoe three weeks after her arrival, 'to make parties to dine in the Country at a distance of 10 miles. They often carry a cold dinner & return to a dance in the Evening & this in the severest weather which seems as much relished by the English as the Canadians.' On 5 December the prince and such a party had driven the eight miles to the village of Lorette. 'Their partners must be very agreeable or they could never have liked these parties', wrote Mrs Simcoe primly, perhaps having been forced into frigid acknowledgement of the prince's lady. (79)

So the winter passed. 'Supper at Major Stewart's', recorded Mrs Simcoe. 'The Prince was there . . . I gave a dance to forty people. The Prince was present . . . The Prince dined with us, Gen'l Clarke, Mrs Murray & St Ours . . . As the cold weather & the short days leave us people cease to be sociable, & no kind of gaiety is continued but a few dinner partys . . . I met the Prince en carriole.' Did she have to give another frosty recognition to Madame, seated beside the prince? In London, *The Times* had picked up a delightful bit of scandal. 'A certain Royal Colonel has carried into Quebec-quarters a Spanish Lady, in whose arms he means to screen himself from the wintry blasts of that frigid region. Her exquisite beauty so much charmed the inhabitants, that they confessed her to be the *Astraea* of their Hemisphere.' (80)

At the end of December, a pleasant domestic event occurred in the prince's household, which his warm-hearted lady probably found charmingly romantic. His servant, Robert Wood, had fallen in love with a French-Canadian miss, 'Mary Dupuis *dite* Caton', and married her on the 29th. (81)

The road to Montmorenci was stony and hurt the horses' feet, but it passed through the village of Beauport, home of the de Salaberrys, with whom Prince Edward and Madame were developing a fast friendship. On frosty days and sunny, whenever the road was passable, Madame went back and forth to Beauport, sometimes with the prince, sometimes alone to visit Catherine Hertel de Salaberry, newly pregnant with a child expected at the end of June. Here, with the children playing around them on the carpet (baby Amelia was a chubby three-year-old) the two ladies chatted over their embroidery (a talent with the needle was one of Madame's accomplishments : she made all her own clothes). Sometimes there was the company of other ladies. Years later, Madame would recall with laughter the tantrum of a two-year-old, daughter of Captain Alexander Walker of the Royal Fusiliers, when her mother brought her to visit : the little girl 'rolling herself on the floor, having her dress in the greatest disorder', and Madame de Salaberry exclaiming 'Mon dieu! Mon dieu! Mon dieu!' (82)

'Prince Edward makes this place lively', Elizabeth Russell would write in June 1792, passing through Quebec with her brother Peter on his way to his post of receiver-general at Niagara. Like Mrs Simcoe, she thought his officers 'all very Handsome young men'. (83) In the evenings (the prince always believed in early to bed, early to rise) Madame would hear accounts of the day's official activities from which she was excluded. The funeral, perhaps, of their landlord, Adam Mabane, from whose dinner on 'the last Sunday of his life' his long-time friend Thomas Aston Coffin had been absent, because 'being New Year's day Prince Edward gave a dinner to the staff of the Army, when four or five of us . . . were out of respect to His Royal Highness obliged to dine with him'. (84) The jolly gathering in Franks' tavern the day after Christmas, when to the sound of trumpets and preceded by two stewards with white staves the merchants of the Lower-town waited on the merchants of the Upper-town to celebrate THE FIRST DAY of the new constitution, and twenty-three toasts were drunk to everyone and everything the company could think of. What the fashions were like at the brilliant ball given by the Lieutenant-Governor for Her Majesty's Birthday 'for the Ladies and Gentlemen who have been presented', and from which Thérèse-Bernardine would have been excluded. At events like theatre performances, where she did not have to be officially received, there was greater toleration of her presence. (85)

In the regimental pay office, Captain John Shuttleworth scratched out orders to London, to Birmingham, to Mr Dickey (army clothier), to Messrs Hewitsons (Lace men), sometimes noting that the goods were 'for a particular use and to be paid for by the men'. For 738 yards strong white worsted webbing 'for Gallowses for the men's Breeches' :

for 290 yards of red cloth for 360 privates' waistcoats : for 1440 yards edging lace (four yards per private) : for '24 breast plates for officers, yellow metal, same as those sent for the Music, strongly gilt and engraven same except the edge to be perfectly plain', and 24 sword belts of the very best buff leather (intended for the review, wrote the harassed captain, so please expedite). (86)

In London the anti-slave-traders were making a new move : readers of the *Quebec Gazette* learned in March about a proposal to boycott sugar and rum, products of the slaves (the *Gazette* thought the planters would indict the promoters for conspiracy). The Duke of Clarence, it was said, had applied to and received from the executors of the late Sir Joshua Reynolds a cast of Mrs Jordan's leg made by Mrs Damer. Sir Gilbert Elliot, deploring the gambling habits of Prince Edward's two eldest brothers, told his wife, 'If anything can make a democracy in England it will be the Royal Family.' (87) In Quebec, Captain Shuttleworth ordered '48 strong vellum Heads for side drums, two Chinese drums, with a peal of bells to strike with a stick, of the best construction'. A brother of Gaspard Lanaudière was off to downriver parishes purchasing horses for the prince 'who considers himself a great connoisseur in this kind of thing'. (88) Captain Shuttleworth wrote for ten double alphabet sets of the largest two-line small Pica full faced letters, all caps, and half a dozen sieves for giving Horses their corn, they can't be got here, also 200 pairs of buff leather knapsack slings : 'if you could meet with any old buff leather that is tollerably good it would answer well for the purpose if not you must send out new.'

Down in Halifax on the Atlantic sea-coast, they were getting the first rumours that John Wentworth was to fill the place of the dead governor, John Parr. And on 19 April, James Randolph wrote from Milverton, Somerset, to his friend Jonathan Sewell, who would be Solicitor-General of Lower Canada within a year, 'I hope you are pleased with your new Constitution—If it possesses within it the seeds of that contentious humour which its parliamentary midwives were swoln [sic] with, a Lawyer need not wish a better soil to thrive in.' (89)

The Proclamation came a month later, when General Clarke announced the division of the Counties of the Province of Lower Canada, and ordered the issuing of writs to call together the Legislative Council and Assembly. It was the starting gun for an election whose repercussions would go clanging around the province for more than a year to come. (90)

The *Quebec Gazette* blossomed at once with polite notes from candidates respectfully soliciting the honour of their electors' suffrage and promising zealous attention to the public interest. *Probus* warned his fellow-citizens to think carefully, offering to assist them 'in a faithful and impartial discrimination of what characters ought, and what characters ought not to represent the inhabitants of the county and city of Quebec', judging from their principles and past conduct. Handbills fluttered in the streets. Accusations and counter-accusations began to fly. Public notices went up on church doors throughout the province. Hustings were erected in places where the vote would not be taken in a house (taverns or inns were forbidden).

The prince impetuously involved himself, though his involvement seems to have extended only to the spreading of oil on already troubled waters. At Charlesbourg the poll was declared closed ('unexpectedly,' insisted the furious loser afterwards) when the voting stood at 'Salaberry Esq, 515; Lynd Esq, 462; Berthelot, Advocate, 436'. At the demand of any two electors the returning officer could close the poll if more than an hour passed without a voter presenting himself: perhaps on this excuse the hustings began to be dismantled. But Berthelot, Advocate, insisted that sixty-two of his friends were on the spot protesting their right and wish to vote 'even in the building where the election was held, from which they were chased by some gentlemen who demolished it by force, but they continued the protest and finished it in the neighbourhood'.

As de Salaberry's leading position was not threatened by Berthelot Dartigny's sixty-two friends, and the argument had taken a racial turn, it would seem to have been directed against Lynd, and the prince's intervention to have been in the interests of peace alone, not in partisanship. He sprang to the rescue, and 'in pure French, and with a tone of affection and authority', begged the crowd to cease and desist. 'Part then in peace. I urge you to unanimity and concord. Let me hear no more of the odious distinction of *English* and *French*. You are all His Britanick Majesty's *beloved* Canadian subjects' . . . Huzzas rang out, 'the *tumult* ceased, and words of *menace, rage* and *fury,* gave place to language of admiration and applause'.

De Salaberry was safe. He had managed, in any case, to get himself elected in two counties at once, Dorchester and Quebec, and chose the latter. But Berthelot nursed his fury.

'We have witnessed as warm an Election (in comparison) for our Lower and Upper Town and our County of Quebec as ever Westminster or Middlesex experienced,' wrote Jonathan Sewell to Ward Chipman in Fredericton on 7 July. (91) 'At the County Election his Royal Highness Prince Edward signalised himself much to his credit, and to the great confusion of one party who to their disgrace attempted by every means & pitiful artifice to keep alive that odious distinction of

French & English. His Highness harrangued the multitude in a style
that would have received approbation from the tongue of an
experienced speaker, and addressed some gentlemen Canadians, the
heads of the party I just mentioned in such a way as rendered them
the contempt of the public, He secured the election of two worthy
members and excluded a scoundrel (though a lawyer)' wrote lawyer
Jonathan, 'by his well timed address and interference. His language
was so marked to one of the French Gentlemen that he meant to have
commenced an action against the Prince, he was however afterwards
better advised, I wish to God he had for His Royal Highness's defence
would I have every reason to think have fallen into my hands. The
issue of the whole however is a contested return and a Petition to the
House when I am retained for the sitting Members, and will I hope
keep them sitting.'

More than one petition complaining of undue elections were presented to the House. Certain righteous citizens protested the seating
of John Young to represent Lower Town on the grounds that he did
'before and during the said Election open and cause to be opened
several taverns particularly one near the place chosen by him to hold
the Poll, where Hams were sliced and strong liquors given to Tradesmen
and Labourers, who were also influenced by sundry other unwarrant-
able acts of his Servants or Hirelings', and that he treated them 'by
distributing to them Cockades to distinguish his party, got them
Conducted to the Poll by his Creatures, where Ribbons and Oranges
were again given to them to induce them to vote for him . . . that
Assaults insults and battles contrary to Peace and Liberty were the
Result thereof. . . .'
   The petitioners may not have been far wrong. John Young's bills
carry down the years the echoes of electioneering jollity: 18 yards
purple ribbon, 25 yards, 33 yards; 3 Hhds Mild Ale, 15 Gallons of
Rum, 6 Dozen of Wine; 30 Loaves, Turkies, Bread & Chees [sic],
rum & fruit in proportion to the Sugar, 10½ dozens of madeira;
Window Glass Broke; one Decanter and many glasses, Tumblers and
mugs broke.
   But there were only eight names to the petition. Dismissed (92)
   When a new election was called in February 1793 to fill the place
vacated by de Salaberry, Berthelot Dartigny was elected 'without',
said the *Quebec Gazette*, 'any other influence than that of liberty'.
As soon as the election was closed he declared rather ostentatiously
'that he had neither given cocades or liquor, nor opened public houses.'
and at once gave 1,200 livres to be distributed to 'the modest poor'
of the five parishes in the county. He was evidently still smouldering,

though a paper that lay in wait to protest his election on the grounds that he was an alien and ineligible never had to be used. It was annotated 'Quebec 1793: Copy of an intended Petition against the Election of Berthelot d'Artigny had he persisted in his petitions agt others'. (93)

On a rainy Sunday at the end of May 1792, merchant and ship-builder Simeon Perkins took up a dutiful pen in the remote little port of Liverpool, Nova Scotia, to write in his journal: 'The Emperor of Germany is Dead, the King of Sweden Shot & wounded'. (94)

On 20 June the expected de Salaberry child was born, and in her excitement at the news Madame dispatched a messenger post-haste to her friend, known by the pet name of *Souris*, with her most frequently quoted letter.

'Hurrah! hurrah! hurrah! a thousand rounds in honor of the charming *Souris* and the new-born. In truth my head is full of joy, and my hand trembles so much that I can scarcely hold my pen. And it is another boy! How I wish that I was one of those powerful fairies who were able to bestow their gifts in such profusion; how the dear child should be endowed. Unfortunately all this is but an illusion, but never mind, something has said to me that the pretty little fellow has been born under a happy star; kiss him for me, my dear friend, and tell him this prediction of his god-mother. O! no! I was never so happy in my life. I have this moment sent the news to our dear Prince. It is needless to await his reply to assure you how delighted he will be. I know his sentiments too well to have any fear in expressing them. Mrs Staunton will excuse me, and I will go to Beauport to-day about seven o'clock; to-morrow I will go again and every day. Ah! I wish it could be this very instant of my life. I reserve it to myself to congratulate M. de Salaberry in person on the happy event; in the meantime I embrace the whole household without distinction of age or sex.' (95)

Perhaps the same gay welcome eventually crossed the Atlantic to a small Mongenet niece born a week later in Grenoble and christened Louise-Ursule-Caroline-Lucie.

The prince sent his good wishes to the de Salaberrys in a separate letter: and on 2 July the child was baptized Edouard-Alphonse, his godfather Edward Prince of Great Britain, his godmother 'Madame Alphonsine Thérèze Bernardine De Montgenêt de St Laurent Baronne de Fortisson'.* Madame signed herself 'Montgenet de St Laurent Bne de Fortisson'. (96)

---

* Someone has written 'Julie' in the margin of the register.

E

The prince's proposal to be godfather had caused a flutter of dismay among the good priests of Quebec, and seemingly also in the family of the de Salaberrys themselves. The main stumbling-block seems to have been Prince Edward's Protestantism rather than Madame's status. As the law in question was an ecclesiastical and not a divine one, the church fathers were permitted discretion: the prince felt that if nothing but dogma kept the clergy from according with his wishes, he would have his own chaplain perform the baptism. To the delighted relief of the Grand Vicar Gravé, however, the Bishop of Capse was chosen, and the prince explained to the rather embarrassed de Salaberry that he would be godfather not as the son of the King, but rather as son of a Sovereign who had given special protection to the Roman Catholic clergy in Canada.

The harassed Gravé got around the difficulty by a nice mental subterfuge. As the prince did not actually *hold* the child, he wrote afterwards, it could be considered that he was not *really* the godfather. (97)

The acceptance of Madame as godmother to a baby baptized a Catholic has been suggested as evidence that she must have been married to Prince Edward. But there was no reason for realistic church fathers caught in an awkward situation to refuse acknowledgement of the name she used as her own (even if they had their suspicions), or to question publicly the respectability of a widowed Baronne de Fortisson.

In any event, the argument is academic. She was not married to Prince Edward—was, in fact, never married to anyone: and as she did sign the register as godmother to the child, it is apparent that the church fathers made no issue of her situation in the prince's household. Perhaps her status as a member of the True Church made her in some degree acceptable. Or perhaps the clergy, by some twist of mental reservation, were able to persuade themselves that like the prince, she need not be regarded as a true godparent.

If the claim had been true that she was the mother of the child named Robert Wood, one might legitimately wonder if the reverend fathers would have been as acquiescent had she turned up at the 2 July baptismal service (with no husband visible since her arrival in August 1791) eight months pregnant with a baby to be born on 10 August.

And if, indeed, Madame had borne that child, then the suggestion that she accompanied the prince when he left Quebec the following day, 11 August, for the quite arduous trip he made to Niagara, could never have been true.

CHAPTER FOUR

'The stupendous wonder of this country'

Simcoe had left Quebec for his jurisdiction on 8 June by bateau up what he called 'the most August of Rivers', on a fairly leisurely journey, stopping off at Montreal (in a heat wave that shocked his wife) and at Kingston, remaining at the latter place for three weeks. He was still in Kingston when a letter dated 9 July from Francis Le Maistre, military secretary at Quebec, was started on its way, announcing that the prince proposed to leave early in August and arranging for him to be carried from Kingston to Niagara in one of the King's vessels. 'He wishes to be received in a private capacity, but . . . he may express a desire to see the Fifth Regiment under arms.' (98)

Prince Edward was received with fanfare at Niagara, though things were still in a fearful muddle for all the new arrivals. Simcoe, arrived on 26 July, and pitched straight into the complication of an Indian murder, had found himself with accommodation troubles. Navy Hall, 'a House built by the Naval Commanders on this Lake for their reception when here' (99) was in need of repair before it would be habitable, and the Simcoes took up temporary residence in three marquees pitched on the hill above. The new Receiver-General, Peter Russell, had similar difficulties in finding accommodation for himself and his sister a week later, aggravated by the fact that he had to stay indoors watching his strong box, 'which the Governor absolutely refused to take charge of'. (100)

Simcoe had set the carpenters to work on Navy Hall at once, which precipitated a small behind-scenes paper battle. A new Ordnance Store had been authorized and the old one pulled down. To the dismay of Captain Glasgow of the Royal Artillery, sent from Quebec to inspect the stores, only the foundation for the new one had been completed. He therefore refused to sign the inspection certificate. 'The stores from necessity are crammed into a variety of places', the Captain wrote frigidly back to Quebec, 'which renders it impossible for me to see their state at present'. An equally chilly request for explanation from Clarke in Quebec brought letters from everybody to everybody disclaiming responsibility. The Governor, they said, had taken all the carpenters off the work to get his own dwelling put in order. (101)

Simcoe remained supremely unconcerned by the furore. 'As you may suppose, I am miserably off for accommodation in this country', he wrote to his friend Sir James Bland Burges, Under-Secretary of State for Foreign Affairs (penned in a hurry on 21 August 'as it depends upon the winds to stay the vessel'), 'and I am fitting up an old hovel, that will look exactly like a carrier's ale-house in England when properly decorated and ornamented.' He noted in the same letter that 'Prince Edward is just arrived here, but not yet landed, on a visit to the stupendous wonder of this country. There are also the chiefs of our Indian neighbours, who, coming to compliment me, luckily will have the opportunity of seeing the "Son" of "their Great Father".' (102)

Preparations had preceded the prince all along the route, and he was fêted at every stop. While there is no direct evidence that Madame was one of the party, her later habit of journeying with him, and what Governor Wentworth would call her 'intrepid fortitude' make her presence on this trip seem likely. The prince's request to be received privately, and a comment by Clarke to Simcoe that he travelled with 'a larger suite than I wish attended him from an apprehension that it must occasion some embarrassment' hints strongly of a possible social contretemps in the reception of Madame. (103)

The prince seems to have travelled from Quebec to Montreal by road, along which the distinguished travellers from overseas would absorb every new experience with the same observant curiosity shown two years later by the Bishop of Quebec, Jacob Mountain, following the same route in the course of his Visitations. 'The road lies for the most part, along the lofty bank of the River St Lawrence', wrote Mountain in his diary, 'but sometimes deviates and leaves the bank to the distance of eight or ten miles. The prospects are inconceivably grand and beautiful, and the cultivated part of the country thickly sprinkled with white farm-houses (for every house in this country is white), and waving with the most abundant harvests, [are] contrasted with the deep woods and lofty mountains that lie beyond that country, on the one hand, and with the sylvan and romantic scenery of the river on the other.' (104)

The 'travelling apparatus' for the Bishop would be less elaborate than for the prince and his party, but complicated enough. It consisted of 'a mattress, etc., and little bedstead for each, with gauze curtains to keep off mosquitoes. Trunks of robes and clothes; hampers of Wine and porter, hams and tongue; a coop with four dozen chickens; a box fitted to hold, without breaking, tea equipage, glasses, plates, dishes, spoons, knives and forks; a travelling basket for cold meat, and other dressed provisions . . .' The prince took with him his curricle, perhaps for Madame's comfort and convenience. A carriage was a luxury the Bishop may have foregone, relying on public transport for the land sections of the journey.

'Our mode of travelling here is not like anything that you have experienced', continued the Bishop, recording his impressions for young friends back in England. 'Our carriages are extremely different and when we choose to stop, either for refreshment, or to sleep, we go to the house of some Habitant (so all the farmers are called in this country), where there is generally a spare room, or two, with beds, for travellers; and where we are sure of meeting a hospitable reception, although they have rarely anything to offer but milk and eggs. . . . They live almost entirely upon milk, bread and eggs, with a soup made of herbes; and now and then a slice of salted pig's head—carrying their veal, mutton, pork and poultry to the nearest market. They make too at home almost every article which they have in *daily* wear. . . . They also make their own hats, of straw, for both sexes, and a sort of shoes of leather tanned by themselves after the manner of the Indians which they called *moccasins*. These are very easy to the feet, and by no means of an ill shape. . . .Upon Sundays or holidays, they are always dressed, not in these home-made materials, but of such as are brought from England. And the women have then, almost universally, a neatness of appearance which I never saw equalled. Their caps . . . have a peculiar propriety which I can't describe, and which is increased by their having no ribbons, which people of their rank are not allowed by their priests to wear. . . . They almost all wear a white jacket, and short white petticoat, white gloves, with a fan, white cotton stockings, and black stuffed slippers. A party of them thus dressed and going to Church, have a neatness and prettiness of appearance that you can scarcely conceive. . . . The men too upon these occasions, make a very smart appearance, and being unrestrained, are much gayer than the women.'

The Bishop was received with welcome and hospitality. The Prince received a more ceremonious welcome. At Berthier, for instance, he was met at the Post house of York by 'the five Captains of the Militia who were known to be loyal Subjects to His Majesty', their men arranged 'in a handsome column on each side of the road' with the Seigneur of Berthier, Mr Cuthbert, at their head. The prince and his suite were escorted to the Manor house for an elegant entertainment, the Union Flag was hoisted and a salute of twenty-one small cannon fired. After dinner and presentations, the royal party left at four o'clock, everyone charmed with his Royal Highness's 'condescending affability'. Background music was supplied by the bells of Mr Cuthbert's chapel, which pealed during the entire visit. (105)

From Montreal the royal party would probably, like Bishop Mountain, have begun to alternate between road and river, transferring from calèche to bateau 'fitted with an awning and all conveniences'. (106) Like the Bishop after them and Mrs Simcoe before, they would have been entranced by the rapids known as The Cascades just past the junction of the Ottawa river with the St Lawrence. Here the whole river, wrote the Bishop, 'falls over a very sloping, rocky bottom, and is dashed and agitated to such a degree as to resemble a sea in a violent storm, only that the billows here are of course much smaller.

'These rapids are very frequent in this river, but this is the most violent of them all, and the only one in which voyagers are obliged to quit their bateau, both in ascending and descending the stream. The men get out and tow their boat up along the side of the bank, which yet they could not do, were it not for several locks, constructed at great expense, and defended on each side by long mounds of piled rock, to keep off the force of the water.'

The Bishop was delighted with his watermen. So too would be the tall English prince and his slender French lady, with their mutual love of music. 'Their manner of singing is extremely pleasing. The man at the helm generally leads—though, by the way, a bateau is not steered by a rudder, but with a paddle, which the man, standing upright, uses alternately on each side of the bateau, with great address and grace, and keeping exact time with the oars. They do not sing in parts but in dialogue—the one leading . . . and the rest answering, he singing the first division of the tune, and they the second. As the time is always measured by the stroke of the oars, the movement is consequently slow. It is almost always in a minor key. They sing in a soft tone, and their voices are almost universally pleasing.'

At Oswegatchie (Ogdensburg) Prince Edward and his suite found awaiting them a Royal Barge, for the fitting up of which Simcoe had earlier dispatched Mr Peter Clark with orders to the Deputy-Commissary-General at Kingston to release the necessary supplies from His Majesty's stores. Ten yards of sheeting for an Awning: eight Fathom of small Rope, for main Sheet etc. etc.: three quarts of Linseed oil: six pounds of white, two pounds of red, and one pound of black paint: a few yards of Bunting for a Jack. (107) In this vessel his Royal Highness and party threaded their way through the Thousand Islands.

'This was by far the most beautiful part of the whole voyage . . . such a prodigious multitude of islands, of every imaginable form and size, from some miles in length or breadth . . . now ranged in close and intricate labyrinths, having the tops of their trees meeting over the narrow streams that divide them; now placed in beautiful distinct groups, in a lovely, spreading sheet of smooth water; now so placed that you can see twenty or more at a time, with the water bending and winding and curling among them . . . then again confining you between narrow, winding, bewildered shores, with steep rocks and lofty trees hanging over your head, and excluding entirely the rays of the sun. . . . The length of Mille Isle is, I think, about thirty miles.'

Colonel Simcoe had issued orders as early as the 13th for Prince Edward's reception 'with every respect due to his illustrious Birth', and Captain Glasgow had been requested to send over 'some Field Pieces . . . to form a saluting battery at Navy Hall, in case His Royal Highness shall land there.' At Kingston he had boarded the eighty-ton *Onondaga,* one of the two armed topsail schooners used for transporting troops and provisions on the lake. Only four days before the royal visitor's arrival Peter Russell had reported to his sister Betsey the 'Violent storms that blew down almost all the Tents'. He concluded gloomily that there was 'no possibility of getting any comforts in this place'. The Simcoes had been equally worried about whether to give the prince 'the Marquees for his residence, or the damp House'.

The colonel was on hand to welcome him, though the prince's visit had upset his plans for an early visit to Detroit. Standing near the cannon when the salute was fired, however, he was afflicted by such a pain in his head that he took to his room for the next two weeks. It may have been a welcome escape from the social awkwardness of Madame's presence.

But the prince (and suite) was well entertained during the five-day visit. Simcoe had been informed by Clarke that as Prince Edward wished to see the Indians, he trusted he would 'give such directions for this Interview as you may think proper and least likely to occasion expense'. (108) The prince wrote dutifully to his father that 'a very large deputation . . . of all the neighbouring nations came to Niagara to wait my arrival. . . . Their professions of attachment to your Majesty and the British Government were extremely warm.' (109) He reviewed the 5th Regiment at six-thirty on the morning of the 23rd, and admired the men of the Queen's Rangers so much that he asked for volunteers from that regiment to transfer to his own Royal Fusiliers. All men five feet nine inches and over were requested in General Orders to parade on the 26th, 'perfectly clean' : but Simcoe was careful to assure them that any such transfer would be purely voluntary. (110)

One does not go to Niagara and not visit the Falls. The grandest sight imaginable (Mrs Simcoe). Tremendously magnificent (the Bishop, by now practically speechless). Without doubt Prince Edward and his suite were equally impressed by their thundering majesty and grandeur, though he made no mention of this part of his visit in any surviving letters. To his father after his return to Quebec on 6 September the prince repeated what he had written to Sir William Fawcett on the 8th. He had visited, he said, 'every post occupied by his Majesty's troops both in Upper & Lower Canada between Fort Erie & Quebec, excepting Oswego, which I was prevented from doing by a very violent storm which overtook us on Lake Ontario & render'd it entirely impossible for me to get ashore at that post.' He had, he said, 'seen whatever it was either necessary, or proper for me to see, both as a professional man & as a traveller.' (111)

But despite the aura of flattering excitement with which he was surrounded, the prince was finding his colonial experience irksome, feeling isolated from where the real action was going on. In England that passionate humanist Samuel Romilly was writing in horror to his friend Pierre Etienne Dumont : 'How could we ever be so deceived in the character of the French nation as to think them capable of liberty? . . . One might as well think of establishing a republic of tigers in some forest of Africa as of maintaining a free government among such monsters.' (112) On 31 October, Simeon Perkins in Liverpool, Nova Scotia, had confided to his journal the shocking news of 'Terrible Riots, & Mobbs in France, the King Dethroned, his Palase Stormed by Cannon, & Broke open, his furniture, Wine, etc., Destroyed'. In England the Prince of Wales had closed Carlton House in an effort to cope with his debts, but carrying the implication of a public rebuke to his father, who had been adamant in his refusal to help unless he saw some signs of a proper economy. Bad weather had damaged the harvest, causing a rise in the price of bread. Even the trivia of daily events in London and in England would have been more welcome to Prince Edward than all the deference of the colonials.

Only three months after his first arrival in Quebec, the prince was trying to set the limit of his exile by a request that the King would permit his return in the summer of 1793. On 8 July 1792 he confided his problem to his eldest brother. 'I must own that though this country is preferable to Gibraltar, by the liberty one enjoys of ranging about . . . yet it is a sad tiresome séjour for any person who looks up to greater enjoyments than those of traineaux parties. I dread the next winter, as I am convinced that it certainly will be still more stupid & insipid than the last.' (113)

With little to occupy his time and interest but to fuss over his regiment, the young prince threw himself furiously into detail again. Orders continued to flutter across the Atlantic for alterations in the uniforms. When he heard that the Duke of York had altered the dress of his Drum Major and band since his return from Germany, he requested a pattern of half of each coat, in coarse cloth, with white cotton to represent the silver lace, yellow the gold, to be sent 'very secretly'. The helmets for officers, sergeants, musicians and drummers were all sent back, properly named, to be altered, the officers to have the bearskin put on a wire 'worn so as to raise it higher than present caps'. Instead of the blue silk turban now surrounding the cap, there was to be one of fur about one-third inch deeper than the blue. . . . (114)

His inability to show to anyone who really mattered—particularly his father—what he had done with his regiment was a nagging disappointment, in a day when the regiment was a rich man's hobby and in many ways an extension of his ego. He had ventured to ask the King whether he might be allowed to attend him at Windsor with his regiment, and sought his brother's support. 'Whenever I am to return home I hope they will not act so unfairly by me as not to give me an opportunity of shewing my Regt at the same time.' (115)

With the meetings of the Freemasons (to which body he was to be deeply attached all his life, and to whose Quebec lodge he had 'made himself known as an Ancient Mason' the previous December), with concerts (to whose subscribers the *Quebec Gazette* printed admonitory reprimands about talking during the performances, about traffic tie-ups caused by carioles using wrong one-way streets, and about the high caps worn by the ladies in the audience), with convivial dinners at this and that tavern for this and that anniversary, and with the traineaux parties and jaunts to country estates of local personages —with all of this the prince was profoundly bored. Thomas Aston

Coffin, before his arrival, had prophesied to his mother in Boston:
'I think our circle too small for him—a prince of the Blood cooped up
in Quebec I imagine will be uncomfortable himself & make those
around him so too.' (116) In the company of Madame and in the
satisfactions derived from perfecting his regiment, the prince found
his greatest consolations. But at the end of December 1792 his self-
confidence would be sorely bruised.

CHAPTER FIVE

Mutiny

Prince Edward's army career, naturally enough, was the centre of his interest, and his regiment the outward expression, to the world, of his ability and his devotion to duty. The reputation for cruelty with which he has been saddled by certain superficial and possibly politically slanted judgements in his own day, and through the printed pages of biographies since then must appear unjustified to a researcher who looks with any degree of care at contemporary records. The letters from Gibraltar written by Craufurd, Symes and O'Hara during the prince's first term on the Rock not only carry no hint of disapproval of his methods or his behaviour with his men, but actively approve his performance as a military officer: and such court-martial records as survive clearly show, by the uncritical acceptance of the sentences, savage in today's terms, ordered for seemingly minor offences by military courts everywhere, that people in general thought of them as justice rather than cruelty. In fact, the verdict of one of the few courts-martial the young prince was allowed to preside over at Gibraltar was considered too lenient by O'Hara, and it is perhaps significant that this was the last one to which he was appointed as president. (117)

Courts-martial, in any event, were not conducted by the officer who brought the charge, but by a president and a court composed of impartial officers, and sentences were passed in strict accordance with the laws governing the various offences and under the authority—usually carefully exercised—of the Judge Advocate-General. The most that can be charged against the prince is the imposition of too many petty rules and regulations. Once an order is disobeyed, however trivial it may have been, a military offence has been committed and must be punished.

It was not possible under the law for an officer to order casual floggings for his men, though he might by unbending discipline create a climate of unrest in which there would be more rebels, earning such floggings more frequently than in a regiment under easier control. In his zeal to show the world a perfect regiment from every point of view, Prince Edward created just such a climate, to his own intense surprise. Even then, the two mutinies he was to face in his career—in a time when military records are full of far more deadly and dangerous mutinies, and sentences of far greater severity—were ill-organized and spontaneous, sparked by irresponsible men of lower than average intelligence (in the case of the second mutiny, also by undisciplined men who resented the re-imposition of discipline).

So the Colonel of the Royal Fusiliers fussed about his men. Kept their off-duty hours short so that they would be out of the taverns and into bed early. Had his officers award extra guard duty to men disobeying the order to wear their caps up, to keep their rifles clean: to men found 'disguised in liquour', to men 'catched with a light on': extra drill to men appearing awkward on the parade ground. Idle men, he thought, were men liable to fall into mischief: and in view of the few spare time interests of most of them, unable to read or write, and the low pay and the number of taverns around town, he was not far wrong, though his remedy had little appeal for many of them.

Even his officers suffered irritating restrictions, though some opinion supported his control. 'I am pleased with your account of his Royal Highness', wrote John Gawler from London to his friend James Thompson in Quebec in 1792, 'his example in the minutest parts of dicipline must strengthen that of the most weighty. But I am at a loss to know for what he restricts the officers from going into the Country without he is wth them; you think He is right because you have some giddy young Gentlemen; I never knew a Regiment without a succession of that description, and I (speaking for myself) should think it hard to be confined to a Garrison in time of peace because there were a few young giddy persons in Garrison with me. If they commit depredations let them be punished for it. In the strictest of dicipline I ever saw there any one might go with a Pass without the escort even of a Subaltern or Noncom.' (118)

Prince Edward's recollections of his own abuse of freedom and its consequent effect on his career must have made a deep impression. Many of his officers, nevertheless, stayed with him voluntarily for years, and there were many who, like Thompson, approved his strict control. Had there been no mutiny in Quebec (or one might better say, discussion of mutiny, for the affair was never more than a disorganized plot consisting mostly of high-sounding bravado by a few disgruntled and unstable men) the prince might well have come down to us as an example of the best kind of military disciplinarian, one who realized the value of precise directives.

After it was all over, the prince wrote his own account of what happened.

'On Saturday evening, December the 22d, Captain Wetherall of the 11th Regt. of foot, one of the gentlemen of my family, inform'd me that an Inhabitant of the Town of the name of Jeffries, formerly a soldier in the 52d Regt., had been with him & had related to him that some men of the Royal Artillery had that morning communicated to him that they had, through some channel or other which they wou'd not mention, discover'd that a plot was form'd amongst some men of my Regiment to mutiny; To force their way out of the Barracks in the night time, and come up to my quarters with the intention of murdering me and burning the house I was in.' (119)

He was, continued the prince, not inclined to credit the story, but instructed Wetherall to inquire further in the greatest secrecy. He took the precaution also of being attended everywhere by 'the whole of the gentlemen of my family', all wearing pistols under their cloaks.

It became evident that 'a very strong spirit of mutiny' did exist, and that a plot which had failed once through the drunkenness of the leader was ripe for execution. No one, however, was prepared to name the conspirators. Two weeks later, therefore, the prince ordered precautions: more frequent barracks inspections, doubled sentry guards, and eventually a parade attended by the Commander-in-Chief and his suite, when Prince Edward informed the ranks of his awareness of the plot and his sense of shock at the discovery. 'As on the one hand I am conscious that I have always studied your comforts, so on the other there is not one of you who can say otherwise than that the delinquents alone have experienced severity.'

He agreed, however, since 'with the best intentions some things may have escaped me', to consider any complaints that might be brought to the officers, and to submit to the Commander-in-Chief's decision any he did not think proper.

The men, pleased with his speech, mentioned several points of hardship they would like relieved, including a new arrangement for getting dinners to the men on guard duty and longer hours of liberty at night, all of which the prince allowed except the later liberty: 'in a country where every other house almost is a Rum shop, and in a Regt. where there is unfortunately so very large a proportion of bad subjects, two hours liberty after night set in, was amply sufficient.'

The affair was then thought to be over. But on 2 January, one of the conspirators, drunk on guard, was foolish enough to let drop his knowledge of the plot.

At the subsequent courts-martial, Private James Shaw, a self-confessed leader of the plot, turned King's evidence. Four men were sentenced : Privates Joseph Draper (death), William Rose (300 lashes) and Timothy Kennedy (700 lashes), and Sergeant Thomas Wigton (400 lashes and reduced to Private). Those sentenced to corporal punishment were to be returned to England 'to be disposed of at His Majesty's pleasure'. One man, Private James Landrigan, was acquitted for lack of evidence. (120)

Draper, an illiterate tailor, and Rose, with a long record of trouble-making, were, with Shaw, the leaders in the plot. The court-martial proceedings, which ran from 11 January to 25 March, give a confused picture, with none of the prisoners or witnesses quite aware of which day what took place—one witness did not know on which day of the month or in which month New Year's Day fell, but placed the mutiny at about twelve days after Christmas, which 'was of a Tuesday'—or where or when they had held their various conversations, often not whispered, the plotters apparently unconcerned about eavesdroppers. At no time was any meeting of all the conspirators held, nor were any of them really certain of the plan of action. Instructions and arrangements for the plan, passed from one to a second and by him to a third, seem to have been accepted without question, and the conspirators had no assurance at any time that any beyond themselves would join the mutiny. It was Draper, so drunk when his time for guard duty at Cape Diamond came up on 2 January that he had to ask a comrade to substitute for the first period, who made the ill-advised revelation that broke the story.

Rose seems to have been the most articulate and active of the group. He had not been silent about his complaints. Witness after witness came forward to testify at his trial that he had been complaining for weeks, that he had 'thought he had suffered enough already, he had been guilty of an error, and that His Royal Highness had punished him enough already, without keeping him at Drill and his name so long on the Gate' : that Joseph Draper had told him 'there was an Affair in hands that might soon acquit him of his discontent, if he . . . would take charge of it, as he thought he was the only Man that was capable of it on Account of the ill usage he had received.'

In a confusion of second- and third-hand evidence the plot was described. Rose was to have displayed from a top gallery window a large handkerchief bearing the words 'General Washington' when the regiment was on parade in the barrack square (he had claimed to have once been Washington's Orderly Sergeant). An old drummer named Baddow was to beat to arms when Draper called on him, at which time the ringleaders would turn down into the square. Sergeant Wigton would then speak to the men and 'get as many over to his side as he possibly could'. Draper and Shaw, seizing pickaxes, were to force the back gate, Rose and his friends to secure the barrack guard, and Landrigan, with the right flank company ('he was almost sure of all of them') to go to his Royal Highness's quarters (which were to be set on fire) and secure his person while Draper took a party 'to secure the main Guard, the Governor and the Chatteau'.

Sergeant Wigton, meanwhile, was to be occupied persuading the Royal Artillery to join in: Rose had said 'he knew the Artillery would join them, and those that would not He would immediately put them to Death'. Shaw and Rose would be busy seizing the Bateaux, loading them with arms and provisions and ballasting them with sand. A party would then join Landrigan guarding the prince, who would be taken to the Château, where Rose would 'lay down the complaints of both Regiments to His Royal Highness, and ask redress for them, with a Pardon for every Mutineer, which if not granted Rose was to begin with killing His Royal Highness and the rest of the Officers were to share the same fate, excepting those who seemed to take the parts of the Men'.

The mutineers would then try to cross the river. If successful, they would force the captains of militia to provide guides 'to the Colonies', where Rose planned to 'take the Regiment up to General Washington, and make him a present of them, and the New Stand of Colours'. In the event of failure 'they were determined to sell their Lives at as dear a rate as possible'.

Details were filled in by other witnesses. Draper had told the corporal of the guard who had discovered his ill-advised revelations that six men 'were to be with loaded arms to go round the Barrack Rooms and that a man of that Party was to be appointed Captain to present a Paper to the Men in the different Barrack Rooms, and he who did not sign it was to be put to Death and such Man as could not write was to put his hand to the Pen'.

Grievances that might have persuaded the Royal Artillery to join the mutiny do not seem to have been strong enough to rouse them to action, and the ill-usage that Rose complained of seems to have been justifiably based on his own past misconduct. The prince had had some right to be suspicious of him. Rose was a Frenchman from the Island of Jersey who had joined the Royal Fusiliers in Gibraltar from the 68th Regiment, and appears to have been a hot-headed and rebellious trouble-maker.

He had been tried in a General Court-Martial just before embarking for Canada because of the mutinous remarks he had been ill-advised enough to make immediately after appearing before a Regimental Court-Martial for an altercation with a sergeant. He had come out of the Officers' Mess where the trial had been held, announcing loudly that 'he would never allow himself to be struck by no person whatever when under arms'. A sergeant major had asked whether he had not seen men struck for trifling offences which had saved them from worse punishment, and Rose had declared injudiciously 'he would be damn'd if he cared, whether it was the Prince, the Adjutant or any other Officer, or Serjeant, he would knock him down; and that he was sorry he had not done something in the morning which would have opened the Eyes of others'. He was promptly hauled before a General Court-Martial ordered by the Governor, Sir Robert Boyd, and earned himself 500 lashes ('by virtue of the second article of the twenty-third section of the Articles of War'), after pleading that not being master of the English language, he might have used words conveying a stronger meaning than he had intended. (121)

Evidence at his Quebec court-martial now indicated that Rose had tried desertion about eight months earlier with two other men (the proceedings of this trial have not been traced), which may well account for the anecdote in the memoirs of de Gaspé about the brave Frenchman La Rose, a special favourite of his royal colonel, pursued into the woods by a search party led by the prince, and earning the latter's admiration by remaining steadfast under a punishment of 999 lashes. De Gaspé wrote the anecdote from hearsay (he was only eight at the time of the mutiny). It has been natural for later writers to assume that any French soldier in Quebec would be a Canadian. (122)

Rose was not only *not* a favourite of Prince Edward, as the story goes, but under constant suspicion as a source of trouble. The award of 999 lashes is improbable. Corporal punishments were awarded in round figures. In any event, they often exceeded 1,000 lashes at that time.

Considerable circumstantial evidence suggests James Landrigan's involvement also, though he was acquitted for lack of proof. Several sources pointed to his having been the man chosen as captain to go round the barracks getting signatures from volunteer mutineers. Unfortunately he got exceedingly drunk on Christmas Night, when the men had had extra pay and every tavern in Quebec was full of inebriated soldiers. The mutiny was uncovered before he was released from subsequent confinement, his hangover next morning having prevented him from going on duty. Landrigan was known as a good man except for his weakness for liquor, and tales about his misadventure had considerably livened the next day's gossip. He had fallen down in the Coffee-house: and a witness remembered meeting Sergeant Wigton rounding up the revellers next morning and telling him 'Your famous champion Jemmy Landrigan has got himself thrashed by a Boy.'

Rose was universally condemned. Clarke warned both Fawcett and Sir George Yonge at the War Office when the proceedings were sent to the Judge Advocate-General ('Rose, a Frenchman by birth, is a clever, daring, dangerous fellow'). Prince Edward himself wrote to Fawcett: 'I look upon La Rose the Frenchman to be one of the deepest, most designing & most dangerous villains that it is possible to meet with.' (123)

As for Sergeant Wigton, his conviction followed his own insistence on a court-martial after having been previously questioned and released. The evidence at the trial so strongly implicated him that his confidence in demanding a trial 'to vindicate himself in his Royal Benefactor's eye' seems founded in stupidity. But his involvement in the plot must have been a shock to the prince, who provided him with a reference during the trial, dated 16 March 1793, endorsing him as 'a valuable regular good soldier, a man in whom confidence was reposed and seldom guilty of those irregularities which the generality of soldiers are apt to fall into'. Only eight days before Christmas—and the mutiny plot—the prince had personally recommended the Sergeant's inititation into the Freemasons' lodge. (124) The involvement of Landrigan and Kennedy too may have troubled him with a sense of disappointment. Both men at their trial acknowledged favours of passes and money from his Royal Highness.

But public opinion was strongly with the prince. Simcoe, in some apprehension, was 'most truly concerned to hear of the mutinous transactions of the Fusileers, particularly as it may be the means of rendering his Royal Highness unpopular amongst the lower class of Men, and that the affair may be exaggerated by disaffected people, so as to occasion other Corps, who may be stationed at more exposed posts, hereafter to follow their example: however, I trust that the Ring leaders may be corrected and punished in as exemplary a Manner as they Merit.' (125)

Only seven months later, Simcoe would show himself less merciful than the prince proved to be, carrying out (with Clarke's official approval) the execution of a seventeen-year-old soldier, Charles Grisler, who, from a similar sense of grievance and much less rebelliously, had deserted his post as sentry over the bateaux. (126) Other court-martial records show Simcoe's approval given to punishments of up to 1,500 lashes.

F

The *Quebec Gazette,* reporting the sentences on 28 March, thought it 'difficult to say whether the folly or the atrociousness of the plot was greatest'. London papers noted that the plan had been formed by a few discontented soldiers, and agreed with the *Quebec Gazette.* 'Supposing that they had been able to have executed their designs in the garrison, they never could have crossed the St Lawrence, for it is no where frozen over this season, and the immense pieces of ice which are continually floating up and down render an attempt to pass it in batteaux extremely perilous if not impracticable.' (127)

Someone in Vermont had heard from someone in Canada (said the *London Chronicle* of 22 April) that 'the cause is supposed to have originated from the repeated alterations in the uniforms and equipment of the regiment, which occasioned many stoppages in their pay'. It is probably a part of the truth. But it is noteworthy that neither this nor any suggestion of cruel or severe punishments were included among the grievances mentioned in all the trial proceedings. It is worthy of note, too, that in February 1794 a former sergeant, William Hinde, who had been invalided home, was petitioning to be allowed to rejoin the prince's regiment. (128)

Lieutenant-Governor Clarke (a former Colonel of the Royal Fusiliers who would later resume the same command) thought the prince had been victimized. He wrote to Sir William Fawcett on 13 February to forestall rumours that might reach England ahead of official information: 'The idea of mutiny seems to have originated amongst ten or twelve soldiers who, I understand, his Royal Highness took pains to get transfer'd from other Regiments at Gibraltar into his own, on account of their size & good looks, previous to his leaving that garrison. These have unluckily prov'd to be men of bad morals & desperate characters; & amongst them, one in particular nam'd Rose, who is a native of France & has been in various services, which, it is probable, he has left with marks of infamy. . . . I am perfectly satisfied that the wickedness I have related did not extend in any degree to above fifteen persons at the most.' (129)

The anonymous writer of *Canadian Letters,* recalling in 1795 a visit he had made to Quebec in October 1792, said much the same thing. Some of the top-ranking officers at Gibraltar had taken advantage of the young prince's interest in a fine-looking regiment 'to get quit of a number of troublesome fellows.' (130)

His experience did not deter the prince from continuing to seek men of good appearance for his regiment. Not three years after the mutiny, Governor Wentworth of Halifax would note: 'The Prince *cannot resist* the temptation of taking a fine Man into his Regt, nor a fine Horse into his stable at any rate whatsoever.' (131)

The prince could not pardon the convicted men—this was the prerogative of General Clarke—but he could intercede for them. Clarke wrote again to Sir William Fawcett on 11 May, saying that the prince's urgent solicitation had induced him to remit Kennedy's sentence. Kennedy was not very bright, the prince thought, and should be pitied rather than punished, as he probably would not have got involved if he had been sober at the time.

'The transcendant humanity of His Royal Highness's heart did not stop here but also extended itself in Draper's behalf, and he became a warm intercessor for his Life, and press'd his earnest desire so forcibly upon me that I could not resist the application.

'Draper, however, was led to the place of execution, and all the awful ceremonious parts gone through, when at the moment of his expecting to sink into Eternity, His Royal Highness went up to him, and having addressed him in the most solemn manner, in a Speech containing wholesome admonitions, whereof I send a copy, he produced the pardon he had procured for him, on condition of his being sent to England to be disposed of with his associates.' (132)

The awful death parade endured by Draper, when, dressed in grave clothes and walking behind his coffin which was covered by a pall and carried by four men, he marched to the place of public execution, has been laid as a heavy charge against Prince Edward by later generations. 'The troops under arms marched slowly before—the music followed playing dirges suited to the occasion, and a vast concourse of spectators attended. When this affecting procession had reached the place of execution, and the convict had prepared himself to suffer, declaring to the last that he was innocent of the crime laid to his charge, and when the critical moment had arrived which was to have landed him into eternity, a PARDON was announced by His Royal Highness. The effect thereby produced in the mind of the unhappy man, which could then have nothing but death in view, as well as on the feelings of the spectators, may be easier conceived than expressed.'

Thus the *Quebec Gazette* of 11 April 1793. In a day when a hanging at Tyburn was an occasion for a family outing, and punishment made as public as possible as a deterrent, the sentence was regarded as eminently just (it was certainly legal) and the grim proceedings considered to be a salutary warning to others. Had not Samuel Johnson said not long before, 'Executions are intended to draw spectators. If they do not draw spectators, they don't answer their purpose'? (133)

The daughter of a respected and kind-hearted colonel (he had been a captain loyal to the prince—by then Duke of Kent—at Gibraltar in 1802) would record a similar 'punishment parade' upwards of twenty years later, when another soldier condemned to be shot went through the same ceremony, unaware—kneeling on his coffin, with his eyes bandaged, and the click of the musket-locks in his ears—of a reprieve that had been deliberately kept from him until the final moment so that he should 'for example's sake, as well as for the purpose of making a lasting impression on himself, go through all the terrible ceremonial that precedes so awful a death'. (134) Draper's experience cannot be taken as evidence of a sadistic tendency either in the prince or in his commander-in-chief. It was normal procedure for the times.

A copy of Prince Edward's wholesome admonitions to Draper was enclosed by Clarke in his letter to Fawcett, but as only the duplicate of Clarke's letter seems to have survived, the original, with the enclosures, may have been lost in transit. However, as much as could be recollected by a public-spirited citizen present at the event was printed in the *Quebec Gazette* of 18 April. The prince concluded by saying: 'May you take warning by this awful scene and so conduct yourself, that by the remainder of your life, you may atone for your past crimes; and that I may not hereafter have occasion to repent having now been your Advocate.'

One may be permitted to wonder if the later adventures of Private Draper ever reached the princely ears. If so, he might have regretted his merciful act. For Private Draper had not entirely finished making his small blots on the pages of history.

CHAPTER SIX

Goodbye to Quebec

Members of the newly elected Houses of the Legislature of Lower Canada were sworn in on Monday 17 December 1792, and His Excellency Lieutenant-Governor Clarke addressed both Houses in the Council Chamber. (The prince's former servant, Robert Wood, had been appointed Doorkeeper to the Executive Council by warrant dated the 15th.) Once in session, the Legislative Assembly began a noisy wrangle about the use of French and English, and impassioned letters from *A Bye Stander* and *A Citizen* appeared in the journals with advice and warning.

At least for the prince, pining for home, this experiment in colonial government provided some variety in a life that but for Madame's grace and cheerfulness was sadly tedious. He was not, however, optimistic about a real integration of English and French. Two weeks earlier he had written to William Dalrymple, then groom of the bed-chamber to the Duke of Clarence, and later his own treasurer:

'In a fortnight, the first assembly of this country will meet; I fear on reflecting on the ignorance, the stupidity & the want of education of the major part of the members of the lower house, we may expect something not unlike a Polish diet. Certain it is, that there is the most inveterate Jealousy subsisting between the French & English inhabitants, & the most sensible & experienced people here seem to fear that the new constitution was not perfectly well timed. The situation of France having occasion'd such a general fermentation, I may say all over the world, it is certainly to be feared that the same spirit which has manifested itself even in England may sooner or later work on the minds of the people here, & be productive of consequences

which can be paralelled only by those thro' which England unfortunately lost the American colonies: I sincerely wish that I may be a
false prophet on this subject but I believe I may say that I am not
singular in my fears.' (135)

A month later (3 January) the sheriff of Montreal, Edward Gray,
writing pessimistically to his nephew Frederick Ermatinger, found himself of the same opinion. 'The house of Assembly met on the 17th
instant [sic] and after setting a week without doing any material
business adjourned to the 7th instant. It is probable when they meet
it will be but for a short time as all the Canadian members are resolutely
determined not to adopt the English language either in the proceedings
or the acts they may pass, in which I am sorry to add there is an
appearance of their being joined by some of the English members . . .
and I do not suppose that the Legislative Councill will receive, or if
they do, that the Governor of an English province will give his consent
to any Act passed in a foreign language, consequently if they persist
in the measure they will be either prorogued or adjourned, which will
throw us into a state of anarchy and confusion as all our existing laws
will expire in six months from their first meeting.' (136)

Worse troubles were looming over Europe. From London Sir
William Fawcett, who had been advising patience in the prince's
unremitting campaign to be removed from hence and from the
boredom of his small social circle, was writing of 'seditious activities in
the country' that would affect the annual relief of regiments in foreign
stations, and, in a later letter, of the fitting out 'with uncommon
Diligence' of a considerable number of Men of War. (137) War talk
was in the air. Lord Henry Spencer, gossiping to his friend Lord
Auckland on 18 December about entertainment provided by the Duke
of Queensberry to 'the French colony at Richmond', had added that
'Well-informed people seem to have hardly any doubt of a war':
though another friend of Auckland's, the engaging Anthony Storer, was
doing some uneasy whistling in the dark. 'How can the French, mad
as they are, be so outrageously insane as to think of war? . . . As I have
seen more than once Mr Pitt at the height of preparation without
coming to acting, I never shall believe in war, at least in one of any
long continuance, till I see the event happen.' Mr Storer deplored 'the
inundation of emigrants which has overflowed the land . . . There are
so many dismal priests in the streets, that, with their sable appearance
and the help of the fogs, our pavement is totally darkened.' (138)

Social life continued, however, with a surface gaiety that covered
hidden apprehensions. While the Quebec garrison was celebrating its
1792 Christmas by drunken parties all over town, the Queen, at

Windsor (anticipating by nearly fifty years the husband of a grand-daughter she would never know) was entertaining local children with 'a German fashion. A fir tree, about as high again as any of us, lighted all over with small tapers, several little wax dolls among the branches in different places, and strings of almonds and raisins alternately tied from one to the other, with skipping ropes for the boys, and each bigger girl had muslin for a frock, a muslin handkerchief, a fan, and a sash, all prettily done up in the handkerchief, and a pretty necklace and earrings besides. As soon as all the things were delivered out by the Queen and Princesses, the candles on the tree were put out, and the children set to work to help themselves, which they did very heartily.' (139)

Life in British North America continued with its small excitements. Levees and balls for Prince Edward's birthday and the Queen's pro-vided bursts of special splendour in the continuing seasonal gaiety. At Niagara, Betsey Russell, not very comfortable in the temporary quarters her brother had finally found, was much mortified that she had had to refuse the invitation of 'a smart little officer' to the Queen's birthday ball because her clothes, still packed in trunks, could not be got at. Mrs Simcoe was also absent, having given birth to a sixth daughter two days earlier. A fire in Quebec's Lower Town market place, where the church roof and two houses had 'catched the flames' was got under control by the exertions of the Citizens, the Fire Society, the Troops, the Officers of the garrison, his Excellency General Clarke and his Royal Highness. The prince went dutifully to funerals, attended Masonic meetings, got Shuttleworth to send to Birmingham for '360 buckles for breeches waistbands of men, of iron, very strong, flat on top, rounded under, account to be charged against men', and fretted over his exile.

He had become reconciled to remaining abroad for at least another year. He had intimated to Dalrymple early in December how greatly disappointed he would be if he were denied the opportunity of showing his father the improvement he had brought about in his regiment, 'toiling day & night to form a crew of the most ragged wretches you ever beheld, into well appointed soldiers'. However, he was resigned to remaining in Quebec until 1794, 'sharing,' he wrote just two weeks before the revolt would disillusion him, 'the fortunes of a corps who have always behaved most particularly well towards me'. (140)

The acclaim accorded the Royal Fusiliers by the local journals after every review must have given their royal colonel one of the few consolations of his exile: and, always, the delighted approval and praise from his lady awaited him in the warmth of his home at the end of each long day.

So, with the court-martial proceedings stringing themselves out through the months of January, February and March, his Royal Highness moved into 1793 : went about his duties and made the best of the limited social opportunities of Quebec, with Madame a warm and joyous source of comfort in his private life. There were quiet evenings for reading—they were both avid readers. A request to his brother Prince William away back in January 1791 for 'maps of N. America, roads mark'd', had included books too—'Novellists Magazine, a small collection of the best French novels', some plays and the works of Rousseau—which he and Madame would enjoy together. The friendship with the de Salaberrys grew and deepened, Prince Edward playing with the children, Madame caressing them, fondling their 'fair sunny hair'.

Down in Nova Scotia, Simeon Perkins was recording with frank and simple delight his visit to Halifax as member of the Legislature for Liverpool. On 2 April he dined with Governor Wentworth : 'His Lady at Table Looked Very gay & was Vastly pleasant'. A week later, dining with the Chief Justice, he had the misfortune to 'Cut my thumb & finger of my left hand, at his Table, opening a Walnut. I blead considerable. Mr Sheriff Clark was kind enough to do it up.' Next day his journal trumpeted : 'Packet from New York with newspapers, French have declared war against English and Dutch 1st February.' The complacent assurance of Lieutenant-Governor Clarke six weeks earlier before the Quebec Legislature that Great Britain was 'happily at Peace with all the World' had been rudely shattered.

Despite his determination to endure without complaint, the young prince had not been able to resist further entreaties to his father even before the outbreak of war, engaging the Prince of Wales also to plead for him 'at this critical moment', and begging his father, since 'the present situation of affairs in Europe is so awful', to be allowed to serve in a more active sphere. But the King remained silent, and Prince Edward cooled his heels in Quebec, 'left to vegetate in this most dreary and gloomy spot on the face of the earth' and to read about the feverish excitement at home.

The war was immensely popular. Men were trying to smuggle aboard transports to get to the Continent, and three battalions of the Guards marched off for an emotional embarkation at Greenwich in the presence of the whole royal family. Sir Gilbert Elliot had got up at five-thirty on Monday 25 February to see them begin their march at Whitehall. 'The King, I think, in the character of an equestrian statue on a fierce white charger, a sufficient gigg, but looking so pleased that one liked to see him. The Grenadiers, when they began their march, sang "God save the King!" of their own accord as they passed by him, which overcame him a good deal. I did not see this myself, but was told so . . . The Prince of Wales was in his new Light Horse uniform, which is very handsome and theatrical, and I daresay delighted him, but it displayed an amount of bulk which entertained Mundy and me, and probably all beholders. The Duke of York is gone with them to Holland. I hear the Duchess is much affected, as she really likes him.' (141)

The Queen and princesses had gone 'secretly', all much overcome, with Princess Sophia fainting and ten-year-old Princess Amelia ('absolutely roaring') refusing comfort from Princess Mary, all of them later revived by an impromptu repast supplied by the understandably flustered governor of Greenwich Hospital.

Another royal son, the Prince of Wales, had also begun to protest against being kept out of action. 'He wishes to serve abroad, and to have his share of the glory that is going,' remarked Sir Gilbert Elliot to his wife. (142) The Prince, who had no better luck than his younger brother with his father, was at least closer to the action, though somewhat remote from its hardships when he attended the review at Warley camp in August. 'A most superb bed had just been Finish'd for the Prince of Wales, and is to be fixed in His Royal Highness's Tent, previous to Their Majesties' visit to the camp. The form of the bed is square, the hangings of a very delicate chintz; a white ground, with a lilac and green cloud. The fringes, tassels, and other ornaments, are very rich and beautiful. The four corners are ornamented with the Prince's Feathers and Motto. The rest of the furniture for the Tent is in corresponding elegance, and will, on the breaking up of the Camp, be removed to the Marine Pavilion at Brighton.' He also faced the rigours of war in a new long carriage for travelling. 'It is so constructed that in a few moments, it forms a neat chamber, with a handsome bed, and every other convenience for passing the night in it, on the road, or in a camp,' (143)

British hopes were running high. The capture of Valenciennes on 28 July with great destruction to a third of the town had heartened everyone, and the Duke of York moved at once to besiege Dunkirk, where, however, initial hitches presaged less success. He was highly vexed with the Duke of Richmond, he told Lady Holland when, passing through the area, she was invited to dine. Richmond had failed to send the ordnance: and the Duke of York was even more annoyed with the artillery officers at Ostend who, in a piece of masterly bumbling, 'have sent down the canals the carriages in one vessel, and the cannons in another, so that they do not arrive together'. Lady Holland, feeling 'odd being the only female among such a party of men', had been terrified when what she thought was rain pattering on the duke's tent afterwards turned out to be enemy fire : but the duke thoughtfully ordered his band to strike up to cover the noise of the volleys and sent her home later with an escort of several light dragoons. (144)

The two younger princes, Ernest and Adolphus, were both engaged in active personal fighting. Early in September, Adolphus managed to acquire a slight wound together with the adulation of his sisters at home while Prince Edward fumed in Quebec and Madame concerned herself with the duties of the home and her private and personal occupations. Sometimes she jotted down, into one of the commonplace books that have not survived, the little verses and epigrams she wanted to remember for future appropriate occasions. Sometimes she practised her singing. Sometimes she took up an expert needle, perhaps to sew some little garment for the next small niece, Alexandrine, who would be born in Grenoble on 11 January, certainly to keep her own wardrobe in good order. Writing to William Dalrymple in mid-July, the prince had complained on her behalf. 'Amongst the different books which did not arrive by the ships, there is one which has been a very great loss to Madame St Laurent, as she makes the whole of her cloaths herself; I can account for none of the numbers of the Journal de la mode. . . .' (145)

Possibly the fashions depicted in the missing copies might have held less appeal than others that year for Madame. At the end of April 1793, Sir Gilbert Elliot had stayed long enough at a ball in London 'to see some of the dancing generation', and was frankly shocked. 'There were one or two instances of the modern fashion of dress for young ladies, by which they are made to appear five or six months gone with child. Perhaps you do not believe this fashion', wrote the astonished nobleman to his wife, 'but it is quite literally true. The original idea seems to have been an imitation of the drapery of statues and pictures, which fastens the dress immediately below the bosom, and leaves no waist. The consequence of which is a slight swell of the figure, as you may see in pictures; but this being attempted by artificial means of pads placed on the stomach is an exact representation of a state of pregnancy. This dress is accompanied by a complete display of the bosom—which is uncovered, and supported and stuck out by the sash immediately below it.' (146)

Eyes and ears were open then, as now, for snippets of scandal. Prince Edward may have been far away, but people at home were still interested in what he might be doing. Few in London, therefore, would have missed the item in the *Morning Chronicle* of 25 April. 'An illustrious Prince, it is said, has formed an attachment with a beautiful Marseilloise, who is highly spoken of for mental as well as personal accomplishments. She is one of the *rank* and *file* in the garrison of Quebec.'

So the royal exile languished, comforted only by Madame: held reviews: visited friends: attended weddings: sponsored a Sunday Free School. A Bishop's See, to be known as the Bishopric of Quebec with jurisdiction in Upper and Lower Canada 'and their Dependencies' was created. In Liverpool, Nova Scotia, Simeon Perkins was having his troubles organizing the militia. 'Some of the officers Seem to dispute paying for their Commissions.'

Governor Simcoe had moved to Toronto (re-named York), and Hannah Jarvis, wife of the provincial secretary, wrote crossly: 'Every Body are sick at York—but no matter—the Lady likes the Place— therefore everybody Else must.' (147) Lord Dorchester came back to a rejoicing Quebec in *Severn,* walking privately up the beach at eleven in the morning on Tuesday, 24 September, though his wife and daughter chose to wait for a carriage. There were reviews, drawing rooms, levees. And Prince Edward still waited for news from home.

His 'beautiful Marseilloise' had been with him now for nearly two years. As a prince for whom 'the choice of a wife was indeed a lottery', with 'very few prizes compared to the number of blanks,' his eldest brother had written in July 1791 with disastrous irony (148), he must have realized that he was among the fortunate in having found so ideal a companion to free him from the temptation of a succession of passing affairs likely to cause unsavoury scandal and cliques. Many more than Colonel Symes at Gibraltar held the same wise and practical view. One French emigré who briefly visited Quebec put it into succinct words. He had met Madame, and liked her.

Bénigne Charles Fevret de Saint-Mesmin, with his twenty-three-year-old son Jules, arrived in the city from Halifax at the end of September 1793, on his way to Santo Domingo (via Quebec, Montreal, St Jean and New York). His visit to Quebec coincided with the return of Lord Dorchester, and he was an interested observer among the crowds flocking to the Plains of Abraham on the bright clear morning of 30 September to see the review of the prince's regiment. 'This young prince gives all his care and interest to the tactics and development of his corps . . . /which/made its manoeuvres with the greatest precision.'

Having brought no direct introduction to the prince, Saint-Mesmin was delighted when Prince Edward expressed interest in meeting him, and by his Royal Highness's gracious welcome, his questions about the visitors' personal circumstances and the reason for the visit.

'Tall, well-built and with a fine figure', Saint-Mesmin recorded afterwards in his journal, 'he speaks our language perfectly and has passed through several parts of France on his way to and from Geneva.

Because of certain dissipations and other youthful amusements, the King made him return to London to go with his regiment to Gibraltar, from whence, after eighteen months, he was sent here. This exile, whose purpose was to develop maturity, seemed to him to be rather long, and he explained frankly to me, a new-comer, that he hoped on his return to England to be placed about the King. Meanwhile, Madame de St Laurent, an elegant lovely lady, relieved the tedium and those problems of a bachelor hard to endure at his age.'

Saint-Mesmin added an eminently sensible footnote about Madame. 'She is French; Prince Edward made her acquaintance at Marseille. [sic] She lived formerly in Paris, where according to what I have been told, she was a kept woman: though she has a well-bred manner, her earlier state is a little apparent: they say a gentleman lent her his name on taking her up. She lives conjugally with the prince, under the same roof, doing the honours of his home and his table at those times when he invites only men. Although the proper ladies of Quebec do not accept her socially, it seems to me that this arrangement is in no way scandalous: this kind of union of convenience is among a prince's privileges, especially in England where the heir presumptive to the Crown lives openly with a well-born lady, Mrs Fitzherbert. For Prince Edward it is an impropriety less licentious than those temporary liaisons a young man of his age tends to form, with all the stir and publicity attached to his rank, especially in such a small community as Quebec.' (149)

The four Royal Fusiliers mutineers under sentence had been awaiting dispatch to England. At the beginning of November they were placed in care of Lieutenant Maxwell on board *Severn*, on which Lord Dorchester had returned to Quebec: the two unremitted floggings had by now been administered. The proceedings of the courts-martial had been laid before the King, and a good deal of anxious paper work had brought the decision that Wigton's previous good character and valuable army experience entitled him to be discharged from the regiment with permission to enlist, with the approval of the command-ing officer, in a newly raised corps. Rose and Kennedy should be transferred to the 60th Regiment of Foot. Draper was to be sent to serve in the New South Wales Corps.

From the Main Guard at Plymouth, where they had been tem-porarily lodged on 12 December, the prisoners were escorted to the Savoy prison, through a country speculating about the destination of Sir Charles Grey and the troops mentioned for the West-India expedi-tion, now thought to be only a blind, as 'the French have scarcely any force in the West Indies and all that we can muster will undoubtedly find sufficient employment nearer home'. (150) British hopes were on the downswing. The siege of Dunkirk had failed, and blame was being laid at a variety of doors. In October, ten months after Louis XVI had died with courage and dignity on the scaffold in the middle of the Place de la Révolution (later to be named Place de la Concorde), his queen followed him to the guillotine, sending a shiver of horror through all except the most fanatical supporters of the Revolution.

The slightest tendency to revolutionary ideas brought whiplash retribution: literally, as in the case of the three soldiers who were flogged at Warley camp for mutiny 'in consequence of having listened to the suggestions of a French Jacobin Suttler': figuratively, but with a savagery that brought cries of shame from the press, to the group of men known later as the Scottish Martyrs, one of whom, the respected clergyman Dr Thomas Fyshe Palmer, was transported to Botany Bay for seven years, and the other four—Thomas Muir, William Skirving, Maurice Margarot and Joseph Gerrald—for fourteen. Earnest men of high principle, they had called for comparatively mild reforms to be brought about constitutionally, but their speeches and publications tended to be inflammatory and were certainly ill-timed.

In the city of Quebec, George Allsopp, a merchant and member of the earlier Legislative Council, was having financial trouble following the loss by fire of his uninsured mills at Jacques Cartier, 'a Loss too heavy for me to support'.

He had proposed what he thought was a good plan to save the property for himself and still satisfy his creditors, in a letter to Brook Watson of the big English trading company of Watson and Rashleigh. He could get no satisfaction from Watson (a personality of the day, an energetic man who had lost a leg to a shark in Havana harbour at the age of fourteen and would become Lord Mayor of London in 1796), who, he found, 'is gone Commissary general to Germany having resigned his seat for London'. He had been equally unable to get action from William Goodall, Watson's representative in Quebec. (151)

By mid-May, nearly three months after the fire, Allsopp had got a pair of temporary stones put into the old mill, 'and I did further trust I should be able to cover in the walls and by degrees refit the Mill on a small plan', but Watson remained adamant. 'Mr Goodall harps on his displeasing Mr Watson by shewing me lenity,' the harassed merchant wrote to his brother-in-law (12 May). 'I do allow Mr Goodall acted so far with lenity—but he has an improper attachment also which displeases Mr Watson & he cant get him home; this is no affair of mine: but I do not think Mr Watson has shewn the least consideration for my services.'

Mr Goodall (who in partnership with Turner would operate the firm from Garlick Hill in the City of London for more than twenty years to come) had indeed formed an improper connection. He had been involved for the past four years with one of the three pretty Green sisters, Eliza, who had borne him her second 'natural' child, a son now three years old. This was the child believed to have been fathered by Prince Edward, but whose birth-date, 28 August 1790 (confirmed by the baptismal record for 19 September in the register of the English Church in Quebec) was supplied by descendants who evidently failed to realize that this was a full year before the prince arrived in Canada.

Goodall's time in Quebec was almost over: he made his final departure on 25 November. His last act, on the day of his sailing, was to leave Jonathan Sewell directions for the collection of some due notes, the agent being named as 'Sexton to the Cathedral Church & lives exactly opposite to the House in which *Miss Green lives*'. The suggestive italics are apparently his own. (152)

In September, General Clarke had written a sympathetic postscript to Simcoe. 'No instructions are come relative to the Prince. We therefore conclude he will remain here—which makes him miserable and really seems hard.' (153) In a letter to his father, the young man tried to make the best of it. 'Although I must own that I have suffered the most cruel disappointment . . . I feel no inconsiderable pride in shewing the World that I know how to submit with the utmost cheerfulness to your command.' (154)

The town had just finished the usual celebration of his birthday with the usual levee, elegant ball and supper at the Château, and with illuminations in the town that indirectly caused the death of George Allsopp's father on 5 November. 'He appeared quite well at dinner and ate with a good appetite on Saturday the 2d day we had an illumination on acct. of Prince Edward's birth day he was desirous of sitting up rather later than usual & going to bed was taken with a shivering.' At his funeral, one of the pallbearers was William Goodall, for whom, in spite of their business disagreements, Allsopp retained a high regard. 'A very sensible and intelligent man,' he told his sons in subsequent years, and sent them to Goodall's London office for business advice. William Goodall would also appear again in the life of Eliza Green. He might have been amused, could a crystal ball have shown him their son being credited with royal birth and a claim to the throne of England.

Things had been stirring at home. The West-India expedition appeared to be on again: Sir Charles Grey had come bustling back from Ostend, the transports with the troops following him to Portsmouth. The fleet under Admiral Sir John Jervis fell down to St Helens. Admiral Hood had captured Toulon in August, and the rejoicing

British public was not yet aware that deep misgivings about holding the port were beginning to be expressed by people on the spot.

Prince Edward helped fight another Lower Town fire, and gracefully accepted an address from the House of Assembly expressing satisfaction at his presence in Quebec. The prince, thanking the Members, said: 'I look forward with anxious expectation to the moment, when, if I am called upon to the more immediate Active Service of my Country, I may prove to You that I shall ever exert myself with redoubled Zeal.' (155) There was a scare when news came that a French fleet of seven sail had left New York carrying pilots for the St Lawrence and mooring chains of a large size, and Dorchester ordered batteries erected and about sixty guns of all sizes mounted. (156) Chief Justice Smith died, and the prince went to his funeral. Admiral Lord Howe was chopping about in the Channel, and General Charles O'Hara, the prince's old commander at Gibraltar, was captured at Toulon by a young artillery officer named Bonaparte. The *Oracle* began to look forward to sugar from Santo Domingo, and announced that the King had bought Cumberland House in Pall Mall for Prince Edward, who would be created Duke of Cumberland on his return to England. The poet laureate, Henry James Pye, had (as usual) written a New Year's Ode, and on being 'much bantered' about its quality, laid the blame at the door of Pitt, who, he said, had not supplied him with a single subject for panegyric exultation.

Relief was in sight for his Royal Highness. On 2 October the rank of major general in the Army was conferred on him by the King, and this information, with orders to serve with Lieutenant-General Sir Charles Grey in the West Indies, was sent off to him post-haste the same day by Sir George Yonge, by Sir William Fawcett (with congratulations), and officially by the Commander-in-Chief, Lord Amherst.

And at last—at last!—on Christmas Eve, forgotten Edward received the news, delayed by Atlantic gales and river ice, that he was not forgotten, had been promoted, his past conduct approved, and would be on his way, as soon as travelling plans could be made, to get his share of the glory that was going.

CHAPTER SEVEN

Action

'I am under the necessity of going by way of Boston, every other route but through the United States being absolutely impracticable at this advanced season of the year . . . The very moment that the roads are passable I shall set off.' (157)

Thus wrote the jubilant young prince to his brother the Prince of Wales. He had long wanted to visit the United States. As early as September 1792 he had put in a request to the King (to which he received no answer) for permission to spend up to two months across the border. Now he made busy preparations for departure. Captain Frederick Wetherall would accompany him as aide-de-camp, with Captains John Vesey and George Smyth of the Royal Fusiliers and Lieutenant George Fisher, Royal Artillery, also in attendance. Lord Dorchester sent an express post-haste through the winter woods on snowshoes to Halifax to order a frigate round to Boston, and the news of the prince's departure—and Madame's—flew through the Canadas.

From Montreal, sheriff Edward Gray passed the local gossip to his nephew Frederick Ermatinger in London on 18 January. 'Prince Edward is to leave this Country for new Brunswick the latter end of this month in order to join the forces in the West Indies, he sets off from Quebec by the way the Courrier go to Halifax and Mr Finlay is to accompany him—his Lady M^{de} St Laurent goes to England by way of the States and it is said that the prince is to conduct her to the limits of the Province before his departure.' And on 25 February, writing after the event to Simcoe in a letter marked *private*, William Osgoode commented acidly: 'Madame is gone with Prince Edward:

Philippe Claude Auguste de Chouly, Marquis de Permangle (1755-1821).
Credit: Portrait reproduced by kind permission of the Marquise de Permangle.

View of the Casernes from the Citadel, Besançon. The Church of St Paul, its tower demolished in 1833, can be seen beyond the Casernes.
Credit: Bibliothèque municipale de Besançon (photo: Jean Bevalot).

General Sir Frederick Augustus Wetherall (1754-1842).
Credit: Portrait reproduced by kind permission of Lieutenant-General Sir Edward Wetherall (photo: S. W. Kenyon).

General Wetherall in old age.
Credit: Photo obtained by kindness of Ealing Public Library.

Captain John Ashton Shuttleworth (1750-1794), Royal Fusiliers.
Credit: Portrait reproduced by kind permission of Lieutenant Commander J. A. Shuttleworth, D.L.

this will be a matter of Animadversion to the Faithful in New York.'
(158)

His Royal Highness had had *two* private farewells to make. His eye
had recently been caught by a charming visitor to the house on St
Louis Street near the royal residence, where Magdalen Green was
living conjugally with Captain George Glasgow of the Royal Artillery.
Her sister, the pretty Eliza, now bereft of her latest lover, William
Goodall, offered a diversion for the bored prince in a life that had been
growing daily more unendurably confined.

'When His Royal Highness recd the information of His Promotion, and going to the West Indies, such a Bustle you would have
been surprised', wrote Captain Robert Walker of the Fusiliers on
25 February to his friend Captain Shuttleworth, recently invalided
home to England. 'There was packing up of all the Brass Drums,
Instruments &c. not to be opened untill he comes back to the Regt.
There was Madam crying her Eys [*sic*] out at Powell Place, and Miss
Green formerly Mrs Goodall doing the same in Town. The Prince
before he recd the Acct. of his going, kept Miss Green at your old
Quarters. We all thought the Prince intended going by way of Halifax,
after returning from seeing Madam as far as St Johns, but to our
great surprise went on to Portsmouth in New Hampshire, and from
that to Boston, where the ship was waiting for him. Madam with all
the servants, carriols, & Horses, &c. proceeded to New York, to take
her passage for England, and I suppose is in London before this.' (159)

Madame, however, was still in New York. Her progress through
the States had been marked by ribald comment in the local press,
the prince's by less ribald but often sarcastic reports (depending on the
political leanings of the publication) along his route to Boston. In
Hartford, Connecticut, on Monday, 17 February, the *American
Mercury* carried an entertaining item. 'We hear that his Royal Highness Prince Edward, son of his Majesty, King George the third, has
lately arrived at Boston, from Canada, with his suit [*sic*]; from whence
he is to embark for the West Indies, to take command of a Brigade—
and', quipped the *Mercury* in a kind of verbal Gillray cartoon, 'that
his Baggage-Waggon, alias Laundress, has arrived at New-York, who,
it is said, far exceeds any of Mother Carey's Chickens for brilliancy'.

The *Boston Mercury* picked up the same item a week later, but
Madame had already arrived in New York, where the New York
Journal of 12 February had also indulged in light-hearted jocularity:
it was *de rigueur*, in this very new republic, to treat royalty with a
proper degree of public ridicule.

G

'It is said that Col. Edward Guelph, fourth son of George Guelph, the present King of England, has embarked at one of the eastern ports, to join Gen. Charles Grey, in his attack on Guadaloupe. One would suppose, that his baggage should follow him.

'Saturday the soi-disant LAUNDRESS of said Col. arrived in this city. Her pomp, equipage, and etiquette, are said to be much more splendid than the *laundresses* in general of New-York. What is the destination of this GREAT PERSONAGE we have not learnt; it is said, however, that she is bound for England.'

The *Journal* was correct. Madame was bound for England, but not directly. Whether from prudence (the proximity of the French fleet being a menace) or inability to find suitable passage, she made her way first to Halifax, probably by the schooner *Providence* which seems to have been the first ship to Halifax from New York, sailing around 19 March, after her arrival there. It was not until 10 May that she found passage for England from Halifax on board the *Portland* packet.

In the *Quebec Gazette* on 23 January, the day after the prince left, *Anglo-Canadensis* published a laudatory poem in Latin: *Ad Edwardum, Principem*. The city would lose much of its glitter with the loss of its royal star, who was by then pursuing a vigorous and happy path over woodland trails and river ice, except for a sad accident that occurred crossing Lake Champlain to Burlington, Vermont. The ice at one point proved too soft, and the prince had the shock and mortification of seeing two of the sleighs, carrying 'the whole of his baggage, consisting of what plate, linen, clothes, &c. he then possessed', fall through the cracking surface into the lake.

There had been a good deal of nervousness in high quarters about Prince Edward's presence in the United States at this moment, when anti-British and pro-French feelings were running high, stirred up by France's ambassador, the young and fiery Citizen Edouard-Charles Genêt. His energy in commissioning privateers to attack British shipping had seriously threatened the neutrality of the United States, precipitating crises within the American government. Possibly, too, long memories recalled Washington's initial support of a plan to kidnap the Duke of Clarence, when as Prince William he had called at New York in 1782. However, Boston welcomed Prince Edward with more than a little awe at having a genuine royal personage in its midst, though a noisy anti-British faction made the visit lively with actual and figurative cat-calls.

There was no frigate—nor any other substitute vessel—awaiting the prince at Boston. Lord Dorchester's man on snowshoes had found the journey to Halifax heavy going. 'It appears that the Person who was sent express from Quebec to Halifax was forty-five days performing that Journey,' the British consul at Boston, Thomas McDonogh, reported later, 'which would be too dangerous an undertaking for his Royal Highness at such a severe season of the year, when Persons can only travel a great part of the way on snow shoes, and through woods without any shelter but such temporary accommodation as the travellers may be able to provide for themselves at Night.' (160)

Governor Wentworth in Halifax had coped well, however, and a ship was on its way on the 8th: not the frigate, but the little six-gun packet *Roebuck,* which would take six days to reach her destination. ('His Royal Highness had found it requisite otherwise to embark in a very unpleasant, and not very safe little Schooner'.) (161) The delay, though it annoyed the prince, allowed time to replace what Lake Champlain had swallowed, to go to a ball and a wedding, to put most of Boston in a flutter. Enthusiastic pens were taken up all over town: Bostonians enjoyed gossip as much as Horace Walpole or Lord Glenbervie. (162)

From Dr William Eustis to the Honourable David Cobb, In Congress, Philadelphia, 9 February: 'My dear Cobb: . . . The day before yesterday arrived in this town Prince Edward—he is attended by four officers & lodges at the B. Consul's. He has made no public appearance as yet. To morrow he goes to the play. In passing thro' the town, the fame of the man & the novelty of his sleighs & cropt ear'd horses, gatherd the boys & some of them hallowed after him— this was not pleasant, but *the Prince did not hear em.* [sic] . . .'

From Henry Jackson to Henry Knox, 10 February. 'Dear Harry: Prince Edward is here—he has been invited to dine with Mr T. Russell and some others but he refuses all invitations—a number of Gentlemen of the town—(that is *the well born*) have called on him and bn recd with great politeness . . . it is said he intends being at the Play this Evening. . . .'

From Mrs S. L. Flucker to Mrs Henry Knox on 16 February: 'My dear Lucy: . . . On Monday I went to the Play, but alas no Prince—he was prevented by the assurance that a large Party was formed in the Galleries to Govern the Music and Preside for the Night—and very properly put himself out of the way of Personal insult—which the Mob Prove doubtless ripe for—for whenever the Box door opened, and he was supposed to enter, there was an alarming opposition between the ragamuffins, Loyalists & Orchestra and Peace could only be obtained by the mortifying submission of the good to the bad. All *Gentlemen* were *silent.* . . . The beginning of the Week the Prince was very unwell and confined—on Thursday he dined at

Mr Russell's—I had the happiness to see him appearing amiable in the view of all. . . . In the Evening we attended him to the assembly where he shone as a Private Gentleman with with [sic] more approved luster than a Crown can give—for he cheerfully submitted to the omission of even *necessary* Ettiquette—he handed Mrs Russell into the room Mrs Gore Miss Talbot his Aids and myself followed—a seat was *found after* he came in, and I had the honor to sit on one side and Mrs R: on the other. The *only* compliments offered him were the 1st Number and the choice of his Partner. Mrs R gained the Prize. She look [sic] very handsome—as did her Royal Beau—who took his regular turns in the setts and danced as a Prince ought, with much ease and Grace. His conversation is affable and the noisiest [? *Pinder*] here has not yet found imaginary folly—his conduct appears the most steady and he talks of and laughs at his youthful pranks— and has shown so accomodating a disposition as even to desire his Servants to take out their Cockades to please the Vulgar. . . .'

From Increase Sumner to the Honourable William Cushing, Phila-delphia, 14 February: 'Dear Sir: . . . The public mind, for want of something more important, has been almost entirely directed towards Theatrical entertainments. Such has been the Rage for this new species of exhibition, that the Gallery Tickets on the first night were sold by speculators for more than twelve times their prime Cost . . . the people in the Galleries, the other night prevailed, after much noise & some confusion to the no small terror of the Ladies, & obliged the Music to play up Ca ira.

'I forgot to mention that Prince Edward, 4th son of George the British King is now in Boston from Quebec, waiting a Ship from Halifax, to convey him to the West Indias . . . I have not seen him yet, but expect to dine in company with him to'morrow. Cousin Polly Cushing . . . saw him last Eveng at a very crowded Assembly where he behaved with great ease & politeness, & . . . he danced gracefully, to the entire approbation of all the Ladies. . . .'

From Henry Jackson to General Henry Knox in Philadelphia, 16 February: 'My dear Harry: . . . The December British packet arrived here on Friday from Halifax for Prince Edward, he embarked yesterday in the afternoon with his suite & saild immediately for Halifax [sic]—he did not incline to wait on Lt Govr Adams, which caused some difficulty—on Thursday he dined with Thos Russell and in the Eveng accompany'd Mrs Russell to the Assembly where there was a display of more than *eighty Ladies* he danced four country dances with Mrs Russell, but she fainted away before she finish'd the last—he danced with no one else. . . .'

The prince had also with his aides attended a wedding in Boston on Thursday, 13 February, when Nancy Geyer was married to attorney Rufus Amory in the elegant home of her father. Their daughter has recorded that he kissed the bride and her bridesmaids. A host of apocryphal stories followed him out of the Green Mountains of Vermont. The one about the landlady at a tavern en route, who struck the prince 'dumb as an oyster' by telling him that the Bible he had noticed on the desk was a favourite book in the United States, but 'when we wish to amuse ourselves we read Peter Pindar'. The unlikely one about an outraged husband who, after being asked 'how it made him feel to have his wife kissed by a *Prince* . . . plied his foot nimbly and repeatedly to his posteriors—asking in turn "How it made a Prince feel to have his breech kicked by a Tailor"'. (163) And the one that tickled all Boston, about his encounter with 'a plain Vermont farmer'. Dr Eustis wrote the anecdote to his friend David Cobb. So did Increase Sumner in a letter to William Cushing.

'At a tavern, an honest New England man thus accosts him— well how do you do Sir, & are you really the Son of King George?— he answered that he was, amazing! s'd the man: & *how does your daddy do*? he was well s'd the Prince when I heard last from him— well now, s'd the honest man, dont you thing [sic] he was wrong in Quarrelling with America as he did. I dont know but he was, s'd the other, but there is no foreseeing, at all times, how Matters will turn out. true s'd the Man, but if it had'nt [sic] been for that plaguy Quarrell I suppose he might have been King here yet!' (164)

McDonogh's report was sent to Lord Grenville on the 17th.

'His Royal Highness Prince Edward arrived here on Thursday the 6th instant from Quebec after a journey of about fifteen Days, in good Health and spirits with the Exception of a Cold only. . . .
'His Royal Highness . . . very much engaged by his affability and condescentions the good Will and Wishes of all who had seen him, and it is much to be regretted that it was not convenient for his Royal Highness to make a longer stay as his Engaging manners and conduct would tend very much to dissipate the Prejudices, with which many in this Country are strongly tinctured against Royalty and princely Blood, and would also unquestionably strengthen the British interest in America.' (165)

McDonogh was right in his judgement. Despite a certain amount of provocation (*A Yankee*, in expectation of the prince's attendance, had publicly urged the playing at the theatre of 'the following pieces of *loyal* music . . .Yankee Doodle and Ca ira', and *A Citizen* had deplored the mutual lack of official recognition between the prince and the lieutenant-governor, Samuel Adams) the visit was eminently successful. Talleyrand would later write to his friend Lord Shelburne : 'Two years ago when Prince Edward stopped at Boston, there was a ball. This year people still recall with gratitude that he never refused an invitation, and speak of his kindness and good nature. The lady who danced with him was overcome afterwards and had an attack of nerves from joy, embarrassment and respect. . . . These things are remembered here. They are recorded in the family register. . . . A few miles from Boston I have visited a man who has horses that belonged to Prince Edward, and who got more prestige than service out of owning them.' (166)

The prince embarked on the 15th and sailed early in the morning of Sunday the 16th for the West Indies. The British ship of war *Hussar,* Rupert George commanding, put into Boston on 12 March, having hustled down from Halifax on the heels of *Roebuck* in case of need, but *Roebuck,* with a fair wind and a reasonably uneventful passage, had landed the prince in Martinique on the 4th. He was plunged at once into the kind of action he had pined for, and though it was all over too fast to satisfy his craving to serve in the field, he was able to show his mettle.

'Major General Prince Edward . . . commands at Camp La Coste, with great spirit and activity', wrote General Sir Charles Grey in his dispatch dated 16 March, and on the 25th he was able to announce 'the complete conquest of this valuable Island ; the last and most important fortress of Fort Bourbon having surrendered to his Majesty's arms at four o'clock in the afternoon of the 23rd Instant ; at which time his Royal Highness Prince Edward . . . took possession of both Gates, with the first and third battalion of Grenadiers and the first and third Light Infantry'. The prince's aide-de-camp, Captain Wetherall, was wounded in the hand in this action, and his Royal Highness himself was reported to have narrowly escaped.

Leaving Fort Bourbon to continue its existence as Fort George, Grey embarked his troops and ordnance on a day of haze and rain for the island of St Lucia, where three different landings were effected on 1 April. The prince's division, under heavy fire from coastal batteries, disembarked at Marigot des Roseaux and marched to invest Morne Fortunée, which fell next day. Prince Edward raised the British colours and changed the name to Fort Charlotte. 'The exemplary good conduct of the brigade of grenadiers, under the immediate command of his Royal Highness Prince Edward, and of the brigade of light infantry, under Major-General Dundas, and indeed of all the troops, affords me the highest satisfaction', wrote Grey.

The small islands known as the Saints were tackled next, falling quickly without loss to the British, and the attack then moved to Guadaloupe. With the formal surrender of the French general Collot and the hoisting of the British colours once again by Prince Edward in Fort St Charles (promptly renamed Fort Matilda) the campaign ended. On 20 May, the Secretary of State for the Home Office, Henry Dundas, moved a vote of thanks in the House of Commons to all involved in the victory, including Prince Edward by name. (167)

'The active service ceasing here for the present', the prince wrote to his father on 23 April from Guadaloupe, 'I shall proceed immediately on my return to Canada, but propose first putting into Halifax, and there remaining till the arrival of the May Packet . . .' He would return to the West Indies at once, he said, if fighting began again; but if not, 'May I hope, after that, Sir, that you will have the goodness to allow me to return to England?' (168)

In Halifax, Madame had been casting her spell on the Wentworths. 'Madame St Laurent (with an hundred names and titles) has been with us several weeks, waiting a passage to England', wrote the governor to his friend John King in London on 8 May. 'You know her connection with Prince Edward. She is an elegant, well bred, pleasing sensible woman—far beyond most. During her residence here, her deportment has been judicious and most perfectly correct indeed. I find she has great influence over him, and that he is extremely attached to her. It is happy, that she is so excellent a character. By her prudence & cleverness, she has restored his deranged finances, and I believe impressed his mind with the best sentiments. She seems faithfully attached to him. I never yet saw a woman of such intrepid fortitude yet possessing the finest temper and refined manners. She is a passenger in the Portland Packet.' (169)

Her prince missed her by hours only. The *Blanche* frigate by which he had come from the West Indies made port at Halifax on Saturday, 10 May. The *Portland* packet had sailed the day before.

He was bitterly disappointed. 'My good fortune would have been complete if on my arrival here I had found my friend Madame de St Laurent,' he wrote wistfully to the de Salaberrys in Quebec. (170) No dalliance with a temporary charmer like Eliza Green would ever threaten the depth of his love for Thérèse-Bernardine. His anxious instructions to hasten her return flew across the Atlantic to John King, penned in Wentworth's emphatic, spiky hand. Madame must be accommodated in the first ship of war destined for this port. She should have passports and certificates 'as a British subject of respectability in case of accidents' (the hazards of war were now added to the hazards of ocean travel). If she should unluckily be taken on her way to or from England, everything must be done to get her back with the least possible discomfort. She must be told immediately should any change occur in the orders the prince hoped to receive. (171)

Meantime, the lonely prince busied himself with a two-week exploration of the district, by land to Annapolis, by the *Zebra* sloop of war across the Bay of Fundy to Saint John in New Brunswick, leaving Halifax on 14 June. His popularity was running high. 'The Prince is adored here, and a perfect confidence is entertained of his military knowledge. His deportment is correct, dignifyed, and irresistably conciliating.' (172)

At Saint John, the adventurous traveller insisted on passing through the falls in the sloop ('a circumstance almost unexampled at that hour in the evening'), and spent the night at the home of Ward Chipman, the solicitor-general, who was greatly impressed. "All you have said of him in your letters falls infinitely short of what I have found him to be', he told his friend Jonathan Sewell. 'He is without exception the most accomplished character I have ever seen, his manners are so dignified and at the same time marked with so much cordialty [*sic*]; he discovered so much good sense, sound understanding and so impressed my mind that I can find no bounds to my admiration of him.' (173)

He was back in Halifax on the 28th, having acquired a reputation for 'violent journeyings' which, it was noted, he seemed to enjoy more than most of his retinue. Passing through Windsor again he found carpenters had almost finished their work on the building of King's College. They hoisted the Union flag from the cupola and gave him three cheers on his way.

In Halifax the armed snow, *Earl of Moira*, had arrived from Quebec with his personal belongings and probably also his band ('No Musick! The People No Souls in this Province!' lamented Captain Smyth, his secretary,* himself an accomplished pianist). He had asked Lord Dorchester to allow the whole regiment to join him, 'a request that has no appearance of being complied with, circumstanced *as matters here* are', wrote Captain Hughes from Quebec to Shuttleworth in England. The prince did get the band, however: Hughes added dismally, 'The whole of our Fusilier music [is] now confined to the Fife and the Drum.' (174)

The prince may not have been so lucky with 'a brace of brass-barreled Pistols' he had had with him in Martinique. On his royal colonel's behalf, Captain Smyth wrote to ask Sewell in Quebec to

---

* It may be of interest to note that Captain Smyth later became Lt-Governor of N.B.

'have the goodness to find out a Man by the name of *Wood* who was His Servant in the West Indies & who lately returned to Quebec to his Wife, & ask him . . . where he put them when he quitted the Prince's service at Martinique, they are remarkable good ones, & H.R.H. anxious to recover them'. It is to be hoped they turned up in due course: Robert Wood informed Sewell's agent that they had been left at Martinique on board a transport with the prince's stores. (175)

Despite the action and the change of scene, the prince was more than ever homesick, after now nearly ten years' absence. Apart from the stirring national and international events, so much of personal interest had happened within his own family since he had left. His eldest brother's liaison with Maria Fitzherbert had grown in depth and intensity: if the prince had met her before his departure for Europe in May 1785, it could have been only fleetingly. His second brother the Duke of York was wed to a duchess to whom as yet he was a stranger. In January an agitated Privy Council had had to nullify the secret marriage of his younger brother Prince Augustus to the Lady Augusta Murray, who had borne him a son only two weeks before the inquiry. And at the end of the same month, all London had been agog, awaiting a child of his brother William Duke of Clarence by its idol 'Little Pickle', the actress Dorothy Jordan. 'The splendid preparations for Mrs Jordan's *accouchement* are still continued. The cradle is enriched with *regal* scarlet, and every article is marked with the royal *insignia*.' . . . 'Couriers are to be dispatched to all the Courts of Europe with the happy intelligence.' . . . 'Mrs Jordan's infant son is named George. The Prince of Wales stood godfather' . . . '[her] infant Son bears the strongest resemblance to his Royal Father. The family complexion, hair, eyes . . . which are not common. . . .' (176)

It was not easy for Prince Edward, one of a family bound in spite of its intermittent disagreements and squabbles by strong ties of interest and affection, to be so long away from home. Nothing he might do, however admirably performed, was under the immediate eye of those on whom his career depended. And besides, as he was well aware, 'Where the King is, there is concentrated all that is delightful in society'. (177)

There was nothing for the prince to do now but occupy himself with military duties, enjoy the music of his band, attend dinner parties and wait longingly for Madame's arrival. A week after the Prince of Wales's birthday, when the harbour had been bright with colours and noisy with guns, his waiting was over. In a letter 'most secret & intirely confidential' to John King, Wentworth was able to report thankfully, 'The Westmoreland packet . . . bro't Mdme St L. in safety to the Prince'. (178)

Madame's visit to England was very short: undertaken, perhaps, because she thought her prince would be proceeding there after the West Indies campaign, perhaps for some private and personal reason. The *Portland* packet landed her at Falmouth on Monday, 9 June, after what must have been, for her, a heart-stopping encounter as *Portland* neared the Channel, when a French privateer chased the packet for two days. *Portland* had just begun to engage the French ship when she suddenly sheered off. Thérèse-Bernardine's too-well-known association with aristocrats and princes could have sent her, had she been taken, to join Marie-Josephe-Rose Viscountess de Beauharnais and Grace Dalrymple Elliott in the Carmes in that year of blood and terror, and even to the ultimate grim fate they escaped.

As well as Madame, the packet brought the mail from New York, with the first news that John Jay had been appointed Envoy Extraordinary of the United States to his Britannic Majesty and could be expected shortly. The appointment would do much to ease the conflict between Britain and the United States over the interpretation of neutrality rights.

Madame found London a city uneasy and questioning: proud of the West Indies victories but depressed by the lack of success on the Continent. Allied armies were in retreat everywhere, and the Navy had not distinguished itself. London mobs were muttering. Less than a week before her arrival, on the very day of the King's birthday celebrations, the *Morning Post* had thought the late losses at sea afforded a very gloomy reflection. 'Lord Howe is certainly resolved to *take care* of the British Fleet; but we could wish that he was sufficiently near to destroy the French Squadron that seems, at present, to ride triumphant on our favorite Element.' In New York, the *Journal* was gleefully reprinting from the *St James's Chronicle*:

'*You know HOW, in some strange way,*
Somehow, somebody, they say,
Lost us once America,
You know HOW.

'*Somehow, too, by some delay,*
Somebody the other day,
Let the French fleet slip away,
You know HOW.' (179)

Overnight, things changed. Madame had arrived at an electric moment, just as the city was galvanized into a state of hysterical jubilation. For some days, hints of something big going on in the

Channel had been filtering through. On the 11th, London papers burst into capital letters and a spate of exclamation marks.

'IMPORTANT NAVAL VICTORY!!!!' trumpeted *The Times*. 'Capture of 6 sail of the line and 2 sunk.'

'A SIGNAL VICTORY OVER THE FRENCH, BY EARL HOWE', chimed the *Oracle*, '—without the loss even of a single British Ship'.

The Duke of Clarence, 'in the ardour of his joy', immediately got into his carriage and drove to Covent Garden to have the Manager announce the victory to the audience. The band struck up *God Save The King* and *Rule Britannia,* everyone shouting, cheering and calling for encore and encore.

Madame saw a London gone wild over the next few days. What stories she must have had to carry back to her homesick prince! The day's paper carried, as well as the first sketchy flash of Howe's victory, a dispatch from Admiral Lord Hood with a full account of the capture of Bastia in Corsica. There were fireworks from Drury Lane theatre. Houses were lighted from top to bottom. The very poorest set up a rush candle in the window.

Even this was not enough for the shouting crowds thronging the streets. Gangs ranged all through the West End demanding more illuminations, smashing windows with abandon, and almost wrecking the home of Lord Stanhope, who was absent in the country. One London resident, 'a poor loyal German', fearing for his windows but yawning himself to sleep, gave up at last, doused his little farthing candle and pinned a note on the door. 'Two o'clock, gone to bed. If I am to light again, pray be so obliging as to ring the bell'. The *Oracle* reported that 'the whole body of Glaziers was next morning in a state of requisition', and the Quakers, fearing they might lose more than window panes, stuck up bills all over town explaining their failure to illuminate by their religion, which forbade rejoicing at any event involving bloodshed.

Howe's dispatch, with the details, arrived late on Friday the 13th. The whole fleet, with the six French prizes, was moored at Spithead. Rejoicing London papers warned the manager of the pleasure gardens at Ranelagh to lay in tea, coffee and rolls for at least 5,000 people expected to turn up for the big fireworks display on Monday night. By Thursday the Gentlemen of Lloyd's Coffee-house had collected £8,000 for the widows of the gallant dead. Vauxhall Gardens went into gala display, and ladies appeared garbed 'à la Howe'.

The following week their Majesties and the princesses journeyed to

Portsmouth to review the victorious fleet. The King presented a diamond-hilted sword to Howe on board his flagship, and was rowed around each ship, boarding the French vessels (some of them lashed together) by ladders lined with scarlet cloth. It was noted at the morning levee that one of the two French captains present wore the white cockade of the Bourbons.

How Madame occupied her time in London one may only imagine. She went shopping: Prince Edward's letter of 11 November to his old friend Major Walter Cliffe thanked him for the trouble he had taken to order the shoes which she had received while in London, though she had had trouble with the shoemaker, who had made them —though 'extremely neat'—without the heels she had requested. (180) It is hard to believe she would not have gone to the theatre, especially to Drury Lane, to carry back to her prince a description of his brother the Duke of Clarence's newest love, Mrs Jordan, who (with a heavy cold 'which severely checked her utterance') gave a Benefit for the widows and orphans of the naval battle. She would not have neglected the pleasure gardens during the festivities, and if it is true that she had been in England before, there would be old friends to visit, perhaps some among the French emigrés (but not her former lover the Marquis de Permangle, who, it would transpire, was at that very time languishing in the dank and hideous dungeons of the Carmes in terror of the guillotine).

It was, at any rate, known she was in town. Noting on Monday, 14 July, that the *Westmoreland* packet had sailed for Halifax the previous Wednesday, a keen *Oracle* writer reported: 'In the latter went passenger a certain FRENCH LADY, said to be *la chere amie* of a ROYAL PERSONAGE, whom she expects to meet there . . . Madame La Baronne de Fortesson [*sic*] and five servants.'

If Prince Edward was destined to be unlucky in the fate of his various outfits sunk or captured on the transatlantic passage, he was at least fortunate in the safety of his own and Madame's personal journeyings. *Westmoreland* brought her safely and in health to Halifax on 19 August, after an absence of just over three months.

CHAPTER EIGHT

Sojourn at Halifax

'The harbour [of Halifax] by which the port of this town is entered . . . is one of the prettiest, best and safest in the whole continent of America. . . . It is only forty-three years since the first buildings were erected in this town. . . . The citadel which dominates it is strong only by its situation, but the fort which occupies the small island at the entrance of the port, and several batteries in front, on the coast, make a landing difficult for enemy ships. . . .

'It is surprising the growth that has already taken place in the buildings of the town, its population and its commerce. It is estimated that the residents amount to about 4,000 souls. If to that are added three regiments and a few companies of artillery, constantly in garrison there, even in peace time, also a more or less considerable number of transient sailors, its usual population would be from six to seven thousand. . . . .

'Considering the modest extent of the town of Halifax it is inhabited by a number of rich people, some obtaining their money from their positions, others making it in commerce.'

This was the Halifax to which Bénigne Charles Fevret de Saint-Mesmin came in June 1793. This, not much changed in 1794, was the Halifax in which Prince Edward and Thérèse-Bernardine Mongenet were to spend five full years of their life.

Though here, as in Quebec, Madame would be eyed askance by many of the town's social leaders, and certainly not received at all by others, her life here was happier, gayer and freer from social snubs than it had been in Quebec. There, while no one would be too critical

of a mistress kept decently hidden, few were willing to accept a lady,
however charming and circumspect, who had by-passed the rules,
especially in a society led by Lady Dorchester. In Halifax there was
one big difference. Madame was received—even welcomed—by the
governor and his wife. (The *American Mercury* of Hartford, Connecticut, had reported sourly—and erroneously—on 16 June 1794: 'Prince
Edward, we hear, has arrived at Halifax from his West-India expedi-
tion, with 80,000l. sterling as his share of the plunder; and has made
a compliment to the Governor's *Lady* of 10,000l.')

'I am persuaded her society will be extremely useful', Wentworth
had written realistically to John King in his letter dated 19 May, just
after Madame's departure and the prince's arrival. 'In several conversations with them both, they declare that they have not the least
idea of marriage, not only because it would be disagreeable to
their M's, wh. he says he will for ever avoid, but because they both
consider it nugatory and foolish.' (181)

Not only the comforts of a prince's estate, but the reward of a
prince's love more than balanced for Thérèse-Bernardine the forfeit
of her reputation: she never lacked for friends among the warm-
hearted and the discriminating. She was neither ambitious nor pre-
suming. Her dignity and tact earned respect and acceptance from
many who might have scorned her. She was never flamboyant. A
natural grace and talent for friendship, a natural instinct for good
manners made her an endearing companion.

The prince and Madame found the governor and his wife to be
most congenial company, though at this time they were both in their
fifties. As a young girl, Frances Deering Wentworth had been a wilful
and passionate Boston beauty, first married to her cousin Theodore
Atkinson, and on his death to John Wentworth, also a cousin and her
first love. Both were high-spirited and gregarious, keenly enjoying
ceremony and elegant hospitality. The presence of royalty with a
beautiful companion added sparkle and zest to a town noted already
for its lively entertainment.

As well as bringing Madame, the *Westmoreland* packet also brought
Prince Edward the orders that gave him the command of the forces
in Nova Scotia and New Brunswick. While he would have preferred
England, or better still, active duty on the Continent, he was, as
Wentworth commented, 'perfectly pleased with obtaining the military
command here'. His performance in the West-India campaign had
received special mention in dispatches and a public vote of thanks in
Parliament, but though the command in Halifax was better than
nothing, he still felt deprived of adequate recognition ('This seems to be

the opinion of the army & navy who served with him and give him the highest praise', wrote Wentworth). (182) Perhaps only the permission to leave North America altogether would have totally convinced him that he had regained his father's full favour. He grumbled, but set to work without delay to do a competent job in his new situation.

'He and his whole family, from six to twenty six, are still with me', Wentworth wrote to John King in his letter of 24 August. 'Since her arrival they sleep at my little Country house, & come to town in the morning. To-morrow they commence dining there, as I have given him the House, furniture and farm, &c. during his stay in the Province. He still retains rooms in the Province house, with me, as it saves him the expence of hiring and furnishing [indecipherable] House, and dines with me whenever he stays in town.'

Wentworth saw the prince, deservedly, as both competent and conscientious in his profession. His liking and admiration for Prince Edward was based much more genuinely on the prince's real intelligence and personal charm than on the sycophantic admiration for royalty of which he is sometimes accused. Over the years he learned to be critical of certain of the prince's shortcomings (his financial incompetence, for instance), but always understandingly. He never had cause to change his high opinion of the prince as a man and a friend.

His behaviour towards his royal friend, indeed, was based on sound policy. 'It is highly necessary, in these democratic times, that every possible distinguishing respect should be paid to the Royal family. For if it is once suffered for the people to think any part of the R family to be within the circumstances of any other Man, be he what he will, either Govr. Admiral or Genl., they will soon think it unnecessary to have any R. family. I therefore sedulously endeavour to surround him with the impenatrability [sic] due to his high Rank, which is sufficiently attempered by his gracious condescension, flowing from the finest temper any Man ever possessed.' (183)

The little country house offered by Wentworth stood on the edge of the great sweep of Bedford Basin, six miles away. Here, on a steep rise of wooded land, so that the carriage drive curved sharply upwards, stood the pretty lodge where Madame, now thirty-four, would spend happy years with her twenty-seven-year-old prince. There were no official quarters for the General commanding in Halifax, and no house could be found that would cost less than 2,000 guineas to repair and decorate. The loan of 'Friar Laurence's Cell', as Wentworth called it, which could be made adequate to the prince's needs for about £800 (though much more than this sum was actually spent on

it) was therefore a godsend, apart from its delightful location. The
prince also had apartments in Government-house for transacting his
military business.

Out at the Lodge, the prince and his lady set to work altering,
decorating, landscaping to their hearts' content. Prince Edward's
passion for building was given full rein. Across the road and on a
small shaded knoll, he built the Rotunda, surmounted by a flashing
golden ball. The strains of music from the band would come gently
up the hilly slope over lawns and winding paths and formal gardens
to the flat-roofed two-storey wooden Lodge with its two wings spreading
on either side.

Behind the Lodge a tiny island lay in the centre of a heart-shaped
ornamental lake. Behind the lake, miles of woodland paths twisted,
where Madame and her guests could walk in the leaf-shadowed sunlight. Little wooden benches were set in clearings where they might
wish to rest. Latticed summer-houses, rocky grottoes and tiny Chinese
temples tinkling with bells dotted the estate. It has been said that
the walks through the woods were laid out to spell the name *Julie*.
(184)

When not engaged in military duties, the prince—essentially domestic
by nature—lived here like a country squire, informal with his staff,
though never relaxing the dignity of his rank to allow of untoward
liberties, visiting the workshops—the gardeners' potting sheds, the
smithy, the carpenters' and painters' shops—to keep an eye on
progress and order. With Madame he was always gentle and con-
siderate, treatment earned by her own conduct. Always she behaved
with a perfect and natural propriety that never embarrassed their
relationship or fell short of his expectations.

In London, plans for the marriage of the Prince of Wales to the
Princess Caroline of Brunswick were going ahead, but awaited the
arrangement of his affairs. Pitt estimated his debts at £552,000, and
offered the suggestion that the income from the Duchy of Cornwall, if
applied to their discharge, could clear them in twenty-five years. (185)
Lord Auckland, writing to his friend Lord Henry Spencer a month
earlier, though he deplored the waste from the Prince's extravagance
and the heavy taxes to be imposed, was generally cheerful about the
state of the nation. 'Provisions are plentiful in the country, the trade
is immense, and the internal prosperity great, and the spirit of anti-
Jacobinism as high as ever.' (186)

On the other side of the world, four victims of the spirit of anti-
Jacobinism, the Scottish Martyrs Muir, Margarot, Palmer and Skirving, were nearing the end of a dreadful eight-month voyage. Notwithstanding press mutterings (after the trials in Edinburgh the *Morning*

Gibraltar, c. 1790.

Quebec from the south-east, c. 1778.
Credit: Print from the Atlantic Neptune. John Ross Robertson Collection, Metropolitan Toronto Library Board.

Ignace-Louis de Salaberry, Seigneur de Beauport, Quebec.
Credit: Reproduced by kind permission of the de Salaberry family.

Lieutenant Colonel Charles de Salaberry (son of Ignace-Louis).
Credit: Reproduced by kind permission of the de Salaberry family.

These miniatures are believed to be portraits of Catherine Hertel (Madame Ignace-Louis de Salaberry) (left), and one of her daughters, perhaps the little Amelia, a favourite of the Prince and Madame.
Credit: Reproduced by kind permission of the de Salaberry family.

Post had impudently asked the Lord Chancellor and Dundas, Secretary of State for the Home Office, 'how they would feel themselves, if for any offence, it pleased His Majesty to transport them for fourteen years to Scotland'), and despite an appeal to Dundas by Richard Brinsley Sheridan, Sir Charles Grey and the Earl of Lauderdale on a legal point, their sentences had not been commuted. They had, in fact, suffered further indignities. It was reported that they had been handcuffed when taken to Newgate and the prison hulks at Woolwich, and, because their baggage had not arrived, that they had been dressed in convict jackets and had their heads shaved. In mid-February they were put aboard the 400-ton transport *Surprise*, and given to the tender mercies of a rogue captain, Patrick Campbell.

On board the transport went also sixty female and forty male convicts; two free settlers with their families; Mr James Thompson, going out to the colony as assistant surgeon; and eighteen soldiers, mostly deserters, who were being sent as recruits for the New South Wales Corps.

Six of these were in irons. One of them was Joseph Draper, about to involve himself in another mutiny.

From the port of Rio de Janeiro at the beginning of June, Captain Campbell penned an impassioned letter to his London agents reporting an attempted mutiny on board *Surprise*, with which he enclosed the accounts of several purported witnesses. (187) On Monday, 2 June, Draper had put his mark to a lengthy statement sadly reminiscent of the plotting at Quebec, that 'about the beginning of April, the Ship then lying at Spithead, Messrs Skirving and Palmer asked him if he knew if the Convicts . . . wou'd be on their side to Attack the Centinel, and kill or heave him overboard, then rush on the Quarter Deck and secure the Captain, Officers, the Arms and Ammunition, and then, those who did not side with the party were to be Shot or hove overboard . . . That Mr Palmer told him he had a man to direct the Ship, and that he cou'd get numbers of Sailors to join them for Money as he had plenty. That several times at Sea within this fortnight it has been spoke of by those concerned, that as soon as the Ship parted from the Fleet, the scheme was to be put in execution; and that he had been liberally supplied with Spirits, Tea and Sugar by the above mentioned Gentlemen. . . . That he got Money from several persons who came to see these Gentlemen, particularly one Gentleman a relation of Mr Palmers gave him money several times, which he considered as an inducement to make him Active in their favour. That he was called by Mr Palmer . . . and that he was caused to stand still, till the Gentlemen had seen him, and he was told by Mr Palmer "that, that was all"—He also says that Mr Skirving the first

H

night he came on Board, asked for him by name as the person who came from Prince Edward's regiment, and that being informed he was the man, Skirving gave him a Bottle of Wine, Mr Skirving also gave him a Silk Handkerchief and other wearing apparel.'

The convict William Neale added his testimony that the plan was to have sailed the ship to France. John Grant, transported for forgery, testified he had overheard the deserters plotting 'in the Irish language'. Campbell added that Muir and Margarot had taken no part in the affair at all (it was to transpire that Margarot, who had broken with his colleagues, had become intimate with the captain and joined him in his vicious accusations).

The more probable version of the 'mutiny' came out when Dr Palmer gave his vastly different account of the affair, published in detail three years later, and supported by statements from witnesses considerably more reputable than those supplied by Captain Campbell. (188)

For the sake of appearances, Campbell had put Draper in irons with the rest of the suspects at first: but in a flamboyant scene on the quarter-deck, where Campbell strode around armed with a sword, a dagger and several pistols, Draper appeared unshackled and publicly accused Palmer and Skirving of instigating a mutiny. Money that Palmer had paid Draper for work on his clothes (Draper had been put into Palmer's room for some time and there had worked at his trade of tailoring) was represented as bribery, as also was another sum of eighteen shillings lent to Draper by Palmer's friend Ellis to buy articles at Portsmouth for use in carrying on his business at Botany Bay. 'Poor Mr Skirving, from the benevolence of his temper, and his readiness at all times to do good, advanced him between thirty and forty shillings, which Draper engaged to work out. Little did he suppose that this would be construed into a bribe for the purpose of murdering Campbell and the principal officers.'

The surgeon, James Thompson, and Ensign William Pattullo, who carried a commission (overruled by the arrogant Campbell) to command the detachment of the New South Wales Corps on the ship, were among those who made sworn depositions on landing, exonerating Palmer and Skirving and expressing their horror at the behaviour of Campbell, 'who was upon terms of intimacy with this Jos. Draper'. Draper had been up to his old tricks. Thompson confessed that he had 'believed in the truth of this mutiny plot till about the time that he arrived at Rio, when the improbability of it more and more struck him; such as there being only one original witness, and the rest dropping in one by one afterwards.'

Corporal Timothy Ryan of the New South Wales Corps remembered hearing Draper say 'after the discovery of this pretended plot . . . that for what he had done, Campbell was to give him his liberty, and take him home with him'. Another convict, John Stirling, had refused a bribe of 'seven yards of printed cotton, a ruffled shirt, a striped waist-coat piece, and many other articles of wearing apparel' laid out in tempting array on the round-house table, although threatened by a pair of pistols. 'Since he has been on shore,' he stated, 'on the 22d day of November, he asked Draper if he had got any of the fine things that had been promised him, he said no, he could not expect much now for telling lies, for every word he had said against Mr Palmer and Skirving were lies. . . .'

Draper's name appears as a private on the pay lists of the New South Wales Corps up to 1799. In the records of history he appears to have run his course in villainous stupidity.

Early in December, James Bland Burges, Under-Secretary of State at the Foreign Office, wrote a gloomy letter to his wife about the miseries of the royal princesses, uninformed about current events and 'treated hardly better than children in a nursery. . . . I do not believe there is a more unhappy family in the kingdom than that of our good King. . . .The ill-success and disgraces of the Duke of York, the wounds and ill-health of the Princes Ernest and Adolphus, the bad conduct of Princes Edward and Augustus, and the strange caprices and obstinacy of the Prince of Wales—all these causes are perpetually preying upon them, and make them miserable. . . .' (189)

A strange comment about Prince Edward, who had won public laurels only eight months earlier. If his long absence had kept alive in public memory only the disgrace in which he had left England in 1790, it is no wonder he was eager to be home where his public character could be judged by his more recent behaviour instead of by the memory of his disgrace. But if at home he could not live down his boyhood scrapes—his debts, his flight to London, his illegitimate daughter—in Halifax he was enjoying repect and admiration. On 3 November his birthday was celebrated by a grand ball and supper, for which 300 cards of invitation had been printed. The prince's 'passion for building' and his ability to indulge it made this period of his life a reasonably happy one, though he found the climate barely endurable, racking him, as well as Madame, with rheumatic pains and colds almost as severe as they had suffered in Quebec. But between these bouts of discomfort they managed to find diversions.

Inveterate playgoers, they patronized the theatre in Halifax, to its great advantage. A very crowded and brilliant audience on Tuesday 30 December 1794 responded to the prince's attendance at the season's opening with what the Halifax *Journal* reported as reiterated shouts

and ardent enthusiasm. *God Save The King* and *Rule Britannia,* in
which the audience enthusiastically joined, were rendered at the close
of the play by 'a handsome file of men of the Royal Fusiliers, beautifully
accoutered,' who arranged themselves, with arms, on the front of the
stage, all the performers drawn up behind.

To strengthen the defences of Halifax was a matter of urgent
concern to its new commander, with the French fighting to control the
seas and ranging dangerously near the isolated little colony to the north
of a powerful and unsympathetic neighbour. A letter found on a
captured ship brought into Halifax pointed up the fanatical forces
arrayed against the Allies.

'My dear Brother', an American citizen named Joshua Barney,
headed for Paris, had written from Bordeaux just before Christmas.
'. . . The French are preparing for a severe campaign by sea next
Spring; they will have out by the 1st of May 55 ships of the Line from
the Ports on the Atlantic and 20 ships of the Line on the Mediterranean, which will make their Enemies look sharp besides near 60
Frigates, some of which I think the finest in the world. Unless the
Dutch make a peace this winter, Amsterdam must fall into the hands
of the Republic before Spring, for the French do not know anything
about going into winter quarters; and if the Dutch are foolish enough
to overflow the Country, and the winter should be severe, the French
will overrun them upon the Ice, for no weather or difficulties stop
them. In fact, how can it be otherwise, conceive to yourself fourteen
Armies, consisting of 12 hundred thousand men, from eighteen years
of age to twenty-seven, all well cloathed and fed, commanded by
Officers who would rather die than retreat, Armies who have nothing
but to conquer; composed (not as other Armies are of Vagabonds) but
men of Character, fortune, and a high sense of liberty . . .' (190)

His predictions were lamentably fulfilled. The wife of General
Harcourt, with the British in Holland, had been writing painful letters
home in ink that had to be melted before it could be used, disciplining
frozen fingers in a room where even a fire could not raise the tempera-
ture above thirteen degrees. The troops, in wretched huts, were short
of food and blankets; her husband was trying to get comforts and
rations at least for those on duty. A frost had begun to close the Waal
river, never frozen since 1785. 'The ice is beginning to come down from
Germany in large islands, and as soon as that attaches itself to any part
of the banks, or fixes in any bend of the river, it soon will accumulate,
unite, and form a bridge for our enemies. Meantime these flakes, as
they are called, have another dreadful effect; they prevent the passage

of our magazines, and the army is nearly without provisions, for all navigation on the river is stopped.'

In mid-January the Royal House of Orange, fleeing to safety, arrived at Yarmouth in fishing boats. The blonde, untidy, garrulous Princess Caroline of Brunswick, on her way to become the Princess of Wales, was delayed and detoured by the weather. Though she had started out at the end of December, it was not until early April that Mrs Harcourt, who had been appointed to travel with her, could thankfully record journey's end in sight, 'about four miles from the dear English shore'. With tragically ill-founded optimism, she had found the Princess 'So affectionate . . . a little treasure.' . . . 'If [the Prince] is loved, as I think the Princess must love him, he will make the best husband in the world.' (191)

Down in the little port of Liverpool, Nova Scotia, Simeon Perkins, recovered from the disorder in his ears that he was satisfied had been cured the previous autumn by an application of roasted onion, was observing to his diary that the papers from abroad carried 'a great deal of News and not much to the advantage of our Nation'. Prince Edward, far from these events and still resenting his enforced exile from action, consoled himself with his plans for Halifax, and nursed a fervent hope of having his command extended to all the British forces in North America.

He had every reason to expect the appointment. Still wearing his West Indian laurels, he was aware that Lord Dorchester was on the point of asking for recall, and that after his Lordship, he was the senior officer in rank in North America. Every letter to his friends the de Salaberrys at this time indicated his high hope of succeeding to the military and even to the civil part of the command should the two appointments remain with one person. When Lord Dorchester gave him advance notice of his intention to leave Canada, he read it as his Lordship's wish to facilitate his Highness's chances to succeed, and made immediate application for the appointment. He wrote to the Duke of York (now Commander-in-Chief), to Sir William Fawcett, the Adjutant-General, and—as early as January 1795—to his brother the Prince of Wales, to ask his support in his request to the King.

Wentworth also was anxious to see the prince as Commander-in-Chief, and in January 1795 he sent an earnest testimonial to the Home Secretary, the Duke of Portland.

'His Royal Highness acceded to the command of this district under Lord Dorchester, & performs the dutys of it, with professional regularity, exactness and ability hitherto unknown, yet I can perceive He would be seriously distressed should any other Commander in Chief

be appointed over him, to the North American command, and would
scarcely think of remaining in this Country after such an event. . . .
It may be acceptable to your Grace to be informed that this Prince
is possessed of considerable abilitys, a mild and benevolent temper,
an active, discriminating mind, retentive memory, and quick percep-
tion, unremittingly diligent in his profession, methodical, exact and
punctual in all his arrangements, to the minutest precision, both in
command and in example, temperate in eating, drinking and sleep,
almost to abstemiousness, &, altho' possessing a full sense of his high
dignity, it is maintained with a condescending attention, that wonderfully attaches every person. . . . He will return to England with
excellent dispositions, active for business, detesting every sort of play,
and gives very little time to Company.' (192)

The social life of Halifax did its best to emulate the life of high
society in the world's greatest city, and the prince dutifully attended
all the official functions. There were levees. There were balls and
drawing rooms. There were anniversary dinners. In May a very
special and magnificent levee honoured the award on 11 April of
a baronetcy to Governor Wentworth. Captain Daniel Lyman, loyalist
from New Haven, Connecticut, who had settled at Fredericton,
happened to be with the prince when the latest papers from England
arrived with the news, and was dispatched to the new Baronet of Great
Britain with a message of congratulations. 'The Baronet takes it very
cooly [sic] and as a dispensation of providence, but her Ladyship is
all smiles & joy.' (193) Her Ladyship has been accused of snobbery
and easy morals, but in both she would have been very little different
from most of the aristocratic ladies of the day. She was not, moreover,
a self-seeking upstart. Both she and her husband were well-connected,
of not inconsiderable social standing in the American colonies and
related to the great Fitzwilliam family of England.

June saw a sumptuous entertainment to honour the King's birthday, given by Sir John to the principal officers of navy, army and civil
departments. The theatre, which in February had been putting in
extra stoves in case of extreme cold weather, was advertising in July
that 'every means will be taken to Ventilate the House, so as to make
it cool and comfortable.' It was not to be expected that the season
could pass without A Lover of Theatrical Amusements asking the
ladies to dispense with feathers, it being his misfortune 'not to be born
six feet high'.

Thérèse-Bernardine does not appear to have suffered much from
the ostracism of those more strait-laced members of Halifax society.
Her personal charm won her enough warm friends to defeat either

loneliness or embarrassment, and she was too secure in the prince's heart to worry seriously about any temporary rivals. She had chosen her way of life, and its rewards had turned out to include love and respect as well as comfort and protection. If the puritan element in Halifax affected to despise the prince because of her, both of them could afford to ignore its opinion. It would never have affected either of them to know of the old lady, born seventeen years after his Royal Highness died, who was reported to have expressed pity in her old age for Queen Victoria: 'You know, she had such a disreputable father.' (194)

Chief Justice Andrew Strange was one of Halifax's proper people who spurned Madame. When an invitation to dine at Government House came to Mr Strange, he 'made it clear that he would only accept the invitation if the lady in question was not present. She accordingly absented herself and the good-natured Duke apparently bore the nice-minded Chief Justice no ill-feeling.' (195) Another chief justice shared the same attitude. Writing to Simcoe from Quebec on 23 September 1794, just after Madame's return from England, William Osgoode sympathized with the social problems faced by the nice-minded Strange. 'He hints at some Disagremens [sic] that have taken place at Halifax that make him desirous to quit; I suspect that the return of Mad St Laurent who is rceived [sic] by the first Female in point of Rank in the Settlement & I hear is established in one of the Government Houses may have made matters unpleasant.' Passing on an assortment of rumours to Simcoe in Upper Canada, Osgoode continued with fore-boding: 'Nay report goes further that Mrs W.s Sister who is married to the Commissary at Halifax and whose Habits are Equally pliable, is also with her Husband to be removed to this Place in order to complete the Arrangement of Madame St Laurent—so that the City of Quebec may again witness that Relaxation of Morals that formerly distinguished it under the French Intendants.' (196)

The royal commander had planned to establish his headquarters at Halifax unless specifically ordered to locate at Quebec, and a good deal of behind-scenes action started at once, letters posting between the communities of Lower Canada, juggling for appointments and opportunities that might develop should his Royal Highness's authority increase. James Monk, Chief Justice of Montreal, had a house at 16 St Louis Street in Quebec he was eager to rent should the prince require it. His portly brother George, superintendent of Indian affairs in Nova Scotia, loyally pushed his brother's interests in Halifax, ears wide open for nuances and inflections at dinner-table conversations, especially since Madame had suggested that James delay renting his house, just in case.

'HRH was sitting on Mrs Wentworth's left, I was on her right directly opposite to him & Madam D St Loran on my right so that he could not but hear what she said, however, to make it the more certain I repeated her request by way of showing that I comprehended it & that so loud that HRH must have heard it. She then added that the P & she had already planed [sic] the addition of one story & other improvements in case they should return to Canada. The P did not notice the conversation in the least either in confirmation or contradiction but continued talking English to Mrs W and when M S'L & I went into another subject HRH joined our conversation in French. I am thus particular because it appears very singular if HRH wished to have such a message sent to you that he did not himself lay his commands upon me as the mention of your House arose from a conversation between him & me respecting our family &c. & the cause of such a vast difference in size between you & me (he often diverts himself with my Falstaff appearance) . . . I shall take an early oppy of telling Madam in the Prince's hearing that I have forwarded her Message &c.'

He added a warning:

'The Govr assures me the P has no knowledge whatever or expectation respecting his being removed from here but what I have been already informed of & have communicated to you—the desire to succeed Ld D.—and that what I have noticed in his arrangements are general precautions in case of being called away . . .' Two months later Monk had little further to report except that 'He still entertains expectations of seeing Canada again . . . I did as I mentioned in my last I would respecting Madam's Message to you and with the fairest opportunities that could be wished for but HRH continues silent.' (197)

The house was fated to remain uninhabited by royalty, and little more than a year later (September 1796) it suffered serious fire damage caused by children playing with squibs and gunpowder in a nearby stable. 'I am truly sorry for his Misfortune', Madame wrote amiably to his brother George, undoubtedly turning to her commonplace book for an apt quotation, 'but Nothing is to be said on such an occasion for, *Before an affliction is digested Consolation ever comes too soon, and when it is digested it comes too late*'. (198)

Among those who set less store on social convention, Madame earned admiration and friendship. The manner in which she set at ease an embarrassed Major Monk early in 1797, when he had inadvertently opened a letter entrusted to him for delivery to her, is a perfect example of her graceful tact. 'You are so extremely attentive in apologizing for what I never should have discovered, I mean the accident of your opening the cover of Mrs Northup's note', she wrote, 'that I feel quite ashamed you should have given yourself so much trouble where I am sure there was not the least occasion for an excuse'. (199)

Almost twice-monthly performances of a variety of plays gave Thérèse-Bernardine an opportunity to shine in public, recipient of glances both envious and admiring. In the *Halifax Weekly Chronicle* of 13 February 1796, someone burst into effusive verse.

> 'On Seeing Mme St L—— dressed in
> *DIAMONDS at the THEATRE*
>
> *Let other Beauties, less divinely fair,*
> *With costly Jewels ornament their hair;*
> *Those living Sapphires, her bewitching eyes,*
> *The Diamond's feeble ray outvies;*
> *Bassora's Pearls her lovely teeth disclose,*
> *And on her fragrant lips the Ruby glows:*
> *No aid from ornament can she receive,*
> *Who must to Dress its taste and lustre give.'*

Was it poetic licence, or were her eyes really blue?

One *Observator*, who addressed an acid letter of criticism to the Managers of the Theatre in early 1796 deploring the quality of the performances, paid tribute to her talent. 'I have constantly attended the Theatre with some part of my Family ever since it opened, and invariably have seen more to be disgusted with, than pleased at . . . In the name of all the Gods at once, what can induce you to act Operas? Is it to convince us what dismal singers you are? The P——e certainly has too much judgment, as well as regard for the reputation of the Theatre, to wish you should so expose yourselves for his amusement; and M——m D- S- L——t is too exquisitely fine a singer herself to relish the discordant pipes of a P——e or a S——r. From such singers (if singing you call it) Good Lord deliver us!' (200)

By now the garrison was showing the effect of the prince's reorganization. 'You would be surprised, could I describe the improvement of this garrison since the Prince's command', wrote Wentworth, who had been at loggerheads with the previous commander, General Ogilvie ('Of all men, he is the most untractable, and implacable . . . He never intimates a syllable to me, even about my own Regt.—ungraciously & with manifest intention to show me disrespect—leaving me to find out from garrison orders'. Wentworth feared that 'no good would happen to the service, should he ever command again'). The garrison under Prince Edward was, by comparison, 'now regular, military & efficient. Complete discipline pervades the whole command, without rigor or severity. Both Officers & Men do more duty with perfect satisfaction, & without a murmur or jealousy. He has represented the Garrison and works necessary for this province, certainly with great judgment. He is in the love & full confidence of Army, Navy, Militia, Church & State—except', added Wentworth with a touch of humour, 'M.G: Ogilvie, who he yet holds up, & in some cases advises with.' (201)

Wentworth was justified in his opinion when he gave it, six months after the prince's arrival, though he was to discover that his Royal Highness's judgement in certain areas—especially financial—was not as good as he could have wished. But though the governor would write to John King six years later, 'I am satisfied/the prince/is unequal to cope with the personal views that naturally surround a man of such high rank, and means of reward' (the prince's friendship for the deputy-commissary-general had caused him to be 'artfully deceived' into misguided approval of costly changes in purchasing procedures) he softened his criticism with a repetition of his 'great regard for H R H and a good opinion of his zeal & industry in the minutiae of tactics, architecture, & domestic oeconomy'. (202)

The later criticism that has washed around the prince, arising in great measure from attitudes and morals of an age quite different from his own—and, it must be admitted, frequently from ignorance of the actual facts of his life—has obscured his obvious qualities of intelligence and experience. He was, after all, commander of a garrison vulnerable to attack during a war with a powerful enemy. It was certainly his responsibility to make as impregnable as possible, as he pointed out, 'the only Port and Dock yard the British have in North America'. (203)

With his engineers under command of Captain James Straton, Prince Edward proceeded during the next few years to rebuild and reorganize the defences of Halifax, especially the Citadel on the low hill that dominated the town. Work on this fort extended from mid-1795, when extensive plans and estimates were sent to the Secretary of State for War, until its completion in the autumn of 1798. Along with this project, the prince employed the militia on various works in the town and its environs: and after the arrival in Halifax of a group of sturdy maroons from Jamaica, he made use of their labour too. Some of them were formed into militia companies and several received commissions.

As well, the prince supervised the construction of a star fort with blockhouse, barracks and storage cellar on George's Island lying in the harbour close to the town, alterations to batteries surrounding the town, and various barracks buildings. Three solid Martello towers were also built, following the interest in this form of defence after resistance to bombardment had been demonstrated by a similar tower in 1794 at Mortella Point, Corsica. Prince Edward was always quick to adopt new ideas, keeping himself keenly up to date on all such matters, from defence innovations to the style of his bandsmen's uniforms.

He had tried without success to persuade Lord Dorchester to let him have another regiment from Quebec. Scares of French fleets in the vicinity occurring from time to time (no doubt endorsed by the captured letter written by Joshua Barney) made him acutely aware of the decayed state of the fortifications and the undermanned garrison. 'He is not well pleased that his request of a Regiment from Canada has been refused', wrote George Monk to brother James in his letter of 23 May 1795, 'and in consequence declines parting with the Company of the 4th that are here without a positive order for it tho' Ld. D. has expressed his desire that they should be sent to Quebec. Indeed if I am not greatly mistaken he is not much disposed to be pleased or to comply with any thing from your Chief.'

A year later, when his Lordship passed through Halifax on his return home, Monk had another comment for brother James. 'The Prince presented me . . . I therefore called on him, &, contrary to my expectation, he received me, & was quite facetious & *Inquiring*—there I evaded—but I am convinced that he condemns the public works carrying on here.' (204)

It seems evident that Dorchester disapproved of Prince Edward: perhaps from personal incompatibility (private letters show he was incompatible with other Canadian colleagues as well), perhaps from jealousy, perhaps as an offshoot of his wife's social and moral censure of Madame. Whether his opinion, asked or given, had weight, or for whatever other reason, the prince had to write to de Salaberry on 2 November—his birthday: '*My fate is at last decided*, and I am to remain at my present post till the close of the war. My Lord is succeeded by General Prescott, who is perhaps with you already, at least my letters lead me to think so. He is a brave soldier, and a man, firm, unchangeable and without ceremony.' (205)

A bitter pill indeed, and one of many he would be required to swallow during his lifetime, but he accepted it without much protest and with generosity to the successful General.

CHAPTER NINE

'The bells rang for an hour'

The deep friendship with the de Salaberrys in Quebec had been faithfully continued by correspondence, and on 2 July 1796 the prince was able to advise them that their eldest son Charles, who had been posted at the age of sixteen to his regiment in the West Indies, had arrived unexpectedly in Halifax.

Young Charles did not return to the West Indies until a full year later, after a brief visit to his parents, a shipwreck on Prince Edward Island (still at that time called the Isle of St John), and some temporary duty in Halifax. Meantime his arrival was a source of pleasure to both Madame and the prince, though he turned up at a time when, being on the point of leaving for a tour of New Brunswick, they were both in a bustle of preparation for the journey.

Prince Edward was attended on the tour by George Monk, at whose home in Windsor the prince 'very civilly called and had all the children paraded'. Three of them were just recovering from a bout of scarlet fever, but the royal visitor made appropriately flattering remarks to the proud father, and one can imagine Madame going down in a billow of skirts to embrace them one after the other. The tour lasted just over a week, and one admirer at least was happy to welcome Madame back to Halifax. In the *Weekly Chronicle* of Saturday, 23 July, lyric words appeared under the heading: *On the return of Madame —— from a Country Excursion*. Five florid verses praised her 'angelic face' and 'sweet accents', and ended:

> *'Exult, my heart then, in thy grateful fires,*
> *And speak the joy her glad return inspires.'*

Though she would not get the news until much later, a child of her own flesh and blood had been born on 15 July in the small French town of Chambéry, to which her brother Claude-Charles had now removed as chief engineer of highways: her first nephew, the little Charles-Benjamin Mongenet, who would be a comfort in later years and at her bedside when she died.

Behind the façade of parades, reviews, work on defence projects, Prince Edward faced a continuing problem not peculiarly his own, but one being faced by army officers all over the world. 'The habits of the garrison were *very dissipated*', an eyewitness, one of the prince's protégés, would write years later, '. . . Among the military/the prince/ soon put an end to it by parading the troops every morning at five o'clock; and as he always attended himself, no officer could of course feel it a hardship to do so. The improvement which thus took place among the military, gradually extended to their civil acquaintances; and His Royal Highness thus became instrumental in improving both . . ./His/discipline was strict almost to severity. I am sure he acted upon principle', concluded the writer, Sir Brenton Halliburton, with what may have been hindsight fifty-odd years later, 'but I think he was somewhat mistaken in supposing such undeviating exactitude essential to good order'. (206)

Many of his contemporaries thought so, too. Many others did not. The martinet image is partially justified, but his interpretation of discipline must be judged by the standards of his own day, not of this. He would be criticized in his time even by his most devoted friends and officers—but for an obsession with trifling detail, not for cruelty.

It is worth recalling again that not one of the complaints at the Quebec courts-martial (as also during those following the naval mutinies of Spithead and the Nore) referred to the punishment of flogging, only to more trivial irritations. Cruelty was accepted as necessary to punishment, and punishment necessary to deter the criminal. This view operated with as much public acceptance in civil life as in the military world. On 1 November 1796, Halifax watched without any apparent horror while a young man convicted of forgery stood in the pillory for an hour and had an ear cut off.

The military régime everywhere was harsh. Soldiers everywhere, illiterate, poverty-stricken and often criminal, were accustomed and resigned to discomfort, hard work and punishment. Desertion was common. Long lists of court-martial verdicts record desertion and mutiny from British army stations all round the globe. In Canada the soldiers took to the woods, skipped down the coast, stowed away on ships. Amnesties were constantly being offered. Admiral Murray, at the beginning of 1795, set a time limit within which deserters could return with impunity and recover lost wages. Prince Edward would pardon any who joined the Fusiliers, the King's Own or the Royal Nova Scotia Regiment within a set period of three months. General Prescott himself advertised pardons for deserters in February 1797, over a period up to the following August.

During the year 1798, when Halifax is supposed to have been recoiling from the cries of the prince's victims, court-martial records from other army posts would show a long list of floggings and seventeen men shot or hanged (four of them in Martinique for desertion and joining the enemy) for such a variety of other causes as desertion, robbery and threats. In Prince Edward's own Garrison Orders Book for the period 28 August to 20 November 1798 (the only one that seems to have survived from his term at Halifax), the most common misdemeanour was drunkenness which got anything up to 200 lashes. Only four men were ordered 1,000 or more lashes (these for desertion) and one at least of these was remitted part of his sentence. Of the minor punishments, some were pardoned, some commuted to a lesser punishment, some suspended. Out of the total, nearly half of the punishments were never administered.

With the Wentworths the royal soldier and his lady continued in friendship and respect. Two years after his Royal Highness's arrival in Halifax, Sir John was still happy with his prince. 'H R H Prince Edward is infinitely assiduous in fortifying; everything great and good in his profession and command may be reasonably expected from his spirit and talents. It is of infinite importance and particularly in such exigencys as the present, that the commanding General so generously cooperates with me—God Almighty send that whenever his illustrious Rank may call him to St Js' [sic]—he may be succeeded by a Genl. of equal kindness, liberal conduct, and other accomplishments.' (207)

Prince Edward was not so fortunate in his relations with his brother Frederick, Duke of York. His recommendations for places and promotions for his officers and protégés were frequently ignored, and the tensions were building between the brothers that would seriously divide them a few years later. He had also experienced a continuation of that unfortunate series of accidents by which his debts, despite his best efforts to clear them, were increased to a point where payment of the interest alone was a struggle. A £2,000 outfit ordered from England to replace the one lost through the ice of Lake Champlain, dispatched aboard the *Antelope* packet in August 1794, had been captured by a French fleet. A duplicate replacement sent by the packet ship *Tankerville* the following December suffered the same fate. In a third try, the French took the *Recovery* transport in 1796, with fourteen tons of stores worth £4,000. No wonder the prince began to feel that family, fate and now fortune were all determinedly inimical.

Levees and balls (even one like Lady Wentworth's at Government House in honour of a naval achievement by Captain Beresford of *La Raison,* when the ladies wore navy blue cockades and bandeaus with the hero's name in gold): the major military undertakings (even the fortifications, which were turning Halifax into a stronghold): the reviews, the parades, the garrison responsibilities—all together were not enough to pacify the young prince's sense of neglect. True, he had been promoted to Lieutenant-General on 12 January 1795, but his April letter of thanks to his father moved abruptly into the usual plea for permission to return. Observant Wentworth shared his disappointment.

'He cultivates the highest sense of duty & veneration as a Subject, wherein None can be more zealous & decided, & as a Son is impressed with unbounded filial respect, affection & obedience to His Royal Parents, so seriously, that he is, not unfrequently, distressed & almost sinking, to need even my feeble consolation, when, on the arrival of a mail he does not receive some expression of parental consideration, tho' in all other cases I observe his mind is firm, unyeilding [*sic*] in what respects himself, and inclined to enterprize.' (208)

He was to have another jolt in April 1797. 'The *Highest* Friend I have'—Wentworth to John King in a letter marked *Secret*—'has been much dejected since the packet arrived, and he saw in the Gazette the promotion of General Prescott. I was afraid He was not quite well—we were alone—He said yes he was well, but was tho'tfull. He asked if I had heard of the appointment. I said I had heard such a report—but, said he, I have seen it in the Gazette. I think it very hard after so many years service abroad to have any body put over my Head, in this Country. It implies to the public, disapprobation & censure of me. I am not conscious of having deserved it. Therefore I cannot with honour serve any longer in this Country. I must now of necessity return to London. I am now near thirty, am the only one of the Brothers kept abroad, and now the only situation fit for me is given over my Head, while I am on the spot. It is so pointed against me, that I cannot stay in the Country with any satisfaction, or regard to my own Honour. I endeavoured to do away these impressions, but it is impossible. He is too much mortifyed and not a little chagrined and distressed. He cannot be persuaded, but that it is intended to greive [*sic*] him and that it will degrade him in the opinion of the world, & particularly of all Military People, of which He is delicately tenacious. Notwithstanding the deep impression this event has taken on his mind, He never uttered an hasty or resentful word, but spoke with calm firmness and in a dignified manner, such as I never before saw him exercise.

He said he had not wrote to the D of P on the subject. He did not wish to add any difficultys to the King's Ministers, but beleived he should soon be obliged to write. I do not think he will go home, untill he has formally applied for Leave. But he is much hurt, and seriously resolves to return to England.' (209)

The prince had had high hopes when the Duke of York became Commander-in-Chief—'As I understand that my brother has expressed his intentions of pleading my cause warmly with His Majesty, I hope and trust, knowing his weight with the King, that I shall shortly feel the good effects of it', he wrote to Walter Cliffe in May 1795. But in June, James Monk had a letter from his affectionate brother George saying, 'The P. is more than ever dissatisfied with his Brother of York', after promotions he had urged for two of his officers had gone to other candidates. (210) He had probably also hoped he might now receive the longed-for summons to come home at last.

Nevertheless, despite his deep disappointments, the prince was not one to make a hasty move. He must be credited with the virtue of patience: his father's reaction to his Geneva escapade had made a deep and lasting impression, and his whole life from that point on was directed towards regaining and maintaining the King's good opinion and redeeming his lost reputation.

The King could hear the squibs of information about his fourth son filtered through from various sources. Prince Edward was beloved by all ranks of people in Canada . . . his conduct was exemplary, his goodness of heart acknowledged by all . . . he was receiving addresses of gratitude from this little community and that. But even these could be easily damned with faint praise by any with the King's ear who wished Prince Edward to be continued in a state of probation.

So the prince composed himself, gritted his teeth, and doubtless went to Madame for comfort and sympathy. (He would write later that during this period of his life she had been 'almost the only comfort of my existence'.)

From home, news of events that were exciting the country was received with each arriving mail. The Princess of Wales had borne a daughter, an Heiress Presumptive to the Throne: the Prince, it was said, had been much agitated during his wife's long and difficult labour. But only a month later, grassfire rumours of a serious rupture between the royal couple snaked through the City, and London buzzed with heated partisan discussions.

Charles James Fox had been elected to Parliament in June 1796 and carried to Devonshire House in a gilt state chair decorated with laurels, preceded by banners and a dozen butchers with marrow-bones and cleavers. Apprehensions of invasion by the French were excited by

an abortive landing of 1,200 men at Fishguard in Wales. The country
was aghast in shocked reaction to the naval mutinies at Spithead and
the Nore. Prince Edward's elder sister, the Princess Royal, was married
to the Prince of Wurtemberg, and was unable to make the journey to
Europe by the route planned because the mutineers would not allow
the frigate to depart from Sheerness.

The trappings of ceremony that did their best to give importance to
military reviews in the small Halifax garrison could not compete with
a grand occasion like the display on Wimbledon Common in June
1797 when the Light Horse Volunteers 'were reviewed without accident
or disgrace' before their Majesties, the Princesses, the Prince of Wales,
the Duke and Duchess of York, Prince Ernest and the Prince of
Orange. Prince Edward grieved that his regiment, at the top of its
form in appearance and precision of performance, was denied an
opportunity to parade before his royal father.

His association with Madame could hardly have been the cause of
his father's silence, unless she had been misrepresented by unkind and
prejudiced tongues. It was, as Colonel Symes had remarked years ago,
unrealistic to expect celibacy in a young man of Prince Edward's age
and restricted marital opportunities, and his circumspect domestic life
gave rise to no scandal except among the pursed-lips moralists. The
King, moreover, had not repudiated the Duke of Clarence, whose
association with Mrs Jordan was public and prolonged : and though
Dorothy Jordan was a loving and loyal woman, she lacked the dignity
and air of breeding that always distinguished Thérèse-Bernardine.
Whether from his own judgement, from a judgement influenced by
others, or from his own wholly practical conviction that his fourth son
was needed where he was while the war lasted (he was not, at least,
denied the money for the necessary strengthening of the defences), the
King gave no sign or reply to the prince's pleading letters.

'Eleven years are now nearly elapsed since I first quitted the parental
roof, in all which time I have been but once permitted to come into
your presence . . . I feel confident that if your Majesty will not
condescend to grant my request, you will not be offended with me for
having made it . . .' (23 April 1796). 'I trust the time is not far distant
when I shall be permitted once more to approach you . . . the heigth
[sic] of my ambition is to merit your good opinion, your regard, and if
I may be allowed the expression, your love' (25 September 1797).
'. . . be pleased to accept of the assurance of my perfect readiness . . .
to obey your commands, with the utmost chearfulness . . . At the same
time . . . I cannot but regret that I am the only one of your sons,
who, after so long an absence, is precluded from the happiness of

I

serving more immediately under your own eye. . . .' (19 November 1797). (211)

Life went on in Halifax. All sleighs were ordered to give the whip hand to each other by keeping on the left hand side. Horses were not allowed to gallop through the streets. Wheels of carriages laden with lumber were required 'to conform to such as would not injure the roads'. Mail delivery was speeded up by putting the post-messengers on horseback and being strict about pick-up time. In the winter, the prince sent soldiers to help clear the snow-blocked Windsor road for thirty-five cattle destined for the Halifax market and marooned for two weeks. Someone wrote a poem for the royal birthday: 'Come celebrate with me/Edward's nativity/Here's gen'rous wine.'

Young George Landmann, son of the professor of fortifications at Woolwich Academy, was posted to the North American colonies in 1797, and while in Halifax awaiting passage to his new duties as a second lieutenant in the Royal Engineers was invited by the prince to dine at the Lodge. Other guests were Sir John and Lady Wentworth, Captain Thesiger, Captain Daniel Lyman, and members of the prince's staff, Major John Vesey, Captains George Smyth, Thomas Dodd, Richard Wright, and Lieutenant Mercer of the Royal Artillery.

After dinner the gentlemen enjoyed three glasses of wine and went to join the ladies—Madame, Lady Wentworth, Mrs Dodd and Mrs Wright—for coffee and tea. Later, with the musical Captain Smyth as accompanist, the prince and Madame delighted the company with a duet. Before the young soldier left (his journey took him the long way round to Quebec, via New York), the prince gave him introductions to two New York friends, Mr Beech and Mr Badcock, and a commission from Madame to deliver a present of harp-strings for 'Madame de Buc' in Greenwich Street. (212)

By two weeks young Landmann missed the storm that blew the forty-four-gun frigate *La Tribune* to tragedy on the Thrum Cap Shoals in Halifax harbour, with only twelve survivors of more than 240 men, with some women and children, despite the most courageous efforts of groups and individuals. It was a night of horror and heroism, which the people from the town spent beside fires lighted on the headland, so near the sinking ship that they could talk to survivors clinging to the foretop. A thirteen-year-old boy got two men off in a tiny skiff and shamed his elders into a belated but successful trip in the jolly-boat of the *Tribune* to get off two more. Some of the rescuers themselves were lost, including Lieutenant James of the Royal Nova Scotia Regiment, whose funeral with military honours, organized with the utmost sympathy and tact by Prince Edward in person, was one of the more pathetic aftermaths of the tragedy. Three Royal Fusilier lieutenants, Brenton Halliburton, Donald Campbell and John Mervin Nooth, were publicly honoured for bravery. The prince ordered immediate provision for families of the soldiers who had drowned, and a public subscription was started to help the widows and orphans.

The Wentworths, like Prince Edward and Madame, were constant sufferers from the climate. Sir John's letters to John King, and the prince's letters to the de Salaberrys, record recurring miseries and bouts of illness. Lady Wentworth particularly had been very unwell, on and off, for more than a year. 'Much impaired in her health, from her late illness', wrote Wentworth in December 1797, '& exceedingly distressed for the declining health of our Son,/she/intends taking passage for England in the ship, Indian Trader, bound to Liverpool, sails about the 25th Jany.' Her departure for the healing waters of Bath and Bristol and to visit their son Charles-Mary, ailing at Oxford, was delayed until 13 March. The ship *Indian Trader* had been 'fitted up with every possible convenience and kindly presented by the Merchants who own her, for Lady Ws accomodation', her husband wrote in shaky writing, confiding to the kind offices of King 'these the dearest . . . nay, let me rather say, essential parts of my existence'. (213) It would not be hard to imagine the envy with which the prince saw the governor's wife depart for the homeland from which he was yet excluded.

On 11 February 1798 the King sat down and wrote a long-awaited personal letter to his homesick son. On 23 April, the prince recorded the moment he had received it as 'one of the happiest of my life'. He was overjoyed to know his conduct had been approved by his father, understood perfectly that Halifax was the scene where he could be most usefully employed, agreed that his long absence from home had probably kept him out of many difficulties. He had not hitherto, however, troubled his father with the miseries he had suffered from the climate of Halifax. Might he now take the liberty of explaining that 'the most respectable medical gentleman of this country' had advised him not to risk another winter here? He was asking for neither a peerage nor additional income. He would serve anywhere in Great Britain or Ireland, where he could demonstrate his virtues of punctuality and zeal, or in Hanover if employment at home was not approved. But could he please leave Halifax? (214)

He had now passed his thirtieth birthday. At the same age his brother William Duke of Clarence had already been receiving an annual parliamentary allowance of £12,000 for six years—a total amount of £72,000 that was never made up to Prince Edward. Was it possible that the example of dissipation set by his three elder brothers had convinced the King that he was saving from a similar fate, by keeping him so many years out of temptation's way, a younger son who had shown early tendency to the same sort of life? There was no reply to the prince's letter. The King might have admired, had he thought about it, the strength of mind and determination that kept this son so respectful and patient in the face of so many disappointments and such weary waiting.

The war was straining Britain's resources. Subscriptions to relieve the exigencies of Government had been initiated in London, as well as the unpopular income tax. 'The voluntary contributions already amount to near 600,000l . . . In the circle in which I live, we are all giving about a fifth of our incomes, including our additional assessments,' noted Lord Auckland. (215) Not to be outdone, Halifax poured £4,000 into the fund in the first week. The Young Gentlemen of Halifax Grammar School, some under six years old, contributed £23.18.00 from their pocket money.

A public fast and humiliation to implore God's blessing and deprecate His wrath was proclaimed in June. The prince presented colours to the Royal Nova Scotia Regiment. Someone stole three of His Highness's Turkey Hens from his Town Residence, one 'remarkable large size, quite white except tip of Wings & Tale five guineas reward'. Simeon Perkins came up from Liverpool to attend the General Assembly: heard a 'Very pritty discourse' at St Paul's Church: dined with the Governor, where His Royal Highness was 'very sociable but soon left the Company': noted (on a 'V. warm day') that in view of the Prince's preference, the House had resolved to buy him a Star instead of the Sword for which they had voted 500 guineas: was amused by the hassle over the wording of the address to be presented to the Prince by the Council and the House of Assembly ('I think it was not much bettered by the Amendments'): went to the play ('I cannot say much in favour of the performance. Perhaps I am not a Compitent Judge, it being the first I ever saw'): and went sturdily home to Liverpool, not much impressed by big city life. The prince thanked everyone graciously for the address, which said how much respect and attachment was felt for him by the whole province. He would not receive the Star until a good deal later.

Towards the end of June, replying to a 'truly kind and affectionate letter' from his eldest brother, Prince Edward made another impassioned appeal for release from his exile. 'It is but too true that I cannot help considering it as rather hard, to be kept after thirteen years absence from home, in this dreary and distant spot, at a period, too, above all others, when every consideration would render it so essential for me to be at home; but alas! I fear the dye is cast, and until the war is over, I apprehend I am but too well fixed here.' He had told the King, he said (and the Queen, and the Duke of York) of 'the bad consequences I had reason to apprehend, if compelled to pass an eigth [sic] winter in this trying climate, from the changeableness, and severity of which I have for the three last suffered incredibly . . . if it should be in your power to do anything in my favor, I feel confident you will never consider any exertions as too great to serve me.' His family was aware of the place Madame occupied in his heart and home. 'Madam de St Laurent is highly sensible of your flattering remembrance, and has charged me particularly not to omit offering you the assurance of her best wishes.' (216)

On 8 August the whole picture changed. By what he must have considered a miracle, an event occurred that gave the prince the excuse he needed to leave Halifax. Cantering through the town, the heavy and powerful horse he was riding went through a small wooden bridge over a drain and fell, rolling twice on top of his left thigh and crushing it into a pile of rocks in the ditch. Though painful, the bruising was not allowed to keep him from business as usual for a few days. He attended the Prince of Wales' birthday review on Monday, 13 August. But the pain and the bruises persisted, and the injury was not improved after some days of rest and various medicinal applications.

By 25 August, when he wrote to his friend the banker Thomas Coutts in London, the prince was beginning to think of the accident as a heaven-sent opportunity for escape. 'My late accident renders it still more requisite to get away from hence, as one of the principal complaints I suffer from is rheumatism; and the contused limb will naturally offer it a mark where to settle. At present a very large swelling has settled itself in the thigh, of the nature of which our surgeons here seem unable to determine, for after having tormented me for several days past with powerful bitter applications, I am now precisely in the same condition in which I was, when first they took me in hand.' He wished he had the King's permission to return : 'For I would willingly have born with the inconvenience attending the leaving the Limb in it's [sic] present state for a few weeks in order to put myself into the hands of Mr Rush on reaching home, who I am sure would instantly have understood the cause of the injury. . . .' (217)

Members of the Faculty in Halifax were understandably nervous. If a son of the King should develop a permanent limp, would they be held accountable? Would it not be safer to suggest more experienced opinion from leaders of the medical profession in England? For the prince, while he undoubtedly shared the same fears, the overriding importance of this decision lay in the promising possibility of a legitimate excuse for returning home. But even now, the once-bitten prince was being twice shy about making an unauthorized journey. Before taking the irreversible step, he forestalled assault on his decision with unassailable outside opinion.

Afraid that the shipboard rest and quiet might find him arrived in England with no evidence to disprove that 'the whole was an invention of my own brain, or at least a cunning trick to effect my return . . .' he asked General Prescott for formal permission to leave if the verdict of Dr Mervin Nooth, Inspector-General of Hospitals, for whom he had sent to Quebec, should agree with that of the Halifax doctors. (218) Nooth's certificate, forwarded to the King on 26 September, confirmed material injury to the limb and the need to try the waters of the hot pump at Bath.

On 15 October, the prince wrote joyously to de Salaberry. 'Madame de St Laurent desires me to say that she wished to write, but feeling so entirely occupied by preparations for our departure, you will have to excuse her till she can give the news from London.' Official addresses of regret were presented. George Monk wished them both godspeed from the little provincial town of Windsor and offered to keep the prince in touch with local happenings. General Murray was left in command of the garrison. The prince's aide-de-camp Major John Vesey went ahead in the *Thetis* frigate to superintend the landing of the royal baggage, which was travelling on several vessels and included 'two or three carriages, built in London, and six or eight beautiful poneys which . . . he intends to present to her R Hs the Duchess of York'. (219)

At nine o'clock on a rainy Saturday, the prince thankfully embarked with his suite under a royal salute on board his Majesty's ship *Topaze*. It was windy and raining less than a month later when *Topaze* moored at Spithead on 14 November, and on the advice in a letter awaiting him from the Prince of Wales, he sped straight to royal Windsor with all the speed he could manage. On his arrival, the bells rang for an hour.

CHAPTER TEN

The Duke of Kent

His family had shown deep concern about Prince Edward's condition. The Queen had written with motherly anxiety to the Prince of Wales from Weymouth on 2 October: 'The accounts of poor Edward's fall are much more serious than was expected. The physicians & surjeons are of oppinion that an abcess is forming in his *thigh* of which the matter lies very deep, &, being sensible of their own ignorance, rather wish him to be moved to England in case any opperation should be performed. . . . I wish the wind would favour the arrival of the mail, as I fear the longer his coming over is put off, the more danger there will be. The Duke of York will do what he can upon this subject & is very desirous to hasten the orders, but must wait till the arrival of other letters. Ceci est entre nous.' (220)

To her friend Lady Harcourt, preparing to leave on a visit to Bath, the Queen wrote a month later: 'Perhaps my son Edward may meet you [there]. We expect His arrival every hour; & tho' I am sorry for the cause of His return, which is owing to a fall from, or rather with His Horse, I rejoice to see Him for He has been absent for Thirteen years. He bears a very Amiable Character abroad; & I hope He will have sense enough to see the Necessity of supporting it in His Native Country.' (221)

The homesick prince was warmed and gratified by his reception. He had been received with honours in Portsmouth, met by the Mayor and Aldermen, a ringing discharge of artillery round the harbour and the garrison, and 'the shouts of a vast concourse of people of all descriptions'. The family gathered about him at Windsor with joy and affection, and suppers and grand dinners honoured his return. He was (he recalled to his friend Walter Cliffe a year later) 'received at Windsor by their Majesties and the whole of my family in a manner that far exceeded my most sanguine expectations'. Did the memory of his disgrace at their last time of meeting still hang so vividly between father and son that even nine years of good behaviour could not entirely free the prince from diffidence?

Though the *Mirror of the Times* thought a week after his arrival that 'the prince walks very lame, and his constitution seems much impaired from his long residence abroad', he told Cliffe that 'In the course of two months the surgeons set me up again, and from that time I have been able to walk as well as ever I did in my life. There is, however, an almost imperceptible contraction left in the limb, and it retains a fulness where the principal contusions were, but excepting these inconveniencies, and its being a barometer upon every change of weather, there are none of the effects of the fall remaining.' (222) He did not go to Bath.

He was now basking in the pleasure of a society far less insipid and (for him) more important than that he had endured in Halifax. On 22 November the Prince of Wales gave a grand dinner in his honour, attended by the Dukes of York and Clarence, the Prince of Orange and the Hereditary Prince, and a host of noble and military guests. He had taken a furnished house in St James's Street for a month while apartments at Kensington Palace were fitted up, and though Madame would live with him at Kensington in later years, he would not have dared to introduce her into one of the King's palaces, especially at this delicate point in his career, newly returned to his father's favour. It was at this time that he bought the house in Knightsbridge (known later as Kent House). The press, even during the term of his tenancy in the St James's Street house, reported his return from Windsor 'to his house in Knightsbridge, where he resides for the benefit of his health, by the advice of his physicians, till Kensington Palace is put into compleat repair'. On 2 December the *Observer* said more specifically that 'Prince Edward has taken the house at Brompton lately occupied by Mr Palmer'.

It was a most elegant mansion, its balconies overlooking Hyde Park to the north and the Surrey Hills to the south. In its lofty dining room, measuring forty feet by twenty-six, Madame met the royal brothers, to whom she would later send many an affectionate greeting in postscripts to Prince Edward's letters. The two drawing-rooms, warmed by fires in the beautiful statuary marble chimney pieces, received a variety of guests for conversation, cards and music. The morning room and the music room, richly decorated in white and

THE DUKE OF KENT

gold, were for less formal, more intimate parties. Spacious and airy bed-chambers, dressing rooms, boudoirs and family apartments occupied the upper floor.

On fine days there was the garden with its sloping lawn in front, and flower beds and shrubs set among gravel walks. In showery weather, guests could enjoy the thirty-eight by thirty-foot greenhouse. The nearly three acres of grounds provided produce from a neat kitchen garden and numerous fruit trees. There was standing for three carriages, stabling for twelve horses, servants' apartments and all the offices needed for the operation of a gentleman's residence. The beautiful daughter of the Besançon engineer must have considered her reputation well lost. Beyond these advantages of comfort and elegance She had earned respect and love. (223)

It is unlikely that their Majesties or the carefully secluded princesses met Thérèse-Bernardine during this year, though the prince's brothers were enchanted by her sparkle at private dinner parties. Certainly Prince Edward and his lady went incognito to the theatre and took discreet drives together. Madame would undoubtedly have been given opportunities to see, if not to speak to, her royal lover's family from favoured locations: Queen Charlotte's stern sense of royal decorum may even have been sufficiently overcome by curiosity to allow her son to point out to her (among the spectators on some public occasion, or as she rode in the park in her carriage) the lady who was his comfort and his joy. But it is quite impossible to believe that the Queen who, many years later, would not receive a daughter-in-law legally wed to the Duke of Cumberland because of the blemish of divorce in her past, would ever have condescended to formal reception of a French courtesan, however charming and well-mannered she might be, or however dear to her son.

It was early surmised by the public prints that Prince Edward and his next-youngest brother Prince Ernest would receive appointments to the peerage. The guess was the dukedom of Cumberland for Edward and of Lancashire for Ernest. In the meantime, Prince Edward journeyed between London and Windsor (on one occasion the object of an attempted hold-up by highwaymen), waiting on the King, breakfasting with the Queen, visiting his ailing youngest sister Princess Amelia, calling on old friends, and entering fully into the social life he had been pining for. The ball given by Lord and Lady Cathcart on 3 December was typical, pitifully eclipsing the pretentious little gaieties of Halifax. The whole royal family attended. There were country dances and a sumptuous supper in different suites of rooms brilliantly decorated with coloured lamps, wreaths of flowers and leaves, arches of shrubbery illuminated from behind. Prince Edward was where he belonged, a part of his family, a part of high society where the power and wealth resided and to which he had been born.

The Queen and princesses took coach to Kensington Palace to look over the preparations for Prince Edward's occupancy, and the prince wrote his father to ask for the same indulgences Prince Ernest had at St James's Palace—'the breakfast, fuel, candles, and household linen, together with the necessary attendance of maid servants to keep the apartments in order, and a porter to wait at the door'. He also asked hesitantly for the same privileges allowed to the Duke of Clarence—the table provided by the Board of Green Cloth (the accounts committee of the Royal Household), and stabling and forage for his horses at Kensington. He estimated his need for his duties about the King at ten saddle horses, fourteen coach horses and four footmen's hacks, the cost of any additional horses for his own pleasure to be met by himself. The number of horses, he pointed out, was the same as the establishment allowed him at Luneburg and Hanover. (224)

He took up residence in Kensington Palace at the end of December, though the decorating did not come up to his expectations. 'The King has given to Prince Edward a suite of apartments in Kensington Palace . . . [He] ordered that they should be painted and whitewashed only, Prince Edward expressed a desire to Wyatt to have some new chimney pieces and other alterations—but did not choose to ask the King, saying He *had once been a bad boy*, and *wd not be so again*—or subject himself to a refusal by asking what the King might not approve'. (225)

The penance he served for his early irresponsibility was long and costly in terms of both money and confidence, and of a greater severity than his fall from grace warranted. It was a penance, moreover, which would never totally absolve him in his father's eyes.

On 7 January a delegation of gentlemen from Halifax headed by Charles-Mary Wentworth waited on the prince with the Diamond Star of the Order of the Garter from the inhabitants of Nova Scotia. Lady Wentworth had been presented at Court on 5 July the previous year by her kinswoman the Countess Fitzwilliam. (226) (There is no evidence to support the belief that she was made a lady-in-waiting to the Queen with permission to reside abroad and a salary of £500 a year.) Until her return to Halifax with her son on the packet ship *Mary* in mid-June 1799, her Ladyship undoubtedly helped to entertain Madame's time in London with her animated company.

Fitting easily and smoothly into his place in the family and in society, Prince Edward was thankfully sure he would not have to leave Britain again soon. He wrote jubilantly to tell de Salaberry on 9 April. 'It appears that His Majesty has not the least intention to send me on service out of England at present, but has thought proper to appoint me to the command of the army of the interior, and I will immediately establish my Headquarters in the centre of the County of Hampshire, in command of the troops there in cantonment, for the defence of Portsmouth and the Isle of Wight, in case of attack.'

On 26 April, the Lord Chamberlain's office received a warrant signed by the King 'that two new seats should be made in the House of Lords for their Royal Highnesses Dukes of Kent and Cumberland'. (227) On the previous Tuesday, at the levee, the princes Edward and Ernest had kissed hands as Dukes of Kent and Cumberland, their parliamentary establishment fixed at £12,000 a year. The news prompted a letter of outraged protest to his father from the next-youngest prince, twenty-six-year-old Augustus. The reasons of wartime economy that had delayed establishments for his brothers Prince Edward and Prince Ernest until they were thirty-one and twenty-eight respectively were not, he argued, a precedent for delaying the establishments for himself and Prince Adolphus, a year younger. (228)

The new royal duke was now concerned about ensuring Madame's financial security. Though his own money problems remained severe, he gave instructions to Coutts to establish a fund that could be built into a nest-egg for Thérèse-Bernardine. 'As to the other point, that of settling something on Mad. de St Laurent that will put her at least so far in a state of independence as not to reduce her to the necessity of begging her bread should anything happen to me, I own I shall never sleep a night easy until *that* is adjusted, while I yet have in my power the feeble means of doing something towards it.'

He therefore instructed Coutts to add to Madame's account, 'from my own little pittance in the stocks', an amount that would regularly increase her small capital. When the stipulated total was reached, Coutts was to continue with quarterly payments towards Madame's capital, apart from her regular pin-money allowance, 'however trivial the sum may be . . . until', he explained, 'in the course of revolving years (if I live so long)' a still larger income could be assured to her. 'As you cannot oblige me more than by giving the earliest attention to this interesting settlement which I have so much at heart, I beg to recommend it earnestly to your care.' (229)

It now became apparent to him, however, that he was not going to receive the coveted supply of candles, fuel and food (which he later estimated to be worth £4,000 a year) that had been allowed to both his elder and his younger brothers, the Duke of Clarence and Prince Ernest (excepting for the latter's dinner). The expense of living in England while the debts remained to be cleared now began to appear prohibitive. Hearing that Sir Alured Clarke planned to leave his latest command in India, the duke applied, without success, for the post. Then learning that General Prescott was vacating the command in British North America, he reluctantly put in a bid to succeed him.

'I have reason to think that it is not unlikely I may yet go out early in the Summer as Commander in Chief of the forces in British North America,' he told Coutts; if he did, he expected terms that would enable him to reduce his debts. 'It certainly will be a severe sacrifice to give up again three of the best years of my life to pass them in that dreary quarter of the globe, but I think it is a point of honour to clear off my incumbrance.' (230)

'I own I was very backward at first in coming into this measure,' he told his friend Walter Cliffe later, 'for I am not fond of a northern climate, and I had had enough of this in a seven years residence.' But his terms were met, his promotion to General in the Army followed, and on 10 May he accepted the appointment as Commander-in-Chief of the forces in British North America. (231)

The excitements of life in the North American colonies had been continuing in the duke's absence. Mr Scavoye, Master of Prince Edward's band, had been giving concerts, and advertised a final one in expectation of being called home by the prince. Colonel Wetherall, preparing to depart, was selling off a variety of goods, including spices, teas, sugars, Truffles, wax candles, Pickles, polishing and plate brushes, Figgs, Almonds, Fish Sauce, Mushroom powder, Single and Double Gloucester Cheese, 14 hogsheads choice London porter, some gallons of Neats-foot Oil and Jarrs of Olive Oil—all the supplies of which it was necessary to lay in large personal stores so far from home. General Prescott left and was succeeded to the civil appointment of Lieutenant-Governor by Robert Milnes, 'highly spoken of—his predecessor entre nous will leave the Province unregretted except by the very few on whom he has bestowed favours or to whom he has held out hopes of them. It was impossible for things to remain in the state they were', wrote Thomas Aston Coffin to Ward Chipman. (232)

In England, the duke was making the most of his few months in the homeland. He travelled to Worthing to see his youngest sister Princess Amelia, convalescing in the south-coast resort. He visited his brother the Prince of Wales (with whom he was on the most affectionate terms) at his rented Dorsetshire estate. He attended the races at Ascot Heath, the Montem at Eton, led down the country dances with the Princess Augusta at the Duchess of York's fête, went riding with his sisters and his father (but not hunting—the duke was never fond of the chase). The military duties of his command took him from time to time to Winchester, his headquarters in Hampshire; this year, the duke was able to take his proper place among the Illustrious Personages at several splendid military reviews.

In Halifax, every move he made was recorded in the journals with possessive enthusiasm. The news of his peerage, and later, his appointment as Commander-in-Chief of the forces in British North America, was hailed with joy.

On Thursday, 11 July, the frigate *Arethusa* began loading the Duke of Kent's furniture in Portsmouth. Thirty-two horses were sent from Southampton a week later (seven would die before reaching Halifax), while the duke and Madame were making their farewells in London. The duke had been acting as emissary for his eldest brother with Mrs Fitzherbert ('The Prince has given up Lady Jersey, and is now trying to renew with Mrs Fitzherbert', Lady Holland confided to her journal. 'He ought to try and make his peace with heaven if he has any account to settle, as he does not look long for this mortal life'). (233) The Prince of Wales had been writing agonized, hysterical letters to 'the wife of my heart and soul . . . My Maria, my only life, my only love': and to his distressed brother, the duke wrote on 17 July, 'I am just returned from Mrs Fitzherbert's where I went agreable to your wishes, and with whom I have had a very long tête a tête. If I am any judge at all of the business, your wishes will ere long be accomplished, but it seems there are some points which she did not enter into the discussion of with me, which she says you must give up to her. Not knowing what these are, it becomes not *me* to advise, but believe me', wrote the duke out of his own knowledge of love, 'a reconciliation with a woman who possesses that attachment for a man which I am well convinced *she* does for you, is worth any sacrifice'. (234)

The duke (as well as the whole royal family) remained devoted to Mrs Fitzherbert. It can surely be assumed that the Prince's love would have received his younger brother's love kindly, a woman in much the same position as herself, though Maria Fitzherbert's aristocratic birth and private awareness of a marriage sanctified if not legalized could not have failed to give her a sense of superiority over a *bourgeoise* from provincial France living without benefit of clergy.

On Tuesday, 23 July, the duke said goodbye to the King at Windsor as he mounted his horse for his morning ride, to the Queen and Princesses at the Queen's Lodge, and to all the servants. 'The Royal Family seemed much affected at his departure,' said the press. With his suite he boarded *Arethusa* at one o'clock on 25 July. It was a long and tedious forty-one days before they saw 'the land of Nova Scotia beaming North', another two days before the guns began firing as *Arethusa* tacked up Halifax harbour and the 'long and anxiously expected arrival of His Royal Highness', signalled in advance by telegraph, was announced to rejoicing multitudes. With bells, illuminations and a carpet spread from the Slip to Government House, Prince Edward came back as Duke of Kent to North America.

With headquarters to be removed from Quebec to Halifax, the duke now found himself deluged with the kind of detail he was tirelessly happy to cope with. He and Madame were again resident at the Lodge—one of the pleasures of their return—though Wentworth, who had been enjoying its comforts after his royal friend's departure, was not quite so eager this time to relinquish the house on loan to the returning duke. Here, when Madame was not busy managing domestic arrangements, entertaining her friends or presiding over the duke's table, she would turn to her commonplace book to note down in her delicate, legible handwriting such epigrams and anecdotes as she wished to keep for reference or quotation. '*Lodge le* 26 8*bre* 1799', she wrote on an October Saturday on the first left-hand writing page of a fine red-leather-bound book with her name (MADAME DE St LAURENT) stamped in gold across the cover.

All 226 pages in the book were filled by shortly after 1805. The first twenty-three pages were written in Halifax. On the twelfth page Madame copied lines from Shakespeare :

> '*No, no! 'tis all Men's office to speak patience*
> *to those that Wring under a load of sorrow;*
> *but no man's virtue or sufficiency*
> *to be so moral, when he shall endure*
> *the like himself. Therefore give me no Comfort.*' (235)

Was this perhaps in January 1800, a wry comment when she was enduring the discomforts of a fall sustained on the 9th? 'Madame de St Laurent . . . would have written to you herself', the duke added to his letter of the 10th to de Salaberry 'but she has just had a very unpleasant fall which will prevent her from doing so for several days : wishing to hurry from one end of the room to the other in the dark to call a maid yesterday, the day after our arrival in town, she stumbled over what we call in English *a fender* that the servant had carelessly left across the door. As a result, she fell with all her force against the wall and chairs, and though she has, thank God, suffered no real harm, she is so badly bruised from head to foot that she will have to stay in her room for several days.' (236)

Though he had accepted the command in British North America, the duke had high hopes of leaving within the year. The prospect of the Union with Ireland offered the possibility of a command post opening up in that country. To the Prince of Wales he wrote nine days after his arrival : 'The contrast between the comforts and the beauty of England, with the want of every resource and the drearyness of Nova Scotia is certainly very glaring . . . I look forward, not without some hope, to the possibility of the union with Ireland taking place in the course of the next Session, for I believe I mentioned to you that Mr Pitt had promised me in that event to suggest to the King the appointing me Commander-in-Chief there, on withdrawing the Lord Lieutenant. I am sure I need not urge *you* (should it be in your power) to exert your interest to forward this favorite wish of mine, for I have too often experienced your friendship not to be very certain that whenever you can serve me you will be ever ready to do it unasked.' (237) Telling Coutts about his hopes, he said: 'I think myself certain of it, unless indeed Mr Pitt has held out to me a prospect for my provision in which he was not sincere; but I cannot suppose this possible.' (238)

As it turned out, the duke's stay in the drearyness was short—but not because of the Irish appointment he had hoped for. A letter written by his brother the Duke of York on 13 December, and by the mischances of communication in those days not received by him until 15 April, left him deeply affronted by its tone of high-minded wiser-than-thou censure. His reply, admirably controlled in the face of his brother's provocation, gave spirited rebuttal to the accusations implying indiscretion and folly in his private behaviour.

First, the Duke of York tartly explained the military position. 'In the first place you do not seem to be thoroughly aware of the situation which you wish to obtain, and I should imagine, think that the Chief Command in Scotland and Ireland possesses the same powers as the one which you at present fill, which is by no means the case in either of those situations, as the Command in Scotland is merely considered, as a district completely as dependent upon the Chief Command here, as the Southern or any other district in England, and the Chief Command in Ireland is at present totally dependent upon the Lord Lieutenant, and should the Union take place you may depend upon it that it is the intention of Government to put it upon the same footing as that in Scotland, for many obvious reasons.

'At the same time, my dear Edward, I trust that you will not take it ill if I state to you very fairly, that if either of these situations were such as you would wish to accept, Ministers would feel a delicacy in venturing to recommend to his Majesty to appoint you to one of them, under your particular circumstances at this moment.'

Then, with a bluntness singularly offensive to one whose domestic life, except for the sanction denied him by law, was unexceptionable, the Duke of York continued: 'It is not the business of anybody whatsoever to interfere in the private connection of any person, as long as they are not brought forward to public view, but a great deal depends upon appearances in this world, and every person in a public situation must avoid doing anything which may shock even the prejudices of the public.

'I am the last person in the world to preach or to wish to meddle in your private happiness or connections, but at the same time I must fairly say to you you can have no idea how much the world talked of the public manner in which you went everywhere accompanied by Madame de St Laurent. I am perfectly well aware that this may be done abroad, but you may depend upon it that it cannot be done at home, and therefore I advise you as a friend to consider this subject well over.

'I must again repeat to you that I trust that you will not take ill what I have written to you, but I thought it much the fairest proceeding towards you, to state to you honestly what people's feelings are concerning you, and leave it to your own judgement to decide.' (239)

The Duke of Kent, probably steaming but still trying to maintain a semblance of politeness, replied in a private letter on 19 April 1800. After preserving the amenities of brotherly affection, he went on to explain that he had been well aware of all the points his brother had raised in regard to the possible command in Ireland, and that his power and authority there would be less than in his North American command . . . 'But believe me, ambition never was, is not, and never will be a predominant passion with me'.

He then turned to the last part of his brother's letter.

'From the moment I got home in the fall of 1798, having no one reason to shake off a connection which had then lasted eight years, and which, in many of the most painful moments of my long absence from my family, under the pressure occasioned by the apparent total loss of parental affection, had been almost the only comfort of my existence, I studied nevertheless to regulate my conduct in that particular so as to avoid giving offence to the prejudices of the world. This motive alone induced me to establish Madame de St Laurent in a residence altogether separate from mine, where she was attended by a distinct set of servants, and from the same principle we mutually agreed upon, never appearing together in the streets of London, in the Parks, or any place which could be termed public, or where there appeared to be the slightest chance of incurring either censure, or even an unpleasant observation on the part of the most rigid, precise

and formal. To this resolution I can solemnly declare that the most
faithful adherence was observed: for if I except driving her out now
and then in an open carriage, in doing which we were careful to make
choice of the most private rides, and going to The Prince's loge grillée
at the two theatres (a part where I always understood no one was
subject to the prying of impertinent curiosity) I am confident there
is no person who can assert having seen us anywhere together. For my
own part, so perfectly convinced was I of having fully succeeded in
not exposing myself to censure by any part of my conduct with respect
to her, that on leaving England, it was one of the most pleasing
reflections to me, and I felt the more confident in this belief, as
I never once was able to find out that even in the most scurrilous public
prints the shafts of satire had been levelled either at her or at me.

'You will easily conceive, then, what must have been my mortification at reading that sentence in your letter in which you say that
"I can have no idea how much the world talked of the public manner
in which I appeared everywhere accompanied by Madame de St
Laurent".'

The gossips of London may well have chattered in their drawing
rooms and scribbled in their diaries: romantic involvements were, as
always, subjects of intense interest for members of aristocratic society.
But the duke was right when he said he had found no allusion in the
public prints. There is not a whisper in any that have survived to
today, and if there were private journals that mentioned the liaison
at the time, none of these has publicly appeared. Except for a passing
reference over the next sixteen years, Madame might hardly have
existed. Lords and ladies of the social world had too many far more
juicy scandals to titter over within their own circle.

'That *some* people have spoken in this manner, I cannot have a
doubt, after what you have said', the Duke of Kent continued, carefully
determined not to quarrel with his brother, 'being satisfied that you
can only have mentioned it from motives of friendship and affection
for me. I therefore am sure you will not be offended if I say that I
cannot help feeling that *no* one had a *right* to make this observation,
as the assertion on which it is grounded is wholly unfounded. The
remark made by you "that you/were/well aware such things might
be done abroad, but I might depend they could not at home" leads
me naturally to say that I so fully felt this myself that I did on landing
in England totally and entirely alter my mode of living with Madame
de St Laurent. Here she always did, and does now again, live in the
same house with me; she therefore presides at my table, goes every
where into company with me, and it is a rule with me never to accept

K

of any invitation where there are Ladies, unless she is asked: but I never looked forward to a similar plan of life at home, and she never had an expectation of the kind. I should have thought the little insight which you would unavoidably get into our mode of going on, by seeing how things were managed when you did us the favor to dine at Knightsbridge, would have been sufficient to convince you of the injustice of the animadversion you have heard passed upon my conduct on this point. But as it is but too clear to me that the case is otherwise, it is in vain to attempt by any comments of mine to undo the past: as it is, however, necessary that you should perfectly understand, and have it from under my own hand, what are my intentions with respect to my future conduct on this point, in the event of my being named to the Command of the Troops in Ireland, Scotland or one of the districts in South Britain, I will communicate the plan I had intended, and which I should still propose to pursue in that case.

'I would in the first instance join my Command *un*accompanied by Madame de St Laurent, and establish my own residence in such place as might be pointed out for Head Quarters. This done, I would take a house for her in the Country at some little distance off, where her ménage would be totally separate from mine. *She* would, of course, not appear at *my* house on the days I gave my public dinners, and when *I* went to *hers*, I should consider myself as *her* guest, and I should avoid being seen with her at any place of public entertainment that might be in the neighbourhood, unless I could so manage matters as to be there in a private way, and without exposing myself to be criticised for so doing. But in all this arrangement I desire it may be understood that not only she is the first to acquiesce, but that she has been uniformly averse to anything that brought her into public view.'

Separation from Madame was too much to ask. She meant more to her royal lover than his ambitions. 'Should this detail be deemed . . . a sufficient assurance of the perfect propriety of my conduct, you may depend upon my strictly abiding by it, but if more is expected, and I am to understand it is the intention to make my separation from Madame de St Laurent a term without which I am not to be employed on the other side of the Atlantic, which, however, it is repugnant to my feelings to credit, I must at once declare that it is one which I will not admit to be dictated to me, and to which, were I to subscribe, I should consider myself as meriting every contemptible and opprobrious Epithet to which those expose themselves who commit mean and despicable actions.'

Having issued this ultimatum, the duke went on to another one. Explaining that his health would not stand another winter in the North

American climate, he asked his brother for a twelve-month leave of absence to recover: and if that were refused, 'I am under the painful necessity of desiring you *in that case* to lay at His Majesty's feet my resignation of that situation to which he was pleased to appoint me in this Country . . . I cannot but cease to feel myself happy in it, the moment I am compelled to be convinced that in order to obtain the honor of serving nearer His person, which you must know I would prefer above everything, the sacrifice of my private comfort and happiness, that cannot possibly injure any one, is to be made the term sine quâ non—a condition which I am confident never sprung from *His* breast, and I trust never could spontaneously have arisen from yours.'

The letter was personally delivered to his brother by Lieutenant-Colonel Wetherall (who had already served the duke faithfully for many years, and in later years would prove to be his closest confidant and perhaps the best friend he ever had). An official letter went at the same time, 'should you think it advisable to lay that before The King, as motives of delicacy may prevent your communicating the contents of *this* to *him*'.

He would wait, said the duke, until around 20 July, by which time word should have been able to reach him about permission for leave. If neither alternative (leave or appointment in Britain) was acceptable, he would consider himself 'reduced to the cruel alternative of being compelled to resign that situation which I now hold'. (240)

CHAPTER ELEVEN

Farewell to drearyness

The eleven months of this second term in Halifax had been busy ones, with tours to various parts of Nova Scotia, in which Madame invariably joined him. A special event was the visit (with his two brothers) from the twenty-six-year-old Duke of Orléans, later Louis-Philippe, King of the French, who would become a close and faithful friend of both the duke and Madame. The Commander-in-Chief's duties were undoubtedly arduous, covering a very large territory, and as he pointed out, the Commissary, the Barrack and the Engineering Department as well.

Rheumatism, his *bête noire*, had confined him to bed for the last forty-eight hours before his departure from England at the end of July 1799, and though he escaped a severe attack during this Nova Scotia winter, he was at the time of his April letter to his brother, suffering from 'a very troublesome humour which, after shewing itself in several parts of my body, at length settled in my leg; indeed at this moment I am writing, one of my eyes is nearly closed from the same cause'. Nevertheless, he coped with the duties, the climate, the ills of the flesh and the social round as his position and rank demanded, with superabundant energy, and whatever certain levels of Halifax society may have thought of the duke's domestic arrangements, he earned approval for other facets of his behaviour. 'H : R : R : the Duke has had a great hand in this drinking reform', wrote Captain Lyman to Winslow on 6 January 1800, 'he used once to Drink 3 glasses after dinner, now he only takes one.' (241)

Before leaving London, he had tried, in a letter to Windham, the Secretary at War (and again to Portland in September from Halifax), to get permission to delegate authority for approving sentences of all courts-martial, without restriction, to the General Officers commanding the various districts under his command, 'in such cases of sudden and unforeseen emergencies, in which alone I would sanction the calling a Court together, such as Mutiny or Desertion under circumstances loudly calling for a serious example'. For the want of such powers in the hands of General Officers, the sentences of prisoners who should have been immediately executed, he said, were often, in the absence of the Commander, commuted to transportation from long confinement. The request was refused in a letter dated 6 November: the duke was to be the only person authorized to approve the sentences. (242) This ruling may have impelled him to a course that biographers in later years have interpreted as further proof of sadism—to keep in touch by a telegraph system when absent on tours of duty. 'There was a continual communication kept up of ordering and counter orders while he was away even to the approval of courts martial and ordering the men to be flogged', wrote an astonished Captain Lyman from Halifax to Edward Winslow on 3 February 1800 . . . 'So though an hundred miles off, the Duke still was acquainted with what was going on, and given orders the same as usual.' (243)

Though we have learned to be far less severe in our punitive legislation today, the legal position is still the same. A sentence duly and legally passed is put into effect without delay. To postpone the punishment of a soldier convicted by a legal court under the requirements of a Mutiny Act or other properly constituted legislation, unless he were to be reprieved (an action often taken by the duke), would be sloppy administration. One may deplore the savagery of the punishment, but one cannot criticize adherence to the law. The duke was acting responsibly if he thought it a part of his duty to see that the law was properly and promptly administered.

He had hoped to inspect the whole of his command in due course. As early as mid-October, before starting out on his Nova Scotia tour, he was planning to visit Upper and Lower Canada, but he saw little hope of making the journey before the following June. Even the plan to continue the Nova Scotia tour into New Brunswick had to be postponed because weather conditions made the Bay of Fundy crossing difficult. Newfoundland and Cape Breton were to be first on the list in the spring.

In January, Thomas Aston Coffin was still holding out hopes to Winslow of a royal visit to Saint John before the planned trip to the Canadas (still scheduled for June): but early in April, he added a postscript to his letter to a friend: 'I have just come from an interview with his Royal Highness who told me he had given up the idea of visiting Quebec this year. He proposes to go to New Brunswick, Newfoundland, Cape Breton and Prince Edward Island and to defer the Canadian jaunt till next year.' (244)

But he was fated never to see again the Quebec to which he had come young and happy with his new-found 'beloved companion'. Wetherall came back to Halifax on 17 June, bringing with him the King's permission for his son to return to England for reasons of health, and the duke would write regretfully to de Salaberry on 28 October: 'I fully participate in your regret at your not having seen me during my late sojourn in America. I know not if I shall ever return to that country, but you may depend on this, that there can be no place in which I will not preserve the most kindly remembrance of you and your family.' (245)

'Preparing a cabbin for Duke of Kent', noted the captain of his Majesty's ship *Assistance* in his log on 22 July, and at nine o'clock on a showery Monday morning (4 August), the ship, flying the Royal Standard, 'slipt moorings and made sail'. When with his suite the duke had embarked the day before, Halifax gave him a royal send-off, with officers and civic dignitaries in ceremonial attendance and citizens crowding windows and roof-tops.

A week after his departure (the Halifax *Royal Gazette* reported) eleven soldiers under sentence of death went through the grisly ceremony that preceded execution, dressed in white, accompanied by black-painted coffins on a little cart and the slow solemn music of the band. All had been convicted for mutiny or desertion. It has been implied that these unfortunate men were left to suffer the ultimate penalty in order to satisfy the Duke of Kent's personal sadism. Eight, in fact, were reprieved. The three who were shot were guilty of major military crimes: Garret Fitzgerrald [*sic*] (convicted of mutiny, desertion and firing on his apprehenders), Edward Power and James Ivory (guilty of mutiny on the schooner *Venus*, capturing the sergeant in charge and placing him in irons, forcibly taking possession of the vessel, and deserting with purloined ammunition). (246)

The duke's complaints of ill-health had been genuine. Though he began to feel better on the voyage, he told the Prince of Wales on arrival at Plymouth on 31 August that he still suffered from violent headaches and a constant pain in his chest. The Halifax doctors had recommended sea bathing. When *Assistance* was obliged by contrary winds to put into Plymouth instead of Portsmouth, he decided to go straight to Weymouth where the Royal Family was then in residence. Approaching Weymouth he was astonished to meet the carriage of the Queen, who happened to be taking an airing with the princesses. The duke continued his journey in his mother's carriage, with his sisters fluttering excitedly around him.

Madame had gone direct to London, to 'the house that was Colonel Stanhope's in North Row, Park Lane,' he told Coutts, adding that she would be delighted to receive him if he should care to call any morning. (247) The Prince of Wales had taken a kindly interest in her welfare. 'I am sure', his younger brother wrote to the Prince on 14 September, 'if Madame de St Laurent knew how kindly you had spoken of her in your letter to me, she would be very much flattered. I am quite pleased to find that you think the house she now occupies is a passable pied a terre en attendant that we can do better for her.' (248) The duke still owned the Knightsbridge house: perhaps it had been rented during his term abroad. It was not long after this that he purchased from Maria Fitzherbert the estate at Ealing called Castle Hill Lodge, which he would own until his death, and where some of his happiest years were spent with Madame. (249)

At Weymouth the duke was once more happy in the company of his family, going to the play, riding out on royal visits to the big country estates in the neighbourhood, and taking the warm salt baths which immeasurably aided his health.

The duke had been coping as best he could with his financial problems. Long ago—in April 1792—he had cleared up his Gibraltar debts out of the savings he had made from his Quebec income by a reduction of his expenses. (250) Perhaps Madame's influence deserved the credit for this. Wentworth, after all, had written in glowing terms in May 1794 of the prudence and cleverness with which she had 'restored his deranged finances'. From time to time he was able to write from Halifax authorizing Coutts to place various instalments of his income towards reduction of old debts in England. Unfortunately, new ones replaced the old, despite his best efforts—these new debts, he must often have thought with some degree of resentment, due in great part to what might be termed acts of God.

The loss of his equipment through the cracking ice of Lake Champlain in 1794 was certainly one such. The latest staggering blow was the loss of the *Francis* transport on Sable Island in 1799, when £11,000-worth of equipment was lost. The *Francis* was found in May 1800 by a lieutenant especially dispatched by Wentworth to search for the long-missing vessel; he found the sands scattered with packages, trunks, papers and the body of a woman. With the *Francis* the duke lost more than money: the surgeon of the Royal Fusiliers, Dr Copeland and his family, several officers and men of the Halifax garrison (including Captain Holland, son of the Surveyor-General) and some stableboys of the duke's household. His library of 5,000 books and irreplaceable maps and his cellar of choice wines were also casualties of the disaster. (251)

On all the debts that had accumulated, the interest appallingly climbed. Though he regularly made payments to Coutts, the total continually increased as various immediate necessities of travel or change of accommodation created fresh overdrafts.

But no matter to what other purpose the duke directed his income, the amount credited to Madame's annuity, as well as her quarterly allowance, was faithfully paid. He was thankful, he wrote Coutts on 26 May 1800, that it had been possible to place a regular quarterly sum towards her trust. When completed, he added, 'it will be a great weight off my mind'. (252)

Madame had stood the voyage home better than the duke had expected, but was now slowly recovering from a severe cold caught in London, occasionally taking the air in her carriage, visiting and receiving visitors, among whom was Mr Coutts, happy to explain to her the intricacies of financial investments. With true French thrift, she pored over the statements he gave her so that she might fully understand the details.

'The Departure of the Duke of Kent has not occasioned any irrecoverable Grief among those who are left in Command', wrote William Osgoode in an echo of the comments that followed almost every departing official, his letter remarkably catty about nearly everyone mentioned in it. 'All his Arrangements in the Indian Department are I believe set aside.' One of these was the removal of de Salaberry by Lieutenant-Governor Robert Milnes from the post of deputy superintendent of Indians, in favour of his own candidate. Milnes had written a 'most private' letter to the Duke of Portland on 4 November 1799 complaining that the Duke of Kent seemed determined to regard all places in British North America as at his disposal, and hinting rather spitefully that several applicants for civil appointment had no qualifications other than that they were entitled to favours 'from their attentions to *Madame St Laurent*'. (253) It would be unrealistic to suppose that the duke would not tend to give her the pleasure of seeing people she liked considered for appointments he could offer, but there has never been the slightest hint that she used her influence with him in any active way to interfere. This was an age when (as George Allsopp wrote to his son five years earlier), 'interest you know is the predominant passion in mankind', with each succeeding official trying to obtain advantageous places for his friends. Milnes, of course, had his own favourites with whom he wished to replace the duke's: one may ask, perhaps, if there has ever been an age when interest and patronage were not a predominant passion. In that period, in fact, there was almost no other way for a person to obtain any kind of paid employment except through the benevolence of someone in whose power it

lay to fill a particular post. The duke explained convincingly and
successfully to Portland that while the position from which de Salaberry had been ousted was now indeed subject to the civil authority,
it had been properly a military appointment when he made it. (254)

The duke went up to London from Weymouth on 24 September. He
and Madame probably congratulated themselves on being where they
were when *The Times* of 4 October printed a letter from Halifax (28
Aug): 'This has been a remarkably unhealthy season here, we have had
no rain these two months, and the woods are so much on fire all round
the country, that we have not seen the sun these three weeks for the
smoke, and the smoke has been most painful to the eyes.' At the end
of October he spent a day or two at Brighton with the Prince of Wales,
with whom he was still on the most affectionate terms. Existing correspondence indicates the exchange of frequent letters between the two
brothers. The Prince of Wales, indeed, seems to have had a tender spot
for the junior prince. He entrusted him on more than one occasion with
delicate and intimate commissions.

As well as the duties of attendance upon the King and the necessity
of appearing at functions and ceremonies, there was much settling in
to be done; at Kensington Palace, where on 13 December the duke
had requested the King for additional work to improve the comfort of
the apartments, the Lord Chamberlain (adhering to the letter of his
Majesty's order) having refused to do more than make them wind
and water tight: at Ealing, where with his usual fervour for building,
he was to bring Castle Hill Lodge to that state of elegance which alone
could satisfy his fastidious taste.

The King had given everyone another scare. At the end of April
1801, the duke wrote to de Salaberry: 'Our winter has been generally
very dull, especially since the beginning of February, for the King has
been indisposed for three months, but now, thank God, we flatter
ourselves that he is entirely convalescent and that he will be spared us
for many years. You will know from this that we abstain from any
amusement whatever, which cannot fail to make the time hang
heavily.'

In mid-February a note of anxiety had appeared in diaries throughout the kingdom. Lord Malmesbury (17 February): 'King got a bad
cold; takes James's powder. God forbid he should be ill!' George
Rose (21 February): 'The King so unwell as to induce several persons
to make inquiries after his health.' Sir Gilbert Elliot (now Lord Minto)
(23 February): 'The King is *really ill;* he has been unwell for some
days, and it is called cold and bile. . . . There can be no doubt of its
having been brought on by the late events.'

The late events by which the conscientious King had been agitated were the possibilities from Pitt's implied promise (which led to his resignation) for Catholic Emancipation at the time of the Union with Ireland: the King felt it was in direct opposition to his coronation oath and popular opinion certainly supported his stand. On a cold and snowy Friday (12 February) the King had returned chilled from a long session in church, it being a fast day, and came down with 'cramps all over him'. Addington (who would become Prime Minister officially on 17 March) found him still suffering a week later, huddled in his chair and wrapped in a black velvet cloak. Three months of worry followed.

Whatever caused the King's illness—his mental worries or a metabolic disorder (the generally accepted diagnosis today) (255)—it threw the country into agitation too, with party alignments splitting both the politicians and the Royal Family itself. Lady Malmesbury told her sister Lady Minto that 'everybody has behaved well, even Opposition'. Lady Holland reported that 'Opposition declare he is as mad as the winds'. Malmesbury thought the Duke of York 'was himself, as usual, all kindness, right-headedness, and uprightness', and the behaviour of the Prince of Wales 'right and proper'. Mrs Harcourt disagreed: the Prince's behaviour, she thought, was very bad; he always went at a time he was sure he could not see the King and then complained of being slighted. The Queen held a Drawing Room on 26 March 'and looked like Death, and all the princesses crying and the pictures of Despair'. (256)

With the spring ('a sweet westerly wind, a beautiful sun, all the thorns and elms just budding, and the nightingales just beginning to sing', wrote Fox to his nephew Lord Holland from his country estate in mid-April) the crisis had passed.

The Duke of Kent spent a busy summer, travelling between London, Kew, Windsor and Castle Hill Lodge, his estate at Ealing, through a countryside perfumed with honeysuckle, bright with laburnum, 'the thorns like enormous periwigs'. At the Lodge, standing in about thirty acres of parkland on Castle Bear Hill, with extensive views of the surrounding countryside, Madame was to be the chatelaine, with the exception of one year only, for the next sixteen years.

The house was simple in style, a neo-classical building with shallow wings abutting at either end, seven french windows opening from the main front on to tree-shaded lawns, and four Ionic columns supporting the triangular pediment of a tall portico in the centre. The carriage drive entering between handsome park lodges passed through pleasure grounds, plantations, lawns and shrubberies to the garden entrance and a central hall measuring thirty feet by seventeen, from which the Grand Staircase rose to the upper floors. To the left were a morning room (twenty-four feet by seventeen), a library, a dressing room and withdrawing room. On the right was a spacious breakfast parlour and the great oval dining room, forty-four feet by eighteen, beyond which one passed through folding doors into a thirty-foot music room and a billiard room almost the same size. From the billiard room one could step directly into the pleasure grounds.

On the upper floor was another library, a drawing room and state bedroom, with folding doors between each that could be opened up across the whole hundred-foot frontage of the house. Strategically placed stoves with flues for hot air warmed the building, and all main rooms had marble chimney pieces, some beautifully carved and decorated. The doors were of Spanish mahogany. East and west wings held a series of bedrooms with dressing rooms and closets, a boudoir and dressing room adjoining the state bedroom. This floor was equipped with six Patent Water Closets.

Beneath the house arched vaults and cellars held coal, beer and ale, a dairy house and well-house. A fire-engine house was a necessary safeguard. The stable and coach yard accommodated ten carriages and apartments for coachmen, grooms, postillions and yard boys. Extensive domestic living and working apartments for the staff were in the main building. Sitting and sleeping rooms for outdoor staff were in separate buildings, together with the various workshops, sheds, washhouse, ice house and other necessary amenities. A farmyard and two walled kitchen gardens planted with fruit trees formed the practical part of the gardens.

Here, for at least six months every year, the Duke of Kent lived as a country squire, with his still-enchanting French lady as gracious hostess to his guests. (257)

He had had to steer a somewhat tricky course during his father's illness, unwilling to break the bond that held him closely to the Prince of Wales, yet concerned about his father, of whom he was also fond as well as somewhat in awe. The Duke of York remained his father's favourite son, and acted this time (as he had not done in 1788) with careful discretion.

During the period when the Prince of Wales had little contact with his father, his brother of Kent kept him informed about the King's progress and anything that would be of special interest to him. The duke had been acting for a second time as a go-between for his eldest brother with a lady, but this time it was the Prince's detested wife the Princess Caroline. In several letters to his brother (for which the Prince of Wales wrote to thank his 'dearest Edward') he explained what he had done to help arrange a reform of the Princess's expenditure. He persuaded her to several reductions, in staff, in entertainment, and (ironically, in view of his perpetual difficulty in curbing his own exuberant projects) in alterations and repairs to buildings.

In August he went to Weymouth again to join the Royal Family, and enjoyed the welcome he received ('Edward arrived Wedy. morning which I was very glad of', wrote his youngest sister Princess Amelia to the Prince of Wales): but he tried to get out of going to Brighton because of Madame. 'You know . . . how I feel upon the subject of all absences from home, situated as I am. Indeed you were kind enough to express your approbation of my sentiments on that point . . . Therefore as it is really essential to my comfort to be otherwise as little from home as is practicable, I trust if you can make it convenient to yourself to see me at Carlton House, you will dispense with my going to Brighton.' (258)

'Situated as I am' meant his inability to take Madame with him at such times. He did, however, go to Brighton at the end of October, when an arrangement was made for several of the royal brothers to celebrate his birthday on 2 November with a dinner at Castle Hill Lodge. Back at Ealing, however, he found that Madame, in a lovingly arranged surprise for him, had invited 'sixteen or eighteen of our old American acquaintance'. In a fluster, she tried to put off the guests, but the duke, sure that his brother would not wish this, suggested that he come on the following Friday instead, 'on which day Frederic has been for some time past engaged to dine here'. The American guests, he thought, would be embarrassed in the presence of the Prince of Wales, though 'had *you* proposed to come *alone* over on Monday I should not have thought it necessary, from the knowledge I have of your affability and readiness to accommodate yourself to *any* company, to have made any alteration'. He felt, however, it would be unkind to subject a group of innocent colonials to 'the remarks of either Frederic, William or Ernest' on account of their sarcastic dispositions. (259)

At the end of May, the duke's leave of absence was extended for another year. Meantime he busily wrote letters to officials in England and North America on behalf of protégés (not always successfully but very willingly); to his friends in North America, notably the de Sala-berrys; to government, pleading for relief from the debts incurred by his heavy losses at sea from storm and enemy action. (In 1806 he would write a total of 3,850 letters, and estimated a total of 4,500 for 1807.) A typical kindness was one he extended to a Negro servant in 1803, who 'was my servant in the West Indies when he joined me spontaneously the day I landed in Guadaloupe, and a more faithful or cleverer attendant upon a single Gentleman without a family I never met with'. He had served the duke in Halifax until it became apparent that discrimination by the other servants was troubling him. 'Were I in your place, I would take him as a Serjeant at once', wrote the duke to the colonel of a regiment shortly to go to Canada. (260)

In Canada, Milnes had fallen out with Osgoode, who, wrote Milnes to John King (King must have been the repository of more confidential gossip than almost anybody else of his day), 'from the first moment of my coming here has wished to govern and act independently of me . . . I have formed a very indifferent opinion of him as a public man, he is vindictive, passionate and rarely or ever allows his judgment fair play and holds himself up as the only man in the Province who has honour or honesty.' (261) Osgoode had been involved in controversy with Milnes' predecessor, Prescott, as well. The rift was too deep to mend. Osgoode was pensioned off, and James Monk, with the duke's support, was appointed Chief Justice of Lower Canada

In Europe the youngest of Madame's brothers, Jean-Claude, had married Louise Antoinette Russier, a twenty-six-year-old Calvinist, born at Rolle in Switzerland, and now began a restless wandering that would keep him moving from city to city in Europe and from house to house in Geneva for the next thirty years. Their first child, Louise Sophie, was born in Prussia some time in 1801. Jean-Claude would be a problem brother to Madame, always in need of financial assistance, and never turning to his kind-hearted sister in vain.

On 21 August the Duke of Kent had been appointed Colonel of the Royals (1st Regiment of Foot), and though he regretted severing his thirteen-year association with the Royal Fusiliers, he told the Prince of Wales 'it is flattering at any time to receive a public mark of the King's favor, & considering it in that light, I thought I could not decline the offer then made me, although it almost broke my heart at the time.' (262)

The war with France had been dragging on with only a few brilliant flashes of victory to lighten the gloom, and except for Sir Ralph Abercromby's defeat of the French in Egypt in March, all naval ones. While London had been whispering anxiously about what might be happening to the King and trying to read between the lines of official bulletins, Nelson outside Copenhagen was exercising his right to be blind. 'I really do not see the signal,' he said just before two o'clock on 2 April, and started a battle that cleared the Baltic for the British and lit joyful lights in London again. If no British soldier stood on the soil of Europe, at least the Union Jack flew proudly over the oceans.

But Napoleon (the Monster, the royal princesses called him), who had made Europe a French stronghold, and now named himself First Consul, was busy cleaning up the administration, consolidating what

he held, and making enough mysterious bustle on the Channel coast
to give another case of invasion jitters to the people of England.
Thomas Aston Coffin, in England as controller of public accounts to
the forces in North America and badly wanting to visit his family in
Boston, wrote that though the Duke of Kent's permission had been
very civilly granted, they were expecting invasion at any moment, and
'to quit the Country at this moment would look like running away'.
(263) Nelson went into the Channel and had a try at tempting the
French vessels out of Boulogne, without success, but he discovered
that French invasion preparations were not yet a threat.

On 1 October, peace preliminaries between Britain and France were
signed. They were to drag on for six months before the shaky Treaty
of Amiens was signed, and William Cobbett, now editor of *The
Porcupine,* wrote disgustedly to Windham : 'The Duke of Kent, and
the Prince, and all the younger princes, are shocked at the terms of
this abominable peace.' (264)

Troops from the victorious Army of Egypt and from Malta were
arriving in Gibraltar, reported General O'Hara, who had returned to
the Rock as Governor in 1795 after two years of imprisonment in the
Luxembourg. He was just beginning six months of painful dying from
old wounds that kept breaking out, and the duke saw an opportunity
for service again. On 20 March 1802 the Prince of Wales wrote to
the Duke of York: 'The Duke of Kent has just call'd upon me, &
acquainted me that O'Harra's Aid de Camp is just arriv'd with the
accounts of my poor old friend's death, which I confess I am very sorry
for, & Edward desires me at the same time to mention to you how
anxious he is to succeed o'Harra in the Government of Gibraltar.
You best know how far this is an arrangement that can take place;
all I can say is that I shall ever truly participate in anything that can
afford him satisfaction.' (265)

The Duke of York, replying from Bath and feeling affable (he had
just sold his house in Piccadilly) agreed to place his brother's wishes
before the King and trusted they would be gratified.

He was not so affable ten days later, after the duke had received
the appointment, arising from what seems to have been an almost
inevitable failure of understanding and communication between these
two brothers. The Duke of Kent, who had evidently asked for a short
postponement of his departure for Gibraltar in order to settle some
urgent personal affairs, was scornfully reprimanded in a caustic letter
from the Commander-in-Chief, who expressed surprise that a 'paultry
private inconvenience would have been laid hold of, as an excuse to
procrastinate your stay in this country'. (266)

In view of the number of appointments held by absentee officers, the Duke of Kent's request for delay seems to have deserved a politer refusal. His reply was dignified and placating.

'The moment I read the footing upon which you urged my earlier departure, I mean, that the good of the King's service and the state of the place where I am to command rendered it indispensably necessary, I felt it a point of honor to set aside every *other* consideration and to sacrifice *everything* to *that* object, satisfied that at a future day it will *not* be forgot that I had done so at a time when everything combined to render a hurried move from home peculiarly hard and oppressive to me. As such I shall make a point *now* of leaving London by the 17th of April. . . .

'As the feelings of men differ, I am willing to suppose some of the expressions in your letter that were very poignant to mine, were not meant to be so, and therefore I will not allow myself any observation upon them, except just to notice that you wrong me essentially if you conceive I ever sought a subterfuge to delay my departure.'

Friends who knew of his pecuniary difficulties, due to losses while serving abroad, he said, could vouch for the sacrifice he would make in hastening his departure at this time. (267)

At the time of the duke's departure, the King is reported to have said : 'Now, sir, when you go to Gibraltar, do not make such a trade of it as you did when you went to Halifax.' The report comes to us at several removes from its source, in the account by John Adolphus of Lady Charlotte Douglas's record of a remark made by the Princess of Wales some years earlier. One may ask how the not notably truthful Princess happened to hear of the King's remark in the first place, and to mention it to the not notably truthful Lady Douglas, whose other evidence at the time was totally discredited. It is hardly likely that the duke confided such a comment to her, equally unlikely that she was present when the King spoke to his son. But this reproof has become another label of fussy incompetence hung on the Duke of Kent, unquestioned, by posterity. (268)

Down in Falmouth the artificers and painters were busy fitting up the cabins and sprucing the ship for reception of the Duke of Kent and suite. On Tuesday, 27 April, on a breezy day under flying clouds, sailed for Gibraltar his Majesty's ship *Isis*, Captain Thomas Masterman Hardy. With the duke, as usual, went his dear and faithful companion who had shared his life 'in all climates, and in all difficulties', Thérèse-Bernardine Mongenet, Madame de St Laurent.

CHAPTER TWELVE

Disaster at Gibraltar

'"I consider it my duty"—thus wrote the Duke of York, then Commander-in-Chief, date 21st of April, 1802—"on your assuming the command of the garrison at Gibraltar, to make your Royal Highness aware that much exertion will be necessary to establish *a due degree of discipline* AMONG THE TROOPS; and which, I trust, you will be able gradually to accomplish by a moderate exercise of the power vested in you."'

The duke received another and more detailed instruction from his brother. '"It is essential that your Royal Highness should be made aware, previous to your assuming the command at Gibraltar, that too great a proportion of the garrison has been usually employed on duties of fatigue; that, in consequence, discipline has been relaxed, and drunkenness promoted; that it will be the *duty* of your Royal Highness to *exact* the most minute attention to all His Majesty's regulations for disciplining, arming, clothing, and appointing of the army, from *all* of which not the most trifling deviation can be allowed."' (269)

It must have been with poignant memories that the duke and Madame saw the towering mass of the Rock lie against the sky as *Isis* came into Gibraltar Bay on 10 May, almost eleven years to the day since their embarkation for departure in 1791. 'After having served thirteen consecutive years in all the English colonies where we have troops except India, and having crossed the Atlantic ocean seven times, I find myself here through a singular sequence of events, in command of this famous place where I began to learn the rudiments of English military service in 1790', he would write in November, reviving a correspondence with a friend of his Geneva days, François-Auguste-Maurice de Vasserot, baron de Vincy, (270)

The royal salutes and the ceremonial welcome were the same as in 1790, but this time there was the added tribute of deference to the top-ranking officer of the garrison. There was also, as it turned out, a resentful muttering and apprehension stirring among the officers and men, who had heard of the duke's severity and strictness and did not relish curtailment of their free and easy habits. But in the first few months, the royal commander had little thought of serious trouble.

He had been appalled by the state of the garrison and the town. Only a few months earlier, another visitor had been equally critical, and would publish his comments early in 1803. 'If water be scarce, wine, on the other hand, is in such abundance, and so cheap, that in no part of the world exists such repeated scenes of intoxication. It is indeed distressing to see whole bands of soldiers and sailors literally lying in the streets in the most degrading state of inebriety. Drunkenness is no crime in the garrison, except in those who are on duty, and every man coming off a working party is ordered to be paid eightpence on the spot, which he immediately proceeds to spend in a kind of bad wine, called black-strap. Houses for the sale of this pernicious liquor are found at every step, and furnish no small part of the revenue.' (271)

Major-General Barnett, second-in-command, had been disturbed by the general slovenliness of the soldiers even before the arrival of the duke. Orders such as 'in future the Sentries are not to be allowed to Dine on their Posts,' and criticism of the 'very slovenly custom/that had/crept into the Garrison of Officers appearing without powder on their hair', seems to indicate a level of discipline well calculated to shock a military commander far less particular than the Duke of Kent. (272) Soldiers—officers and men alike—stationed at the garrison of Gibraltar probably faced more hardship and boredom than at any other station. Space was restricted, rations were short, little entertainment could be found. The Garrison Library offered some occupation to officers, but not to the men; and many of these had come direct to the Rock from the war in Egypt 'covered with their glorious and well-earned laurels . . . six months in arrear of pay'. With nowhere to go and nothing to do, the only fun to be had was to get drunk, and on bad liquor at that.

Even with the excuses of boredom, restraints and discomfort, this was no way for soldiers to behave. For two weeks his Royal Highness did nothing but observe the behaviour of the garrison with mounting disgust and dismay. The narrow, twisting, sharply rising streets were unsafe for civilians, especially women, and especially at night. The rape of two Spanish lady visitors who had been admiring the scene in the Bay was the trigger for action.

L

Seeing drunkenness as a major cause of the laxity and riotous behaviour, the duke first closed thirty, and later twenty more of the ninety wine-houses, mostly the ones in back alleys and near the barracks. He set up a regimental canteen for every corps, where (strictly for cash) non-commissioned officers and privates could purchase, at specified times, wine, malt-liquor, cider and beer, unadulterated and at a controlled price. All but three taverns in the town were declared out of bounds, and a brewery was established at Europa Point.

The reforms instituted were sensible and practical (also injurious to the duke himself, as he cut off much of the revenue from wine-house licences, hitherto a large part of the governor's income). Civil reforms regulated and licensed carters, porters, and boats for hire, licensed and set standards for bakers, ordered control of hawkers and pedlars, and were gratefully received by the harassed citizens of Gibraltar.

The duke had always believed that idleness bred mischief, that busy men would be happier and healthier. He began tightening the military routine of both officers and men, regulating work-hours and duties, insisting on immaculate appearance, neatly shaved faces, neatly cut hair, clean uniforms, regular drill and exercise. ' "The officers were taken from backgammon to manoeuvre their companies; from making bar-points to points of duty; from entering men, to drilling them . . . they were called from surrounding the hollow square of a billiard table, to learn the formation of one in the field; they were withdrawn from knocking about *red* balls, to be taught how to direct hot balls; from making a cannon to using one . . . there was some difference in the occupations, doubtless; but it was incumbent on the Governor to point it out; and it was the duty of the officers to obey him." ' (273)

Drill and manoeuvres had fallen off so badly that the officers were often at a loss to know the correct moves and orders. The duke ordered some of them to take drill practice, and took personal command of many of the parades of his own regiment. It is easy to understand (though not to excuse) the seething resentment that bubbled below the surface among officers made to work, men made to keep sober, and wine-sellers deprived of their customers.

The first case on which the duke was required to pass sentence as governor has been quoted as an example of his cruelty. Two Spaniards found guilty of stealing goods worth £500 were sentenced to hang. The thieves had been traced to Algeciras across the Bay, 'taken up by the Orders of the Spanish Governor', and returned to Gibraltar. The Deputy Judge Advocate, Edmund Nugent, presided over the trial by jury (six Protestants, six Catholics, the latter all Spaniards) at which complete evidence, with witnesses carefully examined, was presented.

After the address from the Bench, his Royal Highness concluded a short speech by saying : 'It can hardly be necessary for me to add any thing to/the judge's/Statement, except that, if you shall see the smallest reason whatever for doubt or hesitation, as to the sufficiency of the Proofs in support of the Indictment, you are to recollect that you ought to lean to the *Side of Mercy*.' The jury took half an hour to return a verdict of *Guilty*. The sentence passed by the duke was mandatory in view of the verdict. (Theft of as little as five shillings in specific circumstances was punishable by death in England at that time.)

In the subsequent trial of the receiver of the stolen goods (who, recommended to mercy, was eventually exiled from Gibraltar) the duke stated the principle that guided him in every similar situation : 'that, though he must then proceed to pass the sentence of the Law, it would be afterwards considered how far it could be mitigated.' (274)

There is no record to tell how Thérèse-Bernardine filled her days during this year at Gibraltar. She was, as always, with her prince. He sent her best wishes to the Prince of Wales in a letter dated only a month after his arrival, and frequently mentioned her in later ones. One has only imagination to call on to see her happily chatelaine of the spacious and airy residence of the governor known as the Convent, a fifteenth-century Franciscan monastery with cool inner courtyard and wide windows overlooking the high-walled garden. Here on smooth lawns, under the shade of pepper trees, palm trees, orange trees, and among bright tropical flowers, she would work or entertain her friends. As well as correspondence, her embroidery and the constant task of making her own clothes would occupy much time. There would be the intimate dinner parties the duke enjoyed so much, at which she would play her part, musical interludes for his pleasure and delight, when he would join her with his pleasant voice, and quiet games of whist when he could find time from the work that sometimes kept him busy for seventeen hours at a stretch.

Along with his work, there were diversions. Formal visits were exchanged with the officers of the Spanish camp at St Roch [San Roque], formal dinners were held, attended by the commanding officers of the English, Portuguese and American squadrons in the Bay. The duke was proud to be patron and protector of the Garrison Library. He sent presents home to the Prince of Wales : some wine, a Spanish horse. Less than a week after his arrival the *Mermaid* frigate had brought his brother Augustus, Duke of Sussex, for a month-long visit from Lisbon, where he had been living for reasons of health (he suffered from asthma). This prince had been worrying his family and the government by rumours that he was proposing to join the Roman

Catholic Church. His elder brother, with his usual amiable willingness to straighten out family problems (he has been accused of meddling too much in personal affairs, and perhaps out of good will he did, though as his aid was so often sought by request, the accusation loses some force) was able to reassure the Prince of Wales that the young man had no such intention. The monks who visited him were a medical man and a music teacher; and his visits to the Catholic church, he explained, were to meet a lady barred from receiving him in her own house during Lent.

It was now that the duke resumed his friendship with the baron de Vincy, a correspondence that would last until his death. The baron, fallen on unfortunate days, had evidently sought advice and help from his friend, for the duke, after expressing his delight in hearing of the baron's continued existence, suggested in his letter of 3 November that he might be able to find a place for him in de Rolle's regiment just arrived on the Rock from Egypt. He then gave the baron a summary of his life since their last meeting, adding that de Vincy would probably not recognize him now, 'as first of all I have lost nearly all my hair, and then I am heavier by nearly a third'.

Among the letters that survive in this collection, the first one to mention Madame is dated 22 December 1816, in which the duke wrote that the pleasure of the simple life he was then living was increased 'with the help of a very respectable and pleasant companion with whom my liaison has lasted for more than twenty-six years, and who has shared all my long and trying voyages, which from 1790 to 1803 were of no small importance'. It is clear from this statement that the baron had never met Madame in the Geneva days shared by the two young men.

Ironically, only two weeks before the mutiny that broke out at the end of December, the duke had written a cheerful letter to his friend Coutts, thanking him for passing on 'the favourable accounts you have heard from various quarters of my efforts to put matters into some sort of decent order here'. It was particularly flattering, he had said, 'as it has ever been my ambition by the faithful and diligent discharge of my duty, in every station in which I have been placed, to merit the good opinion of my friends.' He was even daring to hope that the frightful burden of his debts might at last be rolled away, so that he would no longer be forced to live on less than half his actual income. If only Ministers would grant him an allowance (and in due course make up for his losses at sea) to replace the revenue sacrificed by his attack on liquor sales, so that he could live without touching his parliamentary income, 'I shall be able to return home next spring two years, without owing a shilling to any man.' Madame, he added, desired to thank Mr Coutts for his kind remembrances. (275)

In this happy state of optimism, confident that he was doing a good job, with evidence around him of safer streets, satisfied citizens, better-regulated commerce, healthier soldiers, more disciplined military order, the Duke of Kent was now to see his future demolished before his eyes, though at the time he could have had no premonition of the length of the shadow this second Christmas mutiny would cast.

On 3 January 1803, when the tumult was subdued and control once again established, an observer—Captain Charles Sidney Davers, senior officer of his Majesty's ships and vessels at Gibraltar—sat down at his table in the privacy of his cabin on board *Active* and penned a shocked account of the uprising to the Secretary of the Admiralty, Sir Evan Nepean.

'On the night of the 24th Decr a very serious & disgraceful Mutiny broke out in the Garrison of Gibraltar—at 7 o'clock on the evening of the 24th the Royals or 1st Regt of Foot broke from their Barracks and assembled before the Doors of His Royal Highness the Duke of Kent's House with arms loaded and bayonets fixed demanding His Royal Highness's Person and using much threatening and abusive language, saying that they had been used worse than Slaves & would no longer bear it, and that they insisted on his embarking on board ship & leaving the Garrison. The other Regts were immediately got under arms apparently disposed to support His Royal Highness & the Artillery with two six Pounders marched down to the Duke of Kent's House and placed themselves between it and the Royals, on which General Barnett came down to the Royals & after an hour's conversation with them & entreating them to return to their Barracks with promise of redress for all grievances they might have, they at length marched off, on their way home about 150 filed off for the 54th Regt's Barracks at the South, hoping they would join in the Mutiny, & on their arrival there demanded the question, on which the Grenadiers of that Regt fired and wounded 5 of the Royals, the rest then returned to their Barracks & that night passed quiet. The next day great discontent was manifest through the Garrison, but nothing publicly appeared till the 26th when at 9 o'clock on that evening part of the 25th Regt broke from their Barracks with their arms loaded & bayonets fixed, & marched for the Royals Barracks, but on their arrival were disappointed, as the Royals refused to act with them, and declared they would support His Royal Highness, as they had no longer any grievance. The 25th then marched for the Duke of Kent's House, & were met by a party of Artillery, who finding the 25th determined to persevere were ordered to fire, when 2 men of the 25th and one of the Royals were killed and 6 of the 25th wounded, the

man of the Royals was killed by accident & was in the act of assisting
to repel the 25th, on the Artillery firing the 25th returned to their
Barracks and were tolerably quiet during the night, but on the
morning of the 27th they again turned out in their Barrack yard under
arms without orders, but were soon persuaded to lay them down when
fourteen of the Regt were selected and are now on trial by a General
Court Martial, from every information that can be obtained the soldiers
in general (except the Artillery) conceived their duty more severe than
necessary, & their chief intention of thus breaking into open rebellion,
was to oblige His Royal Highness to be less severe; all the Regts at
present appear well satisfied except the 25th who I understand threaten
much if those men on trial should be executed.' (276)

   The mutiny, which called him from the dinner table on Christmas
Eve and stirred up the Rock like a stick in an ant-hill, shook the duke
to the roots of his self-esteem. At no time did he question the rightness
of his policy : but for a painful moment he looked inwards, asking
himself whether his own personality could be somehow at fault. There
had been men as strict and severe as he. Why were they followed and
beloved when the Duke of Kent's men rose up in a riotous rabble?
In a dejected letter to his favourite brother the Prince of Wales, whose
good opinion he valued above all others, some of his self-doubt
appeared, and a sense of injustice that his careful and devoted labours
to bring the garrison back from licentious insubordination should be
thus rewarded. He had need of Madame's loving sympathy at this
time. What endless hours of self-examination, self-recrimination she
must have soothed, over 'those events that have almost broken my
heart . . . the most cruel I ever yet experienced . . . the dreary gloomy
scene which this place must now ever be to me. . . .'
   He asked his brother the Prince of Wales to intercede for a leave of
absence, to start only after he had been given a few months to recover
lost ground—if the officers 'will with cordiality and zeal *now* support
me'—so that he could with pride 'deliver my trust up into the hands
of some abler and more *popular* man than myself'. (277) To the Duke
of York, as Commander-in-Chief, he sent a long account, differing
from that of Captain Davers only in small details. This he entrusted
to his secretary, Captain Thomas Dodd, who embarked on the sloop
of war *Cynthia*, but was delayed by a month's unprecedented wind
and storm, which on 10 January blew some fourteen ships ashore.
Dodd sailed at last on 31 January. He returned on 16 March with a
peremptory order, not for leave of absence, but for recall to England,
'upon the consideration', wrote Lord Pelham, the Home Secretary,
to the Duke of York, under command of the King, 'that it might be

desirable that the different departments of His Majesty's Government at home should have the advantage of some personal communication with His Royal Highness, upon the recent events in Gibraltar'. (278)

The mutiny had been followed by courts-martial of the ringleaders from the 25th Regiment. The Royals, who had refused to enter into the second riot, saying they now had no grievances, were let off with a severe lecture on the intercession of General Barnett and in view of their wounded and killed : though the duke felt strongly that the Royals, who had coldly planned a mutiny, were far more guilty than the 25th, whose outbreak had been caused by drunkenness. (Three wine-sellers who had been supplying free liquor in order to inflame the discontent were imprisoned as a result.)

Thirteen mutineers were court-martialled. Eleven were sentenced to be shot, the other two to receive a thousand lashes. Of the eleven, only three were actually executed. The remaining eight were respited 'until His Majesty shall be pleased to signify his commands respecting them'.

On Tuesday, 4 January, the three under sentence of death were executed in the manner set down by regulation. At eight o'clock the garrison under arms marched without drums or music to the Grand Parade. The firing party of twenty privates chosen by lot from the regiment of the convicted men, with a subaltern, two sergeants and two corporals, escorted the prisoners to the place of execution, and carried out the sentence with the usual awful solemnity. The duke, apparently, did not attend. In General Order No. 1 for this day, he called the attention of the men 'to the crimes which brought these men to their untimely fate,' and warned them 'to prove . . . that they are sincerely penitent for the past and determined to prove the sincerity of their contrition (the appearance of which during their attendance at the execution this morning Major-General Barnett has reported to His Royal Highness)'. (279)

A soldier of the 25th Regiment is said to have made a witnessed statement two years later attesting his knowledge of the involvement of garrison officers in originating the mutiny. 'The mutiny was formed, and conducted by the officers of the garrison . . . of the first rank . . . A committee was form'd, for the payment of those more immediately active . . ./the ringleaders/attended this committee, and received money from them.' Henry Salisbury, on board the 'Dedam Prison-ship, Medenia river, Isle of Wight' [sic] signed a document with this information on 26 November 1804 'in the presence of three Gentlemen, who are alive, two are officers now serving/the King/, and the third a surgeon in/his/service'. There is no reason to doubt that such a statement was made. But Salisbury was not one of the mutineers tried in January 1803, nor was Francis Fell, who with Isaac Seville and

Peter Clarke [*sic*] was mentioned in the body of the confession. (280)

Two of the men who were shot were Dutch: the third was Irish. 'It appears clearly', the *Morning Chronicle* of 29 January reported, its Gibraltar correspondent writing with great satisfaction on the 3rd, 'that the whole of the late mischief and disturbances, both in the Royals and 25th regiment, originated solely in the foreigners and drafts, none of the old soldiers having been at all accessary [*sic*] to the business.'

Five months later, Garrison General Orders (26 May) contained the copy of a letter from the Judge Advocate General, confirming that the remaining eight executions had been respited to transportation for life. In addition, the two sentences of flogging were remitted, and the men transferred to a regiment stationed in Africa.

The garrison may have resented the duke's discipline, but army officers are expected to behave with military obedience and dignity, and men in the ranks are expected to follow orders and keep out of mischief. The officers at Gibraltar, following the example apparently set by General Barnett, 'were very unguarded in their terms of displeasure, and even at their messes enveighed against the orders. Some of the Captains who had been twenty years in the service were the most loud in their invectives, and the smallest reflection must therefore point out the natural consequences that would follow. The waiters at the messes hearing their Officers loudly blaming and enveighing against the new system, communicated the same to their comrades in the barracks at night. The opinion of the Officers too much coincided with that of the men, and thus engendered the hydra that made its appearance at the ensuing Christmas holidays, and stifled all the fine feelings and characteristic greatness and attachment of the British soldiery at Gibraltar.' (281)

This was the opinion of Major-General David Douglas Wemyss, who had been Deputy-Lieutenant-Governor at Gibraltar just before the duke's arrival and remained there until about two months before the mutiny occurred. Afterwards the duke was to be accused of carrying out the reforms (a duty he had been specifically ordered to undertake) with too great haste. Since the mutiny did not occur until almost eight months after he had taken up his command, it may be permitted to ask how long he should have gentled the offenders and allowed them to set their own standards of behaviour in the garrison. General Wemyss, with first-hand knowledge of the situation, had no criticism of the methods the duke used, nor of his timing.

He laid himself open to criticism under other headings, however, though not justifying the severity of the reaction at home. He now proceeded to busy himself with preparation of the Code of Orders for the garrison, which he worked out in such minute and finicky detail that even his friends were dismayed. His secretary, Captain Richard Wright, took the liberty of writing him a letter 'equally painful for me to write, as it probably will be for your Royal Highness to read'. At a time when, as he said, the utmost prudence should guard against offering his enemies a pretext to justify their behaviour, it could be fatal to issue a work that needed much more time for revision before publication. The implication would be, he felt, that time spent on such minute details had been at the cost of attention to more important matters: worse, some of the orders would be interpreted as far more severe than they were in actual practice. Respectfully, though with urgency, Wright begged his Royal Highness to reconsider.

He then sat down next day—in a further effort to justify his royal commander, for whom it is evident he had a strong attachment and respect—and sent off a heartfelt plea to William Cobbett, whose *Political Register* had now been running for a year. The volatile and outspoken Cobbett had met the duke in Halifax early in June 1800 on his way back to England from the United States. Wright was deeply concerned for the duke's reputation, which he knew did not deserve the condemnation it was receiving, and beyond that, for the fatal effects any discredit of his policies could have 'on the discipline of the British Army, the safety of our colonies, and even on the fate of the Royal Family itself'. He explained with urgent sincerity the real cause of the mutiny—the discontent of men in a crowded space denied the decencies of living, the disappointment of victorious troops denied their expected return to England, the permissiveness of the former governor, O'Hara, with its resultant licence and excesses which had taken firm root in the garrison, and the prejudice fostered against the duke before his arrival by those who knew they would be checked in their free and easy régime.

Wright gave facts and figures to support the improvement effected by his Royal Highness. The annual deaths had averaged 140 over the last six years: in the six months just past there had been only thirteen. Even the number of punishments had been reduced by fifty per cent.

Wright could speak with authority of the officers' failure to support the duke. 'His Royal Highness has been accused of severity; we on the contrary condemn him for a mistaken lenity in not making a severe example of some of those Officers who were most forward and active in opposing his measures and censuring him & his orders.' He was appalled, continued Wright, by a situation in which an officer specifically sent to restore order in an unruly garrison, who quelled a mutiny attempted by opponents of his efforts, and who accomplished his mission by a complete restoration of order and tranquillity, should be immediately recalled to answer for his actions.

'With regard to his Royal Highness's conduct as Civil Governor of Gibraltar', he concluded, 'let enquiry be made of every merchant in the city who trades to Gibraltar what their correspondents there say of his conduct to the inhabitants.' The citizens of Gibraltar, almost as one man, gathered spontaneously to present a reassuring address to the duke on 1 January, expressing their respect and satisfaction with his régime and gratitude for restoring order to their streets and safety to their persons. In fact, a second address had to be prepared (it was presented on 6 January) at the request of most of the Roman Catholics at Gibraltar, who had not had an opportunity to subscribe to the first one: and 1,200 guineas (reported Wright) were collected in only a few hours 'to present him with a diamond star as a small parting tribute of the universal affection and admiration they felt for his character and person, and the services he had rendered them'. (282)

[The 'star' was eventually delivered to the duke in the form of a piece of plate and a Garter, as Dodd explained in a letter of thanks to the Committee dated 8 July 1803 and published in the *Gibraltar Chronicle*. 'As HIS MAJESTY, in token of approbation of HIS ROYAL HIGHNESS'S Conduct, had graciously presented him with a handsome George, and the Inhabitants of Halifax with a Star, I thought I could not do better than to add, from those of Gibraltar, the Garter to complete the insignia of that Order.'] (283)

By the time Wright's letter to Cobbett reached London, carried by Captain Dodd, the public furore had died down, and Dodd decided not to arrange its publication. But press reaction, when the news of the mutiny first reached London at the end of January, was in general favourable to the duke. The *True Briton* of 20 January—five days before the mutiny story broke in its columns—had, in fact, published a report from Gibraltar containing Wright's statistics about improved health and fewer deaths. 'Such are the effects of regularity and discipline, and a proper attention to the health of the troops, which, indeed, has always been a most conspicuous trait in the conduct of His Royal Highness the Duke of Kent, wherever he has commanded.' Afterwards (25 January) the *Morning Post* wrote editorially: 'It is ever the fate of those who enforce strict duty to be calumniated as oppressors, but bold and honest men are not to be deterred by slander. No man has been more calumniated than Earl ST. VINCENT for the strictness with which he has enforced duty in the navy. Had every other officer been equally attentive, we should have heard of none of those mutinies which alarmed the country and disgraced our fleets.'

If the duke had had the support of the government, and especially the Duke of York, he might have survived the calumny as Earl St Vincent did. St Vincent, indeed, was one of those who defended him. And as late as July the following year some small balm came from General Harcourt, to whom the duke sent thanks for compliments on the appearance of his men. 'While there are officers of experience and judgment like yourself who have the goodness to express their opinion of my humble though zealous endeavours in a manner so gratifying and consoling to my wounded feelings I am sure whatever my thoughts may be I ought not to complain.' (284)

Sir William Fawcett, the adjutant-general, also complimented the duke on his Code of Orders. It was the government, and particularly his brother the Duke of York, who remained hostile, adamant, and unapproachable.

CHAPTER THIRTEEN

Into the Wilderness

The *Amazon* frigate, Captain William Parker (a nephew of Lord St Vincent), came expeditiously out from England and arrived at Gibraltar mid-March 1803, with a returning Captain Dodd and the letters that ordered the Duke of Kent home. He was to resign his command to Major-General Barnett until the arrival of the Lieutenant-Governor, Sir Thomas Trigge.

Insult to injury. Having calmed the garrison, the duke had no intention of handing over until his successor and subordinate could see it in the state of perfection to which he had brought it. So when Trigge came into the bay, he was astounded (and, it seemed, affronted) to see the Royal Standard flying, indicating that his Royal Highness was still very much in command.

The duke received him 'very graciously', paraded the troops in succession, and explained what he had done and what he proposed doing.

'But I foresaw the impending evil', wrote Trigge darkly, and not a little treacherously, to John Sullivan, Under-Secretary of State for War, when a few days before his departure, the duke notified him of the code of standing orders he proposed to leave and wished enforced in every detail. 'This places me in no pleasant situation. I have not yet fully determined what I shall do : but before I had read many pages I had determined what I should not do, that is, that I should not attempt to enforce or execute the orders . . . I probably shall think it prudent in a very few days to annul or suspend some of the most obnoxious parts, lest by a longer delay what ought to appear as the effect of my own opinion and free choice might assume a less pleasant appearance. The colour that will be given this matter is that the discipline of the garrison has been for four months conducted on this system without difficulty or the appearance of discontent. *The orders may have been issued, but if ever it should be necessary, I believe I can make it appear that they have not been executed.* [Author's italics.] A bad state of things. I am myself fully persuaded that the quiet state and satisfied appearance of the Troops for some time past which the Duke will dwell upon, may be dated from the time he announced his intention of leaving the garrison. They now look with expectation and anxiety, but at the same time with more hope than fear, to the line I shall take; were I to announce an intention of rigidly enforcing the orders, the effects would soon be seen. If you should ever look at the code you will judge whether the execution of it can be attended with any advantage to compensate for the certain effect of producing discontent at least, if not disaffection in both Officers and men. In the difficult situation in which I am placed I am fortunate in having the cordial assistance and support of General Barnett, a very sensible zealous and active man. I have written this under the idea that you may be glad to know how things are. . . . After having more fully considered the matter, I believe I shall acquaint the Dukes of York and Kent with my proceedings. The first will I think approve; the second will become my enemy, to this there is no remedy.'

In November, under the prospect of receiving a home appointment he had asked for long ago, Trigge wrote to protest urgently that in the present circumstances 'it would very much hurt my feelings to be removed from this Command; and it would be a great discredit, if not considered as a disgrace by people in general'. (285) The public consequences to the Duke of Kent of his summary removal may have presented a horrid warning to Trigge.

Parker, *Amazon's* captain, had been very proud of his assignment, and the command of his 'charming ship'. Before leaving Spithead he had given his father a preconceived opinion of the Gibraltar situation and his views on discipline, especially as it applied on board ship. Though dispassionate, he tended at this time to be a bit critical of the duke.

'The garrison, reduced to the worst state of relaxation from inebriety while under the command of General O'Hara, wanted a reform; still the Duke of Kent has, I fear, been too violent, and wanted to bring about immediately what time and a regular system of discipline would have produced. I believe many of his regulations are tiresome and trifling, but his zeal was considerable.

'This unfortunate business, I understand, has been principally occasioned by some of the wretches whose liquor-houses he shut up (notwithstanding he thus deprived himself of his principal emolument), and, by distributing wine amongst the troops, and when inflamed with liquor, incited them to mischief . . . I admit my sentiments of discipline are strict, but in all cases of mutiny the ships behaved worst where the discipline was relaxed and the *officers courted popularity.*' (286)

The seven-week stay at Gibraltar gave the young captain of *Amazon* a chance to make an on-the-spot assessment, which began to veer strongly in the duke's favour. In April, to his mother: 'The late mutiny in this garrison has occasioned much commotion . . . However, I fear their behaviour was much aggravated by the imprudent and improper conduct of some of the officers, who did not cease to express their sentiments most fully at their mess tables, and sometimes honoured the Duke with most opprobrious epithets in the presence of their servants. This I mention confidentially, having, indeed, heard it from some of the disinterested officers of the garrison; but I believe the Duke of Kent is well aware he did not receive that support from the officers in suppressing the mutiny, that he must have been led to expect.'

There were to be many whose opinion coincided, and the duke had just cause to maintain for the rest of his life the grievances he frequently voiced. But no one with the authority to give redress ever took action. His departure from Gibraltar began the journey into a limbo of official rejection in which he would never be given an opportunity to clear his name.

After Trigge's arrival, Parker wrote:

'H.R.H. made a point of reviewing all the regiments before Sir Thomas, and showing him the whole garrison, that he might be convinced of the order in which everything was on his resigning the command. It certainly surpasses everything I have seen; and he has spared neither exertion or pains to accomplish it, attending to everything himself, and never in bed after 4 o'clock in the morning.

'I fear the string was wound up rather too tight; but nevertheless, his enemies have made the story much worse than it is; and he says, from the neglect of the officers, he was under the necessity of taking steps he would not otherwise have done; at all events, he reasons soundly; his disposition is the most perfect I ever met with. Nothing can put him out of temper or ruffle him, and I have witnessed some trying scenes, in which his forbearance was most conspicuous; by this means he never commits himself by any improper expression; and his most bitter enemies cannot accuse him of having ever been personally uncivil . . . His judgment is sound and good, and reckoned superior to that of most of the Royal Family; but he is wrapt up in his profession, which he studies night and day; and his maxim is, that nothing is well when it can be better. He is a most perfect gentleman, which demands of all his acquaintances the most perfect respect, and at the same time has a reserve about him which prevents the possibility of any one becoming familiar with him.'

An eloquent testimonial indeed from a man of good judgement and observation.

Though Parker seems to have discreetly avoided mention of Madame (almost everyone discreetly did not mention Madame), he must have enjoyed her company. The duke offered him the freedom of his table during his wait-over, and his account seems to indicate small intimate visits rather than formal dinner parties. 'I . . . availed myself of his offer whenever I was at liberty from the numerous invitations I received . . . and always found his table excessively pleasant. Our evenings were generally passed at Cassino.'

The duke had inspected *Amazon* on 19 March and explained his accommodation needs. 'He will embark with a large suite,' Parker confided to his mother, 'which (*entre nous*) occasions a long passage to be very irksome and inconvenient. I am, therefore, praying that we may be favoured with a wind.' Eight days took them to Lisbon and a visit to the Duke of Sussex after their 2 May departure from Gibraltar. The five-day visit was described by the observant Parker. 'His Highness of Sussex is as different a temper as possible, all gaiety and good humour, extremely affable, lives in the highest style . . . and indeed gives a hearty welcome to everybody, spending away money without *thinking out of whose pocket* it comes, and surrounded by a parcel of *sharks*, who are (unperceived by his openness of heart) eating him out of house and home. The Duke of Kent is as much his favourite as he is the Duke of Kent's. The family of the latter was uncommonly well arranged and neat; and I believe he cleared away some of his brother's gang for him on his arrival at Lisbon.'

From Lisbon, where Parker had been intrigued by fine mosaics in the churches, the climate, the opera and the pomp of local royalty, *Amazon* headed into twelve days of stormy weather. Meeting an American ship outside Lisbon, she 'fired three Musq' and two guns . . . to make her pay proper Respect to the Royal Standard'. On 25 May, she spoke a man-of-war which turned out to be HMS *Acasta,* and was told that the Peace of Amiens had ended and Britain was at war again. Two days later, in a heavy fall of rain, *Amazon* made Falmouth and the duke and Madame were home again.

Bursting with explanation and justification, the duke had come

home cut to the quick, but supremely confident that his day in court
would clear away the shadow hanging over him. He did not get
it. A first letter to his brother the Commander-in-Chief remained
unanswered, a second, a third. With mounting consternation the duke
began to understand the forces arrayed against him, to realize slowly
that he was not going to be allowed to give to his accusers his version
of the mutiny.

On 17 July he wrote direct to Lord Pelham, Secretary of State for
Home Affairs. Having vainly tried to obtain a hearing, he said, by
repeated letters to his brother, 'on the 29th ultimo, I received a letter
from the Duke of York informing me, that your Lordship not having
received any Commands from His Majesty upon the subject of my
letter of the 6th which had been laid before him, you had no enquiries
to trouble me with in your own Department'. He now had to try
another approach. 'Thus precluded from an opportunity I had been
anxiously seeking to vindicate my Character from that Stigma which
at present attaches to it in the Eyes of the World at large, in those of
my Profession, and more particularly of that part of it which compose
the Garrison of Gibraltar', he had naturally asked the Duke of York
which department of government might be willing to hear his defence.
On being informed that only the Home Department would be able
officially to discuss his problem, he now requested an interview with
Lord Pelham. (287)

His friends, angry, and muzzled because no court-martial would
allow them to speak, tried to help him. Major-General Wemyss, awaiting departure to take up a command in Ceylon, wished to appear as a
witness. Charles Greenwood, the duke's military agent, twice saw the
Duke of York to try to obtain a reversal of his implacable decision not to
let his brother be heard. The interview with Pelham on Saturday, 23
July, resulted in a promise to call the Cabinet, an arrangement first
postponed by what looked like Pelham's convenient indisposition, and
finally followed by an official communication from the new Home
Secretary, Charles Philip Yorke, that the Cabinet 'could not, consistent
with their duty, interfere in it at all'. (288)

Two subsequent interviews with the Duke of York (more than a
little heated despite the Duke of Kent's heroic efforts to hold his
normally controlled temper in check) made no dent in the Commander-
in-Chief's armoured ruthlessness. At the first meeting 'he condemned
my conduct from first to last as marked by cruelty and oppression.
To those causes, he said, he ascribed the origin of the mutiny, and
intimated his intention of submitting to the King Sir Thomas Trigge's
report upon my Code of Orders, and recommending it to his Majesty
to authorize him to confirm the alterations which the Lieutenant-

The town and harbour of Halifax, Nova Scotia, in 1777, looking towards Bedford Basin from George's Island. Left: the Citadel.
Credit: John Ross Robertson Collection, Metropolitan Toronto Library Board.

Ruins of the Lodge, Bedford Basin, near Halifax, owned by Governor John Wentworth, and residence of the Prince and his lady for about five years in the 1790s.
Credit: John Ross Robertson Collection, Metropolitan Toronto Library Board.

Madame's commonplace book, begun 26 October 1799 Halifax, and completed in London some time after 1805.

Credit: From the book in the possession of Professor André Br... direct descendant of Madame's brother Claude-Charles Monge... (Photo: Ivan Kotul... Toronto).

The church of Saint Paul, Besançon, in which Thérèse-Bernardine Mongenet was baptised.
The building is today the Musée Lapidaire.
Credit: Jean Bevalot, Besançon.

Governor had made in many articles, and to cancel those which he had provisionally suspended. A hint followed this, that probably under such circumstances it might not be pleasant for me to return, and that it was supposed I should not like to retain the Government.'

At the second interview, the duke learned that his brother's intentions had been put into effect. 'With evident confusion and the greatest awkwardness I ever beheld in any man, the Commander-in-Chief communicated his letter to Sir Thomas Trigge, which exactly corresponded with what he had at our prior meeting intimated to be his intention . . . *My name*, however, was totally left out in it, and he took much merit to himself for his forbearance. His Majesty's name being made use of in the dispatch, I felt it my duty, having fortunately a perfect command of myself, to state that I should ever bow to *his* commands with humble submission and without remonstrance, but that I must deeply lament that misrepresentation, dictated by malice and *conveyed in the dark*, should have had weight enough upon the Duke of York's mind to induce him to recommend to his Majesty to sanction an act *the most cruel*, the *most unjust* and the *most arbitrary* any Officer had ever experienced. I then with great composure observed to him that however I might feel after what had passed, it was still my wish that he should report to the King my readiness to go out to Gibraltar *whenever he thought proper*, that I was ready for it *at the shortest notice*, and therefore only waited for his commands to that effect. The surprise evinced when I made use of these words is not to be described (for it was fully expected that I should throw up the Government at once). However, as I began to feel rather roused beyond what it might have been prudent to shew, I then withdrew, leaving the Commander-in-Chief, as I have since found by his own confession to one of my sisters, perfectly confounded at the coolness and determination with which I had received his communication to me; and *thus matters stand at this moment between him and me*.' (289)

So London tongues chattered, and the words *cruelty, severity,* were whispered around, while the duke simmered in impotent anger. Only his powers of controlled patience enabled him to make the necessary adjustment for living a life in which his most passionate interest was to be denied him, and in which he must now continue publicly (if unofficially) convicted of crimes he was sure he had not committed. It was a painful blow to a proud and conscientious man, and one that might have embittered a lesser man and soured the rest of his life.

'It is incredible the number of enemies he has in this Country, his Severity is in every person's mouth, man, woman & child; and I much fear the Comr in Chief's language is, that it is not safe to employ one

M

so obnoxious to the Army', wrote Dodd in England to Wright in Gibraltar on 28 September: and later (13 November), 'The Gibraltar business has been most fatal to him in every way.' (290)

Dodd was right. Later assessments of the duke's character and abilities have all been tarred with the brush of the Duke of York's accusations, which his brother was never allowed to answer or refute. No matter that his government of Gibraltar may have done far more good than harm, and the mutiny have been a rising fostered by the very evils he had been sent to remove. No matter that there were many military men who approved his actions, and that other mutinies were occurring where the commanding officer was not dismissed, but supported. Any references he made in later years to the injustice of his situation, to his undeniable grievances, and to the injuries he had suffered without redress in his income and his career, have generally been interpreted as a whining self-pity. It is only surprising that under so mortal a blow to pride and usefulness, the Duke of Kent did not indulge in an acrimonious railing against fate, burning himself up with a brooding resentment. Any man in his position would have had to be superhuman not to mutter from time to time. The duke's mutterings were wry and disillusioned. They were seldom rancorous or virulent, as well they might have been.

Realizing that the surrender of his Gibraltar government would be construed as a tacit admission of guilt, he clung firmly to his appointment, and the King never demanded his resignation. So, with dignity, the duke retired to private life, dividing his time between Kensington Palace and Castle Hill Lodge, living in a full and vigorous domestic happiness with Thérèse-Bernardine (once again 'almost the only comfort of my existence'), and turning to social problems the energy and attention he was not now allowed to give to military ones. But he never ceased trying to obtain a hearing.

CHAPTER FOURTEEN

The quiet years

In between his social, domestic, and charitable engagements over the next few years, the Duke of Kent persistently but quietly brought to the attention of everyone with any authority his eagerness to return to his command. It was not from any wish of his own, he made clear, that he was kept at home, and he pressed the growing urgency of the war with France, the possible danger from Spain, and any other relevant aspect that might keep his situation before the public eye and put him back into active service.

It was evident that nearly everyone was backing away from real commitment. The duke, who had come home fully believing that the words in the letter of recall had meant just what they had said, continued to be met with shuffling evasions. 'The words used by the late Secretary of State for the Home Department,' he was now told pompously, '. . . were the same always used to Governors or Commanders-in-Chief when it was judged expedient to call them home from their commands from motives of policy, without attaching any censure to their conduct, and consequently without intending to require or allow of an investigation.' (291)

There was, therefore, a certain tendency to calm the duke by smooth and non-committal phrases that would not seem to bang the door entirely shut in his face, and into which he (naturally enough) read the most optimistic meaning. On 5 February 1804 an embarrassed Lord Pelham received from the Duke of York a private and confidential letter demanding peremptory explanation of 'correspondence which has passed between the Duke of Kent and myself upon the Subject of his wishing to return to Gibraltar. . . . As you will probably

remark how differently he represents what passed between you and
him from what I understand from you, I should wish much to know
whether I am right in my conception of the conversation, in order to
frame my answer accordingly'.

As the Duke of Kent would never have been foolish enough to
misrepresent deliberately to his brother any opinions he knew could
be immediately refuted by application to Pelham, his Lordship must
have had some acutely uncomfortable redrafting to do before his final
reply emerged. Evasive comment to escape the devil of the Duke of
Kent's wrath had nearly tossed him to the deep blue sea of censure
from the Duke of York. Now, when confronted with the need to
make a clear interpretation of what he had said, he had little choice
but to stick with the more powerful brother. He set unhappily about
the business of trying to explain that what he had said was not *really*
what he had said. 'Your Royal Highness will I hope excuse me if I
say that I do not think either of the Letters contain an accurate
statement of what passed between the Duke of Kent and me. . . .

'I told His Royal Highness in that conversation that I did not
conceive His Majesty's confidential servants would be easily induced
to give an opinion upon a subject which was purely Military in itself,
altho' they had taken a part in the first instance in consideration of
the peculiar circumstances of ye Persons immediately concerned; that
Y.R.H. the Commander-in-Chief being Brother to the Governor of
Gibraltar and that both being sons of the King, there were many
considerations which not only influenced their conduct at the time, in
stepping, in some degree, out of their line by making the first communication of ye disaster at Gibraltar to the King, but also in deter-
mining me to take the King's Pleasure about the letter to be written
to your R:H: communicating His Majesty's pleasure that ye Duke
of Kent should return to England.

'I did undertake to state to the Cabinet His R.H.'s sentiments &
Feelings & I called His Majesty's confidential servants together for ye
purpose, but I was prevented by Illness for attending them & the only
other Cabinet I was present at before I was removed from Office, was
upon the first Advices from Ireland concerning the business of July
23rd.

'I can as certainly say that I never gave the Duke of Kent the least
intimation of my entertaining an opinion that it was likely he would
return to Gibraltar, or that he would receive any mark of His Majesty's
approbation of his conduct which was also very strongly urged.' (292)

The Duke of Kent was in some degree compensated for the rebuffs
from his brother by the welcome from the rest of his family. 'The

kindness I receive from the Queen, the Prince, and every member of
my family, and all my old military friends, is not to be described, and
the personal goodness of the King was never more marked than it has
been from the moment of my return, and continues to be, which is
as much as a tacit avowal that he laments in his heart the part they
make him take.' (293) To Addington he wrote on 9 February to thank
him for his friendly support, to which he attributed the King's agreement to continue his pay and nominal position as Governor of
Gibraltar.

'This was still enhanced by the King's condescending to express how
sensible he was of the zeal I had evinced in his Majesty's service. All
this, you will easily understand, was like balm to my feelings; and I
never can forget that it is to your manly . . . and friendly interference,
that I owe this.' (294)

So the duke went back and forth between Windsor, Ealing and
Kensington, carried out commissions for the Prince of Wales, began
to involve himself in that support of charitable institutions for which
he rightly came to be honoured and respected. But he did not enter
into the social life of London, preferring to go home to Castle Hill
Lodge, Kensington Palace, or sometimes to the small town house at
Knightsbridge which he did not sell until 1808, and where occasionally
his brothers and other friends came to dine.

The situation in which he was placed with Madame demanded that
they visit places or attend events privately. Society was ready to make
no noisy scandal of what was tacitly accepted, but the duke and
Madame could never expect publicly expressed approval. When the
unfounded rumour of Mrs Fitzherbert's death in Bath had sent the
Prince of Wales into what was reported as a fit in February 1799,
The Times readily paid a compliment to 'a circumstance so creditable
to the sensibility of the Prince of Wales', even though everyone knew
that if they were actually married, as was suspected, it was certainly
not a legal union. But society as a whole—and particularly royalty—
was not ready to go further than a lip-service admiration of this kind
of faithfulness. Reality was different. In May 1803, Lord Malmesbury
had noted the Duke of York's uneasiness 'lest the Duchess should be
forced to sup at the same table with Mrs Fitzherbert, at the ball to
be given by the Knights of the Bath on the first of June . . . says the
King and Queen will not hear of it; on the other side he wishes to keep
on terms with the Prince. I say I will see Lord Henley, who manages
this fête, and try to manage it so that there shall be two distinct tables,
one for the Prince, to whom *he* is to invite, another for the Duke and
Duchess, to whom *she* is to invite, her company.' (295)

But though the duke's thoughtful care of Madame was never
flaunted (nor did she ever seek to enter doors closed to her), she had
much reason to return the love and devotion with which he surrounded
her. Aware that her social opportunities were limited (and also,
obviously, because her companionship was more satisfying to him than
that of anyone else) he made it a practice to be away from home as
little as possible. When he wrote to the Prince of Wales in mid-January
1804 to let him know the most convenient date for attending a ball at
Brighton, he added a proviso. 'With respect to the ball, if *agreable*
to *you*, Thursday the 26th will be the day *I* should wish, and it
will be perfectly agreable to William also, who is disengaged for *that*
day . . . and/we/depend on your indulgence to permit us on *my*
account to return the *next* day, as it is *that* fixed for my taking possession of Kensington, et vous êtes trop gallant pour ne pas sentir quelle
seroit la dureté de laisser Madame de St Laurent veuve pour la
première nuit.' (296)

Did she ever, privately, see that charming, exotic and palatial
residence, the Pavilion at Brighton? Others, with a facility for
observant description, were penning ecstatic accounts to friends and
relatives.

'The pavilion, you must know, is now so completely fitted up *à la
Chinoise,* that the Emperor of China, whenever he pays us a Visit
will find himself as much at home in it as if he had not left Pekin. Last
night it was illuminated from one end to the other, and the whole
thrown open except the Supper room. At nine the Company assembled
to the Amount of three hundred and thirty strangers. . . . The French
Dukes opened the Ball, and performed, as it appeared to me, as well
as they possibly could. The dancing went on till twelve, when the
Supper room was opened, as brilliant and magnificent and with as fine
a Supper as could be imagined. Only one hundred persons could be
accommodated at once, and none but Ladies sat down in the first
instance. I luckily found my Way, with his Grace of Norfolk, into a
Side room, which was but little known, and less talked of, where about
twenty of us supt [*sic*] at ease, with some of the principal beauties.'

Thus Sir Philip Francis to his daughter-in-law Eliza Johnson. (297)
For the whole of 1804 England existed in a state of anxiety. A new
invasion scare swept over the land, keeping apprehension alive in every
heart. 'I find some well-informed and sensible men thinking very
seriously of the invasion,' wrote Sir Gilbert Elliot, now Lord Minto,
to his wife. 'They consider the means prepared for transporting and
landing the troops as well calculated for the purpose. . . . It does seem
as if we should have prepared something similar to the weapon that

is to be employed against us . . . a great number of vessels capable of *rowing*, as theirs are.' Sir Philip Francis sounded out Sir Sidney Smith in July, and received cold comfort. 'He says that, granting them a calm of 24 hours, we have no naval power that could stop them: and he has no doubt of their making the Attempt.' (298)

In mid-August, three months after having been declared Emperor, Napoleon reviewed the Army of England collected at Boulogne, sending more shivers down English spines. In October, Lady Bessborough wrote apprehensively of strange events on the Channel coast. 'We have been out the whole evening staring at the sky in common with all the good people of Hastings, who cover the beach from one end to the other. I never saw so extraordinary an appearance: it began before nine and is going on still at past one. The sky is as red as a glowing setting sun, and bright streaks of light darting from every part of it in various shapes. . . . The people here are in the greatest alarm, thinking it Portends the end of the world *or*—the invasion.' On Guy Fawkes Day (perhaps because the weather had by now removed most fears of invasion) Channel residents found some light relief in defying the edict of the town crier, who in Hastings had been 'employ'd all morning in forbidding bon fires, on pain of great penalties, especially on the heights, lest they should be mistaken for signals of invasion; and if nothing had been said they would probably have burnt Guy Fawkes in the Market place very quietly, but, in consequence of this, every cliff round Hastings is in a blaze, and especially ours, with a fallot on the top of a long pole so like the signal for the French, that I should not wonder if the whole coast was in alarm and the people under arms from here to Dover'. (299)

The King's health had once again deteriorated, and once again there was uneasy taking of political sides. He had maintained a precarious balance of sanity in the early part of this new attack, but as he grew worse, the Royal Family itself, with tempers frayed by worry and weariness, broke out into 'strange schisms and cabals and divisions among the sons and daughters'. Rumour said that the Queen, the Princesses Augusta and Elizabeth, with the Dukes of Clarence, Kent and Sussex, were siding with the Prince of Wales, while the Dukes of York, Cumberland, Cambridge and the younger princesses took the part of their father. (300) The Duke of Kent was certainly very close to his eldest brother at this time—with reason, for the Prince had been extremely kind and sympathetic during several difficult periods of his life. But he continued a dutiful attendance at Windsor. It was not in his interest, apart from any other consideration, to alienate himself from the King. He was thus also able to keep the Prince in touch with developments at Windsor: a reconciliation between the King and his eldest son was not effected until the end of the year.

Madame spent a happy summer. While her duke attended to family duties, wrote his voluminous private and business letters—to Gibraltar with suggestion and instruction (he was still governor, though in absentia), to officials on behalf of protegés, to friends—she occupied her days driving out in her carriage with her maid Mrs Mahieu and the footman Thomas Strangethorne in attendance, walking in the lovely gardens of the Lodge at Ealing, or entertaining in the great public rooms hung with curtains of silk and velvet and ornamented with Parisian clocks, china figurines, mirrors and fine paintings in gilded frames.

Sometimes she would read from a book selected from the duke's library of thousands of volumes in French and English, magnificently bound, on subjects literary, artistic, historical, political, military, geographical. At odd moments, as always, she jotted down in her commonplace book the items that interested her : sometimes, despite her excellent English, betrayed into the French spelling of words (sometimes even of parts of words).

A little verse :

> *'à peu de frais, en verité,*
> *les dieux peuvent me satisfaire;*
> *qu'ils me laissent le necessaire*
> *qu'ils m'accordent la santé,*
> *je fais du reste mon affaire.'*

A remedy (in French) for poisonous mushrooms. An anecdote that amused her (one encounters it still, attributed to some present-day famous person). 'A man after having been Profusely extravagant at length resolved to reform, and become very saving ; he Purchased an account Book, and resolved to be very Particular in his items of expenditure ; but on opening his book at the end of the week it Contenaid [*sic*] but two items, viz.

> a lead Pencil £0   0   8
> Sundries 350   0   0'

In French she copied an article entitled '*Sur L'economie*', and out-lined the qualifications for good housekeeping, which one can be sure she put into practice.

'. . . What is the proper role of the mistress of the house? She should know the value of money, and the price and quality of various com-modities : she should establish order in the house, put everything in its place, make use of the qualities, even the faults of those who surround her. She should pay current accounts, keep a weekly budget for comparison of one week's expenditure with another; plan supplies in accordance with the needs of company and the different seasons; give an honest and intelligent look at everything that happens. She should often meet with members of her staff and tell them what she thinks of their conduct, good or bad : she should never criticize them in public—such criticism is of no interest to visitors and offends the staff; she should work with them to increase their efficiency, praise them when successful and point out without recrimination where they have failed. She should never allow them to lack any necessity, but yet not give them too much : expect in return, harmony, good humour and a moderate work-load. She should not allow them to gamble, but care for them when they are ill and persuade them as far as possible that economy is only sought so as to be able to relieve their needs. She should take care to have a well-ordered table, with every-thing clean. . . . She must know all the resources of her domain and turn them to advantage for her house. She should pay her staff well, giving them not profit but rewards . . . a servant who steals one louis from his master becomes accustomed to stealing a little and ends by being a rogue. She should not pay out money to the staff : it offers an opportunity to go to the tavern, where they eat badly, drink too much and upset their health : but she should expect punctuality and good behaviour from them.'

Servants in the household of the duke and Madame (like the army officers of his staff) stayed for a long time. Philip Beck, who went with the young prince to Quebec in 1791, was in the service of the duke when he died nearly thirty years later. The Mahieus, husband and wife, were on the staff together at least from 1803 : the wife was dismissed from Madame's service in 1816, but the husband rode in the coach with Philip Beck at the duke's funeral.

These quiet years passed for Madame with little variation in the pleasant routine of her life. There were the intimate dinner parties, sometimes with only two or three guests, sometimes falling victim to small domestic mishaps, as happened in July 1804. The Prince of Wales had said he would like to dine at Ealing before going down to Brighton, and the duke had arranged to invite the Duke of Orleans and General Dumourier as well. But an unexpected hitch occurred two days before the date fixed. 'A very principal personage in my House-hold, namely my Cook,/is/*hors de Combat* with a violent feverish complaint', wrote the duke ruefully, and asked for a postponement 'until/he/is again able to wield his knife'. (301)

Both the duke and Madame were, all their lives, susceptible to colds.

In addition, the duke was afflicted with repeated rheumatic attacks.
It has been suggested that, like his father, he may have been a victim
of the disease called porphyria, but with fortunately far less severe
manifestations. (302) In their various times of illness they showed each
other gentle consideration. 'Madame de St Laurent's continued indisposition having prevented me from calling on you today as I had
fully intended doing', wrote the duke to the Prince of Wales in
November 1804, 'I am obliged to have recourse to my pen . . .
Tomorrow towards three I will call at Carlton House, having a great
deal to say to you before you go to Windsor, especially as, from the
certainty of Madame de St Laurent being yet confined for several days,
and having *no* other society than mine I know your good heart will
excuse my not leaving her at such a moment, and that you will kindly
excuse my *not* meeting you *this* time at Windsor'. (303)

What the duke gave to Thérèse-Bernardine was security, luxury,
the company of interesting people. She gave him a sense of homecoming, someone waiting, looking for his return. They gave to each
other companionship, shared interests, the comfortable assurance of
understanding. The two books of the Duke's household records that
have survived (for July-September 1813 and January-March 1814)
give a kind of skeleton picture of the simple domestic happiness in
which they lived. The careful daily record of 'Number of Persons
at the Different Meals of each Table' is listed under the three headings
of *H. R. Highness* and *Persons Extra, The Upper Servants* and *Persons
Extra,* and *The Under Servants* and *Persons Extra.* The entry for
breakfast at His Royal Highness's table was usually simply '2', with
only occasionally from one to four 'persons extra'. Mealtimes at both
Castle Hill Lodge and Kensington Palace were more often intimate
à deux occasions than not. (304)

This was a period of continuing dissension in the royal family,
based more on jealousies and jockeying for favours from those in a
position to dispense them than on any real personal antipathies, and
aggravated by the increasing degeneration in the King's health. There
was always a strong bond of affection and interest between the royal
brothers and sisters. 'As dear Edward is writing in my room I cannot
resist adding a few words in the cover to tell you how truly I do lament
your absence, particularly the cause', wistfully wrote the youngest
princess, Amelia, to the Prince of Wales. 'Do, dear love, take care of
your dear self & if possible be here Augusta's or Edward's birthday. It
is ages since *eleven* of us have been together.' 'The loss of yr. society
is no small mortification', wrote the Princess Sophia to the Prince
of Wales in November 1803 when the target of his displeasure
happened to be the Duke of York, 'but believe me *absent* or *present*

I am ever the same, lamenting in silence that any coolness should subsist *between two* I do *dearly love*'. (305)

The princesses especially, because the Prince of Wales was invariably kind and thoughtful for them (and because they looked to his authority for help and support), loved their eldest brother dearly. Their attitude towards their other brothers was often coloured strongly by the degree of the Prince's favour the junior princes enjoyed at any given moment. At this period the conflict between the Prince and the King over the education and control of the Prince's daughter, the young Princess Charlotte, was the subject of much tale-bearing between the brothers and sisters, with a lot of reporting to each other 'entre nous' the latest developments.

The deterioration in the King's sight was worrying everyone. 'A cataract is completely formed in one eye, of which he has lost the use for some weeks past', wrote the Speaker, Charles Abbot, on 4 July 1805. 'He has no direct vision with the other eye; but can see downwards to distinguish what he walks upon. He knows persons at the distance of three or four yards. He has not been able to read a word for some time, but can sign as usual with great clearness and steadiness. . . . It is supposed his eyes may be in a state for an operation in about two months hence.' (306) Madame, who was in a position to know, and shared the duke's distress, wrote two poignant verses of *God Save The King* in her commonplace book at this time.

The King himself seemed to bear up well under his affliction. Lord Henley wrote on 1 November to tell Lord Auckland : 'Our good King continues, mind and body, the sight excepted, better than I have seen him for years. . . . He plays at Commerce without any further assistance than he derives from his spectacles. He was last night in good spirits that he had nearly got rid of his cold without its having affected his eyes, and was cheerful—in short, was himself. . . . This morning I met him in the park at ten o'clock, and rode with him till a quarter past one. . . . We had more than one of his hearty laughs, which I have not heard before for some time. . . . Lady Henley says that he presented the muffins to the ladies last night in his old jocose and good-humoured manner.' (307)

The question of Catholic emancipation had again been bothering the King, and put the liberal-minded Duke of Kent in an awkward position. At the Birthday celebration in June, the King was reported by Lady Bessborough to have 'told the Archb. of Canterbury . . . that he should die in Peace from the Consciousness of having defended the Church in a moment of extreme danger, and that he hop'd the Majority of both Houses had laid the Catholick question asleep for ever. (308) The Duke of Kent, personally in favour of emancipation (not only because of Madame, but from his own liberal principles), and knowing that the Prince of Wales also supported the measure (because of Mrs Fitzherbert?—his attitude would change after he became king), was too dependent on his father to allow himself any personal independence of action at this time. He informed his brother privately that in view of his father's expressed intention of regarding as his enemy anyone in opposition, he would have to go against the proposal, but that he would support it when his brother became king.

At a later date, when his father had descended irrecoverably into his limbo of unreality, and he himself had no longer any expectation of favour from his brother, by then Prince Regent, the duke was freer to express himself on his stand, as he did to the Earl of Buchan on 30 April 1812. 'Adverting to your Lordship's remarks upon the delusive opinions entertained & expressed by the Duke of Sussex, candor requires of me to explain to you that however I may regret the seeing any political point thro' a different medium than your Lordship, *my* mind has imbibed similar delusions (or *impressions* I would rather say) upon the Catholic Question, and I must openly avow to your Lordship, that had I not fear'd the act might have been misconstrued into paltry revenge, for gross breach of friendship towards me on the part of the Prince Regent, I should likewise have felt no hesitation or delicacy in giving my most decided opposition to the Regent's Ministers on that Question, instead of remaining silent & neuter as I have done.' Buchan sententiously annotated the cover of the letter: '. . . So the Royal family falls in pieces again. A family divided against itself cannot stand.' (309)

There was another occasion when the Duke of Kent spoke out on this subject. A painfully constructed draft of a reply by Bishop Mountain of Quebec dated November 1813 to what was obviously a severe reprimand from the duke has survived in the Quebec Diocesan Archives. The phrases stroked through, the interpolations and the substitution of words clearly indicate the mental distress in which the poor Bishop tried to write himself back into favour and explain that he had not meant what the Duke must have read into his letter. (310)

Madame seems to have been able to communicate with her family during the long war with France. Even if the letters had to go via Sweden, they would eventually reach her wandering youngest brother Jean-Claude wherever he happened to be residing in Germany or Switzerland. If she could not find a route for a letter into France itself (though this seemed unlikely) she may have had news of her sister and her other brothers by letters sent by them to Jean-Claude across the nearby Swiss border.

She would hardly, in that case, have missed hearing about the visit of Napoleon and Josephine early in April 1805 to Chambéry, where her eldest brother was engineer-in-chief of highways in the *département de Mont Blanc*. In any event, she would certainly hear about it from the lips of her young nephew Charles-Benjamin when she met him in Paris in 1816. He had seen the event through the eyes of an excited nine-year-old. How could a small boy forget the two days of public ceremony and rejoicing when the Emperor and Empress arrived in Chambéry preceded by fifty-seven splendidly uniformed citizens of the town as guards of honour and were met by a band of thirty musicians and all the town's residents, cheering and singing and throwing flowers?—a small boy aware that Their Majesties had been escorted on the way, to see the great new tunnel at the *Grotte des Echelles* where a monument carried a Latin inscription bearing his father's name: MONGENET, Curator operum? (311)

On the Continent, affairs (from the British point of view) were going from bad to worse in 1805 and rumours were wildly flying. 'The good news I heard yesterday concerning the King of Prussia/that he would join the Allies/is contradicted today. The suspense at such a moment is dreadful', wrote Lady Bessborough to Lord Granville on 3 November. '. . . The D. of York with his two younger Brothers, Edward and Ernest, are going immediately—D. of York to join the Emperor Francis, Ed. to accompany Armfeldt, and Er. heading a party of horse.' Two days later, hearing of General Mack's capitulation at Ulm with 30,000 men, she was 'so terrified, so shock'd with the news, I scarcely know what to wish for you. This man/Napoleon/moves like a torrent'. (312) A suggestion that the royal dukes might be given commands had been deprecated a few weeks earlier by people with whom the artist Joseph Farington had been speaking, considering (in the light of the duke's publicly accepted reputation) 'the personal danger of it to the *Duke of Kent*', who might, they thought, run the risk of being shot in the back by his men, as was suspected in the case of another officer with a reputation for severity. (313)

Trafalgar, a heartening victory, was at the same time a national tragedy. Among the people who milled around the Admiralty awaiting news of husbands, brothers and sons, 'almost every body wears a black crape scarf or cockade with Nelson written on it'. (314) The Duke of Kent, who had written to the admiral only a month before his death on behalf of a young protégé on *Victory*, had indicated 'how proud I should have felt, could I have been thought worthy of being intrusted with the command of the Army that may be employed on any service on which your Lordship might take on yourself that of His Majesty's Naval Forces, being fully convinced that, with such a Collegue, there is nothing almost that might be undertaken, the issue of which would be doubtful.' (315) Instead, he found himself part of the national mourning in the procession to St Paul's after the landing of the coffin at Whitehall Stairs in a sudden and almost supernatural gust of January rain, hail and wind.

Lady Bessborough, watching from a house at Charing Cross, wrote later to Lord Granville Leveson Gower: 'Amongst many touching things the silence of that immense Mob was not the least striking; they had been very noisy. . . . The moment the Car appear'd which bore the body, you might have heard a pin fall, and without any order to do so, they all took off their hats. I cannot tell you the effect this simple action produc'd: it seem'd one general impulse of respect. . . . Mean while the dead march was play'd in soft tones, and the pauses fill'd with cannon and the roll of the muffled drums.' (316)

The winter had been a bad one. Early in November Lady Bessborough was caught in a fog 'which was bad when I set out, grew thicker and thicker, but when I got into the park was so compleat that it was impossible to find the way out. My footman got down to *feel* for the road, and the holloing of the drivers and screams of people on foot were dreadful. I was one hour driving thro' the park; Queen St. it was impossible to find, and as I was oblig'd to come here/to Roehampton/, and it was as dangerous to try to go home, I set out with two men walking before the horses with flambeaux, of which we could with difficulty perceive the flame—the men not at all. Every ten or twenty yards they *felt* for the door of a house to ask where we were—it was frightful beyond measure; in *three hours' time* I reach'd Chelsea, when it begun to clear a little. I find Ly. Villiers who rode to see me, was overtaken by it in her return, and nearly down'd by riding into the Thames.' (317)

Two days before Christmas, Queen Charlotte wrote to her close friend Lady Harcourt: 'May 1806 prove happier to all of us, than 1805 has been from the beginning to the end. . . . The severity of the weather makes every body cough but nothing to signify. I am occupied with my yearly Christmas presents, not fine ones, but just enough to remember that there is such a chearfull season.' (318)

CHAPTER FIFTEEN

Domestic happiness

The duke had finished paying Mrs Fitzherbert for Castle Hill Lodge in 1803; only the mortgage to the original owner, Mark Beaufoy, on which interest had to be paid regularly, remained outstanding. Along with his continued attempts to get reimbursement for his serious losses while abroad, he was—with his usual kindly impulse to be helpful—writing to Pitt on behalf of his brothers, particularly the Duke of Sussex, in similar financial difficulties. When the second of two instalments of a total of £20,000 was paid to him by the King out of the Admiralty Droits in April 1806, he told Coutts: 'I wish I felt any conviction that the payment . . . was to be the forerunner of a general and effectual plan being adopted for my own relief & that of my brothers the Dukes of Clarence and Sussex, who, I fear, stand more in need of it than I do myself.' (319)

The money did him little immediate good, being swallowed up by interest payments and debt reduction, but he was very grateful. To the end of his life he would never get ahead of his commitments. Current living expenses, recurring emergencies and the mounting interest payments kept him constantly running to stay in the same place, a hard fate for a man essentially honest and conscientious, and not extravagant beyond the extent he felt to be his right—possibly also his duty—as a Prince of the Blood.

The irreversible decision of the Duke of York not to allow him to return to Gibraltar, or even to be heard in his own defence, hung over all the Duke of Kent's activities for the next few years: but he was promoted to the rank of Field-Marshal on 5 September 1805, and appointed Ranger of Hampton Court Park, for both of which he was grateful as marks of the King's favour.

In August 1805, the duke had gone to Weymouth to join the family, after another brief visit to the Prince of Wales in the Pavilion at Brighton ('which is really beautiful in its way', wrote Lady Bessborough, enthralled as all visitors were. 'I did not think the strange Chinese shapes and columns could have look'd so well. It is . . . in outré and false taste, but for the kind of thing as perfect as it can be, and the Prince says he had it so because at the time there was such a cry against French things, &c., that he was afraid of his furniture being accus'd of jacobinism.') (320) While the duke was out of town, three of the de Salaberry boys from Quebec arrived in London, beginning a series of visits to the Duke and Madame that would delight all of them over the next few years.

The duke had arranged for two of them, Maurice and Louis (known as Chevalier) to be appointed to the Royals (his own regiment) as lieutenants, and Madame had been looking forward to their arrival since early in the year. In a hasty letter to their father on 5 April 1805 ('I have only a minute left to dress and go out. It is go and come from morning till night') she had written 'I hope you are satisfied with the way our Duke has disposed of both. His Royal Highness has certainly shown very great zeal.'

On the day the brothers had arrived to call at Kensington Palace, Madame was out, but in the Duke's absence at Weymouth she sent a quick invitation to dine the next day, when they all exchanged excited chatter about Quebec and Madame asked a thousand questions. On 3 September she was able to tell Colonel de Salaberry about their next visit to dinner, on 31 August, after the Duke's return to town.

'Our young men have arrived fresh, vigorous and in good health. I will not attempt to express to you the pleasure I had in receiving them. Captain de Salaberry/Charles/is as usual, very well, but the two Cadets, both of whom I last saw when so small, are to me *perfect wonders*. The Duke being at Weymouth with the Royal Family, I myself had the pleasure of doing the honors of Kensington Palace, and I hope they are quite satisfied with the friendly and cordial manner in which I acquitted myself.

'Captain de Salaberry, in whom I am happy to recognize *the true son of his father*, has had the gallantry to say to me, that he found no change in me, I have not failed to let him know I was much pleased with the good intention, which led him to pay a compliment so agreeable to a lady, after an absence of ten years. The tall Maurice and the amiable Chevalier (your living picture) also said they would have recognized me. My dear de Salaberry, you see they are made for the world, and they will be successful without doubt.

Castle Hill Lodge, Ealing, the Duke of Kent's residence, purchased from
Maria Fitzherbert in 1800.
Credit: Greater London Record Office (Middlesex Records).

Kensington Palace, 1819, the Duke of Kent's official residence.
Credit: W. H. Pyne's Royal Residences (Guildhall Library).

Place Louis Quinze, 1821 (today Place de la Concorde), Paris. Here, in that section of the building on the left now the Automobile-Club de France and next to the Hôtel Crillon, Madame died in 1830.
Credit: Cabinet d'Estampes, Musée Carnavalet (photo: Jacques Buchholz).

116 rue de Grenelle, garden façade.
Credit: Photo: Studio France-Eclair (Paris).

'Our dear Duke did not fail to see them immediately on his return, and partook of my enthusiasm in regard to them; he has arranged with them their journey to Scotland, where they will repair immediately by sea. Captain de Salaberry will remain with us during the three months he proposes to remain in England, but till such time as we have a vacant room at Kensington, the Duke has asked him in the meantime (which will not be long) to *mess* every day with us. . . .

'You may believe that I put question on question to these three amiable *sons of yours*, and I have learnt with pleasure that my dear "*Souris,*" my little friends, and my godson, are enjoying brilliant health. Master Edward will, I flatter myself, be lucky enough, for he has made a fortunate entrance into the world, His Royal Highness having already nominated him as a cadet at Woolwich, and you must send him to us next year, when he shall have completed his fourteenth anniversary.' (321)

The year 1806, apart from the lively young visitors at Castle Hill Lodge, Kensington Palace, and the Knightsbridge town house, was not to be much happier than 1805 had been. The death of Mr Pitt in January shocked everyone. Even so staunch a Whig as Lady Bessborough could be overcome.

'When Mr Fox heard it he turn'd pale as ashes, and did not speak for some minutes, and then only in a low voice repeated several times: "I am very sorry, very, very sorry"; and afterwards "This is not a time to lose talents like his." Grey, too—in short, shall I tell you the remark generally made, that to judge by the appearance of people, it would be imagin'd Opposition had lost a dearer friend than Ministers . . . I must repeat Mr Fox's words: no others can convey what I believe every heart feels . . . "Impossible, impossible; one feels as if there was something missing in the world—a chasm, a blank that cannot be supplied.'' (322)

Fox's own death eight months later brought a sigh from Francis Horner, writer and economist: 'The giant race is extinct; and we are left in the hands of little ones, whom we know to be diminutive, having measured them against the others.' (323)

The duke, with his usual quiet persistence, was using every opportunity to press his return to Gibraltar, considering it his duty to keep the subject constantly open. His persistence kept other people on tenterhooks. Edward Winslow, surrogate-general of New Brunswick, sent a word of warning to his son Thomas who had recently been appointed as a lieutenant to Gibraltar. 'A rumour which has circulated here . . .

N

that the D—— of K—— has solicited to reassume the command at
Gib—— & that the Prince of W—— has exerted all his interest to
accomplish this object. I cannot think the event *will* take place
altho the information came from a correct source . . . I mention
this circumstance to guard you against committing yourself to any
disrespectful expressions towards his RH—which, I'm sorry to say are
too fashionable—but which never fail to reach his ears. It is easy to
conciliate him if he comes to the command—anything like contumacy
towards him wou^d be preposterous in the extreme, especially,' he
pointed out with fatherly concern, 'in *your* situation.' (324)

Two major scandals rocked the year 1806: the impeachment of
Lord Melville for mismanagement of Admiralty funds, and the
inquiry known as the Delicate Investigation, when the Princess of
Wales was examined about the possibility of her adultery with several
persons. On 27 June, having just learned that Charles Fox was suffering from an incurable disease, Lady Bessborough was feeling very low
'when in came the P. of Wales in the greatest agitation . . . the
latter end of last year, before Mr Pitt's illness, the Duke of Sussex
sent for him, telling him he had receiv'd a deposition from Sir John
and Ly. Douglas, not only as to the Princess of Wales' general misconduct, but her having had a child. The Prince answer'd he had
heard of it a year before (which is true, for he told it me), but had
forborne taking any notice of it from wishing the subject to be
dropp'd. The Duke of Sussex answer'd: "You may do as you please
for yourself, tho' it is a little hard upon your Daughter; but at any
rate *we* cannot be so passive and run the chance of being cut out by
a stranger." After much conversation he persuaded the Prince to hear
Sir J. and Ly. Douglas's charge. He did so, and then said he would have
nothing to do with it, but if his Brothers wish'd it to be further
examin'd, that he must leave it to them. He, however, ask'd if the
Douglases were willing to write down what they had said with their
names and affidavit. This they did, and he offer'd to shew it to me,
but for once I had the prudence to refuse, fearing if any thing came
out I might be accus'd of it. . . . Soon after the D. of Cambridge told
the Prince Mr Pitt had heard the same deposition from another quarter
and thought them of serious consequence. Mr Pitt's illness immediately
follow'd, and when Mr Fox came in the Prince was particularly anxious
not to commence their administration with so unpopular a measure.
He talk'd to Ld. Thurlow, who answer'd: "Sir, if you were a common
man, she might sleep with the D——l; I should say, let her alone and
hold your tongue. But the Prince of Wales has no right to risk his
Daughter's Crown and his Brothers' claims . . . " ' (325)

The Duke of Kent was involved in this case, commissioned, 'from

delicacy towards her, to be the bearer of this painful intelligence':
chosen, perhaps, because of having been emissary from his brother to
the Princess a few years earlier, and possibly because his unruffled
good manners made him a congenial messenger. Some biographers
have dated his break with the Prince of Wales from this incident: the
Prince was believed to have been angered by a failure on his brother's
part to acquaint him with his earlier knowledge of the Princess's
indiscretions. John Adolphus, historian of the Georgian period, who
wrote the *Memoirs of Queen Caroline,* stated categorically that the
duke was called to explain his early awareness at an interview with the
Prince in his bedroom on 10 November 1805. The oft-repeated accusation that the Prince's anger followed the Duke of Sussex's revelation of
the Duke of Kent's secrecy does not seem to be borne out by fact, as
the deposition from Lady Douglas witnessed by the Duke of Sussex
was dated 3 December, a month after the interview reported by
Adolphus. (326)

In his long and intimate confidences to Lady Bessborough the
Prince made no complaint against the Duke of Kent, and apparently
had been aware, in any case, of what was going on. Amicable letters
were passing between the two brothers after the investigation, and
a full year later (May 1807) Joseph Farington observed them together
looking at pictures at the Royal Academy, and noted that they left
together after dinner. In August 1809, the duke was still visiting his
eldest brother at Brighton.

The two years that followed were (except for the small human crises
that no one escapes) quietly uneventful for the duke and Madame,
filled with visits from well-liked friends—the Duke of Orleans, General
Dumourier, the de Salaberry boys—evenings at the theatre, and (for
the duke) attendance at meetings of the various benevolent associations
he supported with both time and donations. He shared the sorrow of
the Duke of Orleans when his younger brother the Duke of Montpensier died and was buried with ceremony in Westminster Abbey:
visited his talkative aunt (and mother of the Princess of Wales) the
Duchess of Brunswick who had come to England; went riding with his
father and sisters, was fêted on birthdays with ringing bells and gunfire
at Windsor.

The three young de Salaberrys, like lively schoolboys visiting a
favourite aunt, wrote ebullient letters home about Madame's friendly
countenance. Young Maurice had sat down on 3 September (the same
day as Madame herself was writing) to tell his dear papa about their
dinner after the duke's return from Weymouth. 'I assure you, papa,
that we were not too much at ease on entering, but that did not last
long. He received us with such kindness that we were very quickly

put at ease. I don't think he has changed at all, he really is a handsome
man except that he has lost nearly all his hair.' Charles kept pinching
himself. 'His Royal Highness and Madame continue to pay me the
most marked attention. . . . It appears to me quite a dream to find
myself sitting alone between them at dinner, which is sometimes the
case, when there is no company . . . who could have guessed at that
a few months ago.'

They all raved about Madame . . . 'the most charming lady in the
world' . . . 'the most kind, the best natured, and the most amiable of all
women : the beauties of her mind can only be equalled by those of her
lovely person. I must give up speaking of her', wrote Charles at last,
almost out of adjectives, 'for certainly I am unable to say anything that
possibly could demonstrate the excellence of her character.' Chevalier
reported excitedly that the duke, wishing to see them in full uniform,
had actually given them the honour of using '*sa* dressing room',
and had had their hair cut by his own hairdresser. Madame had
asked continually about his parents and sisters, and had given each
of them a military sash. When 'the little Edward' arrived in 1806,
there was more to write home about than ever.

That little gentleman reached England at the end of August after
a narrow escape from Jerome Bonaparte, then commanding a
squadron at sea. Madame, in her usual heart-warming way, showered
with love and gifts the young godson whose baptismal register she had
signed in Quebec so many years ago. 'The boy who came to spend
some days with us here, and who conducted himself with all possible
grace', she wrote to his father on 16 September 1806 from Castle Hill
Lodge, 'has really charmed us and nearly turned our heads. Nobody
could be better bred, more polished or gentle, and his countenance
is so intelligent and open and he smiles so sweetly. You had good reason
to say in one of your former letters, that his pleasing mien would
charm me. I am absolutely carried away, for never did a boy of his
age inspire me with so much interest. He will tell you I am sure how
much I have caressed him—more than he desired—but he endured it
all with the best grace and the most perfect good temper. He permitted
himself to be kissed and questioned without ceasing with great good
nature and without any fear, for it is not possible to spoil him.

'To-day at length we decided to let him go to school, accompanied
by General Wetherall, where we hope he will do well. It is the first
and best school in the country, and there he will remain till such
time as it is judged that he is sufficiently advanced to go to Marlow
and from thence to Woolwich.

'Before placing him under the rod of his master, we could not refuse to show him, in the meantime, the sights of London. He went with us to Drury Lane, and he had our box for *himself and company* at Covent Garden. His company was, Dr Wetherall, the General, Mrs Wetherall, &c. We intend to go and see him in the course of next week, to recommend him favorably to his Academy. I repeat there is not such another amiable boy. During his stay here he played drafts, dominoes, backgammon, &c, and I am happy to say he won our money at all these games. It is impossible, with the intelligence he showed on every occasion, he will fail to carve for himself a brilliant career. He certainly will not fail for want of application, and I hope still further from the great desire he shows to please his illustrious godfather and his tender godmother. He will come to spend the Christmas holidays with us, and you may be sure that from now to then we will not lose sight of him, and the curricle will be employed to see how he gets on.'

Madame ended her letter on a pleasantly domestic note. 'I would write a great deal longer on this interesting subject, but have not time at present, having a large dinner party to-day. I hope that this rapidly traced letter will suffice to set you at rest in regard to the success of our charming little *man in miniature,* who has entirely, absolutely and decidedly made a conquest of us.'

She added her delight at the news that her dear *Souris* 'has decided to try the wig . . . I hope she will wear it for my sake . . . Every body wears it'. She was also sending some 'room paper' for Beauport —'that home dear to my heart, and which I delight to call to mind, as the home of that amiable family that I so much love'. (327)

The little Edward fully reciprocated Madame's sentiments. From Castle Hill Lodge on 7 January the following year he wrote home : 'I have been here three weeks and will be here until the 12th when our vacation ends. . . . . His Royal Highness and Madame de St Laurent show me the same kindness as always. I play cards and other different games nearly all day long with Madame, which entertains me a lot, my dear Papa, and in the evening, Whist with his Royal Highness and Madame. Also I often go to the play, for this place is not very far from London.'

The fourteen-year-old boy was open-mouthed at her generosity. 'Madame de St Laurent gave me a magnificent gold watch that cost thirty guineas, she bought it specially for me, with a chain, a ring and a gold key too, altogether worth about forty guineas . . . she told me she was going to give me a ring with the family crest when I come for my next holidays . . . if you can send me a pair of snowshoes, Papa, I shall be glad, because Madame told me she would like a pair.'

Writing on the little sheets of notepaper Madame had given him ('she says it is no longer the fashion to use big sheets') he described his room to his sister Adelaide, with its bed *à la Turc* ('I don't know if you know what that is like, but it is very pretty'), its two big mirrors with marble cornices, its chest of drawers and its two tables. He could not find words to describe the Lodge—'it is superb, not a château in Canada can compare with it'—and left to Monsieur de Lanaudière, on a visit from Quebec, the task of describing it when he returned.

Madame asked to see the letters he received from his sisters, showing great interest in their progress. She gave him elementary lessons in hygiene. 'Madame told me there is a kind of little worm in the teeth that you can't see with your eyes, but that they are like *toads,* and that if you don't brush your teeth like you should, they will gradually eat them away.'

Madame did not rise very early ('I have not seen her this morning because she isn't yet dressed, though it is eleven o'clock'), but the little Edward had breakfast every morning between eight and nine with his Royal Highness, who had been up since five. He spent much time with Madame in her sitting room ('which couldn't be prettier'), where 'she is almost always embroidering, writing in her book, drawing or reading'. Edward confessed he had learned to enjoy reading more than he did in Canada—'Madame has a fine library'—and he had read Don Quixote and Gil Blas 'and several others I can't remember'. Sometimes she played shuttlecock with him ('she plays very well'). And the gifts kept coming—a gold signet ring with his initials, new clothes: 'a long Prussian coat with trousers and Hessian boots for morning dress, knee breeches with silk stockings for evening, just like *men* wear': and money, all the time, an allowance for his needs, pocket-money, and every now and then extra guineas. The boys had found the cost of living high in England. *'C'est le diable pour consumer l'argent',* wrote Chevalier. (328)

The two older boys, Maurice and Chevalier, had spent a short time in Scotland (which they did not like) with their regiment, and were then posted to Sussex. In April 1807 they had gone off 'in perfect health and high spirits, as became young heroes', as lieutenants of Grenadiers in the duke's second battalion which had been suddenly ordered to India. The eldest de Salaberry, Charles, after doing considerable recruiting for the duke in England, was posted to Ireland early in 1808, where he looked up the family of an aunt, Mrs Fortescue, and fell in love with a pretty cousin.

Their illustrious protector kept a close and fatherly eye on all four boys: urged Charles to study German while he had the chance as aide-de-camp to General Baron de Rottenburg (an appointment the

duke had arranged for him) : went to Portsmouth to inspect the ship
on which Maurice and Chevalier were to travel to India, and saw
them off : supervised the young Edward's studies, personally escorting
him to his examinations at Marlow Military Academy.

In Charles's love crisis, his letter and Madame's were models of
sound advice presented in the kindest possible manner. 'I am satisfied
that no situation is so *unenviable* as that of a married officer, even
when he possesses an independent fortune to enable him to support
his wife and family in the style in which a gentleman . . . not only
would wish but ought to do . . . I leave it to your own good sense to
judge whether . . . it would either be right or honorable to take
away a young woman, for whom you have a regard, from those
comforts she has been used to at home, to share the wretched
accommodation of, at most, two barrack-rooms, if you are so situated
as to be enabled to have her with you ; or, if the imperious call of duty
separates you, to vegetate in some obscure lodging, on the few shillings
which, I contend, you can ill spare from your scanty pay . . . Believe
me , . . you will, to the last hour of your existence, feel grateful to me
for having given you this counsel.'

The young lover heeded the advice. 'Well, my dear de Salaberry',
wrote Madame to his father, 'would you believe it, the dear generous
young man heroically thanked the Duke in the most grateful terms for
his good advice so full of wisdom, solemnly promising to think no more
of marriage, and to write at once to Ireland, excusing himself to
Miss Fortescue, on the grounds of the advice given by his illustrious
protector, and sending at the same time to the young lady's brother-in-
law a copy of the letter which had induced him to change his resolution.' (329)

No wonder Charles wrote home, in an undated letter : 'What a
pair, the more I see of them, the more I have reason to venerate them.'

Only two months after his arrival in London, young Edward could
write home proudly that he had already dined once with the Duke of
Orleans—'a very amiable Prince'. They nearly always spoke French
in the house of the duke and Madame. 'It is very fortunate that I did
not acquire the French as it is spoken in Canada,' he commented with
naïve satisfaction. The eldest and youngest de Salaberry brothers dined
with the duke at Madame's Knightsbridge house for Christmas 1806,
where young Edward spent two days the following February. The
young boy had been awed to find himself a guest along with Louis-
Philippe and his two brothers Montpensier and Beaujolais. (330) If
he dined there again in December 1807, it would have been the last
Christmas dinner in the Knightsbridge house, which the duke had been
offering for sale, with its furniture, since the beginning of the month.

Early in the next year it was advertised in *The Times*: 'To be peremptorily sold by Messrs. Hoggart & Phillips [62 Old Broad Street, Royal Exchange] at Garraway's, This Day, March 10, at 12 o'clock.'

As well as the de Salaberry boys, another young man was also being given the benefit of Madame's kindly interest at this time, and early in the spring of 1807 he wrote her a grateful letter. This was George Monk's eldest son James Frederick, one of the pretty children she had met at Windsor when she accompanied the prince on his 1796 tour of Nova Scotia and New Brunswick. He had been a delicate child and not equipped to enter a profession, and his mother had written to Madame, knowing her tender-hearted concern for the welfare of young people, to ask for her aid in getting him placed. In a draft dated 24 March young James Frederick asked her to thank the duke (the letter was sent later in French) for his appointment as barrack master at Annapolis, adding, 'It is known to me that your friendly Countenance is most highly respected, esteemed and valued by /my/ Parents.' (331)

In February 1808 the duke made another valiant public attempt to return to Gibraltar. He had always conceived that to resign, as the Duke of York wished him to do, would be a tacit admission that he was guilty of misconduct (so far implied only by a whispering campaign against which he had had no opportunity to defend himself). He therefore wrote a letter to the King, with a copy to the Duke of York, asserting once more his eagerness to serve in these dangerous times: stating that on the result of the King's decision, 'every thing most dear to me in life, I mean my *character* as a *man*, and my professional credit as a soldier, are at stake'. (332)

His brother the Commander-in-Chief—whether from jealousy, constitutional dislike of his younger brother, or a hangover of distrust from the days of the duke's youthful follies, though long since amply atoned for—had been unyielding. With his usual lack of grace when dealing with this brother, the Duke of York had written on 6 February 1808: 'I had hoped, from the number of ineffectual applications which you have at different times made upon this unlucky subject, that you would have been prevented from renewing them; and I can only repeat how much I have lamented that no arrangement could be made to relieve you from the embarrassment which you must undoubtedly always labour under, so long as you retain the government of Gibraltar.' (333)

The duke might have replied that the embarrassment he suffered from could be relieved only by a full airing of his case. His stubbornness could match his brother's. Other appointments that might have come his way were refused. To resign from Gibraltar and so make himself available for them would be, for him, silent acknowledgement of a guilt he repudiated. He published his letter to the King, and concluded for public consumption: 'The Duke of Kent conceives that it would be superfluous to add any observations upon the foregoing lines, except *that he is not going out to Gibraltar,* that being a sufficient explanation of the result of his application; and his whole motive of intruding the perusal of them upon the public at this time, being that of *clearing his own character* from the aspersions that must unavoidable [*sic*] attach to it in consequence of his absence from his Government *at such a moment as the present one,* were it conceived to be voluntary on his part, or that he had been passive on the occasion.'

It was a dignified handling of an unofficial verdict he would have to live with for the rest of his life.

So it was back again to the life of a country squire for the duke, and it was fortunate for him that he possessed a capacity for becoming absorbed in the details of the smaller sphere in which he now must function. In July 1808 he presented his mother with a pair of bay ponies to drive her around the gardens of Frogmore, her residence at Windsor. He had become interested in 'Orkney poneys', which he had ordered towards the end of 1806. 'The poneys are, at present, at Hampton Court,' he told Coutts, 'and I destine them, in the first instance, to draw a smart little caravan, which I am building on purpose for them, and intend working between that place, Castle Hill Lodge, and this /Kensington/ to bring over vegetables, fruit, butter and cream; but if they turn out as well as there is every reason to expect they will, I think it very likely that they will rise to a post of higher importance, such as drawing a phaeton or curricle.' (334)

The storms of 1809 that were to assault the already battered duke (but this time his brother the Duke of York more heavily) broke on 21 January with the rising in the House of Commons of one Colonel Wardle, Member for Okehampton in Devon, to give notice of 'a Motion relating to the conduct of the Commander-in-Chief with regard to Promotions, Exchanges, and Staff Appointments, to Commissions in the Army, and Staff of the Army, and to raising new Levies.' A week later Wardle announced that to show the misuse of the half-pay fund and other unwarranted actions, he must draw attention to the establishment of a splendid house in Gloucester Place, where since 1803 a lady named Clarke had kept a variety of carriages, a long retinue of servants and an assortment of luxuries to be accounted for in connection with the colonel's accusations.

For the next few weeks the columns of the London papers were a solid pack of fine print, snatched up eagerly by everyone who could read, and detailing the words, the appearance, the actions and fascinating snippets of biography about everyone involved. The *Morning Chronicle* accused Ministers of being glad of the affair to take public attention from what the editor called the 'blunders and misconduct in the course of last summer'; and printing every delicious word, virtuously deplored the public interest in the scandal 'to the exclusion of all else', explaining that it was forced to print the story because the other papers did. The editor would later congratulate Britain on her splendid free press, 'an example to the world'.

The *Morning Post* detected a conspiracy against the House of Brunswick. 'Who can doubt, that reads the cards stuck in endless numbers on every wall about the metropolis, announcing the publication of libels by an associated gang in every form against some one or other of the Royal Family?' Afterwards the *Morning Chronicle* asked caustically why 'no attempt was made to develop the mystery of the Jacobinical conspiracy which, at the outset, was asserted to exist against all the sacred Institutions of the Country'.

The Duke of York, for what could well have been an uncomfortable interview with the King, splashed out to Windsor at the end of January, where the river was so high that all the families in Eton were living upstairs, and his Royal Highness had to finish his journey in a cart after the water entered his carriage. Most of England was suffering from floods: an undermined street in Bath collapsed, cattle were drowned, bridges washed away, ships blown ashore at Portsmouth and Plymouth. Five days later, Mary Anne Clarke tripped into the House of Commons and 'with apparent composure curtesied to the House. She wore a light blue pelisse', said the *Morning Chronicle* in the best women's-page style, 'bordered with deep lace, a lilac coloured velvet bonnet, partially concealed beneath the foldings of a veil which hung over her forehead, and carried upon her arm a large swan down muff.' She then proceeded to delight and shock everyone by her saucy answers to questions from the House.

Enterprising persons ('the minor caterers for public curiosity', said the *Morning Post* stuffily) produced pictures of the lady, 'price 7/-, coloured 10/-', small full length portraits and views 'reclining on a sofa, and surrounded by cupids, doves, and all the other satellites appropriate to so amorous a constellation'. Mrs Clarke, it appeared, was the daughter of a journeyman printer, Robert Farquhar, who had lived in a small court leading from Fetter Lane to Cursitor Street, and had met Mr Clarke when he was apprenticed to a stone-mason in Cursitor Street. After bearing 'several children' to Clarke, she left him when he gave himself up to an irregular life, and proceeded to embark, much more successfully, on irregularities of her own.

The Duke of Kent, uncomfortably aware that the public knew of his differences with the Commander-in-Chief, felt impelled in the House of Lords to make a statement early in February in support of his brother. 'He wished thus publicly to state, that, however there might have been a professional difference, there was no schism between them. . . . He regarded the Commander-in-Chief with the feelings of a friend and a brother, and he wished to give him every possible support.'

He was not to escape so easily. It was soon noted that one Mr Pierre Franc M'Callum, a gentleman whose name had come up in the inquiry, was 'the author of a pamphlet entitled "*Observations on his Royal Highness the Duke of Kent's Shameful Persecution since his recall from Gibraltar, &c*"' which had appeared the previous year. When it was published, the duke had been distressed enough to consult Samuel Romilly, the solicitor-general, about the wisdom of publishing a repudiation, in view of suspicion that he had sponsored the document. Romilly, on 29 December 1808, advised against the step as giving undue importance to any such suspicion. 'The tone and spirit of the pamphlet must alone convince every rational man that it has never received any sanction from your Royal Highness.' (335)

M'Callum, however, newspaperman and world-traveller, and freely called a spy because of his activities in Trinidad (he may also have been at one time a merchant in Halifax, Nova Scotia), was said to be a friend of the duke's secretary, Major Dodd, and of Mr Glennie, instructor of gunnery and fortifications at the Royal Military College, who owed his position to the duke through the influence of General Harcourt, which brought the duke more positively into the scandal. M'Callum, in fact, was said by Mary Anne Clarke in the book she published later, to have owed his escape from 'the justice of the country' in Trinidad to the friendship of Dodd and Glennie, both of whom were named in the inquiry. It was stated, in fact, by a witness that Dodd had tried to obtain some of the incriminating documents, though Mrs Clarke herself denied this in the House.

In any event, some of the mud slung around during the inquiry spattered the Duke of Kent too, and many of the newspapers reported that Dodd had been dismissed following his involvement in the case. Dodd published a letter in all of them repudiating the report. 'As that statement is altogether unfounded, I must request you to insert this contradiction of so false and injurious a paragraph. I also most solemnly declare, that I never did, directly or indirectly, apply to Mrs Clarke for the possession of any paper or document whatever.'

Despite this publicity, neither the Duke of Kent nor Dodd came under much comment from the papers. What speculation there may have been was apparently word of mouth. Everyone grabbed for the latest paper and devoured the news of what the ladies wore and how they looked. Throngs of fashionable ladies flocked to Hyde Park to see Mrs Clarke take an airing in her coach, elegantly dressed and 'standing the quiz with composure'. The press noted in colourful phrases that the prevailing styles were short coats of orange silk trimmed with gold lace, pelisses of crimson silk embroidered with flowers, and Pilgrim hats with cockle shells in front.

The papers of 20 March carried two important announcements. The Duke of York had resigned, acquitted of dishonesty but censured for indiscretion. Mrs Clarke had announced she would write her memoirs, with the royal letters included.

The Duke of York's choice of a mistress was vastly different from that of either of his brothers the Dukes of Clarence and Kent. He had, moreover, a duchess to whom he was now proved publicly unfaithful. But Mrs. Clarke's pert and calculated self-seeking drew the attention of society to those other very different women, who honestly loved the men they had chosen to live with.

Mrs Jordan was too much London's darling to receive severe censure from the press: in fact, the *Morning Post* took exception to 'the infamous lies, for some time past in circulation, respecting Mrs Jordan and her unoffending and innocent family'. Thérèse-Bernardine, living in her ladylike and almost anonymous seclusion, was fairer game, and she did not escape a smart crack from the *Morning Chronicle* on 20 February. 'The *Villa* of one Duke recently fitted up for a French *Courtezan* is said to have cost 80,000l.—and when brought to the hammer it did not sell for a tenth of the money!'

People in high society, who had more to lose by any relaxation of matrimonial ties, were even less forgiving. On 20 March at least two high-born ladies expressed decorous disapproval.

'Have you heard that the King has insisted on the D. of Kent's removing his mistress from the Palace at Kensington & the D. of Clarence removing Mrs Jordan from Bushy?' wrote Lady Spencer to her daughter Lady Bessborough. 'I do not think it unlikely, & it is certainly a scandalous thing to have two of the Royal dwellings so filled.'

Up in Wales, twenty-one-year-old Sarah Spencer (later Lady Lyttelton) was writing to her brother from Holywell. 'The King has expelled the Duke of Kent's mistress from his palace at Kensington, where she occupied *eighty* rooms, and the Duke of Clarence's from Bushey Park, in consequence of all this bustle. It does the greatest credit to his judgment and firmness, and I am glad he has done it.' (336)

CHAPTER SIXTEEN

Last years in London

For almost a year the Fates allowed the duke a respite from turmoil. With the Queen and three of his sisters he inspected the new Covent Garden Theatre in September 1809: all through the season the 'OP' riots by patrons protesting against higher prices kept things lively. The fiftieth anniversary of the King's accession brought illuminations, fireworks, and oxen roasted whole on the green. In October, the duke's duty took him to Weymouth as usual, and as usual, Madame stayed in London, well occupied with her circle of friends and the tickets to Coutts's theatre box for which her 'dear Duke' always thoughtfully arranged before leaving. At the end of 1809 his friend Louis-Philippe wrote with 'castles-in-Spain' dreams of commanding armies together: the duke replied early in 1810 commenting wryly on 'the repugnance they have here against the employment of princes'. (337)

In May, Mary Anne Clarke's book, *The Rival Princes,* was published in two volumes and was very well received. She had built up her story in such a way that the whole incident now appeared to have been a conspiracy engineered by the Duke of Kent through his secretary Major Dodd, to bring about the downfall of his brother in the hope of himself succeeding to the post of Commander-in-Chief.

The duke, appalled by the renewed and slanderous publicity, was forced into a statement. He had taken the precaution, after the inquiry of 1809, 'with a view to his own satisfaction' (how could he avoid being curious?) of questioning Dodd on 26 July in the presence of Lord Harrington and his own aide-de-camp Colonel John Vesey, who both signed the document, in which Dodd unequivocally denied that the duke had ever been associated with Mrs Clarke in any way, or had ever expressed the slightest thought of either superseding his brother or of damaging his reputation. This statement the duke had, at the time, circulated only among family and friends. 'He had flattered himself that it would be unnecessary to make any appeal to the public on a matter which affected himself exclusively.' None of the reputable papers at the time had shown any sign of taking Mrs Clarke seriously in this implication. The duke had therefore filed the statement for possible future need. Now he felt impelled to publish it, and did so in (among other papers) *The Times* on 18 June 1810.

Major Dodd was certainly involved, though to what extent and how culpably is difficult to discover. Both the major and Mrs Clarke lived in Sloane Street at this time, and had become acquainted by being neighbours. Dodd was one of the little party (Dodd, Wardle and Glennie) joined by Mrs Clarke on a two-day visit to one of the Martello Towers on the Channel coast, but from her account of the jaunt it is difficult to see what end it achieved for Mary Anne. The conversation she reported from that trip seems to have been unconnected with the case except in vague generalities. Nevertheless, as Wardle was at this time building up his evidence, it seems obvious that there must have been some discussion of it. What Dodd's part may have been is not clear, except perhaps a naturally curious interest in any possible mis-demeanour of the Duke of York, whose behaviour towards the duke (by whom Dodd was employed and with whom he had been associated for many years) would rankle in the mind of a faithful servant. He may even have thought (supposing it was ever true that he had tried to obtain the papers Mrs Clarke said she had) that his Royal Highness would appreciate the recovery of any documents tending to cast aspersions on a member of his family. The duke had behaved with high principle on an earlier occasion, refusing all offers to inspect a packet of indiscreet and malicious letters written by the Princess of Wales which had fallen into the wrong hands.

If there was drawing-room and coffee-house speculation about the Duke of Kent's part in the affair, however, the press was not critical of him. Indeed, the criticism and ridicule were all for Mrs Clarke. *The Times*, in a three-column review of *The Rival Princes* on 30 June, dissected the book with interpolation of scornful comment. 'The whole publication . . . does contain such excellent fun, and has amused us so much in the hasty perusal, that we are anxious to introduce our readers to a fuller acquaintance with it.' Some of its contents, *The Times* said, would 'curl the most democratic muscles into a grin'. The review concluded: 'It will be remarked that Mrs Clarke cannot in this, as in other instances, wherin she has been believed, produce a single scrap of a document to support her testimony. The whole of the charge, therefore, that Major Dodd *said* he came from the Duke of Kent, rests upon her naked word; that he *did* so come is a fact more remote from proof still'. And Mrs Clarke's spiteful publication of letters from Lord Folkestone brought a caustic comment from *The Times*: 'This Lady, it appears, has not done clapper-clawing the Noble Lord.'

It seems apparent that Mrs Clarke, had she had evidence beyond her own imaginative malice, would certainly have rushed it into print. The chief loser from the affair was Major Dodd, though *The Times*, editorially perturbed by injustice, went to bat on his behalf on 19 June. 'It is said that the officers of the royal artillery, in which Major Dodd is a Captain, have had a meeting in which it was resolved that they cannot, with propriety, associate with him any longer as an officer or a gentlemen. A representation founded upon this resolution has been drawn up and presented to Lord Mulgrave, who, as Master-General of the Ordnance, is Commander-in-Chief of the Artillery. . . .

'We think . . . that there is a kind of premature officiousness in the representation herein stated to have been made; Mr Dodd is as yet only impeached by Mrs Clarke's book; and this is evidence neither upon oath, nor on examination in open court.'

In his work with the duke, Dodd's official status was secretary to the Governor of Gibraltar, and this position was summarily annulled. He lost his majority, and though the duke offered sympathy and friendship for many years after his voluntary resignation from his Royal Highness's service, his influence was not great enough to afford Dodd any practical relief.

Mary Anne had tilted at Madame, too, in her book. 'As I am in possession of all the circumstances attending the duke of Kent's conduct, while he was governor of Gibraltar', she hinted darkly, 'it is not improbable but I shall publish a curious history of his *courage, military and political actions,* together with an entertaining account of the discovery of st Lawrence!' Later in the book she quoted Mr Glennie: 'He observed, that the duke's affection for his old French lady, whom, he lamented he could not marry, was a proof of his *steady disposition,* and domestic good qualities, added to which, he regularly went to church, and was never *seen inebriated*—a *habit* he always endeavored to check in those, over whom he had any influence.' In a back-handed way, she had paid him a kind of compliment. (338)

But Madame—and the duke—had other things to worry about. The two sums given him by the King in 1806 and 1807 from the droits of the Admiralty had been applied to cancelling a debt originally bonded in 1791. Having failed in repeated attempts to get reimbursement for his losses during service abroad, and having in any case been denied a provision for years longer than his elder brothers, the duke had at last given up the attempt to cope with his debts alone. In 1807 a group of trustees consolidated his debts. To liquidate them he agreed to have the trustees control half his income and to try to live on the remainder. He was badly hit in mid-1810 by the failure of the banking house of Devaynes and Company, at a time when a sum owing to his trustees was in their hands and he was overdrawn by about the same amount, leaving him with no cash in hand for immediate bills. For the duke, budgeting was a month-to-month juggling of income against payments due, and any unforeseen hitch toppled his whole financial house of cards. He had no recourse but to ask for a large advance from Coutts to meet current expenses, adding still further to his interest payments.

The first real tragedy that came into the lives of the duke and Madame struck in July 1810 when a letter lated 4 January from Louis de Salaberry (Chevalier) in India brought the news that the tall and handsome Maurice, second de Salaberry son, had died of dysentery in India on 17 October, 1809. Just over a year later, Chevalier himself fell victim to the same disease. The duke, who had been trying to arrange Chevalier's return from India, at once prepared to ask for the little Edward's posting to Canada when the winter was past, to comfort his parents. But 'the little gentleman', now almost twenty and as tall as his two elder brothers (Chevalier at five foot ten had been the shortest of the four), did not go to Canada, but to Spain to take part in the Peninsular War; and on 24 April 1812, the duke had the heavy task of writing to tell his parents that this third son too was dead, killed at the murderous storming of Badajos on 5 April (the anniversary of Chevalier's death two years before).

'Little did I think', wrote the duke, 'when a few days ago I put into the hands of Mr Ryland . . . the original of the Letter from Lieut. Gordon of my Regiment, announcing the particulars of the death of our poor Chevalier . . . that it would so soon again fall to my lot to communicate what I fear will be a still heavier blow to my old friends . . . an event that has overwhelmed Mad de St Laurent & myself in the deepest affliction, indeed so much so that no powers of language can convey to you the effect it has had upon us.'

Young Edward had perhaps had a presentiment of his fate, or at any rate the generosity and forethought to write, just before the attack, a touching letter to show his love and affection for the godparents who had cared for him so well. The letter was found afterwards among his effects.

'I am ordered to storm one of the breaches this Evening. As the service is rather dangerous, and I may or may not return, I beg leave to assure your Royal Highness as well as Madame, that whatever may happen to me, I shall, at every moment, feel how much I am indebted to you.

'Believe, Sir, that my last moments shall be to wish all the happiness, which you, as well as Madame so eminently deserve—I have the honor to be with eternal gratitude, your Royal Highness' most obedient and grateful Servant. . . .' (339)

It was years before Madame could bring herself to write to his parents, almost prostrated by the triple loss, and by this time (28 September 1814) she could at least congratulate them on the exploits of their eldest son Charles, who had become 'the hero of Chateauguay' in an engagement with the Americans in the War of 1812. 'Your very touching letter, my dear de Salaberry, could not be read by me without the most tender interest and most profound sympathy; it affected me most keenly, and would have given you evidence, my old and dear friend, why I was unwilling to re-open the subject of *our* loss; you would have felt that I ought not to be reproached for my silence. Alas! I had a great desire to write, but I felt that I could not do so without exposing my afflicted friend to a blow that might be fatal. It was necessary to act with prudence, and I have waited till the time would arrive when I might write without increasing her grief . . . I hope . . . that religion in giving her the consoling hope that she will again see her children in a better world, will relieve the anguish of her heart.' Madame continued with the information that she had given to Charles (the eldest and only remaining son) 'many details in connexion with your poor boy . . . I may add that having had occasion lately to converse with an officer on the terrible assault on Badajos, I was positively assured by him, that the fatal shot which carried away the object of our eternal regret, inflicted no pain. This is poor consolation, without doubt, but still it is some.'

Her long letter assured de Salaberry that she would continue to write, valuing her memories of Quebec and 'a friendship which has triumphed over twenty years of absence'. She added: 'All the public papers are full of [your son's] great deeds and . . . I am as proud as if he were my own brother, and I do not fail to say to all who speak to me—"The young man whom you saw here, is *the* Mr de Salaberry who has conducted himself with such heroism."' It was the last letter from Madame to the de Salaberrys that has survived. (340)

The duke had had personal tragedies to face in these years. 'Our beloved Amelia is absolutely going out like a candle', the Princess Augusta wrote to Lady Harcourt on 26 October 1810. (341) The youngest princess, her father's favourite, died on the Duke of Kent's

o

birthday, 2 November, and Lady Aylesbury heard a whisper from the Duke of York, with whom his younger brother had managed to maintain a polite if not cordial relationship over the years: 'Though this is a sad day, I must drink to the health of poor Edward.' (342)

The King, who had kept an increasingly precarious grasp on reality, now gave up the struggle. Though the Regency was proclaimed in February 1811, there was a period of a few months when the King swung tragically between reality and madness, when he walked with his sons on the Terrace, chose—on one occasion at least—the music for the ancient music nights (all excerpts relating to madness and blindness), (343) and once or twice even went riding. For ten more years he would live in a comparatively peaceful solitude, a sad old man playing his piano, singing to himself 'in a voice both sonorous and touching', holding conversations with friends from the past whose answers he supplied himself, silently observed in his blindness from time to time with compassion and regret by his wife and his sons. The Regent told the French comtesse de Boigne of one of these visits. 'The tears ran down his cheeks as he spoke to us of this voice singing the beautiful motets of Handel, and of the constraint which he was obliged to put upon himself to refrain from clasping the venerable musician in his arms.' (349)

The last years he would spend in England with Madame were, despite the duke's lack of professional employment, busy and productive. He was not a man who could live in useless idleness. In these years he built the reputation for social concern for which he would command a growing respect, indefatigably chairing meetings for the benefit of widows, orphans and the under-privileged. His friendship with Louis-Philippe grew stronger, with frequent exchanges of visits between Castle Hill Lodge and Twickenham (at Kensington Palace a special bedroom was furnished for the French duke). Louis-Philippe for some years had been eager to marry the Princess Elizabeth, a match vetoed by the Queen, and wrote at length to Madame (an admirable and sympathetic confidante) about his affairs of the heart both at this time and during his courtship of the Princess Marie-Amélie of Sicily, whom he eventually married in November 1809. (345)

Over the years, Madame had been thriftily adding the interest on her capital and any surplus from her allowance to the purchase of additional investments. She was also helping her youngest brother Jean-Claude in Geneva with an allowance, and in July 1811 the duke asked Coutts to let her have a small book in which she could keep track of her payments and receipts. Jean-Claude, inclined to be an irresponsible sponger on his sister, by now had two more children, Charles born in 1805, and the baby Thérèse-Caroline-Sylvie, a month old. The youngest, Edward, who would be another godson of the duke's, would not be born until 1815. The war with France made communication difficult, but the duke was able to arrange a conveyance through Coutts's Paris correspondent, the banking company of Perigaux. 'It is not intended to add to the annual allowance of Monsr de Montgenet,' the duke explained on Madame's behalf on 1 June, 'more than will make his receipt the net sum of 100 Louis, that is, to make up to him the loss on the exchange between the two Countries, and that it should be paid to him in ½ yearly sums of 50 Louis, instead of (as before) in quarterly sums of twenty-five. The advance of one hundred and fifty Louis Dors is altogether a separate matter, and intended only to be once paid for a particular purpose.' Perhaps, one wonders, for the birth of the baby Thérèse, Madame's namesake and godchild? (346)

It was at this time that Castle Hill Lodge was visited by the effusive Mr Justice George Hardinge, whose long letter dated 15 August 1811 to his brother Sir Richard Hardinge has been quoted (and misquoted) so often. Hardinge's letter was published in a three-volume edition of his 'works' in 1818, and reprinted in *The Times* (4 February 1820) after the duke's death. In its original form and not discreetly cut to suit the conventions of later biographers, Madame is freely mentioned, and not simply as 'a third person', as some biographers have believed.

Hardinge appeared overcome by magnificence from the moment he arrived (on foot) at the iron entrance gates. He babbled about the grounds, the coloured lights on the stairs, the dignity of the staff, the spacious rooms. Shown into the Regent's suite, he rhapsodized about its elegance and appointments, its mirrors, the flowered velvet that covered the steps to the high bed, the hot and cold water, the supply of books, pens, ink and paper for his convenience.

'In about an hour dinner was announced. The Duke led the way. I was placed at the head of the table. The Duke was on my right; Madame L—— on my left. The honours were chiefly done by him. . . .

'The natural civility of an amiable habit in both of them appeared in two little *traits* of it, and which I may as well delineate here, because they occurred at the *table*, and we are there at present, my Reader and I.

'*Louis the XVIIIth* was upon the *tapis*; and Madame, unsolicited by me, desired one of *her* attendants to ask her maid for his Majesty's Portrait in miniature. The Duke, instead of discouraging this alert *galanterie*, in good humour improved upon it, by saying, "Let her give him poor *Louis Seize* and his *Queen* at the same time." It was accomplished.

'They accidentally mentioned the famous *Dumourier*. I said, "that I loved *seeing* those whom I admired *unseen*, upon report alone, and *in the mind's view.*—But I shall never see *Dumourier*," said I, "for he is the Lord knows where (and I cannot run after him) upon the Continent."—"*Not he*," said the Duke; "he is in this very Island, and he often dines *with us here.*"—I *looked*, but *said* nothing. My *look* was *heard*. Madame asked the Duke (for it is a word and a blow with *her*) if it could not be *managed*?—"Nothing more practicable," said he. "If the Judge will but throw down his glove in the fair spirit of chivalry, *Dumourier* shall pick it up." . . .

'A very little after dinner Madame vanished. I flew to the door, and was in time for it, with a minuet step, not unpractised or unrehearsed . . . but whether such an assiduity was *etiquette* or vulgar, is too deep to be fathomed by so humble a conjecture as mine. . . .

'In the morning the Duke shewed me all his variety of horses and of carriages. He pointed out a curricle to me. "I bought that curricle," said he, "twenty years ago; have travelled in it all over the world; and there it is, firm on its axle. I never was spilt from it but once. It was in *Canada*, near the *Falls of Niagara*, over a concealed stump in a wood just cleared. . . ."

'He is no Gamester,' added Hardinge. 'He is no Huntsman. He never goes to *Newmarket*; but he loves riding upon the road, a full swing trot of nine miles an hour.'

Overwhelmed by the attention he received, Hardinge was most deeply touched by one of the duke's typically thoughtful acts. At breakfast next morning, an unseen band of thirty wind-instruments moved unexpectedly from a brisk march into the dirge written in memory of Hardinge's nephew Captain George Hardinge, killed in a naval engagement off Ceylon in March 1808.

The corpulent sixty-seven-year-old Hardinge, who had an alarming tendency to burst into verse at the smallest provocation, had written a flamboyant poem to Madame dated a few months before this visit:

'*A MADAME DE ST L——T*
Etrenne, Jan. 1, 1811
(*C'est l'Hermite qui parle*)

Age has been call'd "a Vale of Years;"
Life, at the best, a Vale of Tears;
Love, as December nights advance,
At least has parted with romance;
But St L——t a charm has found

That Spring has to the Winter bound:
Upon a furrow'd cheek a tear
No more has clos'd the passing year.
For this, her gift—a Fairy's boon—
Is my commission from the Moon;
Prophetic is the potent spell—
I am its Wizard, and foretell:
The REGENT, by an Act of State,
*Shall E****d's trophies reinstate;*
Though it's half-impious to complain
When Love's in the domestic reign.
But in the sun, or in the shade,
Your planet shall be undecay'd;
And you shall both together sing,
With pride of heart, on Pleasure's Wing:
A turf shall mark the Hermit's bed,
On which no tear that Love can shed
Shall reach in fame, that never dies,
The pearl from Julia's brilliant eyes. (347)

Hardinge was apparently impressed by the depth of feeling and understanding shared by his royal host and hostess. But his legal attainments, said to entitle him 'to aspire to the highest distinction', and his speeches 'replete with merriment and wit', did not prevent him from being a bad poet and worse prophet.

Among other welcome visitors to Castle Hill Lodge were old Halifax friends, Sir John and Lady Wentworth. Her Ladyship, writing to her niece Eliza Monk on 28 July 1812, made a fairly obvious reference to one such visit. 'One day last week the weather was beautiful, and Sir John persuaded me to drive out a few miles, and seek for a country House for two or three months, we did, and I stopped at a *friends* House at *Ealing* and took refreshments, and came home early in the afternoon.' She added later in the same letter: 'The worthy Duke is well and Nancy Dennis is a small woman compared to a friend of his: but she keeps up a sort of shape which makes her still look well. I never saw such a sized woman of fashion in my life.' (348) It would seem that Madame (now fifty-two) like Mrs Fitzherbert and Dorothy Jordan and nearly all the ladies of her age at this time, had lost her youthful slenderness, but not her old charm and sense of style.

The Regency was followed by the fever of political jockeying to be expected after so radical a change, but the Prince's friends, justifiably expectant of power, were to be sadly disappointed. 'Whigs coming in at last', wrote John Cam Hobhouse with jubilation in his journal on

27 May 1812. 'Whigs not coming in', he recorded flatly in the next entry on 2 June. (349)

Now that his brother was Regent, the duke submitted appeals for one military post after another—like the Whigs, depending on his brother for a change in his fortunes. A command in the Mediterranean area. Master of the Ordnance. He would even go back to North America, he said in desperation. The Regent at this time was ill and bad-tempered, quarrelling with the Dukes of York and Cumberland and coming to a final break with Mrs Fitzherbert. ('What will become of us if, as well as our King, our Regent goes mad?' asked Lady Bessborough.) The Duke of Kent recalled to his brother, with gratitude, his support at the time of his trouble at Gibraltar, and in May begged Mrs Fitzherbert to intercede for him. But the days of her influence were past. Only a month later, in the face of insult, she refused to see the Prince again.

One might be allowed perhaps, in seeking a reason for the Regent's change of heart towards his brother, to wonder (with, however, little supporting evidence) if the duke's fondness for Mrs Fitzherbert might have led him into an angrily resented appeal on her behalf. There is a hint in his letter to Mrs Fitzherbert of 30 December 1809 that his brother was touchy about any sign of interference or comment in the matter of her relationship with the Prince. Or did he offend his brother by too strongly showing his sympathy for the young Princess Charlotte, against whom, though his own daughter, the Regent was showing a furious unfatherly severity to the point of cruelty?

Whatever the cause, there was no appointment for the duke: and in March 1813 Dodd wrote to Wright in Gibraltar about 'an offer which Mr Parker/the duke's secretary/ writes me has been made to the Duke of Kent to go to Malta, and which he seems to think His Royal H/s will decline through the influence of Madame', though, he added, 'I confess I am not of opinion that such a Command is sufficiently honorable to him, unless it were coupled with Gibraltar'. Dodd had lost none of his respect and friendship for the duke. He concluded disgustedly, 'The Prince ought for once in his life to keep his promise and give his Brother the Ordnance'. (350)

Though the duke's life as a royal prince had to exclude Madame (she never went with him to Windsor or Buckingham House, or to Court functions, or on the family visits to Weymouth), she did on at least one occasion meet the Queen and two of the princesses. On 7 July 1813 the Queen, with the Princesses Mary and Elizabeth, the Duchess of York, the Duke of Cambridge, and their attendants, paid a visit to Castle Hill Lodge. 'Her Majesty and the Princesses arrived at Castle-Hill, the seat of the Duke of Kent, about three o'clock on Wednesday', reported the *Morning Chronicle* on the 9th. 'They were received by the Duke of Kent, the Duke and Duchess of York, Ladies Macclesfield and Poulet, Count Munster and Colonel Desbrow. The day proving remarkably fine, her Majesty rode in her little garden chaise round the pleasure grounds. The Princesses and the rest of the company walked through the grounds and gardens, with which they appeared extremely delighted. The Royal Party, after partaking of an excellent dinner, left at eight o'clock.'

Madame's name does not appear on any record, but she was indubitably there, watching the Duchess of York, as hostess, receive the guests she was forbidden by etiquette to welcome to her own home. She was unmentioned, still the invisible woman not to be acknowledged by anyone, but she was there. The daily record of meals and supplies for this date shows the ten guests (the Duke of York was not present, despite the press report) listed by name and by total number. The Upper Servants' Table had eight persons extra. There were nine extra with the Under-servants. For breakfast at his Royal Highness's table, two as usual. And for dinner—*two* also, with *ten persons extra*. (351)

The Queen might have allowed a small smile to Thérèse-Bernardine as she curtsied when her Majesty passed by. The princesses, kind women, would have put her at ease, including her in conversation as they rambled through the gardens. They knew of Madame and seem to have been happy that their brother had found congenial companionship. Four years earlier, the Princess Elizabeth had written amiably to the Prince of Wales: 'Our dear good Edward I believe faithful to the banks of St Laurence—& as every body must have a Saint it is but fair He should have his.' (352)

The news of Wellington's victory at Vittoria on 21 June, when Joseph Bonaparte was driven back into France, lit up an ecstatic London in July, and was celebrated with a grand fête and dinner at Vauxhall (the *Morning Chronicle* made the radical suggestion on 12 July that Ladies should be allowed to sit down with the Gentlemen instead of being required to look on from the galleries). At the end of July, the Duke of Kent had probably the worst accident of his life when he was thrown from his horse and sustained injuries that confined him to the Lodge for about eight weeks. He fell hard on his temple, tearing his lip and severely cutting and bruising his arms and legs. As late as 23 September he was telling Coutts that though recovered, 'I feel at times a little weakness in my left arm, and my jaw still exhibits in a small degree the remains of the wounds which I sustained.' (353)

The winter of 1813–1814 was excessively severe, with snow, frost, wind and fog, during which the papers published hair-raising stories of celebrities getting lost (including the Regent) and people falling into ditches. On the frozen Thames a lively fair ran for weeks, where dancing and skittles entertained the crowds, and booths were set up, 'distinguished by appropriate signs . . . the Waterman's Arms, the Crown, the Magpye, the Eelpot'. Madame was confined to the Lodge for six straight weeks: the roads between Ealing and London were in a state that made travelling in a carriage impossible.

In this year the duke strongly supported the claim of General Knollys to the title of Earl of Banbury, and when the case was lost, turned to Coutts to help his friend get settled at Rouen, where living was cheaper, by introducing him and his family 'into the best, *quiet* society of the place'. (354) Years later, Madame would reap a reward from this kindness.

The duke now found he had a real enemy in the Prince Regent. Whatever the cause, the Regent had made a complete turnabout in his feeling for his younger brother, listening to the most trivial talk that might give a semblance of justification to his behaviour. Almost anything the duke did was now construed as 'deceit or deep-laid plans'. When the Duke of York had run to the Regent ('out of friendship for him, being the brother nearest his own age'), with a tale of 'a fine carriage building for Princess Charlotte at Birch the coachmaker's', and 'had told him all about this Birch, who was a protégé of the Duke of Kent', the Regent reared up and called on Cornelia Knight, his daughter's 'lady companion' to account for what he seemed to regard as interference. Miss Knight explained mildly that the carriage had in fact been ordered by the Duchess of Leeds, governess to the Princess, who had sought the duke's friendly advice as had been done for years past. (355)

Even to Charlotte herself the Regent ranted against his brother.

'The Prince I find was *very virulent* on the score of the D. of Kent, & went so far as to say he *would not allow* of his *coming here*', wrote the Princess on 7 February 1814. The young girl hardly knew where to place her trust, harassed from all sides, by the Queen, her father and her aunts, and beset with those she called spies. When only sixteen she had written uncertainly to her friend Margaret Mercer Elphinstone (26 October, 1812): 'The D. of Kent I should *be careful* with in a degree, tho' I don't know why I say so, as he has always been *uniformly* kind to me since I have been here/at Windsor/, & whenever he comes he never fails coming to see me & sitting either part of the mg. or eg. with me in the kindest & most friendly manner possible, so that I feel that, & am much obliged to him; & when it has been in his power to do/a/good natured thing by me or for me, he has been alwas ready & happy to do it.' (356)

It is stretching credulity to see in the duke's friendship for this lonely and tormented girl, all her early life a victim of her parents' incompatibility, anything more than his real and demonstrated affection for all young people. How much his reputation for underhanded plotting has been based on this kind of hearsay is hard to assess. Certainly the fact of the Regent's enmity has somehow come to be accepted as reflecting on the duke and not on the Regent: as an infallible proof of the duke's lack of integrity. Most certainly the nickname of 'Joseph Surface' given to us at third-hand by Wellington via Creevey, seems to have been accepted by historians as if it were an unarguable estimate of the Duke of Kent to be swallowed unquestioned, and not the generalization of temperamental princesses, coloured by the judgement of an emotional and biased elder brother who in his time made a thousand ill-judged comments about people with whom he was for the moment displeased.

The Regent's enmity could not, however, ban the duke from taking his rightful part in State events. The electrifying news of the entry of the Allied Sovereigns into Paris on 31 March had been received in London on 5 April, and 'announced to an enraptured public by the firing of the Park and Tower guns, the ringing of merry peals'. (357) Her Imperial Highness the Grand Duchess of Oldenburg (sister of Alexander I of Russia) who had been visiting London and tirelessly inspecting colleges, asylums, galleries, factories and dockyards (an occupation the press recommended to the guardians of the Princess Charlotte), was soon to be joined by her brother. With other Illustrious Personages, he would be escorted across the Channel by Admiral His Royal Highness the Duke of Clarence in one of the royal yachts at the end of the month. In the meantime, there was the public entry into London of a long-exiled Royal Personage, now Louis XVIII of France, in a procession of prancing horses, fluttering white ribbons, and the Guards in full State uniforms.

Shortly after midday on 20 April the Regent had left for Stanmore in his travelling carriage to meet the King. Hyde Park, cleared of traffic, was opened to the people for the spectacle. A guard of honour in white gaiters and wearing white cockades was marched into Piccadilly, and a band played outside the Pulteney Hotel, where the Duchess of Oldenburg was entertaining the Princesses Elizabeth, Mary, Charlotte of Wales, and Sophia of Gloucester.

At Stanmore the whole town was decorated with anything white that could be found, including sheets and pillowcases. The Regent, at

the Abercorn Arms Inn, awaited the arrival of Louis, who, accompanied by anyone who could get hold of a horse, arrived in his carriage
drawn by enthusiastic members of the crowd. He was lifted out (a big,
lame, unwieldy man), welcomed by the Regent and assisted into the
State carriage drawn by cream-coloured horses, for the two-hour
journey to London. The procession was in full royal panoply, the
royal party preceded by a hundred gentlemen on horseback, 'Horse-
Trumpeters in their splendid gold lace dress, a numerous party of
the Royal Horse Guards,' and six Royal Carriages with an outrider
to each one. At Greillon's [sic] Hotel in Albemarle Street, where a
State ceremony of welcome was held, the party was greeted by the
Duke of Kent's band : 'the people unanimously huzzaed /and /the ladies
from the windows waved their handkerchiefs.' (358) Even if she could
not be a member of any official party, it seems unlikely that Madame
would have missed seeing so memorable an event from a vantage point
with friends—the restoration of the monarchy of her own country.

Next day the King of France was invested by the Regent as a
Knight of the Most Noble Order of the Garter, escorted by the Dukes
of York and Kent in their robes of dark blue velvet lined with white
satin. The Regent accompanied the King that night to a Dover gone
mad with excitement, saw him onto a royal yacht superbly fitted with
scarlet cloth, gold lace, and an awning made from the flags of the
Allied Nations, and went back to a London preparing to receive still
more illustrious visitors. 'Night and day, everybody was rushing everywhere', wrote the Countess Brownlow. Illuminations, fireworks,
'frigates firing on the Serpentine for the masses . . . and great parties
and balls for the great people' kept London agog. (359)

Royal cooks were dispatched to serve on the royal yachts, and the
Emperor of Russia and the King of Prussia arrived in London on
7 June. The *Morning Post* on the 9th found the Emperor 'tall, not very
lusty', but with 'an open prepossessing countenance. The upper part
of his head is rather bald'. The royal visitors brought out enormous
throngs. Two thousand got into the Opera without paying,
the press said, because of the crowds at the doors. Well-dressed
multitudes massed in Hyde Park to see the Illustrious Personages
gallop across the green to Kensington Gardens, preceded by the Duke
of Kent. There were dinners, levees, fêtes. The Emperor himself was
more than a little harassed by the enthusiasm. 'The crowd is so great
everywhere he is, that the Emperor says he would willingly stand one
or even two whole days to be seen on London Bridge if they would
let him alone afterwards.' (360)

The sun shone in this wonderful summer, and the Londoners loved
it, even though the austere Samuel Romilly was critical when it was

all over. 'London has for a long time been half crazy with emperors, and kings, and shows, and illuminations, and fireworks,' he wrote afterwards to his friend Pierre Dumont. 'It has at last sunk into a dead torpor, which is very stupid to the few fashionable persons who may be still lingering in town, but which is very salutary to the lower and laborious orders of the people. The mischief which has been done to the morals and happiness of the inferior artisans by the long holidays, which they have been indulged with, is hardly to be conceived. I have been assured that several pawnbrokers have declared that, while these festivals lasted, they lent, on the pledges of the clothes, and furniture, and tools of their poor customers, about ten times as much as they are accustomed to do in ordinary times.' (361)

Among the visitors had come a quiet and modest young man with a vast ambition and a yellow carriage borrowed from his brother-in-law. 'Perhaps I will end up by marrying in England and staying there: that would be odd', wrote Prince Leopold of Saxe-Coburg to his sister Sophie. 362)

CHAPTER SEVENTEEN

Brussels

For the Duke of Kent the summer of 1814 was a busy one. He was here, there and everywhere. On 2 May he was present at the annual dinner of Governors and Subscribers to the Scottish Corporation, supporting his brother of Sussex in the chair. On 4 May he attended the British and Foreign Bible Society's tenth annual dinner. He chaired the fortieth anniversary meeting of the Royal Humane Society on 18 May, and supported the chair on 21 May at the annual meeting of subscribers to the National Education. At the British and Foreign School Society on 24 June, when a poetical tribute written by Mary Russell Mitford was sung, he was again supporting the chair.

Miss Mitford was in the gallery 'to hear splendid speeches and super-lative poetry, and to see—but, alas! not to share—super-excellent eating. Terribly and fearfully gallant is the etiquette of a public dinner', she sighed, 'which considers and treats men as mortals—well-filled mortals— and women as angels—starving angels'. She had an embar-rassed moment of triumph when Lord Lansdowne, the chairman, called for her health to be drunk. The Duke of Kent noticing that his Lordship's voice had not reached all the audience, roared out the toast again 'with stentorian lungs'. A flourish of drums and trumpets from his band, and a 'three times three' with the thundering plaudits of 500 people shook the blushing Miss Mitford, who had mistaken the name for *Whitbread,* though she had wondered a little how that gentleman could be described as 'fair and amiable'. (363)

Between his charitable and State duties, the duke frequently requested the use of Coutts's theatre boxes. 'Desirous of promising Madame de St Laurent who is come up for the first time these six weeks a sight of the new Tragedian at Drury Lane . . .' 'particularly desirous not to deprive Madame of seeing the Opera tomorrow night, as I cannot join her there till late. . . .' 'We are desirous of seeing the new operatic piece called Frederick the great, of which people speak so favourably. . . .'

After the military reviews and the feasts and fireworks were over, he went back to the peaceful retirement of Castle Hill Lodge, and postponed appointments to watch over Madame who had come down with one of her bad colds (she would be confined for weeks with another one in January). 'Madame de St. Laurent not having made that progress in her convalescence which I had been sanguine in hoping she would . . . but rather had an accession of fever, which has made her suffer considerably, I shall prefer not leaving home tomorrow,' he wrote to Sir William Beechey who was painting his portrait. . . . 'If on Sunday or Monday I should feel more easy about quitting her, for a few hours, I will then . . . send you a Note. . . .' (364)

Now that Bonaparte had abdicated and was languishing on Elba, people were flocking to a Paris denied them for so long, and writing home as if they were tourists discovering a new resort. 'Everything here seems to be at about half the price it bears in England, except cloth which is as dear, and wine, which of course is to be had for a third of what we are obliged to pay for it . . . keeping a carriage seems to be quite as expensive as it is in London. We pay twenty-four francs a day, and we find it impossible to do without one for twenty-four hours. The streets are so villainously dirty and ill-paved, that it is unpleasant even for a man to walk much. A woman can never set foot to ground.' (365)

The young Prince Leopold was finding life in London 'frightfully dear', but the prospects of realizing the plan that had brought him from Paris (nothing less than to marry the Princess Charlotte) was looking good even though the Regent, still hoping vainly for Charlotte's marriage to the Prince of Orange to whom she had been briefly engaged, was frowning on him as a suitor for his daughter's hand. Leopold was optimistic and persistent. It was to be, however, more than a year before his suit was successful, a year spent by the Duke of Kent in unsuccessful attempts to retrench and disentangle himself from the binding cords of debt.

He had begun to think of drastic economies. 'The Duke of Kent dined at the Castle Sunday . . .' wrote Princess Charlotte on 31 January 1815. 'His affairs are terribly deranged, & he talks of a visit in the summer to Pss. Royal/the Queen of Wurtemberg/, & then will put his money out to accrue for 2 or 3 years till when he will not return, & when he does it will be all cleared.' (366)

By this time, the Princess Charlotte had evidently discounted her father's rantings and judged her uncle on his own merits. She would be his friend until her death. In the tangle of tales and counter-tales with which the Royal Family was tying itself in knots, she had turned to him as one of those she could trust. 'I got a word with the D. of Kent', she wrote early in January, '& told him exactly what had passed about A/ugustus/& desired he would *convey it to him* in case of misrepresentations & lies that might be made & set about'. (367) A similar sympathy and discretion seems to have been recognized in the duke many years earlier, pointing once again to the family's tendency to turn to him in personal troubles. At the time of his sister Princess Amelia's affair with Colonel Fitzroy, the Queen had advised her youngest daughter in May 1803 'neither directly or indirectly to name a word of this unpleasant business to your Brothers, *nay not even to the Duke of Kent* . . .' (368) This seems to imply a habit in his young sister of making a confidant of the duke: had he been noted for untrustworthiness, his mother would have written '*especially not* the Duke of Kent'.

But before the harassed duke could escape to the Continent, there was to be the enormous shock and excitement of the Hundred Days. 'The tiger has escaped from Elba; the monster spent three days at sea; the traitor disembarked at Fréjus; the brigand-chief advanced to Grenoble; Napoleon entered Lyon; the Emperor arrived at Versailles; His Majesty sleeps this night at the Tuileries.' Thus ran the latest squib from Paris. (369) There was a mad scramble to get out of the French capital. 'The King & family . . ./are/on their way to Belgium, all the *English families* are *arrived* or on their way', wrote the Princess Charlotte from the accounts she had heard. 'People seemed as if they were planet struck.' (370)

Wellington arrived in Brussels on 6 April. On 21 June the young Emma Sophia Cust, alone in the London house of her uncle Lord Castlereagh, rushed to the window at the sudden sound of shouting and saw three of the 'Eagles' of France projecting from the windows of a post-chaise-and-four that drew up in a lather of horses at the door and turned abruptly to head down the street to Mrs Boehm's where the Regent was dining. Hastily dressing after a message from Lady Castlereagh, she went to the house and heard the Regent, with tears running down his cheeks, announce the losses and the victory of Waterloo. (371)

Then there was the marriage of the Princess Charlotte—'that truly English girl, that darling hope of Britain'—to Prince Leopold on 2 May 1816, when the streets 'were literally choaked with people', and a lot of surprised spectators found themselves pushed inside Clarence

House by the crush of the crowd. Female well-wishers patted the young prince on the back, and the sentinels with difficulty dissuaded the populace from removing the horses to draw his carriage to Carlton House.

The Duke of Kent had almost managed to rid himself of Castle Hill Lodge at this time, a residence that, dearly as he loved it, he could not afford. The Regent, supported by the Queen who had admired it greatly when she made her visit there, had thought seriously of acquiring it for his daughter and her husband, but objections raised by Lord Liverpool prevailed. 'To begin with Lrd Liverpool whom I saw yesterday on account of Edward's place in the country', the Queen wrote to the Regent on 6 March, '& stated the particular reasons why you wished to make the purchase, & yr intention of giving it to her & afterwards to settle it upon the Prince of Cobourg . . . The objections he made are various 1st that the situation of the place was not in a pritty country, 2d that the Prince might be a sportsman & could find no such amusement in that neighbourhood, 3d that there was very little ground about the place. Tho' these objections are true I represented to him, that I was sure neither you or themselves would ever find a more convenient & complete house provided with every comfort for either man or woman & in my opinion I should think large enough for the Prince of Cobourg to pursue his love for botany as there is a collection of fine plants made by Acton, a good kitchen garden & a place ready made.' (372)

At the beginning of March, the duke had made a quick trip to Brussels to see about renting a house there. He was grateful for the offer of Coutts's theatre box to Madame during his absence, though a severe cold kept her 'unable to avail herself of it, and I fear, even to explain by note the cause why she could not'. (373)

They left for the Continent on 19 August, Madame (who would never see England again) directly for Dover in the morning, the duke in the afternoon after bidding farewell to his family. After spending the night at Calais, they separated, Madame heading for Paris where she had a touching reunion on the 23rd with her sister Beatrix (now the comtesse de Jansac) after a twenty-six-year separation, 'though she found her much altered'. On the 31st she told the duke 'she had then just hired a House, with which she seemed to be pleased, for six weeks, and wrote in good spirits'. (374) The house—17 rue de Helder —saw a real Mongenet family reunion. Claude-Charles came up from Chambéry, and Madame met for the first time the young man who would be a great comfort to her in her years of loneliness—Charles-Benjamin (now twenty and a law student in Paris), who had been born when she was on tour in far-off Nova Scotia. Even the ne'er-do-well Jean-Claude came from Geneva to see his glamorous (and generous) sister, but as usual he caused problems by coming late and delaying Madame's departure for Brussels. (375)

The duke went to Valenciennes to review his regiment, and thence to Brussels, where he was detained for three weeks 'owing to the non-arrival until the 7th of my servants, equipment and baggage'. There had been considerable servant trouble, even the faithful Beck somehow confusing orders. The duke wrote to General Wetherall in some irritation: 'What he had to do with a passport from the Bavarian Minister to go to Paris, God above alone knows, for Madam de St Laurent only required that of the French Ambassador . . . and as my servant going to Paris he certainly could not require another. This is the more provoking as Madam has been obliged to dismiss Roger on account of his most scandalous inebriety from the moment of his arrival in Paris, and by a letter received today from Mrs Mahieu by her husband, has also parted from *her*, a circumstance I was not surprised at, as I always thought she would be useless lumber to her after she crossed the water, being in fact only fit to stick close to her chair as a sempstress . . . so that until Beck arrives, she will have no other attendant than the little Swiss footman about her, that she has ever seen before.'

The duke himself was not in very high spirits, he told Wetherall, 'but that is an evil I must struggle against I know manfully & I do my best God knows'. (376) At this point in his life, for the first time, he was having thoughts of marrying, and the prospect of parting from Madame lay heavy on his heart.

Years later Henry Greville, younger brother of Charles Greville the diarist, wrote in his own diary a story told him by Madame de Lieven. 'The Emperor Alexander of Russia was very anxious to make up a match between him/the Duke of Kent/and the Princess of Baden, sister to the Empress Elizabeth. The Duke of Kent expressed himself as quite willing to form the alliance, but at the same time told the Emperor that he had not a farthing of money wherewith to travel or pay the necessary expenses of such an expedition. The Emperor said that if this was the only obstacle he would remove it by furnishing H.R.H. with 2,000l., with which he repaired to Carlsruhe, dined at Court, and saw the Princess, and the following morning marched off to Leiningen and at once married the Duchess of Kent; and he never refunded the money or made the Emperor any apology whatever. The only *amende* he did make was to ask the Emperor to be godfather to Princess Victoria, which enraged George the Fourth, who detested him.' (377)

It was not quite that simple, and the story bears the familiar acid of

Jean-Claude Mongenet with his wife and three of his children, Louise,
Edouard, and Thérèse.
*Credit: By kind permission of Madame Botok-Berlioz, direct descendant of Jean-
Claude, (portrait by David).*

Sir John Wentworth (1737-1820), Governor of Nova Scotia.
Credit: New Brunswick Museum, Canada.

Lady Wentworth, painted by J. S. Copley.
Credit: Public Archives of Canada.

Madame de Lieven's tongue. If Alexander financed the journey, he must have known he took a calculated risk in this investment of his money. The whole project could only be speculative: there could be no commitment involved. And Alexander surely could not have expected, for a journey the duke would not otherwise have taken, a reimbursement whose only alternative would be to go through with a marriage from which he recoiled. It was on this journey, however, that the duke put out another tentative feeler that could lead to marriage. It had been a suggestion and wish of Princess Charlotte and Prince Leopold that he might form an alliance with the latter's widowed sister, the Dowager Princess Victoire of Leiningen. Accordingly, he stopped briefly at Amorbach on his return journey before going on to join Madame in Paris.

For the duke, whose love for Thérèse-Bernardine had grown into something more than love—the friendship into which at their age the long experience of warm companionship had ripened—any marriage would mean a poignant loss. But England had already begun making uneasy speculation about the succession of the House of Brunswick. Princess Charlotte was too newly married to have shown any sign of what *The Military Register* of 8 May delicately referred to on her wedding day as 'the hopes which the nation has every right to entertain from the event'. None of the other members of the King's large family had produced a legitimate heir.

There was also, for impecunious princes, the possibility of resolving their financial difficulties by the enlarged allowance they could confidently expect from a grateful country. The Duke of Clarence had given expression to the thinking as early as 1814 when he wrote on 2 January to William Adam: 'For the real sake of the country it is requisite one of us should marry, for fear of any accident to Princess Charlotte.' (378) He had parted from Mrs Jordan in 1811 (amicably and with great generosity), and had made rather a fool of himself at that time looking for a wealthy wife. 'I trust that all the historiettes about the Duke of Clarence are lies and "waggeries",' wrote Lord Auckland at the end of 1811, 'but, when we are told that he first offered himself to Miss Long, and immediately afterwards to Miss Mercer, and then to Lady Berkeley, and that he has made himself a reviewing General of regiments, and an inspecting Commissioner of Dockyards, it is difficult not to apprehend that there may be more business for Messrs R. and T. Willis.' (379)

On his tour in Europe, the Duke of Kent spent about a month visiting family and friends, including his sister the Queen of Würtemberg, whom he had not seen for thirty-one years, and the husband she would lose a month later. He renewed an early friendship with the

P

eldest son of the Landgrave of Hesse-Homburg, whom he had known in Geneva, and who would later marry his sister Princess Elizabeth. He called on his uncle, the Grand Duke of Mecklenberg-Strelitz, who was to die before the end of the year. His journey took him through Liège, Aix-la-Chapelle, Cologne, Coblentz and Mayence, to Frankfort, Darmstadt, Carlsruhe, Stuttgart, and then straight to Paris via Mannheim, Metz and Verdun.

Even the visit to Paris was not free of the criticism to which he was so often subjected. Early in February, when he first contemplated going abroad, Castlereagh had written to ask the Regent to 'lay his injunctions upon the Duke of Kent not to enter/France/. His R. H's habits with the Duke of Orleans might either in the selection of his residence, or of his society lead to misconception equally unjust and inconvenient both to the Duke of Orleans and your [sic] Royal Highness.' (380)

But the eleven Parisian days were light-hearted and unpressured, an interlude when the duke could forget the possibility of parting, and enjoy, almost as a private person, this short freedom from heavy decisions. 'I was most kindly received (in Paris) by all the Royal Family,' he told Mrs Fitzherbert later. 'I had two audiences of the King and dined with him once. I also dined once with the Duchess Dowager of Orleans, once with the English Ambassador, and once with the Hanoverian Minister—all the other days at home. My evenings I generally went to the Theatre with Madame de St Laurent and her sister in a private box, and the mornings I devoted to seeing those objects that I considered most deserving of attention, accompanied by a nephew of Madame St Laurent, a very intelligent young man.' (This was the young Charles-Benjamin, studying law in Paris.) As well as these delightfully informal activities, 'perfectly *incog.*', he visited St Cloud and Versailles, and one day spent three hours at the Hôtel Dieu, where 900 patients were cared for by forty-eight Sisters of Charity. 'In short, the day was never long enough for all I had to do, and I left a great deal to see for another time.' (381)

Leaving Madame with her family (waiting for the delinquent Jean-Claude to arrive) he set off on 19 October for Cambrai, and on the 22nd, with his brother the Duke of Cambridge, he was entertained with balls and theatricals after watching the Duke of Wellington put his troops through a variety of muddy manoeuvres in pouring rain.

Madame joined him at Brussels on 7 November, and now began a bitter-sweet year for the duke, keyed to a pitch of painful expectancy during the slow progress of his marriage proposal, unwilling to contemplate the heartbreak he knew he would bring to Thérèse-Bernardine, savouring the days any one of which could bring him to the final parting. They lived, as at Ealing, a quiet domestic life in the Hôtel de Maldegham, just off the Place Royale, which the duke had rented from its tenant Admiral Donnelly. 'My house, though old, thanks to painting, papering, whitewashing, carpeting and putting up a number of stoves, is very tolerably comfortable, totally *isolé* from any other, not overlooked, and with a very fine flower garden and small shrubbery, a great deal of fruit on the wall and on standards and I have the advantage of having all my horses, equipages and stablemen within my own yard.' (382)

An outside observer, Pryse Lockhart Gordon, confirmed his Royal Highness's own description. 'The duke's taste for architecture, embellishing, and adorning, was well known, and no one was surprised when a host of carpenters were put into requisition; and in a few months the house was so altered and ornamented (and of course improved), that the young count, when invited to see what the royal duke had done, could hardly recognise his late abode. The extensive gardens next attracted his royal highness's attention, and were new modelled and replanted with the choicest flowers and rarest shrubs which the kingdom could produce. The stables and *remises* were furnished with stalls and mangers, and pavements and ventilators, according to the most approved plans in England; and his royal high-ness's stud became the admiration of the public.'

The duke also, at his own expense, transformed a piece of waste ground on the east side of the mansion from a place 'hitherto covered with filth and every sort of abomination' into an area of 'serpentine walks neatly sanded, bowers covered with creeping plants, artificial mounds, and clumps of flowering shrubs; the whole being inclosed with a trellis-work of willow with the bark on, which saved the expense of painting'. (383) If the duke lived beyond his income, it was at least in the pursuit of orderly living to the level of dignity he thought consistent with his rank, and not in dissipation. An inspired landscape gardener may well have been lost to the world in royal Edward.

A stream of letters now poured across the Channel to Wetherall. Instructions for repairs and planting at Castle Hill Lodge. Orders to speed up the delivery of some silk petticoats Madame had ordered, a vapour bath she hoped to purchase, writing paper, some elder-flower water. Would the general please search at Castle Hill 'in her little Sitting Room, that lays between her Bed Room and her Dressing Room in the East front, upon one of the Book shelves adjoining the Sopha', for four small volumes on 'l'Art de conserver la Beauté', and when found, please forward? They were anxious for the arrival of Charles the Cook, as the assistant was incapable except for the servants' meals. Madame was, thank God, 'in good health, and gets out most days when the sun shews itself for an hour, on a good terrace to which she has access by a back stairs that communicate with her apartment'.

To their delight, the duke and Madame now had another young protégé to watch over and care for in Alexander, the young son of General Wetherall, who was at school in Brussels and spent most Sundays at the Hôtel de Maldegham. In return, Wetherall was keeping a watchful eye on Master Charles Mongenet from Geneva, Madame's twelve-year-old nephew, for whose education she had made herself responsible. Charles was enrolled in Great Ealing School under its celebrated headmaster Dr Nicholas, and spent his holidays in the general's home on Castlebear-hill near the Lodge.

'Madame de St Laurent desires me to beg of you to give her best love to her nephew', wrote the duke on 19 September 1817. On 11 October: 'Madame de St Laurent desires me to thank you most kindly for your promise to take care that Charles Montgenêt does not lose his time while staying the holidays at your house, and she particularly requests that every exertion may be made to push him on in his English, as she says she shall feel quite mortified if when she sends for him over here next summer, he has not wholly lost his foreign accent and is equal to hold any conversation the same as an English boy, but she also requests that he may be kept in the habit of writing French, and great care taken to perfect him both in his German and orthography. Alexander is perfectly well. . . .'

Alexander would benefit by some time in a seminary until he was master enough of his French to attend the Lycée. 'Madame desires me to thank you for . . . the good account you send her of her nephew.' Alexander was now good enough in French to be in classes. . . .

The young Charles had been well looked after in London. Sir Henry and Lady Carr (the former Mrs Spencer Perceval) had invited him to their home in Ealing. At Christmas, the General and his wife took him to spend a week of his holidays at Kensington. Madame was grateful. She would like a *shade* done of her nephew in the Strand, to be sent over as soon as possible. When it came, she and the duke were astounded to find that he looked exactly like young Alexander. Did the general think they were really all that alike?

Madame sent Charles £2 for a Christmas Box 'with *full* liberty to lay it out just as he pleases'. She would like her nephew's account closed up to the end of the year, and Mr Coutts to pay the general the required sum. (384)

CHAPTER EIGHTEEN

Parting

The duke now found himself involved in negotiations for a marriage
that might never take place, balancing precariously between the need
for secrecy and the need for action, the need to proceed and yet delay,
the need to dissimulate for purposes of protocol, and the need to
preserve a woman he truly loved from a heartbreak she might not be
called on to suffer.

Under pressure from Princess Charlotte and Prince Leopold, under
pressure from growing public concern about the succession, and under
the pressure of debts that might be cleared by a move likely, as well,
to win approval from everyone, the duke found himself harassed and
torn by warring emotions, seeing in Madame's eyes the apprehension
from which she was never now to be quite free, and aware that he
was in a position where an ill-judged move or an ill-advised word could
rip apart the fragile web he was weaving for his future.

'Of course it is the object of my greatest anxiety', he wrote to
Wetherall on 26 December 1816, 'that the thing should *not* get wind,
till it is all settled between the Party concerned & myself, so that the
first knowledge my eldest brother obtains of it is from *me* : & therefore
I mean to keep the Period of my going to England *open*, till I see my
way clear, or the thing falls to the Ground, for if, after all, for a public
and political object, I am to be compelled to a separation which,
come *when* it will, will *cost me more than words can describe,* I think
you will agree with me, it had better for *both* sides take place after we
have been a little while apart from each other, under the idea of a
short absence, than that it should be effected by a great Explosion
here, for in the former way I hope we might remain the best friends

in the world, and in the *latter* that it would be very difficult if not impossible to accomplish.' (385)

It had begun to dawn on Madame, however, that even twenty-six years of faithful partnership might not make her position secure, that she was now suddenly and unexpectedly facing a danger she must have thought no longer a threat. The marriage of the Princess Charlotte had given her a feeling of assurance. She was soon to learn how ill-founded this assurance was.

To Wetherall on 11 February 1817 the duke uneasily indicated Madame's awareness of the pit that was opening up before her.

'I must beg of you *never* in future to introduce in the letters you write to me upon *mixed* subjects an *iota* that bears upon *that* extremely delicate point the subject of the M——e in contemplation, for I like to read occasionally your letters upon common place Matters to M—— de St L—— & your naming *that* or any other point of privacy between us, precludes my doing so, & then my either *not* showing your letter, or saying I *have* none (one of which I *must* do) leads always to Suspicion. At the present moment this has been particularly *unfortunate,* as about a week since the paragraph you saw in the Morning Chronicle of the 6th appeared here & she saw it, which produced *no* heat or violence on *her* part, but a scene more truly distressing or heartbreaking than *any* I ever yet went thro', yet the whole of which does equal honor to her head & to her heart. Of course as is always done at *home,* even the day before a projected M——ge takes place in high life, *here* I had it contradicted by authority, which has calmed her apprehensions for the moment, but she conceives that the R—g—t & his Ministers, seeing no Progeniture from Ch——e & not wishing that the Crown of either E——d or H——ver should depend on the issue of the D—— of C—b—d are sollicitous for *my* M——g *which I have hitherto resisted,* but that to endeavor to create a subject for quarrel between us they have made some agent at Frankfort circulate this report, just as the ages of the Lady & my own may be considered not to be very much out of proportion, & of course she knows *nothing* of my having *met* the individual during my tour. So the matter rests at present, but as it has made a very deep impression on her, the subject is frequently reverted to & occasions infinitely uncomfortable moments to both. I wish therefore in your next (which I hope you will yet be able to write on *Tuesday*) you would *without noticing this,* write a little common place news such as I can read to her, & then introduce this paragraph. "I dined a day or two since at the military club with some of Y.R.H.'s old friends, when I was questioned as to the truth of a statement that

appeared lately in one of the Evening papers, copied from some
German one relative to a rumor of a M——ge between Y.R.H. and a
sister of Prince Leopold's, but to which it appears that little or no
credit was attached. I of course, felt no hesitation in taking upon
myself to contradict it *flatly,* knowing so well Y.R.H. sentiments upon
that subject, and your unvaried warm attachment for M——, and I
can assure you I had no difficulty in obtaining full credit from my
hearers, several of whom know her personally, and all by character,
and united in saying everything that was most gratifying & pleasing
to me as an old follower of Y R, relative to *both* : but it is really a *pest*
nowadays to see the license the press take with every one's name, tho'
that very excess renders what is so published less attended to or
credited; I only hope, if either Y R H or M. have seen the paragraph
you won't be annoyed by it, as I am confident it has made no impression upon anyone, and that it did not obtain a moment's credit from
any one of those who know how happily you live together. I beg to
be most affectionately remembered to M——e, in which sentiment
my little daughter enters &c, &c. . . . ."

'This will produce a good effect *here,* & I shall be much obliged to
you for it. The fact is that Ch——e, Prince L—p—d, *his* mother, *his*
Brother & all *his* family are very anxious about the thing taking place :
& as one of the most important points was to endeavor to preserve
to the L—dy (who is a widow) her dower, & the guardianship of a
son (heir to the principality) & of a daughter, children by the first
marriage, a reference to lawyers became unavoidable, thro' which cause
(tho' every precaution was taken to insure secrecy) the report has got
out, & I fear *must* infallibly knock the thing up from its coming
prematurely to the R——ts Ears, who (I learn in confidence from
the D. of O——s), is sadly *hostile* to me, on account of my independant
Conduct, and the prospect of so short a term as 3 years more clearing
me of all my *Embarrassments,* without any thanks to *him.* But exclusive
of *this,* it is ascertained that the L——y *must* lose her dower, & therefore without a Parliamentary addition to my income (*which at this
time is unattainable*) the thing could *not* take place *even in common
sense.* But there is *yet* another still *greater* obstacle. I had *always*
flatt'd myself that, if such a circumstance took place M. de St L——
would have accepted an annual allowance from me, and tho' at
a distance have maintained a habit of amicable intercourse by *letter,*
which would have made me feel *comfortable* about her, after the
agony of parting was once passed ; but all she has stated to me of her
resolve puts *that* out of the question ; for she says that knowing, as she
does, that such a separation will all *but* kill her, her only chance of
gradually overcoming its effects on her mind, will be to *annihilate*

the possibility of her ever hearing of me *directly* or *indirectly*: she should therefore immediately draw her little all out of the English funds . . . and *resolving* to *live on that,* she would never accept a shilling from me, in any shape, making it a point of assurance not to take *that* from me, which ought to be reserved for my wife & Ch——n : & that she would *never* suffer a newspaper of *any* sort, *for years* to be shewn her; & as I know her *firm decided* character, I am confident she would act up to this. Judge therefore, my good friend, how *impossible* it must be for *me* to accede to any plan for my *own* interest, thro' which *hers must* so essentially suffer, as my only compensation for losing her, would be the hope of her being *more* happy in her *new* situation than she is in her *present* one, with the means of giving herself *fully every comfort* she now enjoys with me: and from all I have observed in our late conversations I am satisfied *neither* would be accomplished. Under these circumstances therefore, as I never could live without being daily a prey to remorse and self-reproach for having *thus* abandoned my old & faithful companion of now going on *seven* and *twenty* years, I am sure you will see how little prospect there is of an arrangement taking place, which under *other* circumstances, might have been extremely desirable. You see I write in *all* the confidence of *friendship,* which I know you merit from me, and I am satisfied your own honourable & good heart will applaud my feeling.

'Adieu, I rely on your *secrecy,* & remain ever *yours* most devotedly, faithfully & affectionately, E.' (386)

So, at his master's request, the devoted and kind-hearted Wetherall sent the 'shewables' that the duke drafted in the hope that until a marriage was actually signed and sealed, Madame might be spared the consciousness of the threat hanging over her head. The rest of the year was peaceful, though there remained areas of silence between them into which neither dared venture. Perhaps the knowledge that the Princess Charlotte was now with child, and the necessity for the duke to marry not now so strong, eased the sense of pressure for them both. The English press had picked up the duke's denial from the Brussels papers, and Madame could allow her wishful heart to still her fears.

In November Princess Charlotte's time would come, and everything was prepared for the royal *accouchement.* The Queen, who was in Bath on the orders of her doctors, having selected a date well after that expected for the royal birth, had not felt she could postpone her visit, as the City of Bath had been spruced up for the royal presence. Flowers were planted in front of her house. The police were splendidly attired in new scarlet uniforms with blue collars, and hats trimmed with gold lace. Special troops had arrived as a guard, some of them heroes of Waterloo. On 3 November, twenty capital horses were sent to meet the royal retinue, 'the postillions neatly dressed in new buff coloured waistcoats, white pantaloons, round black hats with gold bands, each wearing a tasteful bouquet in his waistcoat'. (387)

But on 6 November a convivial gathering in the Bath Guildhall was silenced by a message from a page, and the dinner came to an abrupt end, guests departing one by one after the Duke of Clarence had left the room in a state of shock. In London the Great Bell of St Paul's tolled for the death of the young princess and her still-born son.

'God knows, from the moment I saw the poor deceased Charlotte advance in Her Pregnancy, I had a bad opinion of Her,' the Queen wrote afterwards to Lady Harcourt, . . . Her Figure was so immense (to me not natural), that I could not help being uneasy to a considerable degree.' (388)

'The nation have many and weighty causes of a public kind, to lament the loss of this amiable Princess', wrote James Perry, editor of the *Morning Chronicle*, next day (7 November). '. . . The order of the Succession to the Crown is now by her death disturbed; and from the age of the Princes in the order of succession, and the state of the illustrious family, apprehensions will occur to every loyal mind. It will be the earnest prayer of the nation, that an early alliance of one of the unmarried Princes may forthwith be settled. There were some time ago rumours of the intended marriage of the truly amiable and excellent Duke of Kent, with a Princess of the House of Saxe-Cobourg, one of the sisters of Prince Leopold, and we have reason to believe there was foundation for the report. Their [*sic*] is no union which the nation would hail with more rapturous delight, and for the establishment of which they would be more prompt liberally to contribute. We trust that this melancholy and unlooked-for event will accelerate the auspicious alliance, which may yet secure the inheritance of the crown to the lineal descendants of his Majesty till the latest posterity. . . .'

The nation was stunned. 'One met in the streets people of every class in tears, the churches were full at all hours, the shops shut for a fortnight (an eloquent testimony from a shop-keeping community), and everyone, from the highest to the lowest, in a state of despair which it is impossible to describe', wrote the Princess Lieven to her brother. In Rome, John Cam Hobhouse heard the news at the house of his friend Lord Byron. 'Poor thing', he sighed to his journal, 'she had just begun to be happy'. (389)

'Indeed I recollect *no* event of my life that has *so* completely overwhelmed me as the catastrophe at Claremont', wrote the Duke of Kent
to Wetherall on 24 November, 'and I feel it will take *time* before
I regain my usual spirits and composure.' (390) Was it partly because
now he would have to face the dreaded decision once more? All
of Madame's fears were—with cause—revived. One morning he had
tossed to her across the breakfast table the most recently arrived newspaper, as was his custom, for her to read while he opened his mail.
Heard a strangled sob. Looked up to find her almost fainting. She had
seen the *Morning Chronicle* of 7 November, with the paragraph Mr
Perry had written.

Only a few days afterwards, in the rather naïve hope of getting some
government allowance to compensate for her years of devoted love,
the duke sent for Thomas Creevey, walking among the winter trees
in the park near the Place Royale, to express some views he must have
hoped the British Member of Parliament would discreetly pass on to
his fellow Members. It was a vain hope: he had chosen the wrong
man.

Creevey rushed home to record what he thought was a hilarious
conversation:

'. . . It is now seven-and-twenty years that Madame St. Laurent and
I have lived together; we are of the same age, and have been in all
climates, and in all difficulties together; and you may well imagine,
Mr. Creevey, the pang it will occasion me to part with her. . . . As for
Madame St. Laurent herself, I protest I don't know what is to become
of her if a marriage is to be forced upon me; her feelings are already
so agitated upon the subject. . . . Before anything is proceeded with in
this matter, I shall hope and expect to see justice done by the Nation
and the Ministers to Madame St. Laurent. She is of very good family
and has never been an actress, and I am the first and only person who
ever lived with her. . . . When she first came to me it was upon £100
a year. That sum was afterwards raised to £400, and finally to
£1000; but when my debts made it necessary for me to sacrifice a
great part of my income, Madame St. Laurent insisted upon again
returning to her income of £400 a year. If Mad. St. L. is to return to
live amongst her friends, it must be in such a state of independence as
to command their respect. I shall not require very much, but a certain
number of servants and a carriage are essentials. . . .

'As to my own settlement, as I shall marry (if I marry at all) for
the succession, I shall expect the Duke of York's marriage to be
considered the precedent. That was a marriage for the succession, and
£25,000 for income was settled, in addition to all his other income,

purely on that account. I shall be contented with the same arrangement, without making any demands grounded upon the difference of
the value of money in 1792 and at present. As for the payment of my
debts, I don't call them great. The nation, on the contrary, is greatly
my debtor.'

For Creevey it was a joke too good to keep to himself. He passed it
to Wellington. He wrote it to Lord Sefton, who also thought it richly
humorous, and wrote back to say so. 'Nothing could be more first-rate
than the Royal Edward's ingenuousness. One does not know which
to admire most—the delicacy of his attachment to Mme. St. Laurent
. . . or his own perfect disinterestedness in pecuniary matters.' (391)

It was far from hilarious to the duke. He had been forced to be
interested in pecuniary matters, originally by his youthful folly, later
by ill-luck, by allowances smaller and granted later than those to his
elder brothers, and all the time by what he considered (not unjustly)
the necessities of his position.

At a time when one of the accepted and freely acknowledged ways
for young aristocrats to gain a fortune or replenish one lost by gambling
and high living was to marry an heiress, reluctant or not, it was
hypocritical to criticize the duke for a money-seeking marriage,
particularly as to this move in his case was added a considerable and
mounting pressure of public approval on account of the succession.
Those who laughed would nevertheless accept the wife and continue
to ignore the mistress. What caused the hilarity was the apparent
contradiction between his professed devotion to Madame and his
willingness to leave her when something seemingly better offered itself.
His age was also a factor. A middle-aged lover no longer carries the
aura of romance that earns such forgiving sympathy.

Before too harsh a judgement is made, one must at least consider
some of the realities. It was entirely possible for the duke to have
rejected the pressures and stayed devotedly with Thérèse-Bernardine
until the end of their lives. The world, which always loves a lover,
would have found the story (after their deaths) a heart-warming one,
and turned it into one of the wistful legends of history. Indeed, to some
extent it has become just that, because it has been believed that the
duke was forced to leave his true love by dire fate. Only a recent
suspicion that his marriage negotiations were initiated a year *before*
the Princess Charlotte's death has begun to cause a certain blurring of
the image. The world despises—or affects to despise—the person whose
head rules his heart.

But the rules of royal marital behaviour were set by the society
that now gossiped about the duke. These very rules had always offered

him the possibility of the action he now contemplated, and opened the way for the social approval they denied to his truly devoted relationship with a woman of charm and dignity. Years earlier, his brush with his brother the Duke of York had taught him the penalties of continuing the liaison, and he had proudly accepted the price at that time. At fifty, with the fires of passion cooled, and the batterings of fortune and debt blunting his resistance, with the opportunity now presented to him appearing partly a call on his sense of duty, partly a way out of financial straits he was desperately tired of coping with, it would have taken a man of heroic proportions to resist the temptation. The duke was not heroic, but a kind and troubled man with a conscience he could never quite appease. Certainly Madame herself understood and accepted what he did. The duke deserved better than Creevey's pitiless caricature and Lord Sefton's incredulous insensitive laughter.

With the aftermath of the *Morning Chronicle*'s rumour of his marriage fresh in his mind, the duke asked Wetherall to get Perry's promise not to commit the same blunder again, but Perry himself replied with a rather pessimistic letter on 12 December. 'Your Royal Highness [*sic*] injunction of silence on the great subject shall be implicitly obeyed—but I fear that without a general interdict of the Journals there may come notices to the eye of the interesting object of your tenderness from quarters whence it is least expected. I have already observed both in the German and French Journals hints and insinuations too direct to be mistaken—and which must come to the eyes of the Lady's friends and correspondents. I venture to mention this to Y R H because you encourage me to speak with frankness—and because the topic is so generally canvassed. Every eye is bent on Y R H and I fear you will find it difficult to keep it totally unsuspected till April next.' (392)

While the Princess Charlotte lived and promised an heir, there had been no need to rush things, and the duke's letters clearly showed the undercurrent of hope that a failure of the marriage negotiations might take the whole matter out of his hands and free him from the burden of decision. His habit of never writing in full the significant words or names—*marriage, the Lady, guardianship, Leiningen, Leopold*—in letters that only Wetherall would see, may have sprung from a subconscious reluctance to set down in black and white, before his own eyes, the bald fact of his desertion of Madame.

On 18 December, he wrote privately and confidentially to his friend.

'We have, ever since the 9th of last month, lived in complete seclu-

sion, not thinking it right while the black glove mourning continued
to see any one or go to the theatre, indeed we have neither of us felt up
to any thing of the kind. But the consequence has been, that owing to
the shock originally given by Perry's paragraph of the 7th, & kept
alive by two or three innuendos in the papers *here,* my poor companion
has been more or less constantly brooding over the chance of my
m——g & it has occasioned us both 5 weeks of more misery than
language can describe : and now she is become calmer *only* from the
expectation that either the R——t may carry thro' *his* plan of *Divorce,*
or that my *naval* Brother will *marry,* in which case she calculates on
my not being applied to on the subject; & she further relies on the
promise I was compelled to give her, that I would *not* go over to
England, unless my friends, who have the management of my affairs
in their hands, state that my coming over is *indispensible* to perform
some *legal* act . . .'

His hesitations still showed. He continued :

'When I *have* got it /the Princess of Leiningen's sanction to speak
of the union/ I ought to be *first* sure that the *Divorce* scheme is given
up & that the *Admiral of the Fleet* is *not* thinking of marrying.' In that
case, he asked Wetherall to send him a 'shewable' which would appear
to be a request to go to England for some legal business connected with
his affairs, which 'will then enable me to go home without it appearing
like a plan of separation, & hard as the task will be for me . . . I must
hope that Providence will give me energy sufficient to shew no signs
that would lead to a suspicion of the contrary; & if so, all will go
on as smoothly as I dare hope in my very trying position, & I flatter
myself I shall in England be equal to determine, as my duty to my
country may *command,* provided I *first* have the means given me
to render my old & faithful friend independent & comfortable *for life;*
for without being able to do *that at once,* I never could agree to the
sacrifice. . . . You who know *my* nature will easily imagine *what*
this system of dissimulation *costs* me, but in the present critical state
of affairs, & with *her* ardent & easily affected mind, this line of proceeding is indispensible.' (393)

He was writing again in agitation to Wetherall on 2 January 1818.
Mr Perry had renewed the rumour in the *Morning Chronicle* that
connected the duke's name with the Princess of Leiningen, and 'again
disturbed the calm and tranquillity which was beginning to return in
my interior, and produced some very painful moments and affecting
discussions, which might be altogether avoided but for such recurrence

to a subject that, of course, never now can be touched upon however slightly, without its being combined with his paragraph of the 7th of November: and I am sure a word from you in my name will obviate the recurrence of the Evil. . . .' (394)

Ten days later he precipitated matters on Prince Leopold's advice, by writing direct to the Princess Victoire to ask for a decisive answer. If the reply was negative, he wrote to Wetherall, 'the matter will be at an end & I will write you how to word yr communication in *that* case. In the mean while *no* words can describe to you the agony I am living in under this constant dissimulation with that excellent and beloved individual, pending the awful decision; for she has alas a presentiment that something is hanging over her, which leads to very frequent allusions to her future prospects, and to the state of misery in which her mind is kept . . . I anxiously pray therefore that Providence may soon terminate for both our sakes this sad state of suspense which is a very severe trial, and for which I am sure your heart will *make you feel.'* (395)

Having taken the irrevocable step and made the formal request to the Princess Victoire, the duke was now forced to add the tensions of waiting to the distressing continuation of pretence. 'In the meanwhile, in every *shewable* letter you had best keep *up* the idea of the Divorce & of this marriage /Clarence's/', he instructed Wetherall, 'as it helps to keep all quiet here, *which is very essential,* as the ardent and anxious mind of my poor friend works a good deal, and we often pass days & nights in the utmost wretchedness from her anxiety as to *her* own future lot, should I be compelled, from political imperative causes, to m——y.' (396)

By 6 February the answer had come, with permission to ask the Regent's sanction for his marriage, and Wetherall was instructed to write the 'shewable' which would call him back to England on an innocent trip to sign some papers. 'You will easily judge how *agitated* I am, & *how my heart sinks* at the *unfortunate line of dissimulation* I have yet to follow with my poor excellent old faithful companion . . . God bless you, I know you will *feel* for me, and it will be a comfort to me in the midst of my agitation to think you do.' (397)

And the tensions continued. More pretence, more shewables. 'Pray be sure in the *shewable* part to keep alive the Expectation of the Divorce being going on, tho' kept a profound secret, and of the Duke of Clarence being to marry Miss Wykeham, *whatever* may be the *real* fact. Be sure at all Events, *not* to *damp* the Expectations my poor companion entertains on *these* heads as *they* mainly support her in seeing me set off, without any *serious* apprehension as to the Result: and we *both* require, after all that the newspaper reports of Feb: 1817

& of last November occasioned in the way of distress to both, *every thing* that tends to do them away, at the moment of our separation. Indeed the whole has been a dreadful stretch upon our feelings, and I still dread the ten days I have yet to encounter, for *fear* of *some* fresh subject arising to renew her suspicions & add to her misery.' (398)

So they spent the last few weeks together: Madame fearful, sensing that the end of the twenty-seven years was almost come, but still hoping: her duke in anguish of spirit, trying to keep from her the despair of certainty until the last possible moment. Did they try to laugh, as English society was laughing, at the marital manoeuvrings of Clarence with the eccentric heiress the papers were calling *High Wykeham* because of her prowess on horseback? Did they fill up the nervous silences with small talk?—exclaim again about that curious coincidence of the likeness between young Alexander and young Charles? Did their old friend Admiral Donnelly, accepting one of their cheerful invitations to dine and play a rubber of whist, wonder at the unaccustomed apprehension in Madame's eyes?

Both of them came down with heavy colds. Madame wrote to her nephew and got back a typical twelve-year-old schoolboy letter from Charles. 'She is delighted to hear that her nephew is so *well*,' the duke told Wetherall, relieved to be on general topics, 'and hopes when next he writes, his letter will be better *written*, and *more to the purpose* than his last was, in which he pays scarcely any attention to a *very sensible* one of admonition from *her* which had preceded it.' Young Charles was a delinquent letter-writer. Only ten days before, the duke had had to add a P.S. to Wetherall: 'Madame de St Laurent desires me to add that Charles Montgenêt should in future send his letters for his Father, Mother and Sister, through *you* to her, in order that she may ensure their safe arrival, as the family complain much of not hearing from him or of his letters miscarrying.' (399)

The weather turned tempestuous and kept them both indoors. Wetherall's 'shewable' arrived on 20 February, with the information that his Royal Highness was required to make a brief visit to London for business purposes, and the duke, the die finally cast, the irrevocable step taken, was left with nothing to do but face the final days before the final parting. He replied to Wetherall with the most heartbreaking letter among those that have survived.

'I now take up my pen to inform you that I communicated *your shewable* to my *poor faithful Partner,* on *Friday,* the day it arrived (and for which she was *certainly* in a degree prepared by the *preceding* one of the *same* nature which you had written some time before). It was however but *too evident,* it shook her a good deal, and that she looks forward to the separation of two months, *which she considers it will be* (or *rather* of 10 *weeks,* for the plan settled between us is for *me* to stay over my sister Eliza's birthday, May 22, & that we should set out from here on the 14th of March) *as ominous of evil*: indeed tho' she behaves *admirably* about it I see her *tears floating down her Cheeks,* and, at *times,* notwithstanding all her Endeavor to struggle & bear up, she lets out her fears, alarms, & suspicions, and *you may* judge how *my* heart sinks *within* me & *bleeds* at every mark of tenderness & affection she bestows on me; at *other* times the rumor of the R——ts divorce, with a view to his new connexion *you once mentioned,* & of the Admirals marriage makes her rally & bear up & think there is no cause for fear, *which gives me a respite*: but how I shall be able to steel myself, so as to betray *no* Emotions, when her Carriage drives off from this, & raise her fresh suspicions, *Heaven alone knows,* & I *must* rely for Courage on *that* Providence which I *hope* will *direct* all for the best. *Certainly* there *is* a *chance* of the present project, tho' advanced so far, *yet* ending in *nothing,* as the point of the G—rd—ship, which is the condition on which my poor friend L—p—d's sister can *alone* consent to the Union, remains to be carried, & is *unquestionably doubtful,* & will, what is more, become insuperable if the R——t *wishes to balk* it: so there is *that* chance, if the *secret* is well kept, as I *trust* it *will* be, of my reverting to my present *quiet & peaceable* home, with my beloved companion of eight & twenty years, & I must try to keep *that* hope alive in my Bosom, while we part. On the *other* hand, I feel I *have* a *duty* to render to my Country *if* my Elder B——r *does not m*——*y,* and if I am *compelled* to make the sacrifice of my poor companion, I hope Providence will turn it to *her* happiness, & support us both thro the arduous trial . . . I *of course conclude* you have had the *great discretion* not to speak of *my coming over to anyone,* &, *if so,* my object will be fully assured *not* to have it talked of, before I come over, or any absurdities put in the papers about it, that would afterwards be copied in the French ones & make my poor companion *wretched* before there is a necessity for the event.'

He added a word to Wetherall about his son 'Allie's' health, and concluded with a warning not to let Master Charles know that his aunt would not be in Brussels, as she did not want her brother in Geneva to find out. (400)

At mid-March neither the duke nor Madame had fully recovered from their colds, and conditions of wind and weather had delayed their departure from the original plan, now moved to the 16th, but on

The house (extreme right) just off Place Royale, Brussels, in which the Duke and Madame lived from 1816 to 1818.
Credit: Bibliothèque Royale, Brussels.

The cemetery of Père Lachaise, Paris, where Madame lies buried with her sister in a grave that weathering, moss, and ivy have rendered unidentifiable.
Credit: Bureau des Cimetières, Paris.

Edward Augustus, Duke of Kent. This portrait by Sir William Beechey
was probably the one owned by Madame.
*Credit: Burlington Magazine: Collection of Duc de Vendôme (Public Archives of
Canada).*

the 14th the duke wrote to Wetherall: 'We hope *both* to be sufficiently recovered, through the steps of [the] regimen we are taking, to be able to set out on the day fixed viz. "Thursday the 19th", *she* for *Paris* and *I* for *England*. . . . I do hope, now the hurricane has ceased, as it blew for above a month, that we may reckon on its being over, and, if so, that I shall be able to cross the Water on the 21st.' (401)

With one further letter written on the 18th, the duke's letters to Wetherall from Brussels cease. *The Times* of Tuesday, 24 March, announced his arrival at Kensington Palace on the previous Sunday. On the 19th then, as planned, the duke had escorted Thérèse-Bernardine to her carriage and watched her driven away, attended by one of his footmen: he knowing, she fearing that it was the last time they would ever see each other. Nothing was said between them that would make an unbridgeable rift in their love for each other. Madame made her exit from her prince's life with the dignity she had shown all through their relationship.

Q

Part Two

Afterwards

CHAPTER NINETEEN

Separate paths

It had been a hard decision. The public applauded, but the duke was never quite free of guilt. The society that allowed him the choice, though it scorned his unsanctified romance and would never have received his French lady, would also privately scorn his sacrifice of it. 'The Duke of Cumberland told me the Duke of Kent's marriage was declared!', wrote Mrs George Villiers to her sons on 5 May from the very house in Knightsbridge, now owned by her brother Lord Morley, where Madame had been happy with Prince Edward. 'What becomes of all his fine sentimentality to me about Mrs St Laurent.' (402)

Trying to check her tears and her fears in Paris, Madame was not the only one whose sorrow bit deep. The duke too was riven with the same sense of loss and heartbreak. He too had made a sacrifice, and must have made it with trepidation: the sacrifice of assured happiness for the uncertainty of marriage to a woman he had met only once and would not be able to discard, should he find her company unbearable, as he would have been free to discard Thérèse-Bernardine twenty-seven years before. If he had made the wrong decision, this time there was no turning back.

What he wrote to her, waiting and fearing, must be imagined. It would be inconceivable to think he kept her in suspense about the parting that was to be permanent. Perhaps he wrote from Calais, waiting for the packet that carried him across the Channel. Certainly he would have written the moment he reached Kensington Palace. Their subsequent correspondence indicates that he had, as he had hoped—a hope to which his whole way of handling the crisis had been directed—retained her friendship and her love.

The first thing the duke did was to arrange that a proper financial
settlement would be assured to her. A document dated 8 May setting
out the arrangements was sent to her together with one annotated
'Additional note for my poor friend.' In it the duke outlined the legal
arrangement by which he had bound himself to make her a generous
annual allowance, with a substantial increase to date from January
1822 : '. . . so that nothing, I hope, has been omitted to give the only
solid proof that lies in my power of the affection I have for her and
the great longing I have that in every way she will be in a position
to undertake all she thinks will contribute to her comfort and well-
being . . . May she find in all this the proof of how dear she will always
be to me, and how much I want her to look on me, to my last breath,
as a true and faithful friend in every eventuality.'

He had asked Wetherall and a long-time friend from Nova Scotia,
James Putnam, to be trustees, and on 19 May he sent another brief
note (written, evidently, while he was en route to Coburg for his
marriage), using the familiar and affectionate French 'tu' in addressing
her : 'The day of my departure for London I finished making legal
arrangements and the necessary papers are in the hands of Coutts,
until you want to have them. Messrs Wetherall and Putnam have the
responsibility in all events that may happen to me, to supervise the
carrying out my intentions.' (403)

On 6 June he was able to write to Wetherall of the 'extremely kind
and affectionate letter which I received yesterday from my poor friend,
dated Paris 23rd of last month'. (404) Perhaps she had just received
the letter of 19 May from the friend in London who has not so far
been indentified, a letter from which she would have drawn both comfort and courage. The letter was signed with a flourish too contracted
to be recognisable. A name?—initials?—Mrs Fitzherbert, perhaps, who
remained a warm friend to the duke—? (but the way she wrote her
initials was different from the signature to this letter, though it looks
vaguely like an M and an F). A copy of the original, perhaps, with the
signature scrawled, since it was familiar to the copyist and not meant
to be exact? (Though not in his handwriting, the letter may have come
from the devoted General Wetherall, who could be expected to write
in exactly this spirit.) No matter—the writer was someone close to both
the duke and Madame, and someone with a warm respect for both.

'I feel sure, Madame', the unknown correspondent wrote to Thérèse-
Bernardine, 'that despite all that has just happened, you have thought
of me and that you almost expect to receive from me a few comments
on the event which changes your situation. You owe me this expecta-

tion, Madame, as I owe it to myself to respond to it, but in what way, in what spirit shall I write? I know your heart, your sensitivity: but I also know the true quality of your soul. The first consideration would suggest recourse to the kind of consolation one usually offers in sympathy for a loss. The second demands that I speak to you in quite other language. If death had bereft you I would offer you sincere sympathy that there remained to you after all your sacrifices only the memory of some happy days accompanied by many annoyances and privations. But it is not so. The Prince lives, but called to a high destiny he cannot fulfil without breaking the chain which bound him to you. You, then, Madame, are called to join in the accomplishment of the same destiny. I do not therefore consider you an ordinary person, nor your loss an ordinary loss. Neither time, nor reason, nor any other consideration of that kind can alone console you, no, Madame. You have the right to a more immediate consolation, to some gesture of compensation. You will find it, Madame, in the very grandeur to which your illustrious friend has been called. It is here that ambition, the very finest of all ambitions, can be promised to you: that of being associated in spirit with all the noble results that spring from the alliance the Duke has contracted. It is you who for twenty-five years of general care have conserved him for this moment. His exemplary conduct which has so justly earned him the esteem of the nation whose hope he is, is in large measure your work. You know well how grand a thought that is! Let it grow bigger still, Madame, to complete your task. Be happy without the Duke: be happy through him and for him. Your tears, your grief make you both unhappy and take from you personally the only indemnity worthy of you: the right to pride yourself in the elevation of your friend and the great destiny of his family. You would belong only to a fugitive moment by giving way to regret, but you will belong to history by triumphing over your sorrow. This, Madame, is the viewpoint from which I look at your situation, and it seems to me to offer more reason for congratulation than condolence. If your womanly sensitivity yearns meanwhile, let me tell you, Madame, that the Duke has been no less distressed than you by the obligation imposed upon him by circumstance. He has honored me with two or three conversations in which he has opened his heart to me: and I am sure that if without his knowledge you had witnessed these talks, you would have rushed to dry with your handkerchief the tears that filled his eyes and joyfully absolve him of any suspicion that he does not share your regrets.' (405)

Whoever wrote this letter, man or woman, was a true friend. No sorrow but could be a little soothed by such a charming compliment.

The duke at least had the rush of events and the stimulation of new faces and new places to keep his mind from brooding. A round of visits to every member of his family included the Prince Regent, with whom at least a formally polite relationship was maintained. The marriage of the Princess Elizabeth to the Landgrave of Hesse-Homburg followed almost immediately on 7 April, which pleased the duke immensely, as he had liked the young Landgrave in Geneva thirty years earlier. On Monday, 13 April, *The Times* reported that the Princess Adelaide of Meiningen had accepted the Duke of Clarence, putting an end to his frantic search for a bride. The Duke of Kent moved busily from Kensington Palace to Castle Hill. He was glad to see once again his protégé Charles Mongenet. The young Charles had been destined for enrolment at Addiscombe, the East India Company's college for cadets training for the artillery or engineering company, with an entrance age of around fourteen. Just prior to the departure from Brussels, a report had arrived from Wetherall about Charles's prospects, and the duke had replied: 'I am sure/Madame/will be much pleased with Doctor Nicolas' report of your visit to Addiscombe House, as that holds out the fairest prospect, if her nephew be but diligent, of his qualifying himself in sufficient time for admission into *that excellent institution* in the way the most gratifying to his friends, and the most satisfactory to himself.' (406)

In mid-April, Parliament began to debate the forthcoming royal marriages. Lords and Commoners in their respective Houses made long platitudinous speeches pointing out that no one could approach them in their loyalty to the Crown, but . . . That the splendour of Royalty of course must be maintained, but . . . That were the times flourishing and prosperity abroad in the land, nothing could have stood in the way of their voting for suitable grants, but . . .

The noble Lords nobly upheld the principle that nothing should be allowed 'to add to the already enormous burdens of the people'. The honourable Members fought honourable battles with their consciences, trying to reconcile their respect for the mystique of royalty with 'the burdened state of the country'. When the incomes of the royal dukes were printed, it transpired that the Duke of Kent's totalled £25,205.4.2. Castlereagh urged that the portion earned as governor of Gibraltar and as colonel of his regiment (as in the case of similar earnings by any of the other royal dukes) should not be taken into consideration. 'If the house did so, they took away all motives to exertion.' Members were generally more inclined to aid the Duke of Kent than the other brothers for whom grants were being considered (the Dukes of Clarence, Cumberland and Cambridge).

Mr John Curwen was among those who opposed the grant. '/It/

could not be necessary, when it appeared that the Duke of Kent
had 25,000l. a year.' He wondered why further support could not
come from the Queen out of her privy-purse money, if it were really
necessary. Henry Brougham pointed out, however, 'that he had heard
from some of the trustees, that the duke's incumbrances had almost
entirely arisen from difficulties in early life, as he had only the allowance
of 5,000l. a year till he was 32 years old, when he received the
allowance of 12,000l. a year enjoyed by his brothers before. The
offices he had held abroad were not mere sinecures,' explained
Brougham. 'He had been exposed to unhealthy climates, and he
believed also to the chances of war. He had been employed in the West
Indies, at Gibraltar, in Nova Scotia, and in Canada for 12 or 14 years,
having no income adequate to his expenses.' He added a self-evident
truth. 'The great losses which he had sustained, had they been incurred
by an ordinary officer, would have found their way into the army
expenditure . . . By the arrangements for liquidating his embarrassments, he had appropriated . . . 17,000l. a year, which must continue
for some years to come.' (407)

The grant was finally set at £6,000, small enough in view of the
additional expenses with which the duke was instantly faced—to start
with, his post-chaise, 'lately newly ornamented with E V painted on
it, with coronet above, in green relievo'. To his voluntary continuation
of Thérèse-Bernardine's allowance would now be added the expenses
of maintaining the appurtenances of a royal duchess. On 16 May
he left for Germany, where, at Coburg, the Princess Victoire and her
mother were palpitatingly awaiting his arrival. 'Dear, good child, she
seems so unperturbed at what lies before her and this almost worries
me,' her mother, Duchess Augusta of Saxe-Coburg-Saalfeld had written
in her private diary on 26 January. 'In a few months' time, she may
possibly become the wife of a man she hardly knows.'

Exactly four months later (26 May) she was writing less anxiously.
'We had only expected the Duke of Kent to-morrow, but hardly had
we sat down to luncheon, when a Courier arrived with the news that
the Duke would follow in two hours. We waited with much curiosity
and poor Victoire with a beating heart. She had only seen him once
before. At 4 o'clock he arrived with the English Minister in Stuttgart,
Taylor, two Gentlemen from the Legation; Knatchbull and Barnard
and Colonel Hervey who is in waiting on the Duke. At first the Duke,
man of the world though he is, was somewhat embarrassed at suddenly
breaking in on our large family circle. He is a fine man for his age,
has a pleasant winning manner, and a good-humoured expression. His
tall stature helps to give him an air of breeding, and he combines a
simple soldierly manner with the refinement of a man of the world,

which makes intercourse with him easy and pleasant. We all had tea here, and went to supper at the Schloss.'

The betrothal on 28 May and the wedding on the next day were performed with ceremony at the Schloss. 'The Duke of Kent was already standing under a velvet canopy, in the brilliantly lit Riesensaal. He looked very well in his English Field-Marshal's uniform and Victoire, charming, in a white dress trimmed with white roses and orange blossoms . . . A salute from the "Festung" proclaimed that the ceremony had been accomplished. We then returned to the State Rooms, after which, rather late, there was a State Dinner. I accompanied the newly married couple to their apartments, which had been charmingly prepared for them.' On 2 June, the night before their departure for England, the Duchess Augusta wrote: 'I hope Victoire will be happy with her really very amiable husband, who only in middle age, makes acquaintance with family life and will therefore perhaps appreciate it all the more.' (408)

Thérèse-Bernardine, weeping alone in Paris, would have been stabbed to the heart had she read what the duchess wrote. Had the twenty-seven years counted for so little? Except for the lack of children of their union, it was *she* who had given her prince the domestic comfort of a real home, and one which he was reluctant to leave. No pretence of convention or social disapproval could ever wipe out the years of their life together. No high-born lady would ever face an emotional shock with more courage than the daughter of the highways engineer from Besançon.

She had friends. Louis-Philippe, Duke of Orleans, who shared her happiest memories, watched out for her interests. Her sister Beatrix, comtesse de Jansac, welcomed her in the apartment she had rented at 116 rue de Grenelle, a stone's-throw from the Invalides. The King, Louis XVIII, gave her the courtesy title of Comtesse de Montgenêt. 'Her direction is Madame la Comtesse de Montgenêt, being her own name, which de St Laurent was not', wrote the duke to his friend General Mallet on 5 July, in a letter in which he asked the general 'whenever you and Mrs Mallet have the opportunity of meeting her, you will bear in mind how much I have it at heart, that you should shew to her to the full, the same polite and friendly attentions that you would have done, if our connexion had still subsisted.' The young Charles-Benjamin, now twenty-two, and 'a very excellent and well conducted young man', was living not fnr away at '21 Rue du Colombier in the same Faubourg'. (409)

But tragedy had not done with Thérèse-Bernardine. 'She had made all her plans to live with her elder sister, the Comtesse de Jansac', the duke wrote sorrowfully to the baron de Vincy on 31 July, 'and every-

thing had begun to get a little settled for her comfort, when this poor
sister fell ill, and after four days' illness, died in her arms.' (410)

Sadly Thérèse-Bernardine buried Beatrix on the hillside in the old
cemetery of Père Lachaise. She was comforted at this time by another
friend from long ago—her old lover, Philippe Claude Auguste de
Chouly, Marquis de Permangle, who went on her behalf to register
her sister's death and the small estate she had left to Thérèse-Bernardine
as her 'sister and sole heir'. Philippe Claude was living not far away,
at 68 rue de Sèvres. He had divorced his first wife and married
Mademoiselle de Peters, daughter of the painter Antoine de Peters,
who had come to the marriage with a dowry of some farms near
Fontainebleau. A young son, born in 1800, had been named Lucien
for his godfather Lucien Bonaparte.

Madame (now fifty-eight) and Philippe Claude (sixty-three) had
much to talk about. After leaving her in Malaga in 1790, the marquis
had joined his brother in the Duchy of Holstein in Germany, but came
back to France too soon for his safety and narrowly escaped the
guillotine. Arrested and held in the dungeons of Les Carmes during
the Terror from 31 May 1793, he was readied for the tumbrils on
24 August 1794, when Barras, an old fellow-student at the Ecole
Militaire, noticed his name on the list and had him secretly removed
by a side door. Eventually, as the Citizen Chouly, he was given a
civil post, first in the Department of Finance, and then successively
secretary-general, administrator, director-general and inspector-
general of the toll-houses of Paris, and finally of several *départements*.
(411)

But her duke was still the centre of Thérèse-Bernardine's life. From
Brussels on 16 June, he was able to report to Wetherall that he had
now received *two* 'most affectionate and feeling letters from Madame
de St Laurent . . . and though they have affected me deeply, they
have also been a subject of great consolation. I have also heard from
the Duke of Orleans relative to her, and he gives me hope that her
excellent sense and the energy of her character will carry her through
the present most arduous trial.' (412)

Even by the tenuous threads of correspondence she clung to him
and to all the souvenirs of their life together. 'A *strong wish* is expressed
that I would send over to her the large full length picture of myself
which is in the Breakfast Room at Castle Hill, and which is her
property : you will therefore immediately consult with Sir William
Beechey upon the best mode of packing it, together with its frame, to
ensure its safe arrival at Paris, and have it forthwith removed and
prepared in readiness . . . and addressed . . . "pour rester en Depôt
chez Son Altesse Serenissime le Duc D'Orleans, au Palais Royal à
Paris, aux soins de concierge Le Blond." ' (413)

Madame had not the least intention of retiring to a convent.

The Duke of Kent and his duchess arrived in London 1 July, after a journey from Amorbach of almost three weeks, welcomed en route by civic dinners and by such gaieties as that offered by the tiny frontier town of Bisschossgeim, when 'all the young girls, tastefully dressed in white, decorated with ribands and garlands of roses . . . strewed flowers before his carriage'. The crowds at Dover hardly glimpsed the new duchess as the royal couple 'got into their travelling chariot, which was drawn up to the water's edge by the slip at the North Pierhead, and drove off for London', but it was noted that 'she appeared a tall genteel figure, and was affable to all by condescendingly bowing out of the coach-window to the many cheers which greeted her from all ranks in passing'. (414)

Did Thérèse-Bernardine, as she had said she would, refuse to look at the newspapers?—or did she see, with a stab of grief, the announcements in *Le Moniteur*?

16 May: *La ratification du traité de mariage de S.A.R. le duc de Kent est arrivé à Londres hier matin. On croit que S.A.R. partira mercredi ou jeudi pour l'Allemagne.* 25 June: *On mande de Calais le 19 juin. Hier, est entré de nouveau dans notre port le yacht le Royal-Souverain, qui doit y attendre le duc et la duchesse de Kent, pour les transporter en Angleterre.* 16 July: *Le mariage de LL.AA.RR le duc et le duchesse de Kent sera . . . celebré de nouveau . . .*

The English marriage ceremony, set for 9 July, had to be postponed because the ailing Queen Charlotte was not well enough to attend. On Saturday the 11th she was wheeled in by her eldest son to see the double wedding (the Kents and the Clarences both) celebrated by the Archbishop of Canterbury before a temporary altar set up in the Queen's drawing-room at Kew Palace. Both brides were given away by the Prince Regent. Crimson velvet coverings and cushions enriched the scene, as well as the 'valuable and magnificent' Communion plate belonging to the Chapel Royal and Whitehall Chapel. The two brides were equally magnificent, the Princess Victorie in a 'rich and elegant dress' of gold tissue, the Princess Adelaide in silver, both dresses flounced and trimmed with Brussels point lace, both robes lined with white satin, a brilliant diamond clasp fastened at each waist, each head crowned with a wreath of diamonds.

After the Carlton House party on the 15th (the card said 'a small party en frocs', wrote Sir Robert Chester, Deputy Lord Chamberlain, 'but I was informed there were 300 cards issued, and suppose there were 600 present'), W. H. Fremantle commented unkindly (and a little unfairly) to the Marquis of Buckingham: 'There was a grand display of all the Royal Duchesses, one more ugly than another. I think the manners of the Duchess of Clarence the best; and the look of the Duchess of Kent—the latter rather *en bon point* . . . All the Princes are delaying, from day to day, their departure abroad, expecting, and looking out for the plunder to arise from the Queen's death.' (415) This was an unjustified comment, as the duke had planned as early as May not to return to the Continent until the end of August.

Still not satisfied with the financial arrangements he had made for Madame, Edward wrote to her again on 10 August. 'You can be sure that before leaving for Germany, I will send you the papers I mentioned to you in an earlier letter, but as neither Putnam nor I have been happy with the way the latter deed was expressed, I had to have it drawn up again, and up to now, because of the illness of my lawyer, I have not received the corrected deed. However, I am writing today to hurry it up.'

He went on to itemize the arrangements, ending with his spontaneous intention to increase her allowance after 1822 (when he hoped to have cleared his debts) in proportion to any increase in his own, 'to prove to you that while the good God gives me life, we have always a common bond . . . I hope I have explained clearly, at least . . . until I can have the papers in question sent to you.'

Less than a month later (4 September) he was writing again to send her copies of the two deeds, one of 16 May 1818 binding him to repay the small sum owed her, and the other of 28 August 1818, replacing the document previously found faulty and covering the allowance he had promised. 'You will note that the first deed was for one payment only, made directly to you, but the other, as it is a continuing payment during my lifetime, has had to be made by trustees, to satisfy legal rules.

'You will note', the anxious duke added carefully, 'that these are certified copies of the note and not the originals that I send you, and Coutts hold the originals of these two deeds. Thus I hope you will remain convinced that I have taken every care in the matter.'

The duke's anxiety about Madame brought yet another letter dated 11 December on the same subject:

'It is necessary for my honour and to justify my unbounded affection for you, that I explain that no lack of personal funds can ever have any effect on the regular payment each quarter or trimester of the small sum you are pleased to accept from the hands of your friend, for, in the distribution of my income . . . Coutts has an order that I made irrevocable by the deed you have a copy of, to reserve for your use that sum which is sent to your three trustees Wetherall, Kirkland and Putnam the moment the allowance comes from the exchequer, and I can no more dispose of that money than if it belonged to a stranger.'

As well as making more than generous arrangements for Madame, the duke wrote to everyone he could think of to urge their continued friendship for his forsaken love. He had written to the Mallets in Geneva. To the baron de Vincy he wrote on 22 June and 31 July, both times asking that his friends—and especially their wives—show their attachment to him by calling on Madame whenever possible, so that she would eventually have around her a small and select society 'of which, I dare predict, she will be the delight'. She had always, he explained, 'been treated by me in every way as if she had been my wife, except in giving her the title'. He longed to know, from letters and personal accounts by all his friends, how she was, whether she had regained the calm and tranquillity to which he was sure her strength of character would restore her. He hoped that the manner of their parting would make sure that the friendship they had shared for so long would never diminish, and that nothing would change the feeling they had for each other.

His wish came true : for nothing did.

At the end of January 1819, almost a year after their parting, the sense of loss was still a source of grief to Thérèse-Bernardine. The duke begged Mallet again, 'should you see the Countess, to bear in mind that her nerves are *still* in a *very* delicate state, and to avoid if possible . . . any allusion to the Dutchess, but if she should know before-hand that you became acquainted with the Duchess from our stopping at your house . . . on our way to Strasbourg, pray touch upon the subject *as lightly as possible* and say no more of the Dutchess than there is an *indispensible* necessity for your doing, remembering that I should *greatly prefer she was not named at all* . . . Although an intimacy now of eight months with the Dutchess has attached me *sincerely* to *her,* in *every* point that regards the Countess de Montgenêt we must *never* lose sight that our unexpected separation arose from the imperative duty I owed to obey the call of my family and my country to marry, and *not* from the least diminution in an attachment which had stood the test of twenty eight years, and which, but for *that* circumstance, would unquestionably have kept up the connexion until it became the lot of one or other of us to be removed from this world.' (416)

It was true that no lessening of love for her had caused her duke to leave her. At this time, as well as the sharp pangs of loss, a conflict of emotions must have exhausted her, wishing his happiness yet recoiling from the knowledge that he could have found it with the woman who had replaced her. She made no protest, nor uttered any reproach. 'Were I to live to the age of Methusaleh', wrote the duke gratefully to de Vincy, 'I would never be able to acquit myself as my heart would wish of my debt to her for her perfect conduct towards me for so many consecutive years, and especially in this last crisis.'

Madame's family continued to remain his concern. He had agreed in 1815 to be godfather to Edward, the youngest son of Jean-Claude, Madame's troublesome youngest brother. Jean-Claude was taking care to ingratiate himself with his sister and his sister's illustrious benefactor, even though they had now parted. He had rushed to Paris as soon as he heard of Thérèse-Bernardine's arrival there early in the year, and in September he wrote to thank the duke for his benevolence to the two boys Charles and Edward. Geneva friends, including de Vincy, seem to have been concerned about Jean-Claude's elder daughter Louise, which brought a letter from the duke to the baron on 19 August 1818.

'About my dear friend's niece, everyone tells me how pleasant and charming she is, the same as my little godson, her youngest brother, who they say is a perfect little cherub : but while praising these charming children, she and I agree about their father's character, who, with abilities and manners capable of making a success in any line he chose to follow consistently, from his total lack of direction is not and is never likely to be good for anything. Also, though his kind sister continually sends him money, she has stayed as distant from him as possible, and is far from wanting to have him in her circle. He is quite different from his two elder brothers, of whom one, formerly in a distinguished post in the *Ponts et Chaussées*, but today living retired in the Château de St Philippe in Savoie near Montmeillan, and the other in a respectable post in the customs at Dôle, are both fine upright men. However, in principles and loyalty I am sure the unfortunate younger brother is far from lacking, and that even in recent times if he had not shown so much aversion to the usurping government, he would have made his fortune better. But there is no doubt that his character is in no way calculated to do honour to the family, and I know that it is viewed that way by all of them, though each one takes an interest in his wife and children, of whom everyone speaks highly.' (417)

Another who worried about the young Louise was Madame Mallet. She had evidently suggested to the duke that perhaps the girl, then eighteen, could go to Paris to live under Madame's care. The duke was dubious. 'Planning to write tomorrow to my dear kind friend the comtesse de Montgenêt', he replied on 14 June 1819, 'from whom I had a letter two days ago, I will undertake to discuss with her what you tell me about her niece Louise, who, I am well aware, is a most

interesting person, but I doubt if she would have the courage to risk
taking under her guardianship so young a girl who would undoubtedly
demand, at the interesting age she has reached, the most attentive care;
but I will see whether I can touch that delicate chord : besides, she
knows very well what her brother is, on account of constantly rendering
him the most essential services, for I do not believe there exists in the
whole world anyone more generous than she is.' (418)

The young Charles, next brother in age to Louise, was still at Ealing
and still an object of the duke's lively interest. Typical boy, Charles
was also still a lazy letter-writer. In January 1819 Wetherall was
instructed to see that he wrote to his aunt regularly. In February the
instructions had to be tightened. 'The Countess de Montgenêt, in her
last letter, requested me to direct her nephew to address all his
letters to *his father*, in future, through me; you will therefore
have the goodness to give him this instruction and to invariably enclose
them to me in your's, telling him at the same time, that I shall expect
to receive a letter from him, for his father, once a month.' In March
he was doing well at school. The duke was delighted with the favorable accounts you give of our young friend Charles Montgenêt, if I
should not come over, pray make him write to *me*, each time he does
to his father, and tell him I shall expect him to do so henceforward,
on the first Monday of every month'. (419)

The care and cherishing with which the duke had surrounded
Thérèse-Bernardine during the twenty-seven years, he now continued,
as far as was possible from a distance, out of both love and guilt. If he
had deserted her physically, he did not, at least, discard her. On 25
November 1818 he was writing to General Knollys, who had suggested taking his daughter to call on Madame. 'I think the *best* plan of
accomplishing a meeting between you, would be, to write a few lines
beforehand, *whenever you mean to go to Paris,* and then state the
wish you have to prove your grateful recollection of all her former
kindness to you, by presenting your Daughter to her : only if she has
spirits sufficient to receive you (which may perhaps be doubtful) I
intreat you to abstain from *all allusion* to my *present situation,* and
to *any* topic (but *that* of my sincere and unalterable attachment for
her) *that can excite one painful emotion in her susceptible mind.*'

Five months later, on 22 April 1819, he was writing to Knollys again
from Calais, on his way to London with a pregnant duchess. Even a
year after their parting, Madame could not bear to hear of the
duchess. 'I appreciate as I ought your kind attempts and those of your
son to see my old friend and companion, but I perceive clearly what
the Duke of Orléans has long told me, that her nerves are not in a state
to see those who had known her in the happy times of our intimacy;

indeed, I know that *last* summer one fell casually in her way, and it occasioned her a shock she did not recover/from/for weeks; this therefore must account for any apparent incivility on your names being sent in. From all the accounts I hear of her proceedings, from those who are well acquainted with them, I understand that every exertion is made to obtain peace and tranquillity of mind by availing herself of the benefit of an extensive society she has formed, but at the moment when all appears to be going on smoothly, some occurrence or another takes place to bring to recollection former times, and again days & weeks pass before her mind is calmed.' (420)

By the middle of 1819, Thérèse-Bernardine was weary of the rue de Grenelle. Too many sad memories were tied to the area. She had begun to think of moving to another part of Paris, and the duke encouraged her. Writing to Mallet on 8 June to thank him for his congratulations on the baby Princess Victoria's birth, and going on, as he always did, to Madame and her welfare, the duke said: 'I trust when she gets into her new house, as it will carry with it no painful recollections whatsoever, and be a total new scene, it will be the means of restoring her to gaiety and good spirits.'

Before 8 November she was installed in the new residence. Again to General Mallet, the duke wrote: 'Most particularly grateful do I also feel to you for the comfortable accounts with which you favor me of our inestimable friend in the Rue de Chantereine, and who, I am happy to perceive from you, is so nobly fulfilling her promise to me of endeavouring to obtain *that tranquillity* and calmness of mind under her altered situation, the knowledge of which is so essentially necessary to enable me to feel *comfortable* in mine . . . I rejoice to think that she is so well lodged, as well as surrounded by a society sufficient to occupy her when she wishes to be so occupied, and it is particularly satisfying to me to learn that you and your Lady are as often with her as possible, for I know she esteems and values you both highly.' (421)

The move to the rue Chantereine (where not so many years earlier Josephine had had her charming house, and today renamed the rue de la Victoire) took Madame to the other side of the Seine and a considerable distance from the rue de Grenelle. Here, with good friends caring for her, among them the Duke of Orleans, General Mallet, General Knollys, the baron de Vincy, the Chevalier de Broval, the marquis de Graves and madame la comtesse de Vertamy—she lived until 1822.

R

CHAPTER TWENTY

Tragedy

After a round of parties, theatres, visits to London institutions (the Houses of Parliament, the Mint, the Law Courts, East India House, the Millbank Penitentiary), the duke and his bride had returned to Amorbach early in September 1818, planning to live there until the duke's debts were finally cleared. The Queen Dowager of Wurtemberg (the Princess Royal of England) wrote to Lady Harcourt on 2 September, 'It must be a great pleasure to my Brothers that the Queen approves of all their Dutchesses, who also suit my Sisters. Towards the end of November I hope to make the Dutchess of Kent's acquaintance, who I am told is very good humoured and pleasant.' (422)

They had stayed at Brussels for some days, and from Amorbach made a journey to Basle, where the young Prince of Leiningen, Victorie's fourteen-year-old son, was residing. On 3 October, a two-day stop at Aix-la-Chapelle saw a meeting with the Emperor Alexander and a brilliant ball given by the City, at which 'Her Royal Highness the Duchess of Kent attracted particular attention by the richness of her dress and the splendour of her jewels'. (423) By the end of October it was apparent that the purpose of the marriage had been achieved: the duchess was pregnant.

As usual, expenses had outrun the duke's expectations and estimates. He had not planned for the trip to Basle and he had been unable to rid himself of the house in Brussels, which he had taken for five years, owing to the refusal of the owner to allow him to sublet. As a result of these setbacks (added to some over-spending on alterations at Amorbach) he was now left without sufficient funds to take the duchess to England for her confinement. As at the time of his proposed marriage, many friends urged him to take the step he contemplated, and pressed the importance of an English birthplace for an English child so near the throne. The duke was appalled to find himself now obstructed by the Prince Regent, who refused financial aid and in fact reacted with extreme displeasure to the suggestion.

It had been the duke's dearest wish to have any children born in England, but now he found there was criticism to face. The *Morning Herald* pontificated on 12 February 1819: 'The *Morning Chronicle* of yesterday tried to make a piteous story of an injunction, which it states the Duke of Kent to have received from the Prince Regent against a journey to England on the approaching *accouchement* of the Duchess. If the tale be true it tends immediately to the honour of the Prince Regent and ultimately to that of the Royal Duke. The praises, which have been carefully and often bestowed upon the latter for a mode of living, which is consistent with the payment of his debts, will certainly not be the less approved by the public, when his Royal Highness shall be seen to have taken no opportunity for interrupting his progress to that honourable result; and it is obvious, that the Prince Regent is benefitting the nation, when he prevents both the expense of an unnecessary journey and the occasion which some indiscreet friends of the Duke might find for endeavouring to transfer his Highness's debts from himself to the public. The birth of a Prince, or Princess, may be attested by sufficient witnesses, just as well in Germany as in England.'

A limit set by nature governed the time by which the journey must be accomplished, and the duke grew more distressed as the days passed. 'The interesting situation of the Duchess causes me hourly anxiety', he wrote to Dr Rudge on 20 March, '. . . the event is thought likely to occur at the end of the month of May. My wish is that it may take place on the fourth of June, as that is the birthday of my revered father; and that the child, like him, may be *Briton born*'. (424)

Desperate, the duke had written his old friend Lord Dundas, with a personal letter also (on 28 January) to Lord Fitzwilliam, whom he did not know so well, but whose aid he had asked Dundas to solicit. When it was almost too late, help came. The good-natured Dundas supported him. 'It is a hard case on him', he wrote to Dear Lord Fitz on 15 February, 'that such opposition should be shewn in a Certain quarter, to his bringing the Duchess to lay in in England. I should like much to assist the Duke of Kent, and would willingly risk a third or a fourth of what he wants.'

He was not ignorant of the duke's financial situation, after a long conversation with Wetherall and a statement from the trustees. With faith and goodwill, both noble lords came cheerfully to the rescue.

'Dear Lord Fitz', wrote Dundas on 5 March, 'I this morning received your draft on Snow & Co for £2500 which I have endorsed, and have given to Genl Wetherall, along with my own to the same amount, he says that there is no Doubt that it will enable the Duke and Duchess to come to England.' (425)

Their landing was noted in the papers, but not with as much enthusiasm as the arrival at the same time of the Persian Ambassador, Mirza Abdul Hassan, and the Fair Circassian, the mysterious beauty who was to intrigue English society for the next few weeks. Thirty-three lines of print from Dover appeared in the *Morning Post* of 27 April, giving the details of her landing on the 25th. Six lines reported the landing of the Kents, 'His Royal Highness /driving/ his own carriage, and at a very slow pace, paying every attention to the situation of the Duchess'.

Their arrival in London was, however, noted at greater length: and on 24 May, through the kindness of Lord Dundas and Lord Fitzwilliam (neither of whom would be repaid in his lifetime) the Duke of Kent's child was Briton born.

People poured into Kensington Palace to present congratulations in numbers so great that occasionally 'the names could scarcely be taken; the whole were incalculable'. Now that it was a *fait accompli,* public opinion cheered the duke's persistence and the press made loud sounds of rejoicing. 'It is an interesting coincidence that the infant daughter of the Duke of Kent was born on the birth-day of our revered Sovereign, which took place on the 24th of May 1738 but was afterwards transferred to the 4th of June, from old to new style', said the *Morning Post.* 'Considering the high destiny of the Royal Infant, there is nothing which is more calculated to enhance the satisfaction of its parents in particular, and the nation at large, next indeed to that of its having having been born in Old England than this event.' The *Morning Herald,* that carping critic of the duke's 'indiscretion' in bringing his duchess to England, had the gall to add complacently : 'If anything can enhance the satisfaction of the Royal Parent, on the birth of his child in Old England, it must be this circumstance ; and, considering the probable destiny of the infant Princess, it is one in which the nation at large must participate.' His instinct had been right, his decision justified.

Did Thérèse-Bernardine, combing the reports of the English *bourse* in the closely printed columns in *Le Moniteur* to find what she sought, read the brief announcement on 29 May, reprinted from the London *Courier,* and feel again the sense of tearing loss? Or did she feel a moment of pride that her loss was so deeply embedded in this moment of national rejoicing? She may have felt happy that her duke's sacrifice of her had not been in vain, but she could not face any public mention of it. *Do not bring up the subject of the child unless the Comtess does,* the duke begged Mallet on 8 June. (426)

On the advice of his trustees, he tried in July to relieve his financial difficulties by selling Castle Hill Lodge through a lottery, since a normal sale would not at this time bring in its valuation price of £50,000. He was balked by Parliament, which was sententiously righteous about the proposal and vetoed it. *The Times,* which could observe with equanimity the duke's struggles in the toils of debt (which it acknowledged were largely due to injustices and ill-luck in the service of his country) felt it would be disagreeable 'to the notions of dignity and grandeur which we attach, and with justice, to Royalty, to see "THE DUKE OF KENT'S LOTTERY" staring us in the face at every corner in London—on every barn-door in the country'. (427)

The baby princess was christened on 24 June : *Alexandrina* for the Russian Emperor, *Victoria* for her mother. The duke had resumed his energetic patronage of charities, and attended public meetings as well as the season's social events, the latter made especially magnificent this year by the Persian Ambassador's gold tissue and diamonds and the numerous 'Circassians' who turned up at the masked balls. The duchess studied English, went to the theatre with the duke, appeared at the Grand Ball at Carlton House on 17 July as Joan of Arc. The duke chaired a meeting promoting the plan of his friend Robert Owen to establish 'Villages of Co-operation' similar to his successfully operated village in New Lanark : his model, which attracted curious attention on display in London, brought editorial reservations from *The Times,* which objected to the parallelogram design 'on mathematical principles'. (The subscriptions failed to reach an effective level and had to be returned.) On 24 July the duke went (in the company of 'some old military friends') to what appears to have been the only military review attended by the Prince Regent that summer, and answered Owen's fears that he was overtiring himself with a comment syntactically complicated but tragically ironic in view of what happened six months later. 'I shall only allow myself to observe, from my habit of temperance and the rule I make of changing my clothes the moment I get home when heated, seldom does anything appear to me fatigue by which others are worn down who live higher and not with the same regularity of hours.' (428)

Around September, he began to think of spending part of the winter in Devonshire, and at the end of October he paid a visit of inspection to various Devon resorts, staying with Mr and Mrs Thomas Turner during his three-day residence in Exeter. Torquay, Teignmouth, Dawlish, Exmouth and Sidmouth were viewed, where the residents sang *God Save the King* 'and other loyal songs', and decorated their houses with laurel. The duke's visit to the Bishop's Palace to dine on the night of 26 October could hardly have omitted a tour of the Cathedral, where his parents had been escorted in August 1798, thirty years earlier. He would not have failed to pause a moment at the memorial to his old friend Colonel John Graves Simcoe, particularly as this day was the anniversary of his death thirteen years before. (429)

Sidmouth was the location decided upon, where the duke rented Woolbrook Cottage owned by the mother of General Baynes. Here, after a short visit en route to the Bishop of Salisbury (his boyhood tutor, Dr John Fisher), the little party arrived on Christmas Eve, and established themselves in 'tremendous weather', gales of wind, driving rain and snow, and bitter cold. By the 30th, however, an improvement allowed the duke and duchess, with the Princess Victoria, to walk daily on the promenade, and the baby princess had her first and much publicized experience of being under fire, when a local boy shooting at birds got near enough to the royal residence to break a window with the shot and just miss hitting the royal infant.

On 15 January, London papers had begun to report, though without real apprehension, that 'His Royal Highness the Duke of Kent is, we are sorry to hear, indisposed with a severe cold, which has confined him to his room since Sunday last'. The weather had been dreadful all over England. Below Kew Bridge the ice was reported to be five feet thick in places, and gale-force winds made communication with shipping at Deptford and Woolwich impossible. By the 19th, *The Times* reported that the duke's illness had assumed 'most alarming symptoms'. A letter from Sidmouth dated the 17th increased the alarm. 'The cold his Royal Highness contracted has terminated in pleuritic inflammation and cough, and besides three copious bleedings from the arm, he has twice undergone the operation of cupping.'

By now, all the papers were running daily bulletins, fluctuating between hope and alarm. On Saturday the 22nd, John Wilson Croker wrote in his diary: 'The Duke of Kent is very seriously ill . . . had rattles in his throat, and was despaired of. He could not live a day. This seems incredible; so strong a man to go in so short a space, and from, in its origin, so trifling an indisposition'.

On Monday, 24 January, *The Times*, with black-edged columns, announced to a stunned and disbelieving nation the death of the Duke of Kent. 'He was the strongest of the strong', wrote Croker to Lord Lowther, 'never before ill in all his life, and now to die of a cold, when half the kingdom had colds with impunity, is very bad luck indeed'. (430)

'His Royal Highness, in a long walk on Thursday se'nnight with Captain Conroy . . . had his boots soaked through with the wet. On their return to Woolbrook cottage, Captain Conroy, finding himself wet in his feet, advised his Royal Highness to change his boots and stockings; but this he did not do till he dressed for dinner, being attracted by the smiles of his infant Princess, with whom he sat for a considerable time in fond parental dalliance. Before night, however, he felt a sensation of cold and hoarseness, when Dr Wilson prescribed for him a draught. This his Royal Highness, in the usual confidence in his strength, and dislike of medicine, did not take, saying that he had no doubt but a night's rest would carry off every uneasy symptom. The event proved the contrary.' (431)

When it had seemed obvious that the end was near, General Wetherall had called aside Dr Stockmar, physician to the duchess's brother Prince Leopold, and asked 'if it would be injurious to speak to the Duke about signing his will'. Taken by the duchess to see for himself the duke's condition, Stockmar 'found him half delirious, and told the Duchess that human help could no longer avail, and that with regard to the will, the only question was, whether it would be possible to so far rouse the Duke to consciousness, that the signature would have legal force'.

A touching scene followed. 'Wetherall then went to the Duke, and the presence of the friend of his youth had a wonderfully stimulating effect on the dying nervous energies. Wetherall had hardly spoken to the Duke, before he quite came to himself, enquired about various things and persons, and had his will read over to him twice. Gathering together all his strength, he prepared to sign it. With difficulty he wrote "Edward" below it, looked attentively at each separate letter, and asked if the signature was clear and legible. Then he sank back exhausted on the pillows. The next morning all was over.' (432)

Two months later his mother-in-law the Duchess of Saxe-Coburg-Saalfeld would grieve to her diary of her 'haunting suspicion that the wretched doctors by their constant bleeding are responsible for the death of that splendid strong man'. (433)

Correspondence between members of the royal family had been showing increasing agitation as the news of their brother grew worse. When his death followed, they were overcome. The Prince Regent, when the news was brought to him by his brother's equerry, General Moore, burst into a flood of tears. As much as a week later, Princess Augusta was writing to tell Lady Harcourt that William 'has been so very wretched with the loss of poor Edward, that He has not been able to bring Himself to come here'. (434)

From Berlin, the Duke of Cumberland wrote to the Regent on 4 February :

'I can safely declare that I never was so struck in my life as with the late melancholy account of poor Edward's death for I had no idea of his being ill till . . . I received a letter from Mary . . . I can hardly persuade myself of the event having taken place. Poor fellow he must have suffered I fear most dreadfully . . . I should have thought he would have outlived us all from his regular habits of life which he has pursued ever since I can recollect any thing . . . I can say that this event has made a deeper impression on my mind than any thing I almost ever felt, for it was the last I should have looked forward to.
'His heart was good, but he was an unfortunate man from his onset in life, and from having seen very little of the world in his youth he got imposed upon by men who certainly did him much mischief.' (435)

Shock and sadness showed through the Princess Augusta's letter of 25 January to her friend Lady Harcourt. 'Rest as my Heart is . . . it is a consolation to my feelings to write to you . . . I must tell you all I have gone through for the last week; it will help to make me shed Tears, and it will do me good.' Sir David Dundas had come from London, she said, 'and related that the Dutchess of Kent was greatly alarmed about Dear Edward; and that She had sent an express to desire Dundas would go down immediately to Sidmouth'. Unaware of her brother's serious condition, the princess had suggested 'some other Person of whose Skill He was confident', in order not to interfere with Sir David's regular attendance on the King, and Dr Maton was dispatched in his stead. But worse news followed worse news, until 'yesterday we received the fatal conclusive letter to this sad Tragedy. Think, my Dearest Lady Harcourt, that yesterday *five* weeks he was here on His way to Sidmouth; so happy, with His excellent, good little Wife, and his lovely child; and within so short a time was perfectly *well—ill*—and *no more*! It's an awfull lesson, even to those who did not know Him; but it's a severe blow to those who loved Him *as I did*. Thank God he was in some degree aware of His danger; for He said to General Moore, "If I should not survive, if it should please the Almighty to take me, go *and give my love to all my Brothers and Sisters separately.*" This is a great consolation to us all; and must be so, particularly under some very distressing circumstances, which you know occurred a little while ago; but happy am I to say, all my Brothers went to inquire after Him, and He was delighted at it. I cannot be too thankfull that this was the case; knowing all their hearts to be so good, it will be a comfort to them as long as they live.' (436)

The bells had hardly finished tolling for the Duke of Kent all over England when the country reeled from yet another shock. The press had been too concerned with the bulletins about the duke to notice by more than a few small entries that the old King was slipping silently away from 'that dreary prison-house of the soul' he had inhabited for the past nine years. On Monday, 31 January, in the issue of the *Observer* that was devoting its five-column front page and half a column of page two to a laudatory obituary of the duke, the press was stopped for 'the melancholy intelligence of the Death of His Majesty George the Third' at half-past eight on Saturday, 29 January, in the eighty-second year of his life and the sixtieth year of his reign.

While his father lay in state, a sad procession brought the duke's body with cavalry escort from Sidmouth to Windsor, his embalmed body in a coffin more than seven feet five inches long, 'one of the largest which has been made for any of the Royal Family . . . and weighing altogether upwards of a ton'. From Sidmouth to Bridport, from Bridport to Blandford, to Salisbury, Basingstoke and Cumberland Lodge, resting at night in the little parish churches on the way, the Duke of Kent was brought home to Windsor. In the dark winter night of Saturday, 12 February, in the smoky light of flambeaux, the last procession made its way from Cumberland Lodge to the Chapel of St George. 'The darkness . . . gave additional grandeur to the pomp and ceremony of the cavalcade, moving as it did amid the red murky glare of so many torches. As it proceeded down the Long-walk, a noble avenue of elms, nearly two miles in length . . . tree appeared in dark succession to tree, as the torch-bearers advanced in their journey, until at length the whole outline of the avenue became distinctly visible. . . . All was silent and solemn as the grave to which it was proceeding, except at intervals, when, in pauses of the wind, the slow tramp of horses, or the tolling of the funeral bell, came upon the air and disturbed the surrounding stillness.'

So to the Royal Chapel of St George came the Duke of Kent, attended by his servants and grooms in full state liveries; detachments of the Royal Horse Guards and the Lancers, every fourth man bearing a flambeau; the trumpets and drums of the Royal Household, the mourning coaches of the Royal Family; the knights, the pages, the heralds, Blue Mantle, Portcullis and Rouge Dragon. In the Chapel 'there was no more light than what was afforded by a dozen tapers: this was just sufficient to prevent the chapel from being involved in utter darkness. . . . The windows were seen, and also the obscurity which covered every thing beyond them, whilst the white pillars of the chapel appeared conspicuous through the gloom. . . . About eight o'clock a detachment of the Coldstream Guards . . . marched into the

chapel with two regimental flags hung with crape. . . . They formed
a single line on each side of the nave, and shortly after their formation
received a large wax taper for every fourth man. . . . On a private
signal being given to their officers, their tapers were almost simul-
taneously lighted, and the chapel as it were by magic, was immediately
filled with a glare of light. . . . The fretted ceiling of the vaulted roof,
with all its numerous architectural elegancies, became as visible to
the eye as it ever was in the broadest glare of noon.'

General Wetherall had preceded his old friend into the chapel. The
coffin was followed by the chief mourner His Royal Highness the
Duke of York and all the Princes of the Blood Royal, in long black
cloaks. All through the service the Duke of Sussex, the dead duke's
closest friend among his brothers, sobbed uncontrollably.

On the coffin a small quantity of consecrated earth was dropped;
and slowly it was let down into the darkness of the royal vault below,
carrying to his last resting place 'Prince Edward, Duke of Kent and
Strathern, Earl of Dublin, Knight of the Most Noble Order of the
Garter, Knight Grand Cross of the most honourable military Order
of the Bath, and Knight of the most illustrious Order of St Patrick,
fourth son of his late most sacred Majesty King George III, of
blessed memory'. (437)

Nearly 4,000 miles away and two months later (8 April) *The
Independent Chronicle and Boston Patriot* recalled to its readers the
young Prince Edward who had spent a week in their city twenty-six
years earlier. 'Private citizens . . . paid him every mark of attention,
and found him a man every way worthy of it.' In Halifax an old
man of eighty-three heard the news and his heart broke. 'Sir John
Wentworth . . . had been failing very gradually through the Winter
past yet he loved this life, and embraced it as very desireable, till the
melancholy and unexpected account of The Duke of Kents Death
was confirmed when Sir Johns spirits sunk, his mind failed and he
expired on the evening of the 8th Instant at half past Ten o clock.'
(438)

The two women who had loved the duke wept and remembered.
In London, Victoire watched over a living child of her husband's
flesh. In Paris, Thérèse-Bernardine had only memories, but they were
richer and covered a span of time and distance, memories of a younger,
gayer prince than his duchess had known, and perhaps more truly
hers.

CHAPTER TWENTY-ONE

Madame alone

Edward's duchess, comforted by her brother Prince Leopold who had arrived in Sidmouth on 22 January, had left the scene of desolation on the 25th, the baby Princess Victoria touching all hearts as she was held up to the carriage window by her nurse. Their slow and sorrowful journey back to London created unfounded rumours that the duchess had been left pregnant.

Wetherall, who had asked permission to stay with his royal friend until the last sad duties were performed, remained behind to make the necessary arrangements and go with the body to Windsor.

'My dear Countess', he had written to Thérèse-Bernardine on 22 January, from Sidmouth, while the man they both loved lay struggling for breath in a nearby room. 'It is with deep regret that I have to communicate to you that His Royal Hss The Duke of Kent is at this time suffering under severe indisposition, so much so that the Physicians in attendance upon His Royal Hss are led to pronounce the Case almost hopeless. It is, however, my earnest hope that a favorable change may yet take place, and that our good and amiable Prince may still be spared to his Friends. To be enabled to inform you of such a change having taken place will afford me the highest satisfaction.

'Your Nephew Charles Montgenet is, I am happy to say, quite well and at present under my Roof. Adieu, My Dear Countess, may I be enabled to give you better accounts of His Royal Hss in my next. In the mean while believe me to remain with sincere regard. . . .' (439)

Another letter reached the rue Chantereine, perhaps at the same time. It was written by the other woman who had loved Edward, his duchess Victoire. It came to Madame by the hand of Louis-Philippe, who wrote in a covering letter dated 2 February: 'Here, my dear comtesse, is a letter for you from Madame the Duchess of Kent that Prince Leopold sent to me, asking me to pass it on to you with the consideration and care your situation requires. I send it to you, however, without delay, so that you can prepare your reply, which I will come for in about three hours if you can receive me, in order to discuss with you what you would like me to write. I am glad the matter has taken this turn, and think it looks promising. It is very good of her, and from everything I hear the Prince of Cobourg is full of good wishes. I hoped this would be the case, but I am delighted not to have been mistaken. You have known for a long time, my dear comtesse, my feelings for you and the cruel loss we have just suffered. Be brave if you can.' (440)

For the letter to have reached the Palais Royal by 2 February, the duchess must have written it almost immediately after the duke had drawn his last breath. Victoire had accepted Madame's place in her husband's life. 'She is not ignorant of my earlier liaison and gives me every reason to believe that she respects it', the duke had written to de Vincy in July 1818.

Thérèse-Bernardine must have been prepared for the news. *Le Moniteur,* which had been carrying increasingly grave bulletins, had announced the duke's death in its issue of 29 January. One may imagine with what heartbreak she would have read the glowing praise of another woman's exemplary devotion to the last moments of the man she had faithfully loved for now nearly thirty years.

Louis-Philippe, too, was desolated. He was to have attended a ball given by the duc de Berri at the Elysée Palace, but the news of his friend's death caused him to send his apologies and seclude himself in the Palais Royal. (441)

For Thérèse-Bernardine, some concern for her own future was added to the emotional shock of the duke's death. He had made sure she would have at least a minimum of financial security, and her own good management had expanded the income she would receive from her 'pittance'. But the sudden loss of a regular and generous allowance, if it were to cease, could not fail to affect her standard of living.

Her friends shared her concern. On 3 February, Louis-Philippe, the Duke of Orleans, acted promptly and wrote on her behalf to Thomas Coutts.

"You will easily conceive how much I am grieved by the loss of the invaluable friend who has been so suddenly wrested from us. You know the unalterable friendship that constantly subsisted between us since so many years, & you will feel that such a loss never can be compensated. But now that the Duke of Kent is no more, I am still more anxious to give every assistance in my power to Mme de St Laurent, now the Comtesse de Montgenet, to obtain the accomplishment, not of what I knew to have been his intentions towards her, I am afraid that is impracticable, but at least of those dispositions which he made for her, & of which you are one of the trustees. I look with confidence to your assistance in what is unfortunately become a duty of affection & friendship to the memory of my lamented friend.

'I saw Mme de Montgenet for the first time since she received the fatal intelligence the day before yesterday. She communicated to me the attested copies which are in her possession of the deeds lodged at your house.'

These, as Louis-Philippe pointed out, appeared to establish Madame's clear right to repayment, out of the duke's life insurance, of a small loan she had made to him; and he added that he was aware of his royal friend's intention—'& indeed he had mentioned it several times to me'—to have continued the insurance in Madame's favour. What steps, he wondered on Madame's behalf, should she take to recover the small sum actually due? He also suggested that some 'proper person' might be appointed 'to watch over her interests & to defend her rights against or with the creditors. But supposing that step to be adviceable [sic], who could be that proper person, is what I am ignorant of & consequently what I could not tell her. Should you be able to give me advice in that respect, you would greatly oblige me, & I am quite certain in so doing you would do that which the Duke of Kent would have wished you to do, if he was still among us.

'The Duchess of Kent having been so good, so generous, & I may truly say so admirable, as to manifest to Mme de Montgenet (since the Duke's death) the interest which she takes in her fate & her good wishes for Mme de M's future welfare, I have informed Prince Leopold of the intentions of our friend towards Mme de M. And besides an extract of the deeds, I have sent him copies which I have attested of certain Notes in the Duke's own handwriting which is of course well known to me, which contain some very important explanation of the manner in which he contracted that debt . . . towards Mme de M. & of his intentions about the continuation of the annuity he made her, & even of his resolution of increasing it, should his means increase. I know, as I already told you, that these intentions cannot be fulfilled . . . but still it was right to give a positive proof of what were the Duke's intentions in her respect.' (442)

What Madame wrote in reply to the Duchess's kind message has
not survived. It would have been a tender and sympathetic letter,
from one heart wrung by sorrow to another suffering the same loss.
Prince Leopold replied for his sister to the Duchess of Orleans on the
13th: Louis-Philippe's Comptroller, the Chevalier de Broval (who
had so often visited the duke and Madame at Ealing and Kensington)
sent a copy to the rue Chantereine. 'For the information of the duke,'
wrote Prince Leopold, 'I beg you to tell him that I have given the
letter from Madame de Mongenet to my sister, the Duchess of Kent,
who was very much moved by it.

'As for the papers, I have given them to Captain Conroy, who, with
General Wetherall, has for the moment the arrangement of all matters
of this kind. He has told me they are quite aware of the bond . . .
and that she will receive her share with the other creditors. . . . I have
heard that the princesses have mentioned the necessity of giving
something from themselves to Madame de Mongenet, but I cannot
answer for it. I will speak about it to the Duke of Sussex.' A second
letter of the same date from Prince Leopold to Louis-Philippe noted
'with satisfaction, that if Castle Hill is sold the total debt . . . can be
paid without loss.'

Madame's interests were well looked after by the widowed duchess,
her brother, and Madame's unfailing good friend Louis-Philippe. An
undated letter written by the Chevalier de Broval kept her informed.
'A conversation has been held between the two princes. It went off
perfectly well. . . . He wants to talk to General Wetherall and other
people close to his august sister and perhaps to herself. There was no
hostility to you, Madame; on the contrary, the most pleasant language
and repeated assurances of a lively interest on the part of the widowed
princess and himself for one who has proved so well and for so long
the true devotion of her heart and her life. After I had learned of this
conversation, I had reason to believe that if they had been rich, or
even comfortably placed, it would have occurred to them before
that it would be a good thing to do something for you. At least your
worries of yesterday are over, also mine and those that an old and
royal friend . . .' The rest of the letter is missing. (443)

Madame's twenty-five-year-old nephew, Charles-Benjamin, had
apparently completed his law course and seems to have moved in to
live with her: the resident at rue Chantereine No. 28 in January 1821
appears in the *Almanach des* 25,000 *adresses des principaux habitants
de Paris* (Dulac) as Mongenet, avocat à la Cour royale. Some time
later that year he moved to Grenoble, marrying there on 5 November

the eighteen-year-old Jeanne Françoise Rose Zoë Perrard, daughter of
a mortgage administrator. He had lost his father (and Madame her
brother Claude-Charles) four months earlier, on 22 July.

By 1822, the address of Madame la comtessse de Mongenet had
changed. She had moved to an apartment at No. 8 Place Louis Quinze
today's Place de la Concorde) in one of the great hôtels built by
Gabriel on either side of the rue Royale.

In England the law was proceeding with slow gravity to sort out
the affairs of the late duke. His debts were not on nearly so extravagant
a scale as his detractors indicated, nor did they approach the totals
reached by his three elder brothers. Nevertheless, they represented a
sum that would considerably embarrass his heirs and creditors. Castle
Hill Lodge was advertised for sale in *The Times* of 7 June 1820:
'The capital Mansion-house . . . comprising suits [*sic*] of noble and
lofty apartments . . . the offices admirably disposed . . . the gardens
. . . encircled by lofty fruit-walls, the vinery and conservatories . . . the
elegant and very splendid Furniture, noble glasses of great brilliancy
. . . beautiful lustres, magnificent Parisian clocks, figures and candel-
abras . . . cellar of the choicest wines, numerous elegant carriages and
harness . . . the valuable Library . . . consisting of several thousand
volumes . . . the splendid and extensive Sideboard of fashionable Plate
. . .' all went beneath the hammer of auctioneer James Denew. Sale
of the house and land was not successful. The rest of the property
brought in only about £14,000. Only after a third attempt, in August
1827, was the property sold—piecemeal: sills and frames, mahogany
stair rails, marble chimney pieces, joints and girders, doors, iron fences,
stone paving. After removing most of it, the buyer became insolvent,
and in 1829, 'knowing the strictly honorable and high-minded intentions of His late Royal Highness with respect to the liquidation of
his debts', the duke's friend General Wetherall, loyal to the last, bought
the property in the hope of settling the estate and paying off the
creditors. The duke may have been unfortunate in money matters, but
he was rich indeed in friends. (444)

On 13 May 1821 a petition had been presented in Chancery on
behalf of George Fournier 'for and on behalf of himself and all the
other simple contract creditors' against the trustees William Allen,
Thomas Pitt and Nugent Kirkland, to whom the executors of the
duke's will (Wetherall and Conroy) had 'duly renounced the probate
thereof'. The trustees admitted the debt and their position as legal and
personal representatives of the testator, and that a considerable amount
of value had been got in, but not sufficient 'to pay all just debts and
funeral and testamentary expenses'.

Administration was held over until the Master of Chancery had made his report, which, after advertisements had been placed asking simple creditors to come forward and prove their claims (totalling £58,664), was handed down on 20 July 1824. By August 1824, Thérèse-Bernardine had received payment of most of the money owed to her. (445)

She had been very ill in April that year, and fearing she might die, she called in her lawyer, Maître Lombard. 'In her bed, sick in body but sane in manner and judgment which is apparent from her conversation,' she dictated her will in a bedroom that looked out on to a courtyard from the second floor of No. 8 Place Louis Quinze. Maître Lombard brought in four local tradesmen from nearby rue St Honoré as witnesses (grocer, fruiterer, dealer in porcelain, dyer): Madame's bequests, apart from those to her legal heirs (her three brothers) and a woman named Marie Anne Eichhorn whose status was not indicated, were all made to members of her personal staff. The will, in the handwriting of Maître Lombard, was read over to her and signed 'T. B. de Montgenet', with her characteristic capital T. (446)

But she was to live for a few more years before the will had to be proved. From this period of her life no document has been traced, though the small traces of her presence can be found here and there. Her old lover, Philippe Claude Auguste de Chouly de Permangle, had died on 19 October 1821, ruined financially by the failure of a bank in the Place Vendôme. In Grenoble, Charles-Benjamin Mongenet was building his career as a successful lawyer and *juge-audietur* of the Palais de Justice de Grenoble. His first child, Anne-Marie, was born on 15 August 1822, in St-Jean-de-la-Porte, near Chambéry in Savoie, probably when he and his wife were visiting his stepmother. (Claude-Charles had married a second time.) A second and third child, Joseph-Bernard-Alfred and Marguerite-Françoise-Isaure, were born in 1825 and 1827. It is not too much to imagine that Madame, with her love of children and her penchant for travel ('a woman of such intrepid fortitude') would have visited them in Grenoble during these years. The young Charles Mongenet who had been a schoolboy at Ealing, and who did not, after all, enter Addiscombe College, may have been part of her household. Records in the Archives d'Etat in Geneva indicate that he left for Paris on 15 June 1825: in 1830 he was 'étudiant agé de vingt quatre ans . . . demeurant même place & No.' (8 Place Louis Quinze).

These last years of Madame's life were probably lived quietly, as indeed she had always lived, with visits from her friends and her family, and drives in her carriage through the streets and squares of the Paris she loved. Louis-Philippe, her old friend in the Palais Royal nearby, would never have forsaken her. The warm affection that had existed for years between them would not have wavered. Generous, protective and interested in her welfare as he had shown himself, who had known her gay and beautiful in Halifax, loving and loyal in London, heartbroken in Paris, it is safe to assume that he sustained her into advancing age with a continuing concern.

The memories that lit her mind in these last years covered a span of time and distance, covered royal events, covered those people—royalty and commoners alike—who occupy the high peaks of our past. She would dwell on those happier days when she was close to the centre of power and fashion, sending intimate inside gossip of the Court to her good friend Louis-Philippe ('The Regent is delighted with your letters that your illustrious friend never fails to send him . . . Lord Bentinck has also written Ministers a thousand flattering things about you . . .'). (447)

Her dying, too, blended into the great events of history. When she fell ill in July 1830 Charles-Benjamin came up from Grenoble to be with her (leaving a wife near her time, who gave him a son and heir in his absence). The two nephews who had been closest to her, who had both known her prince, Charles-Benjamin and Charles-Jean, watched over Thérèse-Bernardine as she slipped slowly away from life. Revolution was in the air again, the people of France stirring under the reactionary government of Charles X, the last of the Bourbon kings. On 26 July Paris erupted into violence. Barricades went up, paving stones filled their time-honoured role as ammunition, and the sound of firing echoed from different parts of the city.

From the Place de la Concorde beneath the windows of 'Madame of an hundred names and titles' the shouts of the people of Paris rose, a fusillade of shots came with staccato menace from the Champs Elysées. Armed men marched, drums beat, as they had when she was a girl in Besançon. A deputation went to Raincy to ask Louis-Philippe—*her* friend—to place himself at the head of affairs. On the last day of July, he stood on the balcony of the Hôtel de Ville, wrapped in the tricolour, and accepted the call to destiny.

Did he know that she was dying? Did he find time, in the midst of tremendous happenings, to say goodbye? She died on 8 August, three weeks before her seventieth birthday. Did she know, did they tell her, that Louis-Philippe had been declared 'king of the French, by the grace of God and the will of the people', just the day before?

S

'*Tuesday, 25 January, 1820*: I was astonished to hear yesterday of the Duke of Kent's death . . . No one in England will mourn the Duke. He was false, hard and greedy. His so-called good qualities were only for show, and his last public appeal to the charity of the nation had lost him the support of the only friends he had—prisoners and City men.' Thus wrote the Princess Lieven to her lover Metternich, adding with typical spitefulness: 'His wife kills all her husbands, though. She would cut an interesting figure now if she had it in her to do so; but, whatever you may say, she is the most mediocre person it would be possible to meet.' (448)

'Pray is the Duke of Kent dead yet'? wrote Mary Russell Mitford anxiously to Sir William Elford on 24 January. 'I want to know very much . . . really, one has a respect for the Duke of Kent. There is something of his old and venerable father about him. His talents, too, were certainly considerable—a fine public speaker—a charitable man.' (449)

Contemporary opinion was kinder to the duke at death than it would be to his brother of York, whose immorality and extravagances were strongly condemned in the obituary notice in *The Times* on 6 January 1827—kinder, too, than most of his biographers would be. Sermons were preached all over Britain (some dozen have survived in the British Museum), extolling virtues well deserving of praise, and most of them more than merely sycophantic.

Stockmar liked him. At the time of his marriage, he described the duke as 'a tall, stately man, of soldierlike bearing, already inclined to great corpulency. In spite of the entire baldness of the whole crown of his head, and his dyed hair, he might still be considered a handsome man.' (Sending a copy of a portrait by Sir William Beechey to the baron de Vincy at this time, the duke had written: 'It is exactly like I am today and not like the twenty-year-old *blondin* you knew in 1787'.)

'His dress was simple, but in good taste, and scrupulously neat and nice', continued Stockmar. 'He had seen much of the world and of men. His manner in society was pleasant and easy, intentionally courteous and engaging, and as he possessed the gift of speech in no small degree, he expressed himself in English and French with a certain degree of eloquence and elegance. The play of his countenance betrayed calculation. He was not without ability and culture, and he possessed great activity. His dependants complained of his strictness, and pedantic love of order. The regulation of his finances, and the perfecting of what English people call domestic comfort and the household system, and an extraordinary love of patronising and concerning himself in the affairs of others (he received almost everyone who wished to see him and who desired his help)—these were his occupations. The Duke was well aware that his influence was but small; but this did not prevent him from forwarding the petitions he received whenever it was possible . . . Liberal political principles were at that time in the minority in England, and as the Duke professed them, it can be imagined why he was hated by the powerful party then dominant . . . The Duke proved an amiable and courteous, even chivalrous husband.' Earlier, Stockmar had remarked him as 'the quietest of all the Dukes I have seen, talks slowly and deliberately, is kind and courteous'. (450)

He was mourned, despite the Princess Lieven. If he was false at times, it was a falsity from which no human being (least of all Princess de Lieven) is entirely free : capable of small subterfuges to protect himself from disaster, capable of calculation (which then and now meant forethought, the ability to think before speaking) : caught up in small palace intrigues at least to no greater extent than his brothers and sisters, whose plotting (if plotting it can be called) consisted of little more than anxious whispering to one of what they learned about the plans of another, all of them dependent on early knowledge of the way things were likely to go, in order to tread with discretion between opposing factions, within and without the family.

He was not hard. Stern in his attitude to duty and not sparing himself from its demands : insistent upon the letter of the law but ready to extend mercy and pardon where these could possibly be applied : perhaps, in his possession of great energy, not understanding the lack of it in others : brave in the face of danger : thorough in his attention to the health and welfare of those who were his responsibility, though they did not always appreciate it.

He was not greedy. What he asked was what he considered his due, and no more : an income equal to that received by his elder brothers, and one that would allow him to live in the manner his rank and position demanded. His letters asking for money do not carry the overtones of whining, of which he is sometimes accused. He wrote often enough to be considered a nuisance by the recipients of his requests, but his requests were based on real grievances and real needs. It is greatly to his credit that he did not become embittered, but turned to activities in which he could be socially useful.

He could not live within his income, and this is a fault from which few people are free, but he manfully tried to meet his obligations on an income smaller than he had a right to expect. ('If you are not to consider him as a Prince', an exasperated Edmund Burke had written to Windham in June 1795 about the Prince of Wales, 'and keep him as such, by an honourable establishment of a Court—there is no reason why you should give him anything on his private and personal merits. What is a Prince without people of distinction about him? . . . He is not, and cannot be . . . a Gentleman. He is a prince or he is nothing.') (451) The Duke of Kent's sense of importance was far less self-importance than a sense of the rank he was expected to dignify.

He may be despised for choosing income and prestige to living out his life with his long-time love. The romantic impulse inherent in all of us would rather read of the lover for whom the world was well lost, though we might not ourselves meet the standards we set for others. But Madame, though she was broken-hearted, had always understood the possibility of separation. It can be counted to the duke's credit that he did not consider for so many years a move that was always his to make with social approbation, and that she—the chief sufferer—did not spurn him for his decision. He must be allowed, too, some motives of duty in his choice. His love for 'his old French lady' lasted until his death, and they were never separated in thought or by letter.

He was a man with a conscience, and though his marriage earned him public appreciation, he could never quite free himself from self-condemnation.

He has been pictured as a man furious against fate, apoplectic in frustration, sadistic, pompous and of dubious taste. He was none of these things to any extreme degree. He was notably good-humoured, not easily angered, capable of self-control under provocation, a rigid but fair disciplinarian, solicitous for his friends and gentle with those he loved. Criticism of his taste (based largely on the peculiar description of Castle Hill Lodge by Mr Justice Hardinge) derives more from Hardinge's florid writing than from the duke's florid taste. His virtues of punctuality, of attendance to correspondence and of insistence upon neatness have often been reduced by derision to the status of petty vices. His other virtues of interest in the welfare of the poor, his unfailing attention to requests for aid or influence, have often been granted to him with a sneer, as some slight mitigation of the failure of his public career. Even his habits of temperance have been used to denigrate him as a man for whom self-importance was the reason for a control that would not allow him to appear drunk in public.

'After this', the King had written to his errant twenty-one-year-old son in 1788, 'it is not a few months that can either make me think your disposition changed nor make me forget what has past'. (452) For the whole of his life it was not forgotten.

He stayed alive, however—almost literally—in the minds of some of his friends. In 1854 Robert Owen, now an old, old man whose generous and energetic mind was betrayed by advancing age, was sure he had been visited by the spirit of the Duke of Kent. In this year, when he was eighty-three, he sent several letters to Queen Victoria 'at the request of the spirit of your royal Father' enclosing copies of his latest pamphlet *The New Existence of Man upon the Earth*, in which the observations made by her father's spirit 'are given for the benefit of Your Majesty and of this realm and of the population of the world'. Owen also wrote in his autobiography, published when he was eighty-six: 'I have had the unspeakable gratification and happiness of being visited by the spirit of his Royal Highness, who communicated with me in precisely his manner and phraseology as when conversing with me formerly, and spoke of his former domestic relations and interests, and gave me more valuable and important information respecting the spheres and past events and personages than I could have conceived to be possible.' (453)

Owen had passionately espoused the cause of that strange woman Olivia Serres, who claimed to be a daughter of King George III's brother the Duke of Cumberland (partly on the basis of another 'remarkable likeness' to the Royal Family) and stated that the duke, recognizing her as cousin, had asked Owen to advance money to her. Owen, gullible and by this time with a failing memory, may have been duped by the 'Princess Olivia' into believing that the impecunious duke had granted her a yearly allowance, with instructions to Owen to pay it for him. As she singled out the Duke of Kent for affection and praise in the extraordinary book she wrote to present her claims, the duke, unfailingly kind and polite, probably offered her a sympathetic hearing. But no one, reading her book, could fail to pity that deluded woman, or to reject her preposterous claim that she had letters in which the duke had settled on her £400 a year for life, promised her a grant of £10,000 from the sale of Castle Hill Lodge and the 'large tract of land he told me [he had] in *Canada*', and even that she had been appointed by him '*guardian* and sole *protector* of my daughter, *Alexandria* [*sic*], should the Duchess of Kent and myself depart this life during my said daughter's minority'. (454)

An anecdote widely repeated tells of an old gipsy woman who is said to have approached the duke in Gibraltar (sometimes in Malta, where he never was) to tell him 'You will have a daughter and she will be a great queen.' If there was ever such a prophecy (no contemporary reference has been traced), the duke was in no hurry to see it fulfilled. He lived with Madame for fifteen years after leaving Gibraltar in 1803 for the second time.

And what of Madame?

Even in her own day she was a woman of mystery. So authoritative a person as the marquis de Beaupoil St Aulaire wrote to Louis de Salaberry from London in 1800: 'I have heard in Canada gossip about Madame de St Laurent. I am taking this opportunity of clearing it up. She is most certainly born Mademoiselle de Montgenest [sic] St Laurent, wife and widow of M le Baron de fortisson, woman of quality, beautiful, agreeable and respectable, on whose account question and censure would never be correct. I tell you this out of respect to the truth and because I know it will please you.' (455)

The marquis was writing in good faith out of his own certainty, no better documented than the traditions that were to spring up many years later. Madame's own manners and behaviour lent credibility to the belief. How could such a fine lady, of such grace and integrity, have been a courtesan, not even of aristocratic birth?

Did her prince know, too, that she was seven years older than he?—or was this a woman's secret, well-kept by Madame over the years? He knew of her past life, though he told Creevey 'I am the first and only person who ever lived with her.' He had paid a pension to the marquis de Permangle (the assets of the marquis at death showed arrears of 2,500 francs owed by the duke, and his name appears among the creditors on the list given to Queen Victoria). (456) A payment was certainly made to the family of de Permangle in the early 1840s, a small sum under 1,000 francs. Descendants have surmized that it might have been a gambling debt, except that the duke never gambled.

There will always be the questions unanswered, matters of human interest about which we would like to know more, but maybe never will. Did someone write to tell the princesses of England in 1830 that their brother's beloved companion was dead? Did the duchess learn about it, watching over the child who lived because the duke had parted from his French lady, and feel a moment's sadness that this link with her husband was gone at last?

Madame's two nephews went to register her death—the lawyer Charles who had been the student in Paris when she made that joyful visit there with the duke; the schoolboy Charles, that schoolboy whose progress at Ealing she had watched over with such loving care. 'On the ninth of August one thousand eight hundred and thirty at half past eleven in the morning—Death certificate of Thérèse Bernardine Mongenet, lady of independent means aged sixty-nine years and eleven months, unmarried (*célibataire*), born at Besançon (Doubs) died Place Louis XV No 8 yesterday at three o'clock in the afternoon.

'Sworn by us Charles Gobillet deputy-mayor in the First arrondissement of Paris, on the declaration of Charles Benjamin Mongenet, *juge auditeur près le Tribunal de Grenoble,* aged thirty-four, Charles Jean Mongenet student aged twenty-four, both nephews of the deceased living at the same place and number, who have signed with us after reading . . .'

On 16 September 1830, Charles-Benjamin appeared before the proper authorities to declare and register her will. After certain personal legacies were made, her property was left to her three brothers or their heirs: Jean-Joseph-Suzanne, who had now retired to Besançon: Jean-Claude, the ne'er-do-well, living at Carouge, near Geneva: and Charles-Benjamin himself, as heir to his late father Claude-Charles. Under the will drawn up on her sickbed in 1824, Thérèse-Bernardine had left the sum of 100,000 francs to one Marie Anne Eichhorn, living at Bürgel near Offenbach. All the members of her staff received three months' wages. Mariette Lavigne, her maid, 4,000 francs: Joseph Pélissier, valet, 150 francs: Fanni Leroi, chambermaid, 125 francs: Marie Selinger, cook, 112.50 francs: Jean Jacques Ruchette, coachman, 112.50 francs: and François Bardé, servant, 100 francs. (457)

Was Marie Anne Eichhorn a friend of her youth, a companion of her old age? There were Eichhorns living in Bürgel (a small community near Offenbach) since at least 1817. In 1823 Gottfried Eichhorn owned House No. 2—a two-storey house, with a ballroom, wine distillery, bowling lane, shooting range, kitchen garden and farm outbuildings. There is mention of a Christoph Eichhorn in the Ground Tax List of 1838. Was Marie Anne wife or daughter of Gottfried or Christoph? These fragments of information and the knowledge that at some point her life touched that of Thérèse-Bernardine, are probably all that will ever be known about Marie-Anne. (458)

The letters left by Thérèse-Bernardine—few discovered, indeed, though doubtless there are others that were penned by her hand now growing faded and fragile in forgotten attics—show a gay brave spirit, worthy of her small place in history. A kind person and loving, one who gave gladly to the man with whom she chose to live. Wanton and wayward, perhaps, in her youth, but faithful and respected when chance brought her to a man she could love and respect. And she made her exit, when it was demanded, with a dignity unsurpassed by any royal lady.

Her 1824 will had stipulated the place of her burial. 'I wish to be buried beside my sister whose body rests in the cemetery of Père Lachaise. I wish the monument at present on her grave to be replaced by another which will cover both our bodies, for the erection of which I assign twelve thousand francs. On this monument I wish my sister's names and mine to be inscribed, with this wording: *Here lie two sisters united in life, whom death could not separate.*' (459)

She was buried on 10 August in a simple and elegant funeral from the Church of the Madeleine, with the solemnity of ceremonial wax candles, holy water and silver candelabra; mortuary chamber, church and cortège draped in black velvet with silver-fringed trimmings, the hearse drawn by two horses plumed and caparisoned. (460)

In a grave listed as Division 27 Line 7 Number 19, *concession perpetuelle* 132 *du 9 juillet* 1818, the Duke of Kent's faithful and beloved companion was laid to rest, high on a hillside in Père Lachaise. Today the old wide-spreading trees shade the area, and the old grey graves crowd together, overgrown with ivy and moss, and on most of them no one can any longer read the inscriptions. Here the two sisters from Besançon lie side by side, anonymous in death.

The facts

INTRODUCTION

'That there were children born to Edward and Julie' (thus a Canadian writer in 1966), 'there seems no doubt. Nor is there doubt that the couple, unlike Edward's brothers with their liaisons, for some reason were determined to conceal the existence of their children, consigning them to various foster parents, while they maintained them generously and rewarded those who reared them. When, in addition, following the death of the Duke, all records of his connection with Julie disappeared, proof of descent becomes very difficult. If documentary evidence is missing, by accident or design, there is however a solid background of private and public tradition, unusual circumstances, physical resemblances, unexplained wealth and possessions, and special preferments which dovetail with historical facts to indicate that one of the world's outstanding romances, in one of the world's most prolific periods, was not barren.' (461)

The traditions were all alike. The villain was an embarrassed and malicious Queen Victoria or her mother, using threats or actual destruction of documents to hide 'the truth'. Missing records, indeed, were a basic part of the claims. Why would they be missing if there was nothing to conceal? Amazing likenesses to some member of the royal family were deduced, often with no resemblance stronger than the wearing of a beard or a widow's cap. Unexplained money was surmised to be a royal pension, despite the duke's well-known state of chronic financial distress.

'So luxuriantly', wrote Elizabeth Longford in *Victoria R.I.*, 'grows the ivy on the bare wall'.

Missing records are evidence of little other than a fire, an accident, the unavoidable depredations of time, the oversight of a recording officer. Human doubles are too often found, even where no possible claim to relationship exists, for this kind of coincidence to carry weight as evidence. (A pertinent example: 'In both looks . . . and voice [Lord Glengall] is so like the poor Duke of York. It is quite wonderful his thick nervous way of speaking and profile, only not so handsome. I asked him yesterday if it had not been remarked and he told me he always avoided going by the gate at Hampton House, when he was going to the House of Commons, as the Guard invariably turned out and that old Queen Charlotte had remarked him at some fete and sent to inquire who it was she took for Frederick.' This was written by one qualified to speak: Minney Seymour to Mrs Fitzherbert). (462)

Madame's own history effectively contradicts the possibility that she mothered this brood of children and left them—in spite of her known love of children and those empty years to fill after her prince's death—in forgotten silence. It is impossible, too, to believe that the duke, with his strong sense of rank and privilege, would unconcernedly see the illegitimate sons of his brother the Duke of Clarence publicly received by the Queen and allow his own to remain in unacknowledged obscurity. Never reticent about his relationship with Madame, he would hardly have been reticent about any children born of the liaison. (463)

Most of the loose ends can now be tied up.

ISABELLA HYDE

'Family legend maintains that the Whyte family was selected by the Duke of Kent'—so goes a Canadian report—'and rewarded with plantations in Jamaica, to provide husband and protection for Isabella; that James, prior to Victoria's accession to the throne, left his honourable post as one of His Majesty's privy council and a justice of assize in Jamaica to establish an estate in the wilds of Upper Canada that would maintain Isabella's line for futurity.' (464)

The Jamaican plantations were not a reward for this self-sacrifice: they had been owned by the Whyte family from as early as 1765. In 1824 (probably at the time he bought his estate of Garbrand Hall) James Matthew Whyte had a map drawn up showing the estates of Garbrand and Mullet Hall in the parish of St Thomas in the East. The map shows three tracts of land of 300 acres each marked with the name of James White [sic]: one of these estates, Windhill, bears the date 1765. Other references on the map indicate that this was the date of the original survey. (465) James Whyte (the name is spelt White from time to time) was the father of John (Isabella's husband) and James Matthew.

After his death on 18 April 1822 at the age of 90, administration of James Whyte senior's will—seven enormous pages of close hand-writing (executed October 1814, with codicil dated February 1817)—was given to Thomas Whyte, eldest son of the deceased James, 'formerly of Windhill in the Island of Jamaica thereafter of Newmains in the County of Ayr and afterwards of Upper Stroquhan'. (466)

The will divided James Whyte's property explicitly between his three sons, Thomas, John and James Matthew, including the planta-tions of Windhill, Cavebottom and Craighead in Jamaica, plantation stock and hundreds of negro slaves, as well as Scottish property.

James Matthew left Jamaica not to establish a home in Canada for a daughter of the Duke of Kent, but for economic reasons. Profits from West Indian plantations had been falling for years. 'Fifteen to twenty years ago', wrote A Retired Military Officer in 1835, 'a good tradesman —mason, carpenter, saddler, etc., would have brought £180 to £200 : an able field negro from £140 to £170 . . . a healthy infant, £20 to £25. During the last seven years, one quarter of the above would not have been offered.' In 1829, he said, he was glad to accept £1,700 for a property worth £6,000 in 1824, in consequence of the immense depreciation in West India property at that time. (467)

In the early 1830s, James Matthew also saw the writing on the wall. He was evidently eyeing Canada as the new frontier of oppor-tunity; a friend signing himself T. Edgar wrote cautiously from London on 3 October 1833, 'I hope you will not lay out your money in Canada without personal inspection of the country—James Christie is coming back again quite disappointed and disgusted'. (468) James Matthew was not dissuaded, however. A permit 'to licence and permit James Matthew Whyte to depart this Island having put up His name in the Secretary's Office One-and-Twenty Days, pursuant to an Act of this Island' was issued to him on 15 March 1834. (469) He settled in Hamilton, Ontario, where on the Mountain overlooking the city he built the home known as Barton Lodge (destroyed by fire in 1930) which, when he died in 1843, he bequeathed to his older brother John.

John Whyte (he was not the Colonel of West Indian battle fame) (470) was listed in London business directories as early as 1816 as a broker operating from 12 Mincing Lane. James Matthew had appeared in Army Lists as a Lieutenant as early as 1806 : Whyte was clearly not a cover name. 'I observe you are at length established in your new house in Chester Street', wrote James Matthew to his sister-in-law, 'My dear Isabella', from Garbrand Hall in Jamaica on 18 March 1827, 'though I fear under very uncomfortable circumstances at the commencement. Tell me how the new square comes on, and whether its neighbourhood has become as much recherché as was expected. . . . Give my kindest regards to your mother . . . also to Christie when you write—or go to see him; for indeed I should not at all [wonder?] to hear of your accompanying Mrs Hyde [across the channel?] for that purpose.' (471)

Mrs Hyde was obviously not Thérèse-Bernardine, Comtesse de Montgenêt, living quietly in Paris at this date. A later reference in the letter to a Mr Sam: Hyde on whom James Matthew regretted he had not called since his return from a London vacation points to other Hyde connections in Jamaica. Mr Sam (who died in 1828) owned Retirement in St Thomas in the Vale in partnership with Charles Nicholas Pallmer (or Palmer): Hyde Hall was not owned by the Hydes but by the Shirley family. (472)

In 1829, operating steadily as a 'wine, spirit and colonial (West-India) broker' from his Mincing Lane address, John Whyte changed his private address to 'Warren House, near Uxbridge'. (473) At this address (the house was on Iver Heath) his name appears in the registers of electors as a resident up to 1834. Some time between 1834 and 1837 he seems to have moved to Brace Cottage, Notting Hill: there is good evidence for believing that he became the enterprising proprietor of a racecourse, the Hippodrome, on the site of what is now Ladbroke Grove, which drew excited praise and interest during its four-year existence. One account of the Hippodrome project appeared in the two-volume *History of the British Turf* published in 1840 by James Christie Whyte. This gentleman seems to have been connected with John Whyte: he appears in the London Post Office Directory for 1848 as a merchant at 9a Mincing Lane, the same address as that given for John Whyte in that year.

After the death of his younger brother James Matthew in 1843 (he is buried beside St Paul's Church in Hamilton), John Whyte, with his daughter Emily, crossed the Atlantic in August of that year to inspect the property he had inherited. Isabella apparently remained in London, and the family as a whole did not emigrate until 1848. In 1853, William Henry Giles Kingston, writer of books for boys, made a honeymoon trip to North America armed (among other introductions) with a letter to 'John Whyte, Esq., of Lake Ontario'. With his bride, Kingston stayed at Barton Lodge for several days with Mr Whyte ('upwards of seventy'), his daughter (now the wife of Colonel William Gourlay) and presumably Isabella, though she was not mentioned in Kingston's spirited account of Whyte's estate. (474)

John Whyte died in 1862, a man of property (his will in Wentworth County Court House lists considerable assets of money and land), survived until 1865 by his wife, who lies buried beside him in Hamilton Cemetery.

And what of Isabella, that legendary 'first-born child' of the duke and Madame? Wherever this child was born, she was not consigned at birth to the care of the Ursuline nuns in Quebec, to whose establishment the prince made the ceremonial visit expected of all important visitors to the city. The name of Isabella Hyde does not appear in the old convent register of pupils dating from 1649 which—though marked with the ravages of fire and water—still is clearly legible: moreover, the convent never accepted children younger than five years old.

A theory is offered as possible explanation for the legend. It will be recalled that the 1798 London journals reported the prince taking 'the house at Brompton lately occupied by Mr Palmer'. Is it possible that the child Isabella (her mother a Palmer, her father a deceased brother of Mr Sam: Hyde, partner to Mr Pallmer in Jamaica) stayed in this house between 1791 and 1798? If so, it is easy to see how residence in the Knightsbridge house later occupied by the prince and Madame could have been misconstrued, especially since information about Isabella's real origin was lost.

Whoever she was, Isabella was not a child of the duke and Madame. Her exact birth-date being unknown, it has been assumed—because the record of her death on 11 February 1865 still to be seen in the original church register at Hamilton says flatly 'aged 74'—that she was born in 1791, the year the royal lovers came to Canada.

But since the duke and Madame did not meet until (at the earliest) the end of November 1790, there was no possibility of a birth from their union before August 1791. To have been already seventy-four by mid-February 1865, Isabella must have been born before mid-February 1791. It is clearly impossible, therefore, apart from other evidence, that Isabella Hyde was the offspring of a union between the young prince and his French lady that had begun less than three months before her birth.

WILLIAM GOODALL GREEN and LOUISA GREEN

Eliza Green, mother of William Goodall and Louisa Green, was a daughter of James Green, butcher, and Marguerite his wife, who in 1790 were living at '3 St roc, Saint Rocks suburbs'. (475) She may have been the eldest of several children, who included Mary, Magdalen, Thomas (born 27 February 1788) and Helena Catherine (born early in March 1791).

On 28 December 1788, a child born by Eliza was baptized in the English Church in Quebec. The register reads: *Eliza Green, a natural Daughter. Mother Eliza Green, Father Mark Pictet, Captain.* Marc-

Louis Pictet, a Swiss national, was 'an officer in the service of England, born 1754, married in Geneva 27 September 1789'. (476): his name appears in British Army Lists up to 1790. He died in 1834: his first cousin, the Swiss professor of the same name, was one of the most distinguished scholars of the day. The Quebec baptismal register gives the name of his child as Eliza, not Louisa: but in view of his own name, Marc-*Louis*, it seems likely that the minister repeated the mother's name in error when recording the event.

After the departure of Marc-Louis Pictet, Eliza found a new lover in the merchant William Goodall, and bore his son in 1790: *Father, William Goodhall. Mother Eliza Green. William John. A Natural son.*

These records clearly prove that neither child was fathered by Prince Edward: and a theory that one of them may have been a child of the prince's brother Prince William is also proved impossible, as the prince was not in Quebec after October 1787.

Eliza's sister Magdalen was married to George Glasgow, a Royal Artillery officer, though she bore him several children in the 1790s before their legal marriage on 27 May 1801. To one of these, named Edward and born in 1794, the prince stood godfather (by proxy, for he was absent in Martinique at the time). Eliza was godmother, and it is possible that the tradition about the royal parentage of Eliza's child received impetus from some later confusion in the telling of this incident. Eliza's own brief interlude with the prince, lasting less than two months, would add some force to the story.

Some of the traditions about Eliza are hard to understand, even though they have no real bearing on her association with Prince Edward. Dunkirk, the small town on the shores of Lake Erie to which she was said to have eloped with the prince, did not exist at that time: it was not incorporated until 1837. 'Most of Western New York in the 1785–1795 period was quite literally a howling wilderness devoid of white inhabitants except perhaps for a few transient fur traders.' (477) Neither the Public Library nor the New York State Library at Albany could find any record of a wealthy and tragically drowned Mr Green —nor, in fact, of any family named Green at that period.

Eliza eventually left Quebec, married Thomas Esdaile at St Marylebone Church in London on 8 July 1809, and was widowed on 25 July 1811. She inherited her husband's property at 72 Baker Street, Portman Square, and Sudley Cottage at Bognor in Sussex. (478) William Goodall, father of her son, who had returned to England at the end of 1793, continued as a partner in the firm of Goodall and Turner at 25 Garlick Hill, London. (Sir Brook Watson, former senior partner in the company, left him £100 in his will.) He first appeared in the land tax records at Tottenham, Middlesex, in 1813. His only legitimate son, William, died in December 1833 at the age of thirty-two. His daughter Eleanor married George Farr of St Margaret, Lothbury (London) on 7 May 1818. (479) As George Farr is stated by descendants to be a cousin of William Goodall Green and his sister Louisa, it is clear that the William Goodall of Tottenham who witnessed Eliza Esdaile's will in July 1818 was the man who fathered her son in Quebec, and that they continued to be good friends.

In May 1831, nearly a year after the real Julie's death, Eliza Esdaile wrote to the Duchess of Kent from Bognor, enclosing copies of correspondence with the duke to support her request for repayment of a small personal loan she said she had made to his Royal Highness. Her husband, she explained, had left her 'a comfortable independance, but through severe & disastrous misfortunes, resulting from the inroads which the Sea made upon my late premises the Marine Cottage, which commenced & increased for the last 12 years, until at length it reached to my very door, the only alternative then left me was to have the House taken down & removed to a Leasehold piece of Ground.' She therefore found herself in distressed circumstances, and presumed to approach the duchess for repayment of that part of the loan still outstanding at the time of the duke's death. Only a copy of the letter remains: the enclosures, at Mrs Esdaile's request, were apparently returned. (480)

Eliza Green Esdaile lived until 2 January 1835, dying at Bognor at an age said to be sixty-four. She would thus have been seventeen when she bore her first child, and twenty-three at the time of her brief affair with Prince Edward. Her daughter Louisa married first, William Grant, a purser in the Royal Navy, and second, a Lieutenant Aitchison, having children by both. (481) Eliza's son William Goodall Green died in Bath of pneumonia on 9 April 1866, aged seventy-five (further evidence of his 1790 birth). He had been deputy-assistant-commissary-general in Quebec, and served later in Nova Scotia, Newfoundland and the Cape of Good Hope. He retired as Commissary-General on half-pay in January 1855. He had married a daughter of John Gray, first president of the Bank of Montreal, and left numerous descendants.

ROBERT WOOD

The Robert Wood who became a servant to Prince Edward and was later said to have been foster-father to the prince's 'son' was believed to have served earlier as a petty officer on a ship with the prince's brother Prince William. Only one Robert Wood appears on the muster list of any of Prince William's ships, a marine private on *Barfleur*, and he was 'discharged 9 September 1780 to Haslar Hospital' —two years before the prince joined the ship.

There was, however, a quartermaster named Robert Wood on *Southampton* when this ship took the young Prince Edward to Gibraltar in February 1790. No. 60 on the muster book, he was a Londoner aged twenty-five. He was discharged in Gibraltar on the order of Admiral Peyton, and it is possible (though there is an age discrepancy) that this man was the Robert Wood who went to Canada as Prince Edward's servant on *Resistance* in 1791. This Robert Wood would not have been an officer. (482)

It is true that no entry in Quebec Diocesan registers records the birth of the child Robert Wood : but there is also no relevant page missing (the pages of the church registers in Quebec are numbered, initialled and certified by a Judge of the Court of King's Bench). His birth-date (10 August 1792) is, however, clearly indicated on the memorial window erected by his son William Frost Wood in the Church of the Holy Trinity (there is not, nor ever has been, a 'Christ Church Anglican Cathedral' in Quebec City).

Even more convincing is the sworn declaration of the child's mother, Mary Dupuis, *dite* Caton, who on the death of her husband (that Robert Wood who arrived with Prince Edward as his servant and who married her on 29 December 1791) presented a petition to the Honourable Judges of the Court of King's Bench in Quebec dated 24 November 1806, asking to be appointed guardian of her children and attesting that 'of her marriage to the said late Robert Wood were issued seven children who are minors, namely, Robert born the 10th of August 1792 . . .' (483)

Perhaps the most conclusive evidence, however, to disprove the belief that Robert Wood was an unacknowledged son of Prince Edward and Madame comes (unwittingly) from one of Robert Wood's descendants, Lieutenant-Colonel William Wood of Quebec. A distinguished Canadian historian, the late Colonel Wood allowed himself to be a little too easily convinced by circumstantial evidence to seek for further *documented* evidence on the subject of his own ancestry.

In 1944, three years before he died at the age of eighty-three, Colonel Wood wrote a memorandum to the Curator of the Quebec Provincial Museum generously offering his entire collection of Canadiana to the Museum. Among the items is the pass signed by Prince Edward, dated at Martinique on 4 March 1794, giving to Robert Wood, who had accompanied him to the West Indies, permission to pass 'without molestation' from Martinique to Quebec.

'This Robert Wood', wrote Colonel Wood in explanation, 'was formerly a C.P.O. in the R.N., and there became "body servant" to the future King William IV, who recommended him to "Edward". He acted as foster-father to the only child of Edward and "Mme St.

T

Laurent", who really was Alphonsine Thérèse-Bernardine Julie de Montgenêt, *Baronne de Fortisson et de St Laurent, Princesse de Normandie, who really had much longer Royal ancestry than the Hanoverian Kings of the British Isles.* But since she was an R.C., and she and the future Duke of Kent were married by (apparently) the R.C. Bishop of Gibraltar . . . their only child (born in 1792 and taking his name from his foster father, Robert Wood) was baptized by the R.C. Curé of Beauport, P.Q. Therefore both mother and child were within the "nor-Est" terms of the British Law, which forbade any possible Heir to the Throne from marrying any R.C.'

Colonel Wood was mistaken in most of his facts in this account; and other information in the Quebec Provincial Archives, indicated as 'Family records supplied by Lt.-Col. W. Wood', contradicts even these facts. This version states unequivocally that 'the Duke of Kent was married to his first wife at Valetta by the Bishop of Malta on 25th September 1791, and a child was born at Quebec, on St Lawrence's day, of the following year . . . The baptism took place in the Bishop's Palace, Quebec, and was performed by Mgr Charles-François Bailly de Messein, Bishop of Capse, and Coadjutor to the Bishop of Quebec.'

Records of the English Church show that the young Robert Wood was godfather to a sister Mary on 19 June 1805, which would seem to indicate that he was a Protestant. It is possible, however, that the record of his birth and a Catholic baptism may yet be found: for though the other children of Mary Dupuis were baptized in the Protestant church, she buried two of them in Catholic cemeteries, Edward in Ste Anne and an earlier Mary in Ste Famille. (484)

Prince Edward was never in Malta. Moreover, on the date given for the 'marriage' he was in Quebec, having landed there on 11 August, just six weeks earlier. Only a week later than the supposed marriage in Malta, he was handing out medals of merit to his regiment in Quebec.

The appointment of the senior Robert Wood as Doorkeeper to the Executive Council was authorized by Lieutenant-Governor Alured Clarke on 15 December 1792, 'having confidence in your Integrity, Discretion and good conduct'. In 1795 he was living at 33 rue Champlain in Lower-town (the *Visite Générale de la Paroisse de Québec 30 juillet* 1792 . . . 15 *May* 1805 lists him consistently as Robert Hood). By 1805 he was living at 40 rue St Jean, Upper-town.

He died 16 November 1806, aged thirty-eight (this would have made him only twenty-two in 1790 when quartermaster Robert Wood on *Southampton* was twenty-five). Robert Wood junior (the supposed

* Author's italics.

royal child) married Charlotte Gray in 1817 : the couple had eleven children. He died at Savannah, Georgia, on 10 April 1847, and was buried in Quebec the following month. (485)

JEAN DE MESTRE

Search for information about this child began in Australia, where the young man was said to have settled on Crown lands given to him by Queen Victoria. The only de Mestre known to the Mitchell Library in Sydney was not named Jean, but Prosper, noted in biographical dictionaries as the first American merchant in Sydney. Current descendants have confirmed that Prosper and Jean were the same person, adding that Prince Edward and his Julie were married not in Martinique but in Quebec, and that the marriage was annulled by the British Government.

The Mitchell Library provided further information—a copy of a letter written on 25 March 1830 by Prosper de Mestre to the Collector and Comptroller of Customs, New South Wales, stating his claim to British citizenship when the legality of his claim to hold a share in a British ship was in question. A contemporary copy is in the Public Record Office, London.

'Gentlemen : Adverting to our Conversation, I beg to state that I claim the right of holding a British Register on the following grounds. My Father an Officer of the French Royal Service, emigrated at the time of the French Revolution, and the British Vessel that took him and my Mother off the Coast of France (in which Vessel I was born) landed us, at the reduction of Martinique (the end of the year 1793) on that Island, where my Father was killed previous to the Capitulation. My Mother married afterwards a British Officer (Captain Armstrong) on that Island, and on the Evacuation of said Island at the Peace of Amiens, I was sent to Philadelphia for my Education, and remained until 1812, when I left it for China, and have been residing in the Isle of France and other British Colonies, and India, and the last twelve years in this place, where I married a British Subject, and have a family of Five Children.' (486)

It will be recalled that Madame spent the whole of 1793 in Quebec, and left at the end of January 1794 for London via New York and Halifax. She was never in Martinique : de Montgenêt estates in that island are non-existent. Madame's parents were born, married and died in Besançon : Jean Mongenet's death certificate and Claudine Pussot's birth certificate remain untraced, but the death certificate of their son Jean-Joseph-Suzanne declared that both parents died in Besançon.

Though there is no record in the Archives de la Martinique of a de Montgenêt or a de Fortisson, there is in fact record of a de Mestre

—that widow de Mestre (mother of Prosper-Jean) who married the British officer Captain Armstrong. The mysterious lady so long thought to have been Julie de St Laurent (Thérèse-Bernardine Mongenet) was actually the Demoiselle Hélène Cotterel, and she came not from Normandy but from Brittany. In the old *Registre des Actes d'état civil* in the Archives de la Martinique the marriage is recorded on 2 March 1795 of 'Messire Jean Armstrong, officer of the sixth regiment of his Britannic majesty . . . and the Dame Hélène Cotterel, of legal age, native of the parish of St-Etienne de [?] in Brittany . . . widow of the late Messire de Mestre, captain of artillery. . . .' (487)

One grain of possibility exists that may explain the tradition. The Sixth regiment in which 'Jean Armstrong' was a lieutenant in 1794 (the Army List gives his name as James) went to Martinique from *New Brunswick*. If the young lieutenant had met the prince in North America and briefly renewed the acquaintance in Martinique, perhaps family conversation about this association became confused in repetition, and the origin of the small de Mestre stepson, whose name was no longer the same as his mother's, became a part of the confusion. (488)

There may have been a de Mestre or de Fortisson daughter named Melanie, but she had no connection with Madame. It has been suggested that de Mestre was a title of the de Fortisson family and that André de Mestre was actually Madame's baron, but the name does not appear in any of the extensive genealogies of the de Fortissons, an old and aristocratic family from the *départements des Landes* and *des Basses-Pyrénées*. It is, in fact, difficult to identify which de Fortisson was Madame's first lover, though it may have been Pierre de Fortisson, baron de Roquefort, who ended his military service as an infantry Colonel in 1770, was granted a royal pension in 1781, married a widow in 1786 and died in 1795 without issue. There is no record of his ever having been stationed in Besançon.

JOHN and MARY REES

Of John and Mary Rees little need be said. The Session Records of St Mathew's [*sic*] Church, Halifax, Nova Scotia, show the baptism on 4 February 1796 of 'Mary Elizabeth born 19th January daughter of John and Catherine Rees' (George Laidler's chart gives the year as 1798). No record has been traced for the birth of her brother John Edward, but it is generally stated to have occurred in 1795. Arriving back in Canada in August 1794, Madame could not possibly have given birth to a child by the prince before May 1795: if she had borne John Edward in that month or later, how could she have borne Mary Elizabeth in January 1796?

The baptismal entry for Mary Elizabeth reads as if John and Catherine Rees were man and wife: yet family information also acknowledges that Catherine was not wife, but housekeeper to John Rees, and that she was actually Mary Catherine Fowsell, a German woman, who died on 4 February 1837, aged seventy-eight, and was buried in the Old Dutch Church on 6 February. (An entry in the register of St Paul's Church for 1787 records the marriage of one John Fowsel to Cath^n Miller. Nothing further is known about these two people, but the names are suggestive.)

Certainly John Rees, who died on 12 February 1828 at the age of seventy-seven, made no mention of a wife in the will he drew up on 4 December 1812, in which he described himself as a butcher, nor did he make any bequest to Catherine Fowsell. He did, however, emphatically describe Mary Elizabeth as his *natural* daughter and John Edward as his *natural* son throughout this document and the two codicils added on 9 May 1820 and 2 January 1827. (489)

It is necessary here to remark that the term *natural* child does not necessarily imply illegitimacy, although it tends to be used in this sense. It does mean 'real' child, not son-in-law, stepson or adopted child. (490)

Under the original will, John was to get the interest and dividends on £6,675 in three percent consols. Mary Elizabeth's legacy was the interest and dividends on the remainder of the stock (£6,683), as well as the rent from property in the town of Halifax. They were to divide the remainder of the property after certain other small bequests had been deducted. The two codicils added the interest and dividends on a further £5,564 and rent from additional property to Mary Elizabeth's legacy. The interest on a total sum of almost £12,300 would more than explain the 'unexplained' source of her pension. It is difficult to discover just how the tradition arose that gave these children Prince Edward and Madame as parents. Not the slightest documentation in any form can be traced.

OTHERS

Not a few public figures, especially royal ones, have been saddled with rumours of illegitimate offspring. As well as the seven whose evidence has been here considered, others from time to time have made an appearance in print as descendants of the Duke of Kent.

Rumour once suggested, for instance, that Nova Scotia's 'Hero of Kars', Sir William Fenwick Williams—later Lieutenant-Governor of the province—was a half-brother of Queen Victoria. This rumour is effectively demolished by a paper lodged in the Public Archives of Nova Scotia by Judge Savary of Annapolis Royal. The judge quotes a letter written from Malta to one of his sisters by Sir William: 'My birthday was the 21st of December 1800, and the day of my baptism late in the next year'. Sir William, writing from memory without the birth certificate before him, made an error in the year: he had actually been *baptized* in 1800 (2 February). (491) The fact that he was exactly the same age as a brother-in-law whose birthday was 21 December 1799 was a matter of interest in his family.

As the duke was in England until September 1799, he could not have fathered a child born in December. Another inaccurate belief may have started the tradition—that Sir William owed to the duke his auspicious start in a military career: an unfounded rumour, Judge Savary points out, as the duke died five years before young Williams got his commission.

Rumour also gave to the duke an illegitimate son in the father of that Constance Kent whose conviction for murdering her young brother was a scandal of the 1860s. This theory cropped up in *Notes and Queries* in January 1907, when *Helga* requested information about the twelve children attributed to the duke and Madame by Lewis Melville in his *First Gentleman of Europe*. 'It seems strange,' wrote *Helga*, 'that while the offspring of Mrs Jordan should be ennobled, these should have been left in obscurity.'

M.N.G. replied, noting that no reference to children was made in letters to the de Salaberry family, but adding, 'The Duke had children by Miss Green, Miss Gay, and other fair but frail damsels, and Lewis Melville may have thought them the children of Madame de St Laurent'. *Wm. H. Peet* wrote flatly: 'The father of Constance Kent (Road Murder, 1860) was said to be a son of the late Duke of Kent'.

M.N.G. then produced a description of Madame not found elsewhere and more than a little suspect. 'Tradition describes her as small, dark, and handsome; and as having a hasty temper, under the influence of which she was known to go into the garden and tear up flowers.' Someone signing as *H.* pointed out that the duke had not mentioned children in his request to Creevey for provision for Madame: *H.* thought this would have strengthened his argument for her financial support.

Another contributor, *B.*, described as 'extraordinary' Mr Peet's report that Constance Kent's father was a son of the duke, though he then went into a pretty shaky argument that there were some grounds for assuming a *French* connection in the family background. *Wm. H. Peet* had little to add. 'I cannot give any other authority . . . than that of persistent rumour. My impression is that what was considered as exceptional treatment of the criminal was attributed to the relation-

ship I have suggested.' Did Mr Peet mean 'exceptionally lenient',
asked *B*.? Constance Kent had been imprisoned for twenty years after
a voluntary confession made years later to clear her father from
suspicion of the murder she had committed at sixteen : *B*. thought this
was certainly exceptional, 'but it is an odd reason for supposing her
to have been related to the royal family'. (492)

The rumours—if indeed rumours did circulate at the time (Mr
Peet, in 1907, was writing of an event that had occurred forty-seven
years earlier)—have been connected with a supposed likeness to Queen
Victoria, one of the most monotonously recurrent pieces of 'evidence'
in all the legends of royal birth. Neither of the two books written about
the murder at the time mentions this rumour : one of the authors, who
knew Mr Kent, says in fact that his father was a London carpet manu-
facturer. (493)

Another odd story appeared in *The Papers and Records of the
Ontario Historical Society* in 1924. This was not concerned with a
descendant. It offered the statement—with absolutely no supporting
evidence—that one of Major Holland's sons, Frederick Braham, was
married to 'Mdle De St Laurent of Quebec and sister of the first wife
of Edward Duke of Kent'. (494) As this is clearly impossible (if for
no other reason than that Madame's family name was never de St
Laurent) the statement illustrates the danger of accepting unsubstan-
tiated legends as historical evidence. Even as basic a proof as a record
of marriage between young Holland and a woman of the name of
de St Laurent is missing. A statement baldly presented in a historical
journal may have deluded descendants of this family into perpetuating
a myth.

MONGENET

On 21 June, 1837, when the eighteen-year-old Princess Victoria
was proclaimed Queen of England, Jean-Claude, the black sheep of
the Mongenet family, had been dead for four years. Jean-Joseph-
Suzanne, now a widower living in Besançon whither he had gone
from Dôle into retirement, had nine more days to live : childless,
apparently, as his death was registered by two friends. Charles-
Benjamin, now to be the head of the family, was a successful lawyer
attached to the Palais de Justice at Grenoble.

On 15 December of the same year a 'List of Simple Contract
Creditors of His late Royal Highness the Duke of Kent' was delivered
to the young Queen 'for Her Majesty's most gracious consideration'.
Among the names appeared *Alphonsine Thérèse-Bernardine de St
Laurent Countess de Mongenet* : and *Mqs de Permangles* [*sic*]. (495)

A statement followed that certain sums were 'supposed to have been satisfactorily disposed of'. In the list supposed satisfied, Thérèse-Bernardine was credited with an amount representing the annuity the duke had bound himself to pay until her death. It transpired, however, that though Madame had received her share (under the original settlement in Chancery court) of the money owed to her, she had not received any of the annuity beyond 15 January 1820. The duke had faithfully paid it until his death : she had received nothing since then.

Did the Queen's advisers communicate with Madame's heirs, now represented by Charles-Benjamin? Perhaps so : this appears to have been the case in the repayment of Lord Dundas. (496) At any rate, with a covering letter dated 6 June 1838 from one Lewis Mansse of No. 2 Laurence Pountney Lane, London, a claim was submitted to the Queen through Lord Melbourne, giving a detailed statement of the sum outstanding. (497) In support of the claim, extracts of letters from the duke to Madame, from the Duke of Orleans, Prince Leopold and others which mentioned letters exchanged by Madame and the Duchess of Kent, were included. These are the letters quoted earlier, 'which passed at the time between the deceased Countess and several Illustrious Personages and others, which will shew the estimation in which she was held. Most of the facts related in the within document, I am inclined to think, are known to Her Royal Highness the Duchess of Kent'.

The Memorial noted that Madame's estate had been excluded from benefits 'altho' strongly urged on behalf of the heirs of the Countess in the Court of Chancery'. The heirs had taken no further action until now, 'being well assured that as soon as these alterations took place, which have since been realized [the accession to the throne of the duke's daughter], the earliest opportunity would be taken to discharge those demands, which every principle of honor and respect to the illustrious dead require should not remain uncancelled'.

A presentation in French in the handwriting of Charles-Benjamin himself, who had come to London to help prepare the Memorial, was included.

'To Her Majesty Victoria Queen of England—

'The undersigned has the honour to present his homage and profound respect and to explain very humbly : that his Royal Highness the Duke of Kent of glorious and cherished memory drew up in favour of Madame la comtesse de Mongenet various agreements whose execution ceased as soon as death, as tragic as unexpected, had taken that excellent prince from his country and from the filial love of your Majesty.

'Circumstances having left no right of claim to Madame de Mongenet, she had to submit to a state of things very different from the wish his Royal Highness had so clearly manifested in the deeds he had executed.

'But Madame de Mongenet never ceased to hope that when your Majesty came to the throne of her illustrious ancestors, whose great virtues give it such dignity, everything concerning the memory of her august father would be for her as precious as it is sacred.

'Having the same sentiments, the heirs of Madame la comtesse de Mongenet beg your Majesty to deign to consider the present request which has for its object the acknowledgement of the undertaking made by his Royal Highness the Duke of Kent in respect of Madame de Mongenet. . . .'

No evidence has been traced to indicate payment of this claim. It is unlikely, however, that the young Queen would have quibbled over fulfilling her father's obvious intentions towards a woman he had loved for so long, whose behaviour had justified his respect, and whose right to be respected had always been acknowledged by her mother the Duchess of Kent.

The two middle children of Charles-Benjamin (Joseph-Bernard-Alfred and Marguerite-Françoise-Isaure) seem to have died in infancy. The eldest, Anne-Marie, was married at the age of nineteen to Alexis Auguste Victor Diday, judge of the civil court of Grenoble and former mayor of nearby Domène, on 16 February 1841. Their son, Victor Maurice Charles, was born the following December: eight months later, he was an orphan, left to be brought up by Charles-Benjamin. His father had died in July 1842, his young mother (just past her twentieth birthday) in September.

Charles-Benjamin lived to be seventy, dying on 15 January 1867 (his wife had died just over a year before) at his town residence in Grenoble, 8 rue St Vincent de Paul (today rue Voltaire). His heirs were his little grandson Charles Diday (by then twenty-five) and his son Antoine Charles Alfred, who had been born while his father was at Madame's deathbed. Alfred, then thirty-six, had married in Tiflis a young widow named Anna de Roth (veuve de Bernet), daughter of the Russian general who was commandant of the military stud farm where Alfred was deputy-manager. (498)

Charles-Benjamin left a prosperous estate. As well as a spacious town apartment and many investments, he had a country property, Boisfleury, at Bachais in the nearby commune of Corenc, where the *maison de maître* he built in 1832 still stands, a part of the property owned by Les Dames du Sacré-Coeur. (499)

The name of the young Charles whose education at Ealing had been sponsored by his aunt does not appear on the student register of the East India Company's college at Addiscombe. (500) Perhaps he did not manage to pass the entrance examination, perhaps the plan for his future was changed. In the Archives d'Etat at the Hotel de Ville, Geneva, it is recorded that he left for Paris on 15 June 1825 and that all trace thereafter has been lost. As he did, however, attend his aunt on her deathbed in 1830, perhaps he had lived with her while attending university in Paris.

His younger sister, Madame's godchild Thérèse-Caroline-Sylvie, married le comte Jean-Marie-François de Saxel du Noyer, fifteen years her senior. Their only child, François, born at Carouge on 31 August 1843, died seven years later on 20 October 1850. Both his parents died at Evian, the comte in February 1865, the comtesse in 1874.

Her elder sister Louise—that interesting young person whom Madame did not feel capable of chaperoning in Paris—married the noble chevalier Hyacinthe de Livet de Moisy, a widower with two small daughters living at Vetraz-Monthoux in Savoie. Her own daughter, Marie-Caroline-Olympie, was born about 1832; Olympie was twenty when on 5 May 1852 she married Pierre Auguste Desiré Berlioz, banker and *conseiller général de l'Isère,* living in Pont-de-Beauvoisin some thirty miles north of Grenoble.

That little godson of the duke, the *petit cherubin* Edouard, died at Carouge in 1845 at the age of thirty, an unmarried gentleman of means. (501) It was left to Olympie and Auguste Berlioz to continue the line of Madame's youngest brother Jean-Claude. Their six children left a large and distinguished posterity: the eldest son, Fernand, who died in 1922, was professor of medicine at the University of Grenoble. (502)

THE MONGENET FAMILY TREE

Jean Claude = Jeanne Claude [Claudine]
MONGENET | PUSSOT
b. 1726–? | b. 1734?–1808

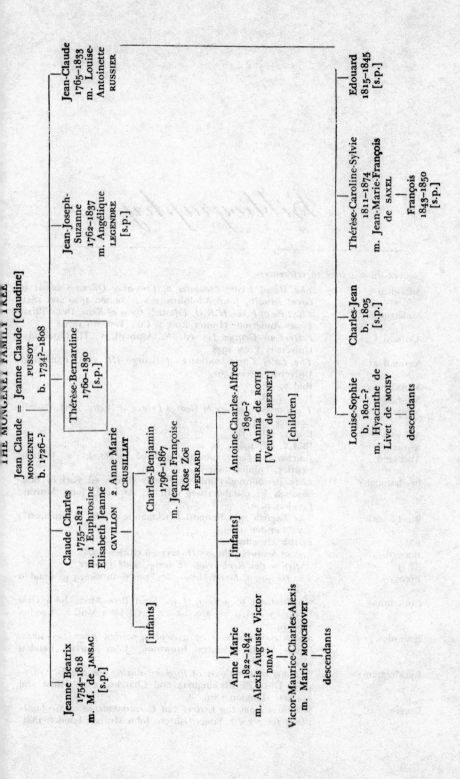

Jeanne Beatrix
1754–1818
m. M. de JANSAC
[s.p.]

[infants]

Claude Charles
1755–1821
m. 1 Euphrosine
Elisabeth Jeanne
CAVILLON 2 Anne Marie
CRUSILLIAT

Charles-Benjamin
1796–1867
m. Jeanne Françoise
Rose Zoë
PERRARD

Antoine-Charles-Alfred
1830–?
m. Anna de ROTH
[Veuve de BERNET]

[children]

[infants]

Anne Marie
1822–1842
m. Alexis Auguste Victor
DIDAY

Victor-Maurice-Charles-Alexis
m. Marie MONCHOVET

descendants

Jean-Joseph-
Suzanne
1762–1837
m. Angélique
LEGENDRE
[s.p.]

Thérèse-Bernardine
1760–1830
[s.p.]

Jean-Claude
1765–1833
m. Louise-
Antoinette
RUSSIER

Louise-Sophie
b. 1801–?
m. Hyacinthe de
Livet de MOISY

descendants

Charles-Jean
b. 1805
[s.p.]

Thérèse-Caroline-Sylvie
1811–1874
m. Jean-Marie-François
de SAXEL

François
1843–1850
[s.p.]

Edouard
1815–1845
[s.p.]

Bibliography

Sources quoted (key to references)

Adolphus: *The Royal Exile: Memoirs of Caroline, Queen Consort of Great Britain.* John Adolphus, 2 v., London 1820 and 1821.

Anderson: *The Life of F.M., H.R.H. Edward, Duke of Kent.* Dr. William James Anderson, Hunter Rose & Co., Toronto 1870

Aspinall 1:   *Letters to George IV,* ed. A. Aspinall, v. II, Cambridge University Press 1938.

Aspinall 2:   *The Later Correspondence of George III,* v. I, Cambridge University Press 1962.

Aspinall 3:   Ibid v. II.

Aspinall 4:   Ibid v. III.

Aspinall 5:   *The Correspondence of George Prince of Wales,* v. II, Cassell, London 1964.

Aspinall 6:   Ibid v. III, 1965.

Aspinall 7:   Ibid v. IV, 1967.

Auckland: *Journal and Correspondence of Lord Auckland,* 4 v., Richard Bentley, London 1861–62.

Bessborough: *Lady Bessborough and her Family Circle,* ed Earl of Bessborough in collaboration with A. Aspinall. John Murray, London 1940.

Blackmantle: *The English Spy.* Bernard Blackmantle (C. M. Westmacott?) 2 v., London 1825.

BM: British Museum.

Boswell: *Life of Samuel Johnson* (Everyman edition 1906).

BRH: *Bulletins des Recherches Historiques de Québec.*

Brooke: *The History of Emily Montague.* Frances Brooke, 4 v., London 1769.

Broughton: *Recollections of a Long Life.* Lord Broughton (John Cam Hobhouse) ed. Lady Dorchester, 4 v., John Murray, London 1909–10.

Brownlow: *Slight Reminiscences of a Septuagenarian from 1802–1815.* Emma Sophia Countess Brownlow, John Murray, London 1867.

Buckingham: *Memoirs of the Court of England during the Regency 1811–1820,* Duke of Buckingham and Chandos, 2 v., Hurst and Blackett, London 1856.

Burges: *Selections from the Letters and Correspondence of Sir James Bland Burges,* ed. James Hutton. John Murray, London 1885.

Camp: *Wills and Their Whereabouts*: Antony J. Camp, Society of Genealogists, Canterbury 1963.

Campbell: *A Mountain and a City: the Story of Hamilton.* Marjorie Freeman Campbell. McClelland and Stewart, Toronto 1966.

Castillon du Perron: *Louis-Philippe et la révolution française*, Marguerite Castillon du Perron, Paris 1963.

Childe-Pemberton: *The Romance of Princess Amelia.* Wm. S. Childe-Pemberton. G. Bell & Sons Ltd., London 1910.

Clarendon: *Life and Letters of George William Frederick, Fourth Earl of Clarendon,* ed. Sir H. Maxwell. 2 v., London 1913.

Clarke: *The Rival Princes.* Mary Anne Clarke. 2 v., London 1810.

Coke: *Letters and Journals of Lady Mary Coke,* 4 v., Edinburgh 1889–96.

Colchester: *The Diary and Correspondence of Lord Colchester,* 3 v., John Murray, London 1861.

Combermere: *Memoirs and Correspondence of F.M. Viscount Combermere,* ed. Rt. Hon. Mary Vtss Combermere and Capt. W. W. Knollys. 2 v., Hurst and Blackett, London 1868.

Coutts: Royal correspondence in the archives of Messrs Coutts & Company.

Creevey: *The Creevey Papers,* ed. Sir H. Maxwell. 2 v., John Murray, London 1903.

Creston: *The Youthful Queen Victoria,* Dormer Creston, Macmillan, London 1952.

Croker: *The Croker Papers,* ed. Louis J. Jennings, 3 v., London 1885.

De Boigne: *The Memoirs of the Comtesse de Boigne 1781–1814,* 3 v., 1913.

De Gaspé: *Mémoires.* P.A. de Gaspé, Ottawa 1866.

Delany: *Letters from Mrs Delany to Mrs Frances Hamilton from the year 1779 to the year 1788.* London 1820.

Detailed Statement: *A Detailed Statement of the Case of H.R.H. The Duke of Kent,* London 1819.

De Vincy: De Vincy MSS, in the possession of the Comte de Wurstemberger. (Some letters have been published in *Le Château et l'Ancienne Seigneurie de Vincy,* Gaston de Lessert, Genève 1912).

Dudley: *Letters to Ivy from the First Earl of Dudley*: Longmans Green & Co., London 1905.

Englishman: *A letter to His Majesty . . . Sketch of the Duke of Kent's Life and Losses . . .* London 1808.

Elliot: *The Life and Letters of Sir Gilbert Elliot, 1st Earl of Minto,* ed. Countess of Minto. 3 v., Longmans Green & Co., London 1874.

Farington: *The Farington Diary.* Joseph Farington, R.A. 8 v ed. James Grieg. London, Hutchinson & Co., 1922–28.

Fitzherbert: *The Letters of Mrs. Fitzherbert,* Shane Leslie, Hollis & Carter, London 1944.

Fitzwilliam: Wentworth Woodhouse Muniments, Sheffield City Libraries.

Frampton: *Journal of Mary Frampton from the year 1779 until the year 1846,* ed. Harriot Georgina Mundy, London 1885.

Francis: *The Francis Letters.* Sir Philip Francis, ed Beata Francis and Eliza Keary. 2 v., Hutchinson & Co., London 1901.

Glenbervie: *Diaries of Sylvester Douglas, Lord Glenbervie,* ed. Francis Bickley. 2 v., Constable & Co., London 1828.

Gordon: *Personal Memoirs . . .* 2 v., Pryse Lockhart Gordon, London 1830.

Graham: *Outlines of the History of Freemasonry in the Province of
                   Quebec.* J. H. Graham, Montreal, 1892.
Granville: *Lord Granville Leveson Gower (1st Earl Granville) Private
                   Correspondence 1781–1821,* ed. Castalia Countess Granville.
                   2 v., John Murray, London 1916.
Greville: *Leaves from the Diary of Henry Greville,* ed. Countess of
                   Stafford, 4 v., London 1904.
Harcourt: *Harcourt Papers,* ed. E. F. Harcourt. 14 v.
Harcourt MSS: In the possession of the Earl of Harcourt.
Hardinge: *Miscellaneous Works of George Hardinge, M.A., F.R.S.,
                   F.S.A., Senior Justice of the Cities of Brecon, Glamorgan and
                   Radnor.* 3 v., London 1818.
Holland: *Journal of Elizabeth Lady Holland,* ed. Earl of Ilchester,
                   2 v., Longmans Green, London 1908.
Horner: *Memoirs and Correspondence of Francis Horner M.P.,* ed
                   Leonard Horner, F.R.S. 2 v., Boston, Little Brown & Co.
                   1855.
Jordan: *Mrs Jordan and her Family: The unpublished correspondence
                   of Mrs Jordan and the Duke of Clarence, later William IV,*
                   ed. A. Aspinall. Arthur Barker Ltd., London 1951.
Kingston: *Western Wanderings,* 2 v., W. H. G. Kingston, Chapman &
                   Hall, London, 1856.
Knight: *Autobiography of Miss Cornelia Knight,* 2 v., 1861.
Knollys: MSS Letters, County Archives, Kent.
Landmann: *Adventures and Recollections of Colonel Landmann;* Colburn
                   & Co., London 1852.
Lieven: *The Letters of Dorothea Princess Lieven during her Residence
                   in London 1812–1834,* ed. Lionel G. Robinson. Longmans
                   Green & Co., London 1902.
Lieven-Metternich: *The Private Letters of Princess Lieven to Prince Metternich
                   1820–1826,* ed. Peter Quennell, John Murray, London 1948.
Leopold: *Letters de Leopold 1er, premier roi des Belges.* Carlo Brenne,
                   Bruxelles 1943.
Lyttelton: *The Correspondence of Sarah, Lady Lyttelton,* ed. Hon.
                   Mrs Hugh Wyndham, London 1912.
Macalpine: *George III and the Mad-Business,* Ida Macalpine and Richard
                   Hunter, Allen Lane, The Penguin Press, London 1969.
Macaulay: *Victoria R.I.: Her life and reign.* Dr James Macaulay,
                   London 1887.
Malmesbury,   *Diaries and Correspondence of James Harris, 1st Earl of
                   Malmesbury,* ed. the 3rd Earl, 4 v., Richard Bentley, London
                   1844.
MHS: Massachusetts Historical Society.
Mitford: *The Life of Mary Russell Mitford,* ed. Rev. A. G. L'Estrange.
                   3 v., Richard Bentley, London 1870.
MTLB: Metro Toronto Library Board.
NBHS: Collections of the New Brunswick Historical Society.
Neale: *Life of his Royal Highness, Edward, Duke of Kent.* Rev.
                   Erskine Neale. Richard Bentley, London 1850.
NSHS: Collections of the Nova Scotia Historical Society.
Owen: *The Life of Robert Owen, by Himself.* London 1920 (published
                   by Owen in 1857).
Owen MSS: Letters in Co-operative Union Library, Manchester.
PAC: Public Archives of Canada.
Palmer: *A Narrative of the Sufferings of T. F. Palmer and W. Skirving
                   during a voyage to N.S.W. 1794 on board the Surprise
                   Transport.* Rev. Thomas Fyshe Palmer, Cambridge, 1797.

PAO: Public Archives of Ontario.

Papendiek: *Court and Private Life in the time of Queen Charlotte: being the Journals of Mrs Papendiek, Assistant Keeper of the Wardrobe and reader to her Majesty.* Ed. Mrs Delves Broughton. 2 v., Richard Bentley, London 1887.

PAQ: Public Archives of Quebec.

Parker: *The Life of Admiral of the Fleet Sir William Parker from 1781–1866.* London 1876.

Princess Charlotte: *Letters of the Princess Charlotte,* ed. A. Aspinall. Home and Van Thal, London 1949.

PRO: Public Record Office.

Retired Military
Officer: *Jamaica, As it was, as it is, and as it may be . . .* Lond. 1835.

Riedesel: *Letters and Memoirs.* Madame de Riedesel, New York 1827.

Romilly: *Memoirs of the Life of Sir Samuel Romilly, written by himself,* ed. by his sons. 2 v., John Murray, London 1840.

Saxe-Coburg: *Extracts from the private diary of Augusta, Duchess of Saxe-Coburg-Saalfeld,* Selected and translated by H.R.H. the Princess Beatrice. John Murray, London 1941.

Serres: *The Princess of Cumberland's Statement to the English Nation . . .* London 1822.

Shuttleworth: Spencer Stanhope Collection, Sheffield City Libraries.

Sidmouth: *Life and Correspondence of . . . First Viscount Sidmouth,* ed. Hon. George Pellew, D.D. 3 v., John Murray, London 1847.

Simcoe: *Mrs Simcoe's Diary,* ed. Mary Quayle Innis. Macmillan of Canada, Toronto 1965.

Stockmar: *Memoirs of the Baron Stockmar,* ed. F. Max Muller. 2 v., Longmans, London 1872.

Strange: *Jacobean Tapestry.* Nora K. Strange. Stanley Paul & Co. Ltd., London.

Talleyrand: *Correspondance Diplomatique de Talleyrand: La Mission à Londres en 1792. Ses letters d'Amérique à Lord Lansdowne.* G. Pallain, Paris 1889.

Taylor: *Relics of Royalty, or Remarks, Anecdotes and Conversations of His late Majesty George III.* Joseph Taylor, London 1820.

Walsh: *Journal of the Campaign in Egypt, including descriptions . . . of Gibraltar . . .* Thomas Walsh, London 1803.

Ward: *Recollections of an Old Soldier. A Biographical Sketch of the late Col. Tidy, C.B., 24th Regt. . . .* Mrs Ward. Richard Bentley, London 1849.

Wetherall: Wetherall Papers, Ealing Public Library.

Windham: *The Windham Papers.* II v., Herbert Jenkins, London 1913.

Winslow: *The Winslow Papers,* ed. W. O. Raymond. Sun Printing Co., Saint John, N.B., 1901.

Newspapers and Periodicals

London Newspapers

1767: *Public Advertiser*: Various
1784: *Public Advertiser*: *Morning Chronicle*: *London Chronicle*: *Morning Herald*: *Parker's General Advertiser*
1785: *Morning Chronicle*: *Public Advertiser*
1788: Various
1790: *Public Advertiser*: *General Evening Post*: *St James's Chronicle*: *World*: *Gazetteer*: *Times*
1791: *Gazetteer*: *Morning Chronicle*: *Public Advertiser*: *Star*: *St James's Chronicle*: *Times*
1792: *World*: *British Gazette & Sun Monitor*
1793: *Morning Chronicle*: *Oracle*: *Morning Post*: *True Briton*: Various
1794: *Morning Post*: *Public Advertiser*: *Oracle*: *Daily Advertiser*: *Courier*: *St James's Chronicle*: *Star*
1798: *True Briton*: *Times*: *General Evening Post*: *Observer*: *London Packet*: *Lloyd's Evening Post*
1799: *True Briton*: *London Chronicle*: *Times*
1800: *Times*
1803: *True Briton*: *Morning Chronicle*: *Morning Post*: *Cobbett's Annual Register*
1807: *Times*
1808: *Times*
1809: *Times*: *Morning Chronicle*: *Morning Post*: *Morning Herald*
1810: *Morning Chronicle*: *Times*
1813: *Morning Chronicle*
1814: *Morning Chronicle*: *Morning Post*
1816: *Morning Post*: *Morning Chronicle*: *Star*
1817: *Morning Chronicle*
1818: *Morning Herald*: *Morning Chronicle*: *Times*
1819: *Morning Post*: *Morning Chronicle*: *Morning Herald*: *Star*: *Public Ledger*: *Times*
1820: *Times*: *Morning Post*
1827: *Times*

Newspapers and Periodicals (other than London dailies):

   Annual Register
   Gentleman's Magazine
   Military Register
   Royal Military Calendar
   Military Magazine
   Military Panorama
   British Magazine 1800–01
   Register of the Times 1794–96
   Jamaica Journal 1824
   Jamaica Magazine 1812
   Jamaica Almanac 1818
   Annuaire Historique Universel 1818–21, 1823, 1825, 1826–1830
   Annuaire Nécrologique 1821–27
   Montreal Gazette 1791, 1794
   Quebec Herald 1788–1791
   Quebec Gazette 1764—
   Halifax Weekly Chronicle 1791–94, 1798–99
   Misc. Halifax Newspapers 1795–1843
   Halifax Royal Gazette 1792, 1793–94, 1795–97, 1798–1800
   Halifax Journal and Misc. 1795
   N.S. Gazette and Weekly Chronicle 1787–88
   N.S. Magazine July 1790–March 1792
   Boston Independent Chronicle & Public Advertiser 1794
   Columbian Centinel, Boston, 1794 and 1820
   Boston Mercury 1794
   Boston Gazette 1794
   American Mercury, Hartford, Conn., 1794
   American Apollo, Boston, 1794
   Independent Chronicle & Boston Patriot, January–April 1820
   Boston Intelligencer 1818
   Boston Daily Advertiser 1820
   Le Beau Monde 1806–08
   Gibraltar Chronicle 1801—
   Affiches et Annonces de la Franche-Comté, 1766–75, 1779–85
   Revue Littéraire de la Franche-Comté 1776, 1866
   Journal de Savoie 1819
   Journal de Grenoble 1798–99, 1803, 1830—
   Le Patriote des Alpes 1838, 1843-45, 1850
   Journal de Genève 1787–91
   Journal des Dames et des Modes 1798–99
   Kentish Gazette 1814, 1816, 1818, 1819
   Lady's Magazine 1790–91, 1800–03, 1808–09
   Sporting Magazine 1837–1850
   Le Moniteur Universel 1816, 1818–1820
   New York Journal 1794
   Weekly Museum, N.Y., 1794
   Diary, N.Y., 1794
   Herald, N.Y., 1794
   Daily Advertiser, N.Y., 1794

U

References

1. PRO: C.O. 217/36, 8 May 1794
2. PAC: de Salaberry Papers, MG 24 G 45, March 5.
3. PRO: C.O. 217/36, 8 May 1794.
4. Longmans Green & Co., Toronto, 1961.
5. Register of St Peter's Church 1864–65, Synod of Niagara Church House, Hamilton, Ontario.
6. The second ship was not *Resolution*, but *Resistance*. Anderson gave the name as *Resolution*, a trap into which I, with other writers, fell before undertaking more precise research. See Adm. 36/11005 (PRO) and contemporary newspapers.
7. *Hamilton Spectator*, 23 October 1965 (this and previous quotation).
8. Prince William's visit was in 1787, not 1789 as Porter says.
9. Evans Brothers, London 1938.
10. The name should be *de Jansac*.
11. Charles X did not succeed his brother Louis XVIII until 1824.
12. Shuttleworth (Letter Book, 60595/3).
13. Charles Sturt at this date had already succeeded his father Humphrey as Member for Dorsetshire.
14. Aspinall 5, p. 61.
15. Aspinall 2, p. 457.
16. Aspinall 2, p. 458
17. Aspinall 2, p. 459.
18. Aspinall 2, p. 467.
19. Aspinall 2, p. 467.
20. Aspinall 2, p. 465.
21. Aspinall 2, p. 468.
22. Aspinall 2, p. 459.
23. RA 45410.
24. RA.45418. The colonel is repetitious in this letter, and I have therefore transposed some sentences in order to make use of the most comprehensive of his statements on the same topic.
25. Aspinall 5, p. 66.
26. RA 45810.
27. AR 45412.
28. These details come from an article in *Transactions of the Quatuor Coronati Lodge*, 1965, by Paul Tunbridge. The pensions were to continue during the lifetime of the father and sister, no matter what happened to the child or to the prince (presumably because the dead mother had been their source of

support). Money paid to Victoire Dubus (and later to 'Madame Barthelemy', apparently her married name) shows up regularly in the prince's accounts with Coutts Bank, and on the Geneva record as late as 1832.

29. RA 45813.
30. RA 46669.
31. RA 46659.
32. RA 46651. This and the previous letter are in a letter book, in French, and published also in Aspinall 5, pp. 113–116.
33. RA 45825.
34. Aspinall 5, p. 131.
35. Aspinall 5, p. 132.
36. Aspinall 5, p. 136.
37. Neale, p. 28.
38. PRO: Adm. 36/11005, muster list of *Resistance*. The prince did not sail on *Ulysses*.
39. This, with other local information, derives from material at the Bibliothèque Municipale de Besançon (ref. 55.032 etc.).
40. Bib. Mun. de Besançon GG 280, f. 22 (archives municipales). All Mongenet references will be found in f.n. 502.
41. List of emigrés 1793: there is some reason to believe that the artillery officer was Madame's youngest brother Jean-Claude.
42. Coke, v. 4, p.120.
43. Ibid. p. 119.
    Ibid. v. 3, p. 82.
44. Papendiek, v. 1, p.60.
45. Delany, p. 63.
46. Taylor, p. 35.
47. Both quotations in this paragraph from Aspinall 2, p. 68.
48. Not in February as indicated by David Duff in *Edward Duke of Kent*.
49. Jewel forming part of the insignia of the Order of the Garter.
50. Aspinall 2, p. 129.
51. Aspinall 2, p. 157.
52. Aspinall 2, p. 152.
53. Aspinall 2, p. 161.
54. Aspinall 2, pp. 164, 187.
55. Aspinall 2, pp. 231, 274.
56. This information comes from the present Marquise de Permangle, whose late husband missed purchasing the 'plainte' by only two hours. Family history contains other references to the association of Philippe Claude with the lady who had lived with the Duke of Kent, and to the existence of personal letters unfortunately destroyed early in this century by the grandfather of the late marquis in a lamentable access of moral prudery.
57. Copy of the petition is in the possession of Madame le marquise de Permangle, Paris.
58. PAC: Smith Papers and Diary (MG 23 G II 14).
59. Brooke, v. 1, p. 9.
60. Riedesel, p. 260.
61. PAC: MG 24 I, 1.
62. PAC: Winslow Papers (MG 23 D 2) (M–147).
63. PAC: James Thompson's Journal v. 4, 14 and 15 August 1787.
64. Georgiana, p. 103, 6 February 1786.
65. PAQ: Henry Juncken Papers.
66. PAC: MG 23 H 1, 1, v. 1, p. 166, Simcoe Papers.
67. PAQ: Mabane Papers.
68. Her father may have died before this date: her mother was a widow when she died in 1808.
69. *Zouaviana*, 2nd edition, pp. 555–56.
    U*

70. Brooke, v. 1, p. 57, and v. 2, p. 76.
71. *Quebec Gazette*, 15 December 1791.
72. Elliot, v. 1, p. 395.
73. Simcoe, pp. 38, 41.
74. Aspinall 2, p. 576.
75. Aspinall 2, p. 562.
76. Simcoe, pp. 39 and 50.
77. Ibid. p. 52.
78. Smith Papers: See f.n. 58.
79. Simcoe, p. 41.
80. 19 November 1791.
81. Register, Church of the Holy Trinity, Quebec (entry No. 446).
82. PAC: de Salaberry Papers, letter from Charles to father 4 December 1805.
83. MTLB: Elizabeth Russell Papers.
84. MHS: Coffin Papers III, 5 January 1792.
85. *Quebec Gazette*, 23 February 1792.
86. Shuttleworth (this and other regimental accounts).
87. Elliot, v. 2, p. 13.
88. PAC: MG 24 L 3 v. 11, p. 6368, Baby Collection (in French).
89. PAC: MG 23 G II 10, v. 3 p. 794, Sewell Correspondence.
90. Election information were not attributed is found in contemporary issues of the *Quebec Gazette*.
91. PAC: MG 23 D 1, v. 3, Lawrence Collection, Ward Chipman.
92. PAC: MG 24 B 4, v. 2, 17 January: v. 3: v. 2.
93. Ibid. v. 2, pp. 43–46.
94. Diary of Simeon Perkins (typed copy, PAC).
95. Anderson, p. 12.
96. Beauport Church Register, Judicial Archives, Quebec.
97. BRH: v. 9, p. 347 et seq.
98. PAC: MG 23 H I, 1, Series 3 Bk 2 p. 141.
99. Simcoe, p. 75.
100. PAO: Russell Papers.
101. PAC (see f.n. 103): various pages.
102. Burges, p. 221.
103. I have not traced the contemporary references to this comment, quoted by Duncan Campbell Scott in *John Graves Simcoe*, p. 183, as having been written on 7 August 1792.
104. BRH: v. 40, p. 125 et seq. Diary of Bishop Jacob Mountain 1794, from which the whole account of his trip to Niagara is taken.
105. *Montreal Gazette*, 16 August 1792.
106. Bishop Mountain, p. 142.
107. PAC: MG 23 H I, 1, v. 1, p. 604.
108. See f.n. 107: p. 608, 30 July 1792.
109. Aspinall 2, p. 618.
110. See f.n. 107: p. 606.
111. Aspinall 2, p. 614.
112. Romilly, v. 1, p. 351, 10 September 1792.
113. Aspinall 5, p. 258.
114. Shuttleworth.
115. Aspinall 5, p. 258.
116. MHS: Coffin Papers III, 20 July 1791.
117. Garrison Orders, Gibraltar, 21 August 1790. The defendant was a young ensign and not in danger of corporal punishment, but of reprimand. The prince refused to hear the testimony of a witness he considered to be an accomplice, and insufficient evidence brought a lighter sentence than O'Hara thought proper.

118. PAQ: James Thompson Senior, MSS Letters v. 1. Undated, but internal evidence places it in 1792.
119. RA 45888.
120. Information about these courts-martial comes from PRO records: W.O. 71/166 (full proceedings of trials of Rose, Landrigan, Kennedv and Wigton): W.O. 72/16: W.O. 81/19: W.O. 1/1062.
121. W.O. 71/163.
122. De Gaspé, p. 40 et seq.
123. W.O. 72/16: W.O. 1/1062.
124. Graham, p. 93, minutes of meeting 17 December 1792.
125. PAC: MG 23 H I, 1 (Coventry Transcripts), 20 March 1793.
126. PAC: MG 23 H I, 1, Series 3: approved 17 October 1793, carried out 29th.
127. *Morning Chronicle,* 20 April 1793.
128. Shuttleworth.
129. Aspinall 3, p. 5.
130. Canadian Letters, p. 6.
131. PAC: Colonial Office Records A 122 Nova Scotia, July-December 1795, 28 October 1795.
132. PRO: W.O. 72/16, 11 May 1793.
133. Boswell, V. 2, p. 447.
134. Ward, p. 136.
135. RA 45878.
136. PAC: MG 23 G II 3 v. 6, 3 January 1792.
137. PRO: W.O. 3/11, pp. 13, 20.
138. Auckland, v. 2 pp. 475, 487.
139. Combermere, v. 2 p. 419.
140. RA 45880.
141. Elliot, v. 2, p. 119.
142. Ibid. p. 125.
143. *True Briton,* 3 August 1793.
     London Chronicle, 23 August 1793.
144. Holland, v. 1, p. 93.
145. RA 45897.
146. Elliot, v. 2 p. 133.
147. PAC: MG 23 H I 3 (2), 25 September 1793.
148. Aspinall 5, p. 174.
149. The original of this diary, in French, of which I saw a copy in the PAC. is in the Edward E. Ayer Collection of the Newberry Library, Chicago. M. de Saint-Mesmin (today spelt St Mémin), in writing of Madame, used the phrase 'on assure qu'un gentilhomme en l'épousant lui a prété son nom': and since the gentleman, had he married her, would have given and not lent her his name—and since Madame was in any case never married—I have translated the word 'épousant' as 'taking up'.
150. *Oracle,* 5 November 1793.
151. This and preceding references to Allsopp and Goodall are found in various pages of The Letter Book of George Allsopp, MG 23 G III 1 (1), PAC.
152. PAC: MG 23 D 1 (1) v. 6, p. 761, Lawrence Collection, Ward Chipman Papers.
153. PAC: MG 23 H I (1), v. 5, 26 September 1793.
154. RA 46683, 4 November 1793.
155. *Quebec Gazette,* 21 November 1793.
156. Shuttleworth.
157. Aspinall 5, p. 409.
158. PAC: MG 23 G II 3 v. 6, 18 January 1794 (Edward Gray Letter-books). MG 23 H I 1, Series 4 v. 5, 25 February 1794.
159. Shuttleworth.
160. PRO: F.O. 5/6 p. 276 et seq. from which this and other quotations by McDonogh are taken.

161. PRO: C.O. 217/65, 25 March 1794.
162. MHS: Cobb Papers 1794. Henry Knox v. XXXV p. 42.
      Ibid. p. 24. Robert Treat Paine Papers. Henry Knox Papers v. XXXV p. 49.
163. *Columbian Centinel*, Boston, 1 March 1794.
      The Weekly Museum, N.Y., 15 March 1794.
164. MHS: Robert Treat Paine Papers, 14 February 1794.
165. PRO. F.O. 5/6.
166. Talleyrand, p. 442.
167. Account of the Martinique campaign from *The Times*, April and May 1794.
168. Aspinall 3, p. 197.
169. PRO: C.O. 217/36, 8 May 1794.
170. Anderson, p. 23, 14 July 1794.
171. PRO: C.O. 217/36, 19 May and 7 June 1794.
172. Ibid., 19 May 1794.
173. NBHS, v. 2 (1905) No. 5.
174. Shuttleworth. For Smyth, see n. 182.
175. PAC: MG 23 G II 10 v. 3 pp. 847, 863.
176. *Morning Post*, 3 and 11 January 1794.
      Public Advertiser, 8 and 19 March 1794.
177. Blackmantle, v. 1 p. 328.
178. PRO: C.O. 217/36, 24 August 1794.
179. *New York Journal*, 17 May 1794.
180. RA 45565.
181. PRO: C.O. 217/36.
182. Ibid, 24 August 1794.
183. Ibid. 16 September 1794.
184. I have not found contemporary references for this.
185. Aspinall, 3 p. 255.
186. Auckland, v. 3 p. 242.
187. PRO: C.O. 201/12.
188. Palmer, various pages.
189. Burges, p. 278.
190. PRO: F.O. 115/4.
191. Harcourt Papers, v. 5, various pages.
192. PAC: MG 23 I, 1 No. 1972.
193. PAC: MG 23 D Series 2, 2 (M–149), v. 10, to Col. Winslow.
194. NSHS, v. 29.
195. Strange, p. 115.
196. PAC: MG 23 H I 1, Series 4 v. 5.
197. PAC: MG 23 G II 19, v. 3, March and May 1795.
198. Ibid. v. 7.
199. Ibid.
200. *Halifax Journal*, 3 March 1796.
201. PRO: C.O. 217/36, 19 May 1794, 12 November 1794.
202. PRO: C.O. 217/37, 6 August 1800.
203. PAC: MG 23 G II 17, v. 3.
204. PAC: MG 23 G II 19, v. 2, 3 September 1796.
205. Anderson, p. 34.
206. Neale, p. 72, letter dated 1 October 1849.
207. PRO: C.O. 217/37, 24 September 1796.
208. PAC: MG 23 I 1, No. 1972 22 January 1795.
209. PRO: C.O. 217/37, 25 April 1797.
210. PAC: MG 23 G II 19, v. 7, 29 June 1795.
211. Aspinall 3, pp. 472, 624, 640.

212. Landmann, pp. 193, 196. 'Madame de Buc' lived at 274 Greenwich Street. Mr Beech is thought to be Theophylact Bache, wealthy merchant and one of the founders of the Tontine Coffee House, where young Landmann stayed during his New York visit. (New York Public Library).

213. PRO: C.O. 217/37, 27 December 1797. C.O. 217/69, 10 March 1798. This effectively refutes an assertion that it was upon hearing of the prince's imminent return home after his accident (which did not occur until the following August) that Lady Wentworth rushed to England in order to take snobbish social advantage of her friendship with a son of the King. She had, incidentally, only one living son.

214. Aspinall 4, p. 49.

215. Auckland, v. 3, p. 386, 12 February 1798.

216. Aspinall 6, p. 439.

217. Coutts 1439.

218. PAC: MG 23 G II 17, 3: Prince Edward to General Prescott, 29 August 1798.

219. PRO: C.O. 217/69, Wentworth to John King, 30 September 1798.

220. Aspinall 6, p. 475.

221. Harcourt, v. 6, p. 63, 5 November 1798.

222. RA 45569.

223. Description of house from advertisements in *The Times* when the house was offered for sale, 1808.

224. Aspinall 4, p. 169.

225. Farington, v. 1, p. 263.

226. *The Times*, 6 July 1798. A possible explanation of the theory about Lady Wentworth's appointment and pension may be found in NSHS v. 20, Life of Sir John Wentworth, in which Sir Adams Archibald states that Wentworth himself, received an annual allowance (specifically stated as not salary) of £500 for several years.

227. PRO: L.C. 1/2 No. 42.

228. Aspinall 4, p. 205.

229. Coutts 1442, 11 April 1799.

230. Ibid. 1443, 4 May 1799.

231. RA 45569.

232. PAC: MG 23 D I (M-154), 26 Pune 1799.

233. Holland, v. 1 p. 258, 30 May 1799.

234. Aspinall 7, p. 57.

235. This commonplace book is one of the two surviving documents belonging to Madame in the possession of André Brun, professor of Law and Economic Sciences at the Université de Lyon, a direct descendant of Madame's elder brother Claude-Charles. The quotation is from Much Ado About Nothing, Act 5, Sc 1, Line 27 et seq.

236. PAC: MG 24 G 45, de Salaberry Papers (in French).

237. RA 45967.

238. Coutts 1444, 28 September 1799.

239. RA 44164.

240. RA 45973.

241. PAC: MG 23 D Series 2.

242. RA 45963, 24 June 1799.
     PRO: W.O. 4/279.

243. Winslow, p. 441.

244. PAC: Commissariat 1800-01, 3 April 1800.

245. Anderson, p. 70. It is clear from this and the foregoing information that a statement in John Ross Robertson's *Landmarks of Toronto*, 1894 (probably picked up from Henry Scadding's *Toronto of Old*, 1873) is without foundation, viz: that in a rude log cabin on an estate north of the garrison, named Oakhill and owned by Captain Aeneas Shaw, the Duke of Kent resided on his visit to Toronto. JRR does not specify the date of the visit: Scadding says 'in his second tour in Upper Canada'. The building did not exist in 1792, the date of the first tour, and there was, in fact, no second tour.

246.   The account in the *Halifax Royal Gazette* of 12 August 1800, from which
       this information is taken, differs in several details from the List of Courts-
       Martial 1796–1825 (PRO W.O. 90/1). This gives the sentences as follows
       (the men were all privates):
           Den^s Farrell, Nfld Fencibles, 29 May, desertion: 1000 lashes
           Thos Segar, 66th Regt, 29 May, desertion: Transported for Life
           Wm Fitzgerald [*sic*], Nfld Regt, 23 June, Mutiny, Desertion, Disobedience
               of orders: To be Shot
           James Ivory, Nfld Regt, 23 June, Mutiny, Desertion, Disobedience of
               orders: To be Shot
           Ja^s Keefe, Nfld Regt, 23 June, Mutiny, Desertion, Disobedience of orders:
               Transported for Life
           T^h McNamara, Nfld Regt, 23 June, Mutiny, Desertion: To be Shot
           Pat^k Murphy, Nfld Regt, 23 June, Mutiny, Desertion: To be Shot
           Edm^d Power, Nfld Regt, 23 June, Mutiny, Desertion: To be Shot
           Jos^h Scammell, Nfld Regt, 23 June, Mutiny, Desertion and leaving his
               post: Transported for Life
           John Serjeant, Nfld Regt, 23 June, Mutiny & Desertion: Transported
               for Life
           Thos McKee, 24th Foot, 14 August, Desertion: 300 Lashes
       Only five had been sentenced to be shot, and of these two were reprieved.
       If the *Gazette* is right in stating that eight were reprieved, the other six
       appear to have had lesser sentences remitted.
247.   Coutts 1447, 7 September 1800.
248.   RA 45990.
249.   Glenbervie, v. 1, p. 258.
250.   Aspinall 2, p. 625.
251.   *Halifax Gazette*, 3 June 1800, and Detailed Statement, p. 53. Some writers
       have confused *Francis* with *Amelia*, whose loss under similar circumstances
       occurred 9 November 1797.
252.   Coutts 1446.
253.   PAC: MG 23 H I 1, v. 5, 4 November.
       PRO: C.O. 42/22, 4 November 1800.
254.   Anderson, p. 72 et seq.
255.   Macalpine.
256.   Elliot, v. 3 p. 205.
257.   Wetherall (inventory for public sales of estate on 29 May 1827). Published
       accounts giving the length of the *library* as 100 feet arise from a misreading
       of George Hardinge's 1811 description: 'This library . . . is the first room
       of a magnificent range, commanding at least a hundred feet.' In fact, the
       whole range of rooms—'Library, Anti-Drawing-room, Drawing-room, State
       Bed-room'—measured 104 feet by 17 (specifications given in the printed
       particulars for the sale).
258.   Aspinall 7, p. 229.
259.   Ibid. p. 238.
260.   Anderson, p. 133.
       MS letter, MTLB.
261.   PRO: C.O. 42/22, 11 June 1801.
262.   Aspinall 7, p. 233.
263.   MHS: Coffin Papers IV, 8 August 1801.
264.   Windham, v. 2 p. 176, 20 October 1801.
265.   Aspinall 7, p. 264.
266.   Ibid. p. 265.
267.   Ibid. p. 266.
268.   Adolphus, v. 1 p. 98.
269.   This and the preceding quotation, Neale, p. 91. The italics and capitals
       are presumably his own and not from the original documents.

270. All de Vincy quotations are from the original manuscript letters.
271. Walsh, p. 7.
272. *Gibraltar's Royal Governor: a memoir.* Dorothy M. Ellicott, Gibraltar, 1961.
273. Neale, p. 103 (quoted without source).
274. *Gibraltar Chronicle*, 30 July, 6 August 1802.
275. Coutts 1465, 9 December 1802.
276. PRO: W.O. 1/701, p. 27 (copy of letter enclosed to John Sullivan, War Office, from Admiralty Office).
277. Aspinall 7, p. 357.
278. Quoted by Neale, p. 136, dated 5 March 1803.
279. Garrison Orders Book No. 13, Gibraltar, 3 January 1803. The men were Saunders, Van Shaghtten, John Sculler, John Reilly, Alexander Pastora, Christopher Cronebury, James Taylor, Theodorus Tymon, John Haynes, Patrick M'Carthy, John Crute, Peter Clark and Isaac Seville (as given in the original entry). Tymon and Reilly are given as Timon and Riley in G.O. 3 of the same date. Neale gives the names as Pastoret, Teighman and Reilly: the *Morning Chronicle* of 29 January spelt the second as Teigman.
280. Englishman, p. 90 (quoted inaccurately by Neale).
281. *Royal Military Panorama* 1814, v. 4 p. 515.
282. Aspinall 7, p. 370 et seq.
     Gibraltar Chronicle, 24 January 1803.
283. *Gibraltar Chronicle*, 7 August 1803.
284. Harcourt MSS.
     13 July 1804.
285. PRO: W.O. 1/289 p. 211 et seq. (4 May): p. 239 et seq. (23 August): p. 267 (3 November) 1803.
286. Information and quotations from Parker, pp. 205–216. Log entry, PRO Adm. 51/1454.
287. BM Add. MSS. 33,133, f. 42 et seq, 17 July 1803.
288. Aspinall 7, p. 412.
289. Quotations in this and preceding paragraph, Aspinall 7, pp. 416–419.
290. RA 46119: RA 46128.
291. Aspinall 7, p. 416, Duke of Kent to Captain Wright, 27 September 1803.
292. This exchange of letters, BM Add. MSS. 33, 133, f. 48 and f. 50.
293. Aspinall 7, p. 419.
294. Sidmouth, v. 2, p. 248.
295. Malmesbury, v. 4 p. 258.
296. AR 46154.
297. Francis, v, 2 p. 563.
298. Elliot, v. 3 p. 312.
     Francis, v. 2 p. 575.
299. Granville, v. 1 pp. 467, 471.
300. Auckland, v. 4, p. 213.
     Colchester, v. 1, p. 526.
301. RA 46217, 20 July 1804.
302. See f.n. 265.
303. RA 46240, 13 November 1804.
304. RA 46789–46880, RA Add. 17/29.
305. Aspinall 7, pp. 437, 438.
306. Colchester, v.2, p.14.
307. Auckland, v. 4, p. 251.
308. Granville, v. 2, p. 76.
309. BM Add. MSS. 34,813, f. 114.
310. Quebec Diocesan Archives, Mountain Papers.
311. *Annuaire Statistique du département de Monte-Blanc pour l'an XIV (1805 et 1806)*, 2me partie, pp. 84–90, Archives de la Savoie.
312. Granville, v. 2, p. 129, 3 and 5 November 1805.

313. Farington, v. 3, p. 112.
314. Granville, v. 2, p. 135, 10 November 1805.
315. BM Add. MSS. 34,931, f. 174, 12 September 1805.
316. Granville, v. 2, p. 155, 9 January 1006.
317. Ibid. p. 131, 6 November 1805.
318. Harcourt MSS, 23 December 1805.
319. Coutts 1491, 4 April 1806: he had received the first at the beginning of the previous October.
320. Granville, v. 2, p. 120.
321. Anderson, p. 98.
322. Granville, v. 2, p. 162.
323. Horner, v. 1, p. 397.
324. PAC:, M–150, Winslow Papers, 5 April 1806.
325. Granville, v. 2, p. 203 et seq.
326. Adolphus, v. 1, p. 71.
327. Anderson, p.111.
328. With a few exceptions which can be found in Anderson, quotations and information in this section come from the de Salaberry Papers, v. 1, 2 and 3 (PAC). All letters except those by Charles were written in French.
329. Anderson, p. 155 et seq.
330. An apparent error of dating exists that makes a second Christmas dinner (1807) extremely dubious. The duke's letter of invitation (19 December 1806, Anderson p. 116) and the little Edward's letter (30 December 1807, Anderson p. 141) must refer to the same event. Edward de Salaberry writes of dining on Christmas Day with the Duke of Orleans and his *brothers*: but by December 1807 the Duke of Orleans had only one brother, Montpensier having died the previous May. Moreover, the boy wrote of going to Marlow the following February, but by 30 August 1807 (Anderson, p. 133) he had already *finished* there.
331. PAC: MG23 G II 19, v. 7.
332. Published in *The Times*, 25 February 1808.
333. Quoted by Neale, p. 167.
334. Coutts 1502, 19 January 1807.
335. Romilly, v. 2, p. 100.
336. Bessborough, p. 184.
        Lyttelton, p. 64.
337. BM Add. MSS. 37,290, f. 132.
338. Clarke, v. 2, p. 85n, 86.
339. PAC: de Salaberry Papers.
340. Anderson, p. 219.
341. Harcourt MSS.
342. Knight, v. 1, p. 176.
343. Horner, v. 2, p. 70.
344. De Boigne, v. 2, p. 70.
345. Castillon du Perron, various pages. The author of this biography had access to the papers of Louis-Philippe in the archives of the comte de Paris, unfortunately unavailable to researchers at this time.
346. Coutts 1546: 1575: 1570.
347. Hardinge, v. 2, p. 396 (letter), p. 152 (poem: *'étrennes'* are farthings, or New Year's gifts). Though Hardinge dated his letter August, he is writing about an October visit.
348. PAC: MG 23 G II 19 v. 4, pp. 1584 and 1591.
349. Broughton, v. 1, p. 40.
350. RA 46551, 9 March 1813.
351. RA 46795, 7 July 1813.
352. RA Add. 11/154, 18 September 1806.
353. Coutts 1628.

354. Coutts 1662, 12 October 1814.
355. Knight, v. 1, p. 274, c. 3 February 1814.
356. Princess Charlotte, pp. 112, 31.
357. *Morning Chronicle,* 6 April 1814.
358. This account is taken from the *Morning Chronicle,* 21 April 1814.
359. Brownlow, p. 108.
360. Frampton, p. 220, 13 June 1814.
361. Romilly, v. 2, p. 346, 17 August 1814.
362. Leopold, p. 57, 31 May 1814 (in French).
363. Mitford, v. 1, pp. 284, 285.
364. RA 45315, 26 August 1814.
365. Dudley, p. 255.
366. Princess Charlotte, p. 189.
367. Ibid. p. 182.
368. Childe-Pemberton, p. 64.
369. Frampton, p. 247 (in French).
370. Princess Charlotte, p. 193, 17 March 1815.
371. Brownlow, p. 117.
372. Aspinall 1, 151.
373. Coutts 1740, 3 April 1816.
374. RA Add. 7/1205, 7 September 1816.
375. Fitzherbert, p. 151.
376. RA Add. 7/1202, 31 August 1816.
377. Greville, v. 3, p. 383.
378. Jordan, p. 261.
379. Colchester, v. 2, p. 347, November 1811. The Willises were the doctors attending George III to treat his 'insanity'.
380. Aspinall 1, p. 147.
381. Fitzherbert, p. 150. Other information from *Morning Chronicle* 21 October 1816.
382. Fitzherbert, p. 152.
383. Gordon, v. 2, pp. 312, 313.
384. Information about this period in Brussels and about Charles Mongenet is found in RA Add. 7/1201–1275.
385. RA Add. 7/1226.
386. RA Add. 7/1246.
387. *Morning Chronicle,* 5 November 1817.
388. Harcourt, v. 6, p. 112.
389. Lieven, p. 34.
Broughton, v. 2, p. 85.
390. RA Add. 7/1268.
391. Creevey, v. 1, pp. 268–271.
392. RA Add. 7/1272.
393. RA Add. 7/1276.
394. RA Add. 7/1286.
395. RA Add. 7/1290.
396. RA Add. 7/1292, 20 January 1818.
397. RA Add. 7/1298.
398. RA Add. 7/1306, 3 March 1818.
399. RA Add. 7/1299, 14 February: 7/1291, 4 February 1818.
400. RA Add. 7/1301, 23 February 1818.
401. RA Add. 7/1310.
402. Clarendon, v. 1, p. 20.
403. RA: Melbourne Paper Box 11.
404. RA Add. 7/1318.
405. Manuscript letter written in French, in the possession of Professor André Brun of Lyon, France.

406. RA Add. 7/1310, 14 March 1818.
407. Speeches reported in *The Times* of April 16, 17 and 24, and 16 May 1818.
408. Saxe-Coburg, pp. 190–193.
409. RA 45332, 5 July 1818. In this letter the duke gave Madame's address as the Hôtel de Ste Aldegonde, 113 (not 116) rue de Grenelle.
410. De Vincy MSS.
411. Declarations des Mutations par Décès, Archives de la Seine. Entry No. 510 (1819), succession de Beatrix de Montgenet veuve de Jansac, signed by the marquis de Permangle: other information from documents in the possession of the present marquise de Permangle.
412. RA Add. 7/1219.
413. RA Add. 7/1318.
414. *The Times*, 27 June and 2 July 1818.
415. PR.: LC 5/8.
       Buckingham, v. 2, p. 267.
416. RA 45340.
417. This letter is in the de Vincy MSS.
418. Bibliothèque Publique et Universitaire, Genève (in French).
419. RA Add. 7/1357: AR Add. 7/1382.
420. Knollys, U 1186, C 2/8 and C 2/9.
421. RA 45344: RA 45348.
422. Harcourt Papers. v. 6, p. 157.
423. *The Times*, 9 October 1818.
424. Macaulay, p. 15.
425. Fitzwilliam.
426. RA 45344.
427. 3 July 1819.
428. Owen MSS, 23 July, the Duke of Kent to Owen. I can find no contemporary evidence to support the statement (possibly originating with Agnes Strickland in *Queen Victoria from her Birth to her Bridal*) that the duke took the young princess to a military review when she was only three months old, and thereby incurred the Regent's wrath. This review was the only one reported by the papers to have been attended by the Regent this summer.
429. Exeter newspapers, October 1819, City Library, Exeter.
430. Croker, v. 1, p. 155.
431. *The Times*, 26 January 1820.
432. Stockmar, v. 1, p. 78.
433. Saxe-Coburg, p. 216.
434. Harcourt Papers, v. 6, p. 225.
435. Aspinall 1, p. 304.
436. Harcourt Papers, v. 6, p. 220 et seq.
437. Details of the duke's funeral from *The Times*, 14 February 1820.
438. PAC: MG 23 II 19, v. 4, p. 1649.
439. RA: Melbourne Papers, Box 11.
440. Ibid (in French).
441. De Boigne, v. 3, p. 14.
442. RA Add. Y/56, No. 30.
443. RA: Melbourne Papers, Box 11 (in French): the two princes may have been Louis-Philippe and Prince Leopold, or Prince Leopold and the Duke of Sussex.
444. Wetherall Papers, Ealing Public Library.
445. PRO: C 13/1726 and C 38/1286.
446. The original will is in the archives of Mᶜ Burthe-Mique, Paris.
447. Bibliothèque Nationale, Paris: Fr. Nouv. Acq. 1309, f. 264, 265. This letter is not attributed, having been signed only with initials, but these appear distinctly as 'J de St L' and the handwriting is Madame's.
448. Lieven-Metternich, p. 3.

449. Mitford, v. 2, p. 83.
450. Stockmar, v. 1, pp. 75, 51.
451. Windham, v. 1, p. 299.
452. Aspinall 2, p. 357.
453. Owen MSS, 2227, 2205.
      Owen, p. 267.
454. Serres, pp. 57, 79.
      Owen, p. 267.
455. PAC: de Salaberry Papers (in French).
456. Archives de la Seine: DQ⁷ 3804 f°92 v° 93 r°, 18 avril 1822.
457. Ibid. DQ⁷ 3431 f°s–161r°–161v°, 16 september 1830. Death certificate: Archives de Paris, Etat-Civil Reconstitué, acte de décès de Thérèse-Bernardine Mongenet.
458. Stadtarchiv, Offenbach.
459. See f.n. 449: will dictated and signed by Thérèse-Bernardine Mongenet.
460. Archives de la Seine.
461. Campbell, p. 145.
462. Fitzherbert, p. 258.
463. E.g., as reported in *The Times* of 2 September 1809, when the Duke of Clarence introduced his sons to the Queen at Egham Races.
464. Campbell, p. 146.
465. West India Reference Library, Institute of Jamaica, Kingston, W.I.
466. Scottish Record Office: Com. Dumfries Inventories, v. 4, p. 141.
467. Retired Military Officer, p. 54.
468. PAC: MG 24 D 18.
469. Ibid.
470. This John Whyte, who was a General by 1811, had died at Walberton House, Sussex, on 30 March 1815 (*Gentleman's Magazine* 1816 pt. 1, p. 377).
471. PAC: MG 24 D 18.
472. Samuel Hyde's Will, Jamaica Archives, Spanish Town: Liber 109 f. 145. The only property named Hyde associated with a family of that name was one patented by an unidentified Elizabeth Hyde and surveyed in 1684 (West India Reference Library).
473. Boyle's Court Guide 1829 (index).
474. Kingston, v. 1, pp. 123 and 318–343.
475. Quebec Almanach 1790 and registers of the English Church in Quebec.
476. Register of the English Church, Quebec: Généalogies genevoises d'Albert Choisy, 1947.
477. Letter to author from Buffalo and Erie County Public Library, 8 June 1965.
478. Will of Thomas Esdaile, 1811 (Somerset House).
479. *The Times*, 9 May 1818.
480. RA: P.P.1/38.
481. Will of Eliza Esdaile, 1835 (Somerset House).
482. PRO: Adm. 36/10971.
483. Judicial Archives, Quebec: Tutelle 24.
484. Registre des baptêmes, mariages et sépultures de Notre Dame de Québec 1795–96: Edouard Wood, buried 8 June 1796 in the Cimetière Ste Anne. 1799–1800: Marie Wood, buried 23 September 1800 in the Cimetière Ste Famille (Judicial Archives, Quebec).
485. 1847 register, Church of the Holy Trinity, Quebec.
486. PRO: C.O. 201/211. (Legend has said that Jean de Mestre was born to Madame on a warship carrying her from Quebec to Halifax in 1794 to rejoin the prince.)
487. Registre des Actes d'état-civil No. 1504—2 E 10/11 de 1788 a 1799, Archives de la Martinique.
488. C. L. Kingsford: *The Story of the Warwickshire Regiment*, 1921.
489. Probate records, Halifax, N.S.
490. Camp, p. xvii.

V

491. Annapolis Register of Baptisms 1782–1817, PANS.
492. *Notes and Queries* 10 S VII, Jan 19, Feb 9, Mar 2, Mar 23, Apr 20, 1907.
493. J. W. Stapleton: *The Great Crime of 1860* (1861).
494. Willis Chipman: *The Life and Times of Major Samuel Holland, Surveyor-General, 1764–1801.*
495. RA Add 7/1485.
496. Creston, p. 471.
497. Mansse was not an attorney. He had operated in London from as early as 1806 at 41 Coleman Street, and from 1821 at the Laurence Pountney address. In 1838 George Mansse appeared at this address as an insurance broker. George and his brother Lewis Albert died bachelors, predeceasing their widowed mother. The family seems to have had only a business connection with the Mongenets.
498. See f.n. 502.
499. Manuscrit inédit du Col. de Guillebon, Notes sur Corenc: Bib. mun. de Grenoble, cote R. 9675.
500. India Office Records L/MIL/9/333 and 334.
501. Archives d'Etat, Etat civil, Carouge, v. 35, année 1845, décès no. 91.
502. All Mongenet records not so far indicated will be found in registers at the relevant archives in Besançon (E 215 f. 28: GG 13 f. 118: GG 161 f. 7: GG 161 f. 11 verso: GG 267 f. 97: GG 274 f. 9: GG 276 f. 8; GG 281 f. 2: GG 283 f. 39: GG 284 f. 18: registre décès 1808, 470: 1837, f. 119): and in the registers of l'état-civil for relevant years in Grenoble, Haute-Savoie, Savoie and Geneva.

Abbot, Charles, Lord Colchester 171
Abercromby, Sir Ralph 141
Acasta, H.M.S. 159
Active, H.M.S. 149
Adams, Samuel, Lieutenant-Govenor of Massachusetts 84, 86
Addington, Henry, Lord Sidmouth 138, 165
Addiscombe 232, 256, 282
Adelaide, Princess of Meiningen 232, 236
Adolphus, Duke of Cambridge 74, 99, 123, 178, 198, 210, 232
Adolphus, John 143, 179
Affiches et Annonces de la Franche-Comté 26-9
Aitchison, Lieutenant 272
Aix-la-Chapelle 242
Albany, New York 6, 271
Alexander I, Emperor of Russia 201, 202, 208, 242, 245
Allen, William 255
Alligator, H.M.S. 40
Allsopp, George 36, 77, 78, 136
Amazon frigate 156, 157, 158, 159
Amelia, Princess 30, 73, 121, 124, 140, 170, 193-4, 206
American Mercury (Hartford, Connecticut) 81, 94
American Revolution, War of the 6, 35
Amiens, Treaty of 142, 159
Amorbach 209, 236, 242
Amory, Rufus Greene 85
Anderson, Dr W. J. 7
Annapolis, Nova Scotia 88, 184, 277
Antelope packet 110
Arethusa, H.M.S. 125
Armfeldt, General Gustav 173
Armstrong, Captain James (Jean) 4, 275-6
'Army of England' 167
Ascot, England 124
Assistance, H.M.S. 134
Auckland, Lord *See* Eden, William

Augusta, Duchess of Saxe-Coburg-Saalfeld 233, 234, 247
Augusta, Princess 33, 124, 170, 193, 247-8
Augusta (royal yacht) 31
Augustus, Duke of Sussex 33, 89, 99, 123, 147, 159, 172, 178, 204, 250, 254, 254n
Australia 5, 275
Aylesbury, Lady 194

Bachais (France) 281
Badcock (New York merchant) 114
Badajos, battle of 192, 193
Baden, Amelia, Princess of 208
Baker Street (London) 5, 271
Bardé, François 264
Barfleur, H.M.S. 272
Barnett, Major-General Charles 145, 149, 151, 156
Barney, Joshua 100, 107
Barras, Paul-François-Nicolas vcte de 235
Barton Lodge 4, 268
Bastia (Corsica) 91
Bath (England) 115, 118, 119, 120, 142, 165, 186, 216, 272
'Bear-keepers' 15
Beaufoy, Mark 175
Beaujolais, comte de 132, 183, 183n
Beauport (Quebec) 37, 45, 181
Beck, Philip 22, 25, 169, 208, 249
Beech (Theophylact Bache) 114, 114n
Beechey, Sir William 205, 235, 259
Beresford (naval captain) 111
Berlioz, Fernand 282
Berlioz, Pierre Auguste Desiré 282
Berthelot Dartigny 47, 48, 49
Berthier (Quebec) 54
Berwick Advertiser 6
Besançon (France) 26-9, 33, 121, 234, 257, 264, 265, 275, 279
Bessborough, Lady Henrietta 167, 171, 173, 174, 177, 198
Birch (coachmaker) 200

Bisschossgeim 236

Blanche frigate 87

Board of Green Cloth 122

Bognor (Sussex) 5, 8, 271, 272

Boileau, René 41

Bonaparte *See* Napoleon

Bonaparte, Jerome 180

Bonaparte, Joseph 199

Bonaparte, Lucien 235

Boston (Massachusetts) 80–6, 250

Boston Mercury 81

Botany Bay 77, 98

Boulogne (France) 142, 167

Boyd, Sir Robert 64

Brant, Colonel Joseph 40

Brighton (Sussex) 73, 137, 140, 166, 176, 179

Brompton (England) 120, 270

Brooke, Frances 37

Brougham, Henry 233

Brownlow, Emma Sophia Cust, Countess 202, 206

Brunswick, Augusta, Duchess of 179

Brunswick, House of 186, 209 *See also* Royal Family

Brussels (Belgium) 206, 207, 210, 225, 232, 235, 242

Buchan, Earl of 172

Buckingham House 14, 30, 198

Buffalo, New York 5

Bürgel (Germany) 264

Burges, Sir James Bland 52, 99

Burke, Edmund 261

Bushey Park 188

Cabinet *See* Government, British

Calais 1, 207, 229, 240

Calvados (France) 2

Cambridge, Duke of *See* Adolphus, Duke of Cambridge

Campbell, Lieutenant Donald 115

Campbell, Patrick 97, 98, 99

Canada 2, 15, 35, 112

Canadian Letters 66

Carleton, Sir Guy *See* Lord Dorchester

Carlton House (London) 12, 56, 140, 170, 207, 236, 245

Carmes, Les 90, 235

Caroline, Princess of Wales 96, 101, 112, 139, 143, 178

Carouge (Switzerland) 264, 282

Carr, Sir Henry and Lady 212

Cascades, The (St Lawrence river) 54

Castle Bear Hill 138, 212

Castle Hill Lodge (Ealing) 135, 137, 138–9, 139n, 162, 170, 175, 181, 185, 194, 195–7, 198–9, 205, 207, 211, 232, 235, 245, 254, 255, 261, 262

Castlereagh, Robert Stewart, Lord 206, 210, 232

Cathcart, Lord and Lady 121

Catholic Emancipation 138, 171

Cavillon, Euphrosine Elisabeth Jeanne 41

Chambéry (Savoie) 109, 173, 207, 256

Champlain, Lake 82, 110, 135

Channel, English 12, 79, 90, 91, 201

Chantereine, rue (Paris) 241, 251, 254

Chapel of St George (Windsor) 249–50

Charles X of France 7, 7n, 257

Charles of Leiningen, Prince 215, 242

Charlotte Augusta, Princess 112, 171, 198, 200, 201, 205, 206, 213, 217, 220

Charlotte, Queen 12, 26, 30, 70–1, 73, 119, 121, 122, 134, 138, 165, 174, 194, 198–9, 216, 217, 236, 242, 267, 267n

Château de St Philippe (Savoie) 239

Château St Louis (Quebec) 37, 39, 41, 43, 78

Chester, Sir Robert 236

Chichester Cathedral 5, 7

Chipman, Ward 47, 88, 124

Cholmondeley, Lord 24, 34

Chouly, Citizen *See* De Permangle, marquis

Christchurch Anglican Cathedral 4, 273

Church of The Holy Trinity (Quebec) 4, 273

Clarence, Duke of *See* William, Duke of Clarence

Clarendon, Earl of ('Lord Clarendon Hyde') 3

Clarke, Major-General Sir Alured 39, 40, 42, 46, 52, 55, 61, 65, 66, 67, 68, 69, 71, 72, 78 123, 274

Clarke, Mary Anne 185, 186, 189–91

Cliffe, Major Walter 92, 120, 124

Cobb, David 83, 85

Cobbett, William 142, 153

Coburg 1, 230, 233

Coffin, Thomas Aston 37, 45, 58, 124, 133, 142

Coke, Lady Mary 26, 29, 30

Collot, General 87

Colonna, Prince Prospero 7

Commonplace books, Madame's 74, 126, 126n, 168–9, 171, 182

Conroy, Captain John 247, 254, 255

Copenhagen, Battle of 141

Cotterel, Hélène 276

Courier (London) 244

Courts-martial 59–60, 62–5 (Quebec), 64 (of William Rose in Gibraltar), 109, 134n, 151 (Gibraltar), 151n

Coutts, Thomas 117, 123, 124, 127, 135, 136, 148, 175, 189, 194, 195, 199, 204, 207, 212, 230, 237, 252

Covent Garden Theatre 91, 181, 189
Craufurd, Captain Charles Gregan 14, 15, 16, 17, 18, 20, 21, 23, 59,
Creevey, Thomas 201, 218–19, 220, 263
Croker, John Wilson 246
Cumberland, Duke of See Ernest, Duke of Cumberland
Cumberland, Henry Frederick, Duke of 262
Cumberland, Dukedom of 121, 123
Curwen, John, M.P. 232
Cushing, William 85
Cust, Emma Sophia See Brownlow, Countess of
Cuthbert, James 54
Cynthia sloop of war 150

Dalrymple, William 69, 74
Davers, Captain Charles Sidney 149
De Beauharnais, Vtesse See Josephine, Empress
De Beaupoil St Aulaire, marquis of 263
De Roth, Anna (veuve de Bernet) 281
De Berri, Charles Ferdinand, duc 252
De Boigne, comtesse 194
De Broval, chevalier 241, 254
De Buc, Madame 114, 114n
De Fortisson, baron 29, 33, 34, 76, 263, 276
'De Fortisson, baronne' See Mongenet, Thérèse-Bernardine
De Gaspé, Philippe-Aubert 64
De Jansac, comtesse See Mongenet, Jeanne-Beatrix
De Jeansan, comtesse See Mongenet, Jeanne-Beatrix
De Jensac, comtesse See Mongenet, Jeanne-Beatrix
De Lanaudière, Monsieur 36, 46, 182
Delany, Mary Granville, Mrs 30
Delicate Investigation 178
De Livet de Moisy, Marie-Caroline-Olympie 282
De Messein, Msgr Charles-François Bailly, Bishop of Capse 50, 274
De Mestre (veuve) See Cotterel, Hélène
De Mestre, Jean See de Mestre, Prosper-Jean
De Mestre, Jean Charles André 'baron de Fortisson' 2, 4, 275
De Mestre, Melanie 2, 7, 276
De Mestre, Prosper-Jean 3, 4, 5, 275, 275n, 276
'De Montgenêt, comtesse', Madame's 'mother' 3
Denew, James 255
De Permangle, Lucien 235

De Permangle, Philippe-Claude-Auguste de Chouly, marquis 24, 33, 34, 34n, 92, 235, 256, 263, 279
De Peters, Antoine 235
De Rottenburg, General baron 7
De St Laurent, Madame See Mongenet, Thérèse-Bernardine
De Salaberry, Adelaide 182
De Salaberry, Amelia 45
De Salaberry, Catherine Hertel ('Souris') 45, 177, 181, 193
De Salaberry, Colonel Charles-René 7
De Salaberry, Charles-Michel 7, 108, 176, 180, 182, 183, 193
De Salaberry, Edouard (Edward) 34, 49, 50, 177, 180, 181–2, 183, 192–3
De Salaberry, Ignace-Louis 7, 36, 45, 47, 50, 72, 87, 107, 108, 134, 136, 193, 263
De Salaberry, Louis (Chevalier) 176, 180, 182, 192, 263
De Salaberry, Maurice 176, 179, 182, 192
De Saxel du Noyer, François 282
De Saxel du Noyer, Jean-Marie-François 282
D'Este family 3
Devaynes & Co. 192
De Vincy, François-Auguste-Maurice de Vasserot, baron 144, 148, 234, 238, 239, 241, 252, 259
Devonshire, Georgiana, Duchess of 38
Diday, Alexis-Auguste-Victor 281
Diday, Victor-Maurice-Charles-Alexis 281
Discipline 59–60, 109, 110, 146, 152
Dodd, Major Thomas 114, 150, 154, 162, 187, 189–91, 198
Dôle (France) 239, 279
Donnelly, Admiral Sir Ross 211, 223
Dorchester, Lady 38, 94, 107
Dorchester, Lord 36, 37, 39, 40, 41, 75, 79, 80, 88, 101, 107
Doubs (France) 26, 264
Douglas, Lady Charlotte 143, 178
Douglas, Sir John 178
Dover (England) 13, 167, 202, 207, 236, 244
Draper, Joseph 62–8 passim, 67, 76, 97, 98, 99
Drury Lane 32, 91, 92, 181, 205
Dubus, Adelaide 13, 19, 20, 21, 21n
Dubus, Adelaide Victoire Auguste 12, 13, 19, 21, 21n
Dubus, Victoire 19, 20, 21, 21n, 23
Duff, David 5
Dumont, Pierre-Etienne 56, 203
Dumourier, General Charles 169, 179, 196
Dundas, Sir David 248
Dundas, Major-General David 86

Dundas, Henry (later Lord Meville) 87, 97, 178
Dundas, Lord 243-4, 280
Dunkirk (France) 73, 77
Dunkirk, New York 5, 271
Dupuis, *dite* Caton, Mary (wife of Robert Wood Senior) 44, 273, 274

Ealing (England) 135, 197, 200, 212, 254, 264
Earl of Moira armed scow 88
Eden, William 70, 96, 116
Edward Augustus, Duke of Kent, birth 26; health 21, 99, 115, 130, 132, 134, 170; early life and education 29-31; departure for Europe 31-32; at Luneburg 31, 33; at Hanover 33; his 'bearkeepers' 15; flight from Geneva 2, 11; father's anger 13, 14; illegitimate child 12, 19, 20, 21, 21n; association with Adelaide Dubus 12, 19, 20, 21n; first term at Gibraltar 2, 15, 16, 17, 18; arrival of Victoire Dubus 19, 20, 21; sends Fontiny to find companion 21; letter to Mlle de St Laurent 22; her arrival 21, 23, 34; supposed meeting with 'Julie de St Laurent' 2; leaves for Quebec, taking Madame 24, 25; arrival in Quebec 35, 37, 38, 39; social life in Quebec 35-44 *passim*, 57, 58, 71, 72, 75; meets Indian chiefs 40, 55; his regiment (Royal Fusiliers) 11 (appointed colonel), 18 (posted to Gibraltar), 44, 45, 46, 57, 71, 100, 141 (relinquishes command); his regimental band 43, 57, 81, 88; Quebec elections 47-8; friendship with de Salaberry family 45, 49, 50, 108, 176-7, 179-84, 192-3; Niagara trip 50, 51, 52, 53, 54, 55, 56; his discipline 59-60, 59n, 109, 110, 146, 152; mutiny in Quebec 61-8; intercedes for Draper 67; views on French-English discord in Quebec 69; domestic happiness 69, 72, 75, 94, 96, 112, 136, 138, 139, 140, 147, 148, 166, 170, 195, 211, 212; pleads for greater activity 72, 76, 79; meets Saint-Mesmin 75; asks for permission to return home 71, 78, 111, 113, 115, 116, 117; ordered to West Indies 79; arrives Martinique 86; fighting 86-7; promoted (to Major-General) 79, (to Lieutenant-General) 111, (to General 124, (to Field-Marshal) 175; affair with Eliza Green 81; passage through United States 81, 82, 83-5, 86; Boston letters about 83-5; British consul's report on 85; arrives in Halifax 87; tours district (Nova Scotia) 88, 133,

(New Brunswick) 88; seeks pistols left with Robert Wood 88-9; sends for Madame 87; Madame arrives from England 89, 92; life in Halifax 94, 95, 96, 99, 102, 103, 104, 105; Wentworth's friendship with 94, 95, 101, 105, 106, 110, 111, 197, 250; resides at the Lodge 95-6 (description) 126; fortification of Halifax 106-7; chagrined by appointment of General Prescott 107, 111; drinking reform 109, 146; relations with Duke of York 32, 33, 110, 112, 127-131, 142-3, 155, 160-4, 184-5, 187, 194; accidents 117 (at Halifax), 199 (in London); leaves Halifax for England 118; buys Knightsbridge house (description) 120; peerage rumoured 12, 121; becomes Duke of Kent 123; apartment in Kensington Palace 120, 122; appointed Commander-in-Chief, British North America 124; returns to Halifax 125, 126; seeks Irish command 126-7; debts and financial problems 2, 43, 135, 191-2; determination not to lose Madame 130; leaves Halifax 134, 134n; buys Castle Hill Lodge, Ealing 135 (description 138-9, 195, 207); his correspondence 140; appointed governor and commander at Gibraltar 142; instructions from Duke of York 144; action to correct bad conditions, civil and military 145-6, 153; mutiny 149-50, 151; recall ordered 150-1; leaves Gibraltar 159; his Code of Orders 152, 156-67, 160; requests hearing 160-1, 163; homecoming 159, 165; views on Catholic Emancipation 171-2; visited by de Salaberry sons 176-7, 179-84; Delicate Investigation 179; retains governorship of Gibraltar 165, 185; Mary Anne Clarke inquiry 187, 188, 189-91; friendship with Louis-Philippe 132, 169, 179, 183, 189, 194, 210, 252-3; relations with Prince of Wales 12, 18, 57, 72, 116, 118, 120, 124, 135, 137, 139, 142, 147, 150, 165, 178, 179, 198, 200, 215, 243, 245n, 247; receives Queen and princesses at Castle Hill Lodge 198-9; nicknamed 'Joseph Surface' 201; charitable activities 204; relations with Princess Charlotte 200-1, 206, 213, 215; departure for Brussels 207; tour in Europe 209-10; visit to Paris 210; his residence in Brussels (description) 211; marriage negotiations 213-222 *passim*; reported in *Morning Chronicle* 217; death of Princess Charlotte 217; talk with Creevey 218; asks Perry to suppress rumours 220; his suit accepted 222; parting from Madame 225; his financial provisions for her 123, 136, 230, 237; marriage grant debated in Parliament 232-3; his wedding (at Coburg) 233-4, (in England) 236; association with other members of Mongenet family 195, 210, 212, 239, 240; residence at Amorbach 242; duchess pregnant 242; struggle to finance visit to England for child's birth 243-4; Castle Hill Lodge lottery plan 245; plans to winter in Devonshire 245, 246; death 6, 246, 247-8; funeral 249-50; settlement of affairs 255; character 259-63; his 'descendants' 1-8, 266-79

Eichorn, Marie Anne 256, 264
Elba (Island of) 205, 206
Elizabeth, Princess 194, 198, 199, 201, 210, 224, 232
Elliot, Sir Gilbert 42, 46, 72, 73, 74, 137, 166
Elliott, Grace Dalrymple 90
Elphinstone, Hon. George Keith 24
Elphinstone, Margaret Mercer 200, 209
Erie, Lake 6
Ermatinger, Frederick 70, 80
Ernest, Duke of Cumberland 74, 99, 121, 122, 123, 140, 198, 229, 232, 248
Esdaile, Mrs 'Julie' See Green, Elizabeth
Esdaile, Thomas 5, 271
Eton (England) 124, 186
Eustis, Dr William 83, 85
Evian (France) 282

'Fair Circassian' The 244
Falmouth (England) 143, 159
Farington, Joseph 173, 179
Farquhar, Robert 186
Farr, George 272
Fawcett, Sir William 21, 56, 65, 66, 67, 70, 79, 191, 155
Fell, Francis 151
Fifth Regiment of Foot 51, 56
Fifty-fourth Regiment of Foot 149
First Regiment of Foot 141, 149, 151, 176
Fisher, Dr John 246
Fishguard (Wales) 113
Fitzherbert, Maria 38, 76, 89, 125, 135, 165, 175, 197, 198, 210, 230, 267
Fitzroy, Colonel Charles 206
Fitzwilliam, Lord 243-4
Fitzwilliam, Countess 122
Flucker, Mrs S. L. 83
Folkestone, Lord 191
Fontiny, Monsieur 21, 22, 23, 34
Fournier, George 255
Fowsell, Mary Catherine 276-7

Fox, Charles James 112, 138, 177, 178
Franche-Comté 26
Francis transport 135, 135n
Francis, Sir Philip 166, 167
Frederica, Duchess of York 42, 73, 89, 198, 199
Frederick, Duke of York 12, 14, 15, 30, 31, 32, 57, 73, 74, 89, 99, 101, 110, 112, 119, 120, 127, 131, 138, 139, 140, 142, 144, 150, 155, 160-1, 163-4, 165, 184, 185-8, 189, 190, 198, 200, 202, 218, 220, 250, 259, 267
Fredericton, New Brunswick 37
Freemasons 17, 57, 65
Fréjus (France) 206
Fremantle, W. H. 236
French Revolution 2, 27, 34, 56, 77, 275
'Friar Laurence's Cell' See The Lodge, Halifax

Gabriel, Jacques 255
Garbrand Hall (Jamaica) 267, 268
Gawler, John 60
General Evening Post (London) 12, 14
Genêt, Edouard-Charles 82
Geneva 2, 12, 13, 15, 19, 43, 112, 141, 144, 208, 210, 232, 238, 256, 264, 271, 282
'George' 31, 31n
George, Prince of Wales (later Prince Regent) 11, 12, 18, 30, 32, 38, 56, 72, 73, 75, 76, 80, 89, 96, 99, 101, 112, 116, 117, 118, 119, 120, 124, 125, 126, 134, 135, 137, 138, 139, 140, 141, 142, 147, 150, 165, 169, 176, 178, 179, 194, 198, 200, 201, 202, 205, 206, 207, 208, 215, 222, 224, 232, 236, 243, 245, 247, 248, 257, 261
George III, King 6, 11, 12, 13, 14, 15, 16, 17, 18, 30, 31, 32, 33, 43, 56, 57, 71, 72, 76, 79, 80, 82, 85, 92, 99, 112, 113, 115, 121, 122, 125, 137-8, 143, 150, 160, 161, 162, 164, 165, 167, 171, 186, 188, 194, 248, 249, 250, 262
Gerrald, Joseph 77
Geyer, Nancy 85
Gibraltar 2, 6, 11, 14, 15, 16, 17, 18, 21, 22, 24, 25, 39, 43, 57, 59, 63, 64, 66, 142, 143, 144, 145, 146, 147, 148, 149-55, 156, 158, 159, 162, 163, 164, 177, 184-5, 232, 263, 273
Gibraltar Chronicle 154
Gipsy prophecy 263
Glasgow, Lieutenant-General George 6, 52, 55, 81, 271
Glengall, Lord 267
Glennie (Glenie), James 187, 190, 191
Goodall, Eleanor, 272

Goodall, William, 36, 77, 78, 81, 271, 272
Goodall, William (junior) 271–2
Gordon, Lord George 14
Gordon, Pryse Lockhart 211
Gourlay, Colonel William 269
Gourlay, Mrs William See Whyte, Emily
Göttingen 32
Government, British 155, 160, 275
Grant, William 272
Gravé, Grand Vicar 50
Gray, Edward 70, 80
Great Ealing School 212, 240
Green, Elizabeth (Eliza) 5, 6, 38–9, 78, 81, 87, 270, 271, 272
Green, 'Laura' 5
Green, Louisa 3, 5, 6, 39, 270, 171, 272
Green, Magdalen (Madeline) 6, 81, 270, 271
Green, William 6, 271
Green, William George 6
Green, William Goodall 3, 5, 6, 78, 270, 271, 272
Greenwich 26, 31, 72, 73
Greenwood, Charles 160
Grenelle, rue de (Paris) 234, 234n, 241
Grenoble (France) 40, 74, 206, 254, 256, 257, 264, 279, 281, 282
Grenville, Major-General Richard 17, 19, 23, 24
Greville, Henry 208
Grey, General Sir Charles 76, 78, 79, 82, 86, 97
Grisler, Charles 65
Guadaloupe 35, 82, 87

Habitants 35, 53
Haldimand, Sir Frederick 42
Halifax, Nova Scotia 2, 5, 6, 46, 66, 72, 80, 83, 86, 87, 88, 92, 93, 95, 99–116 passim, 117, 118, 122, 132, 134, 137, 143, 187, 250, 257, 276
Halifax Journal 99
Halifax Weekly Chronicle 105, 108
Halliburton, Sir Brenton 109, 115
Hamilton (Ontario) 3, 4, 5, 268, 270
Hampshire (England) 123, 124
Hampton Court 14, 175, 185
Handel, G. F. 194
Hanover 15, 31, 122
Harcourt, Hon. Mrs 100, 101, 138
Harcourt, Lady 119, 217, 242, 247, 248
Harcourt, General the Hon. William 100, 155, 187
Hardinge, Mr Justice George 195–7, 197n, 261
Hardy, Captain Thomas Masterman 143
Hassan, Mirza Abdul 244, 245
Hastings (England) 167

Helder, rue du (Paris) 207
Henley, Lord 165, 171
Hesse-Homburg, Landgrave of 210, 232
Hinde, Sergeant William 66
Hippodrome, The 269
Hobhouse, John Cam 197, 217
Holland, Captain Henry 135
Holland, Elizabeth, Lady 73, 125, 138
Holland, Frederick Braham 279
Holy Trinity, Church of, Quebec 4, 273
Hood, Admiral Lord Samuel 78, 91
Hope, Brigadier-General Henry 37
Horner, Francis 177
Hôtel de Maldegham (Brussels) 211, 242
Hôtel Dieu (Paris) 210
House of Commons (London) 186, 232, 267
House of Lords (London) 187, 232
Howe, Admiral Lord Richard 79, 90, 91, 92
Hughes, Captain William 88
Hundred Days, The 206
Huntley, Marquis of 14
Hussar, H.M.S. 86
Hyde Hall (Jamaica) 3, 269, 269n
Hyde, Isabella 3, 4, 5, 267, 269, 270
Hyde Park (London) 120, 188, 201, 202
Hyde, Samuel 269, 270

Independent Chronicle and Boston Patriot 250
Indians 39, 40, 52, 55
Indian Trader (ship) 115
Invasion of England, fears of 112, 142, 166–7
Isis, H.M.S. 143

Jackson, Henry 84
Jacobinism 77, 96, 176
Jacques Cartier (Quebec) 77
Jamaica 3, 106, 267–8, 269, 270
Jansac, comtesse de See Mongenet, Jeanne-Beatrix
Jarvis, Hannah 75
Jay, John 90
Jersey, Lady 125
Jervis, Admiral Sir John See St Vincent, Earl
Johnson, Sir John 39
Johnson, Samuel 67
Jones, Colonel Daniel 11
Jordan, Mrs Dorothy 46, 89, 92, 113, 188, 197, 209
Josephine, Empress of France 2, 90, 173
'Joseph Surface' 201
Journal de la mode 74
Jouve, Mr (bandleader) 42
Juncken, Henry 38–9

Kennedy, Timothy 62, 65, 67, 76
Kensington Palace 120, 122, 137, 162, 170, 176, 185, 188, 194, 225, 229, 232, 244, 254
Kent, Constance 278–9
'Kent House' (Knightsbridge) 3, 120, 121, 135, 183–4, 183n; (Montmorency Falls, Quebec) 7, 42; (Quebec City) 39, 40, 41, 81
Kew (England) 14, 246; (Palace) 236
King, John 2, 87, 89, 94, 95, 106, 111, 141
Kingston (Ontario) 51, 55
Kingston, W. H. G. 269
Kirkland, Nugent 237, 255
Knight, Cornelia 200
Knightsbridge (London) 3, 120, 121, 135, 183, 270
Knollys, General William 200, 240, 241
Knox, Henry 83, 84

Laidler, George 5, 276
Landmann, George 114
Landrigan, James 62–5 passim
La Raison, H.M.S. 111
La Rose See Rose, William
La Tribune frigate 114–15
Lauderdale, Earl of 97
Lavigne, Mariette 264
Leeds, Duchess of 200
Legislature, Lower Canada 4, 46, 69, 70, 77, 79
Leiningen (Germany) 208
Leiningen, Dowager Princess of See Victoire, Duchess of Kent
Leopold, Prince of Saxe-Coburg 203, 205, 206, 213, 217, 222, 247, 251, 252, 253, 254, 254n, 280
Leroi, Fanni 264
Levison (Lewison), husband of Melanie de Mestre 7
Lieven, Princess 208, 217, 259, 260
Limoges 33
Lisbon (Portugal) 147, 159
Liverpool, Nova Scotia 49, 56, 72, 75, 101, 116
Liverpool, Lord 207
Lloyd's Coffee House 91
Lodge, The, (Halifax) 95–6, 114, 126
Lombard, Maître 256
London 12, 72, 90, 135, 137, 138, 161, 165, 199, 201, 202, 203, 236, 250, 257
London Chronicle 66
Longford, Elizabeth 266
Lord Chamberlain 137
Louis XVI 42, 56, 77
Louis XVIII 195, 201–2, 210, 234
Louis-Philippe, duc d'Orleans, later King of the French 29, 132, 169, 179, 183,
189, 194, 194n, 210, 215, 234, 235, 241, 252, 253, 254, 254n, 256, 257, 257n, 280
Lower Canada 46, 69, 103, 133
Luneburg 15, 31, 33, 122
Luxembourg, The 142
Lyman, Captain Daniel 102, 114, 132, 133
Lyon (France) 206

Mabane, Adam 36, 40, 45
M'Callum, Pierre Franc 187
McDonogh, Thomas 83, 85
'Madame' See Mongenet, Thérèse-Bernardine
Madeleine, Church of the (Paris)) 265
Mahieu, Armand 169, 208, 249
Mahieu, Mrs 168, 208
Malaga (Spain) 22, 34
Mallet, General 234, 238, 241, 245
Mallet, Mme 239
Malmesbury, Lady 138
Malmesbury, Lord 165
Malta 142, 198, 263, 274, 278
Mansse, Lewis 280, 280n
Margarot, Maurice 77, 96, 98
Marie-Amélie, Princess of Sicily, 194, 254
Marie Antoinette 29, 42, 77
Marlow, Royal Military College 180, 180n
Marseillles 19, 22, 76
Martello towers 107, 190
Martin, Sally 14
Martininque 2, 3, 4, 86, 88, 89, 110, 271, 273, 275
Mary, Princess 73, 198, 201, 248
Mary packet ship 122
Maton, Dr 248
Maxwell, Lieutenant J. S. 76
Mecklenberg-Strelitz, Grand Duke of 210
Melbourne, Lord 280
Melville, Lord See Dundas, Henry
Mermaid frigate 147
Metternich, Prince Clemens von 259
Military Register 209
Milnes, Robert 124, 136, 141
Mincing Lane (London) 268, 269
Minto, Lady 138
Minto, Lord See Elliot, Sir Gilbert
Mirabeau, Victor Riqueti, marquis de 33
Mirror of the Times 120
Mitchell Library (Sydney, Australia) 275
Mitford, Mary Russell 204, 259
Monaco 26
Mongenet, Anne-Marie, 256, 281
Mongenet, Antoine-Charles-Alfred 257, 281
Mongenet, Charles-Benjamin 109, 173, 207, 210, 234, 256, 257, 264, 279, 280, 281

Mongenet, Charles-Jean 194, 212, 223, 224, 232, 239, 240, 251, 257, 263, 264, 282

Mongenet, Claude-Charles 27, 40, 109, 173, 207, 239, 255, 256, 264

Mongenet, Claudine *See* Pussot, Jeanne-Claude

Mongenet, Edouard (Edward) 195, 239, 282

Mongenet, Jean 27, 40, 275

Mongenet, Jean-Claude 27, 27n, 41, 141, 172, 194, 208, 210, 224, 239, 264, 279, 282

Mongenet, Jean-Joseph-Suzanne 27, 239, 264, 275, 279

Mongenet, Jeanne-Beatrix, comtesse de Jansac 6, 27, 40, 207, 210, 234, 235, 265.

Mongenet, Louise-Sophie 141, 239, 282

Mongenet, Thérèse-Bernardine, birth 27; early life 26–9, 33–4; affair with baron de Fortisson 29, 33, 34, 76; association with marquis de Permangle 33, 235; joins prince at Gibraltar 21, 23, 34; accompanies him to Quebec 24, 25; arrives in Quebec 35, 38, 39; life in Quebec 41, 43, 44, 45, 49, 75; friendship with de Salaberry family 45, 49, 50, 108, 176, 177, 179–84, 192–3; may have gone to Niagara 50, 52, 52n, 54, 55; domestic happiness 58, 69, 71–2, 74, 75, 96, 114, 140, 148, 162, 165, 166, 168, 170; society's attitude to 44, 74, 76, 102, 103, 128, 129, 130, 165, 188, 199; Saint-Mesmin's opinion of 76, 76n; goes to New York 80–2; United States press comment 81–2; to Halifax 82, 87; to England 87; in England 90–2; returns to Halifax 92; resides at The Lodge 95, 96, 126; poems to 105, 108, 196–7; life in Halifax 93, 95, 96, 99, 104, 105 114; letter to George Monk 104; friendship with Wentworths 2, 87, 94, 110, 122, 197; accompanies prince on tours 108, 132 (Niagara tour 52–5, 56); her titles 2, 41, 50, 92, 274 ('baronne de Fortisson'); 234 (de Mont-genêt); her commonplace books 74, 126, 126n, 168–9, 171, 182; leaves Halifax for London 118; established in Knightsbridge house 120; accompanies duke to Gibraltar 143, 144, 147; life at Gibraltar 147, 159; returns to England 159; George Hardinge's reaction to 195, 196–7; visit of Queen and princesses to Ealing 198–9; leaves England 207; visits Paris 210; to Brussels 210; apprehensions of parting 213–14;

alarmed by press rumours 218; last weeks with duke 223–5; final parting 225; receives consoling letter 230–1; sends for duke's portrait 235; death of sister 235; her loneliness 229, 234, 236, 238, 244, 250; friends in Paris 234, 234n, 238, 240, 241; friendship with Louis-Philippe 29, 132, 194, 234, 240, 252–4, 257, 257n; moves to rue Chantereine 241; reaction to birth of Princess Victoria 244, 245; Wetherall's letter about the duke's serious illness 251; hears of duke's death 250, 252, 253; receives letter from Duchess of Kent 252, 253; duchess receives her reply 254; her will 256, 264; her death 257, 263, 264; funeral 265; settlement of her affairs 279–80; petition to Queen Victoria from her heirs 280–81; her interests and accomplishments 22, 72, 74, 105, 114, 181, 182; her thrift 135, 136, 194; her health 99, 115, 136, 169, 170, 205, 207, 211, 223, 225, 256; her role as hostess 41, 114, 120, 129, 139, 140, 169; the duke's love for 112, 128–31, 166, 170, 230, 238, 239, 240, 241, 261; his financial arrangements for 123, 136, 230, 237, 252, 253; her relatives 49, 109, 172, 173, 194–5, 207, 210, 212, 224, 232, 234, 235 239, 240, 254, 257, 263; legends about 2 (birth in Normandy); 5, 274 ('Princesse de Normandie'); 5, 6 ('Julie Esdaile'); 4, 5, 6, 271, 274, 275 ('marriage' to Duke); 2 ('marriage' to de Fortisson); 279 ('relationship' to Holland family); 'descendants' 2, 176 (Melanie de Mestre); 3–8, 50, 78, 266–77 (others)

Mongenet, Thérèse-Caroline-Sylvie 194, 195, 282

Moniteur, Le (Paris) 236, 244, 252

Monk, George 103, 104, 107, 108, 118, 184

Monk, James 36, 103, 104, 107, 141

Monk, James Frederick 184

Mont-Blanc, département de 173

Montmorency Falls (Quebec) 7, 37, 41, 42, 45

Montpensier, duc de 179, 183

Montreal (Quebec) 6, 35, 36, 51, 52, 70

Montreal Gazette 36

Moore, General 247, 248

Moré (Prince Edward's valet) 19

Morley, Lord 3, 229

Morning Chronicle, 31, 74, 152, 186, 188, 199, 214, 217, 218, 220, 221, 243

Morning Herald 243, 244

Morning Post 90, 97, 154, 186, 188, 202, 244

Mountain, Bishop Jacob 52–6, 172

Muir, Thomas 77, 96, 98

Murrray, Admiral 109

Murray, General 118

Murray, Lady Augusta 89

Mutineers (Quebec) *See* Draper, J., Kennedy, T., Landrigan, J., Rose, W., Shaw, J., Wigton, T.

Mutineers 134 (Halifax); 151 (Gibraltar)

Mutiny 61–8 (Quebec); 97–9 (*Surprise*); 148, 149–50, 151, 152, 153–4, 162 (Gibraltar); 113 (Spithead, The Nore)

Napoleon Bonaparte 79, 141, 167, 173, 205

Navy Hall 51, 55

Nelson, Admiral Horatio 141, 142, 173, 174

New Brunswick 80, 108, 133

Newgate Prison 14, 97

Newmains (Scotland) 268

New Orleans (Louisiana) 7

New South Wales Corps 76, 97, 98, 99

New York 79, 81, 82, 114

New York Journal 81, 90

Niagara (Ontario) 45, 50, 51, 56, 71, 196

Nicholas, Dr D. 212, 232

Nooth, Dr John Mervin 118

Nore, The, 109, 113

Normandy 2, 5, 26

Northup, Mrs 105

Notes and Queries 278–79

Notting Hill (London) 269

Nova Scotia 127, 132, 233, 272

Observer, The 120, 249.

Ogilvie, Major-General 105, 106

O'Hara, General Charles 2, 16, 17, 18, 59, 79, 142, 153, 157

Old Dutch Church (Halifax, Nova Scotia) 277

Oldenburg, Grand Duchess of 201

Onondaga (topsail schooner) 55

Ontario Historical Society, Papers and Records of 279

Oracle (London) 79, 91, 92

Orange, House of 101; 120, 205 (Prince of)

Orleans, Duke of *See* Louis-Philippe

Orleans, Island of 37, 44

Ormond, Duke of 29

Osgoode, William 80, 103, 136, 141

Ossory, Earl of 29

Oswegatchie 54

Overture to Victoria 2, 4

Oxford Companion to Canadian History and Literature 3

Owen, Robert 245, 262

Palais Royal (Paris) 252, 256

Pallmer, Charles Nicholas 269, 270

Palmer, Mr (of Brompton house) 120, 270

Palmer, Dr Thomas Fyshe 77, 96, 97, 98, 99

Papendiek, Mrs 30

Paris (France) 1, 76, 173, 201, 205, 234, 250, 263

Parker, Captain William 156, 157–9.

Pattullo, Ensign William 98

Pegasus, H.M.S. 14, 37

Pelham, Lord 150, 160, 163–4

Pélissier, Joseph 264

Père Lachaise, Cimetière de (Paris) 235, 265

Perkins, Simeon 49, 56, 72, 75, 101, 116

Perry, James 217, 218, 220, 221

Piccadilly (London) 142, 201

Pictet, Marc-Louis 39, 270–1

Pitt, William 13, 14, 17, 70, 79, 96, 127, 138, 177, 178

Place de la Concorde (Paris) *See* Place Louis XV

Place Louis XV (Paris) 77, 255, 257, 264

Place Royale (Brussels) 211, 218

Plymouth (England) 14, 76, 134, 186

Political Register (London) 153

Porcupine, The (London) 142

Porphyria 138n, 170

Porter, McKenzie 2, 3, 4, 5, 7, 7n

Portland, Duke of 101, 132, 136

Portland packet 82, 87, 90

Portsmouth (England) 11, 14, 92, 119, 123, 125, 186

Powell Place (Quebec) 81

Prescott, Sir Robert 107, 110, 111, 118, 124, 141

Prince of Wales *See* George, Prince of Wales

Princess Charlotte *See* Charlotte, Princess

Princess Royal, the 113, 205, 209, 242

Princess of Wales *See* Caroline, Princess of Wales

Prussia, King of 173, 202

Public Advertiser (London) 14

Pussot, Claudine 27, 275

Putnam, James 230, 237

Pye, Henry James 79

Quakers 91

Quebec 2, 4, 7, 8, 21, 25, 35–7, 46–9, 52, 57, 58, 60–8, 71, 75, 76, 77, 78, 79, 88, 89, 93, 103, 109, 114, 126, 193, 270, 271, 273, 274, 275

Quebec Gazette 36, 42, 46, 47-8, 57, 66, 67, 68, 82
Quebec Herald 36
Queen Charlotte *See* Charlotte, Queen of England
Queen's House *See* Buckingham House
Queen's Rangers 56
Queen's Regiment *See* Second regiment of foot

Randolph, James 46
Ranelagh 91
Recovery transport 110
Rees, John 276
Rees, John Edward 3, 5, 6, 276-7
Rees, Mary Eizabeth 3, 5, 6, 276-7
Regency, The, 194
Regent, The Prince *See* George, Prince of Wales
Resistance, H.M.S. 3n, 25, 25n, 37, 273
Resolution, H.M.S. 3, 3n
Retired Military Officer, A 268
Reynolds, Sir Joshua 46
Riedesel, baroness 37, 42
Rio de Janeiro 97, 98
Rival Princes, The 189-91
Roddam, Admiral Robert 14
Roebuck packet 83, 86
Romilly, Samuel 56, 187, 202
Rose, George 137
Rose, William 62-6, 76
Royal Academy 179
Royal Artillery 61, 63, 149
Royal Family 5, 6, 31, 91, 99, 125, 138, 167, 186, 247-8, 249 262
Royal Fusiliers *See* Seventh regiment of foot
Royal Gazette (Halifax) 134
Royal Nova Scotia Regiment 110, 114, 116
Royals *See* First regiment of foot
Ruchette, Jean-Jacques 264
Rudge, Dr (rector of St Clement Danes) 243
Russell, Elizabeth 45, 55, 71
Russell, Peter 45, 51, 55
Russell, Thomas 83, 84
Russell, Mrs Thomas 84
Ryan, Corporal Timothy 98

Sable Island 135
St James's Chronicle (London) 90
St James's Palace 30, 122
Saint John, New Brunswick 88
St-Laurent-Sur-Mer (France) 2, 7
St Laurent, Madame de *See* Mongenet, Thérèse-Bernardine
St Lawrence river 35, 51, 52, 55, 66, 79
St Louis Street (Quebec) 39, 40, 41, 81, 103

St Lucia (West Indies) 86
St Mathew's Church (Halifax) 276
Saint-Mesmin, Bénigne Charles Fevret de 75, 76, 76n, 93
St Paul, Casernes de (Besançon) 28
St Paul, Church of (Besançon) 27, 28
St Paul's Cathedral (London)) 174
St Paul's Episcopal Church (Halifax) 6, 116, 277
St Thomas in the East (Jamaica) 267
St Vincent, Earl 78, 154, 155
Saints, The (West Indies)) 87
Salisbury, Henry 151
Savannah (Georgia) 275
Savary, Judge 277
Savoye, Mr (bandmaster) 124
Savoy prison 76
Scottish Martyrs *See* Gerrald J., Margarot M., Muir T., Palmer Dr T. F., Skirving W.
Second regiment of foot 11, 16
Sefton, Lord 219, 220
Sélinger, Marie 264
Serres, Olivia 262
Seventh regiment of foot 11, 18, 24, 44, 56, 57, 60, 61-8, 66, 71, 100, 110, 115 141
Severn, H.M.S. 75, 76
Sewell, Jonathan 36, 46, 47, 78, 88, 89
Seymour, Minney 267
Shaw, James 62, 63
Sheridan, Richard Brinsley 97
Shuttleworth, Ashton 11
Shuttleworth, Captain John Ashton 11, 24, 45, 46, 71, 81, 88
Shy Princess, The 5
Sidmouth (England) 245, 246, 248, 249, 251
Simcoe, Mrs Elizabeth 43, 44, 51, 54, 71, 75
Simcoe, Colonel John Graves 42, 43, 44, 51, 52, 55, 65, 75, 78, 80, 103, 246
Skirving William 77, 96, 97, 98, 99
Smith, Sir Sidney 167
Smith, William 36, 37, 41, 44, 79
Smyrna 8
Smyth, Lieutenant George 80, 88, 114
Sophia, Princess 73, 170
'Souris' *See* de Salaberry, Catherine
Southampton frigate 11, 14, 273
Spencer, Lord Henry 70, 96
Spencer, Lady 38, 188
Spithead (England) 91, 109, 113, 118
Stockmar, baron 247, 259-60
Storer, Anthony 70
Strange, Andrew 103
Strangethorne, Thomas 168
Straton, Captain James 106

Sturt, Charles 11, 11n, 12
Sudley Cottage (Bognor) 5, 271, 272
Sumner, Increase 85
Surprise transport 97-9
Sussex, Duke of See Augustus, Duke of Sussex
Sydney (Australia) 275
Symes, Colonel Richard 15, 17, 18, 18n, 19, 23, 24, 34, 43, 59, 75, 113

Talleyrand, Charles Maurice, Prince de 86
Tankerville packet 110
Telegraph (signal system) 125, 133
Thames river (London) 174, 200
Theatre 45 (Quebec); 99-100, 102, 105, 116 (Halifax); 32, 129, 179, 181, 189, 204, 207 (London); 210 (Paris)
Thetis frigate 118
Thisbe frigate 36
Thompson, James (overseer of works) 38, 60
Thompson, James (surgeon) 97, 98
Thrum Cap Shoals 114
Thurlow, Lord 13, 178
Tidy, Colonel Francis 68
Times, The 25, 44, 137, 165, 184, 190, 191, 195, 225, 232, 245, 246-7, 255, 259
Topaze, H.M.S. 118
Tottenham (England) 271
Toulon, 78, 79
Trafalgar, Battle of 173
Trigge, Sir Thomas 156-7, 160
Triton, H.M.S. 43
True Briton (London) 154
Twenty-fifth regiment of foot 149, 150, 151
Tyburn (London) 67

Ulysses, H.M.S. 3, 25, 25n, 37
United States 80, 82, 90
Upper Canada 42, 133, 267
Upper Stroquhan (Scotland) 268
Ursuline nuns (Quebec)) 3, 270

Valenciennes (France) 73, 208
Valetta (Malta) 274
Varennes (France) 42
Vauxhall Gardens (London) 91, 199
Vesey, Colonel John 80, 114, 118, 189
Victoire, Duchess of Kent 1, 5, 6, 208, 215, 217, 221, 222, 224, 233, 234, 236, 237, 238, 240, 242, 243, 244, 245, 246, 247, 248, 250, 251, 252, 253, 254, 259, 262, 263, 266, 272, 280, 281
Victoria, Queen 3, 4, 5, 103, 208, 241, 244, 245, 245n, 246, 247, 248, 251, 262, 263, 266, 277, 279, 280, 281

Victoria R.I. 266
Victory, H.M.S. 173
Villiers, Mrs George 229

Walker, Captain Alexander 45
Walker, Captain Robert 81
Wangenheim, Lieutenant-Colonel George von 13, 15, 31
War, 70, 72, 100, 107, 116, 141, 142, 159, 173
Ward, Mrs (Colonel Tidy's daughter) 68
Wardle, Colonel G. L., M.P. 185, 190
Warley camp 73, 77
Warren House 269
Washington, General George 62, 63, 82
Waterloo, Battle of 206
Watson, Brook 77, 271
Wellington, Duke of 199, 201, 206, 210, 219
Wemyss, General David 152, 160
Wentworth, Charles-Mary 115, 122
Wentworth, Lady Frances 94, 102, 104, 111, 114, 115, 122, 122n, 197
Wentworth, Sir John 2, 46, 52, 66, 83, 87, 89, 94, 95, 101, 102, 104, 105, 106, 110, 111, 114, 115, 122n, 126, 135, 197, 250
West Indies 4, 26, 35, 76, 78, 79, 80, 81, 86-7, 94, 108
Westmoreland packet 89, 92
Wetherall, Alexander 212, 223, 224
Wetherall, General Frederick Augustus 61, 80, 86, 124, 131, 134, 180, 181, 211, 214-15, 216, 218, 220-1, 223, 225, 230, 235, 237 240, 243, 244, 247, 250, 251, 254, 255
Wetherall, Dr J. 181
Weymouth (England) 42, 119, 134, 135, 140, 176, 189, 198
Whigs 197
White, James See Whyte, James
Whyte, Emily 4, 269
Whyte, James 267-8
Whyte, James Christie 269
Whyte, James Matthew 3, 4, 267, 268
Whyte, John 3, 268, 269
Whyte, Colonel John (later General) 3, 268, 268n
Whyte, Thomas 268
Wigton, Thomas 62-5 passim, 76
William, Duke of Clarence 2, 4, 4n, 12, 14, 19, 21, 30, 32, 37, 46, 69, 72, 82, 89, 91, 92, 113, 115, 120, 122, 123, 140, 188, 201, 209, 217, 221, 222, 232, 236, 247, 267, 267n, 271, 272, 273
Williams, Sir William Fenwick 277-78
Willis, R. and Rev. T. 209, 209n

Wilson, Dr 247
Wimbledon Common 113
Winchester (England) 124
Windham, William 132, 142, 261
Windhill (Jamaica) 267
Windsor (England) 12, 14, 57, 71, 118, 119, 120, 125, 138, 167, 170, 186, 198, 200, 249, 251
Windsor, Nova Scotia 108, 118, 184
Winslow, Colonel Edward 37, 132, 133, 177
Winslow, Thomas 177
Wood, Robert junior 3, 4, 5, 7, 50, 273, 274, 275
Wood, Robert senior 4, 25, 44, 69, 89, 272, 273, 274 (as Hood)
Wood, Lieutenant-Colonel William 273-4
Wood, William Frost 4, 273
Woolbrook Cottage (Sidmouth) 246, 247

Woolmer, John 25
Woolwich (England) 11, 97, 177, 180, 246
World (London) 13
Wright, Captain Richard 114, 153
Wurtemberg, Queen of See Princess Royal
Wyatt, James 122
Wykeham, Miss 222

Yonge, Sir George, 65, 79
York, Duchess of See Frederica, Duchess of York
York, Edward Augustus, Duke of 26
York, Frederick, Duke of See Frederick, Duke of York
York (Toronto) 75

Zebra, sloop of war 88